THE POLITICS OF GEN Z

MELISSA DECKMAN

THE POLITICS OF GEN Z

How the Youngest Voters
Will Shape Our Democracy

Columbia University Press / *New York*

Columbia University Press
Publishers Since 1893
New York   Chichester, West Sussex
cup.columbia.edu

Copyright © 2024 Columbia University Press
All rights reserved

Library of Congress Cataloging-in-Publication Data
Names: Deckman, Melissa M. (Melissa Marie), 1971– author.
Title: The politics of Gen Z : how the youngest voters will shape our democracy / Melissa Deckman.
Description: New York : Columbia University Press, [2024] | Includes bibliographical references and index.
Identifiers: LCCN 2024003378 | ISBN 9780231213882 (hardback) | ISBN 9780231213899 (trade paperback) | ISBN 9780231560085 (ebook)
Subjects: LCSH: Generation Z—Political activity—United States. | Generation Z—United States—Attitudes. | United States—Politics and government—2021–
Classification: LCC HQ799.9.P6 D435 2024 | DDC 324.084/20973—dc23/eng/20240508
LC record available at https://lccn.loc.gov/2024003378

Cover design: Elliott S. Cairns
Cover image: Jacob Lund / Shutterstock.com

CONTENTS

Preface vii
Acknowledgments xix

1 Gen Z and the Role of Gender and Sexuality in Their Politics 1

2 Political Context, Gender, and Sexuality in Shaping the Political Engagement of Gen Z 30

3 No More Old White Men: How Role Models Shape the Political Engagement of Gen Z Women 60

4 "Growing Their Feminist Thing": How Women's Rights and Reproductive Rights Are Propelling Activism Among Gen Z 80

5 How Gen Z Women and LGBTQ Zoomers Fight for Racial and LGBTQ Equality 104

6 How the Fights Against Gun Violence, Climate Change, and Income Inequality Have Become Gendered Spaces 124

7 Gen Z Men and Politics 145

Conclusion: The Possibilities of a More Inclusive Political Future 167

Methodological Appendix 185
Notes 255
Index 283

PREFACE

A political revolution is upon us. Its leaders are barely old enough to vote. They are often women and members of the LGBTQ community, refusing to be marginalized or silenced. Nurtured by family members and school and civic programs that foster their passions, these young activists are banding together across the internet and finding inspiration in role models who now look like them. They have been molded by gruesome school shootings that leave their peers dead; an existential climate crisis that their elders seem to ignore; and the dramatic reversal of women's rights, including the constitutional right to a safe and legal abortion.

Above all, these young leaders have been galvanized by the election and continued relevancy of Donald J. Trump. For the first time in U.S. history, during Trump's presidency, a generation of young women became more engaged in politics than their male counterparts. A reverse gender gap emerged suddenly and markedly in American politics, appearing in Generation Z (also known as Gen Z or Zoomers), those born between 1997 and 2012.[1] Throughout most of our nation's history, it has been men who were consistently more active in politics. But with Generation Z, that

PREFACE

is no longer true. This book explores that gender gap—how it came about, whether it will last, and what it means for both Democrats and Republicans in future elections.

As we will see, the women of this youngest generation were propelled by the 2016 election to engage in politics at significantly higher levels than young men—a phenomenon that warrants a critical examination. The growing gender division within Gen Z extends to partisanship and political views.

The gendered political revolution among the nation's youngest voters includes the LGBTQ community, whose members are participating in politics at greater levels than their straight counterparts. And it is as diverse as its generation, often powered by young women of color.

This book tells the unfolding story of how young women and those in the LGBTQ community refuse to sit passively on the sidelines while their rights, their lives and the planet's future are threatened, and how their activism will likely drive progressive political change in coming years.

The United States has witnessed the power and urgency that Gen Z brings to politics. The March for Our Lives rallies held after the 2018 massacre at Marjory Stoneman Douglas High School in Florida attracted more than 1 million followers nationwide in Washington, DC, and in hundreds of sister marches across the nation. School walkouts and climate strike marches started by Sweden's Greta Thunberg when she was fifteen have since been adopted by many younger Americans. Millions of young people stood up for racial justice in response to George Floyd's murder at the hands of Minneapolis police in summer 2020. These events helped drive high voter turnout among Gen Z in 2018 and 2020. The Supreme Court's *Dobbs* decision, overturning a national right to legal abortion and allowing states to ban the procedure, inspired higher than normal youth voter turnout in the 2022 midterm elections and in normally sleepy state elections for judgeships and ballot initiatives the year after.

While young people have led calls for progressive political change in the past, I argue that what is unique now is that Gen Z women and LGBTQ Zoomers are often at the forefront of the youth-led political groups that

PREFACE

are fighting for a more just, more inclusive, and healthier planet. You will meet dozens of them in this book. Young women such Rosie Couture, who in 2019 cofounded the youth-led organization Generation Ratify when she read about the failed history of the Equal Rights Amendment (ERA). Active in all fifty states, Generation Ratify, which in late 2023 changed its name to the Young Feminist Party, continues to lobby for the ERA while also campaigning for candidates promoting reproductive rights and gender equality. Zikora Akanegbu, the daughter of Nigerian immigrants, founded the online magazine *GenZHER* during the pandemic lockdown in 2020 to promote stories about political and social activism written by Gen Z teen girls. Katie Eder founded Future Coalition, a networking organization that has connected more than one hundred progressive, youth-led organizations under one umbrella and partnered with youth voter turnout organizations, racial justice and gun violence prevention groups, and in particular groups that address climate change.

In researching this book, I spoke with nearly ninety Gen Z political entrepreneurs in individual interviews and many more Zoomers in focus groups for their take on why gender matters to the political story of their generation. These young political leaders and activists do not, of course, represent an entire generation. Relatively few Americans at any age participate in politics actively, let alone create or lead their own political organizations that amass thousands of followers online, influence the policy decisions of elected officials, or bring together legions of young people to march in the streets. Still, they vividly illustrate the forces at play among our youngest leaders.

None of this happens in a vacuum. Political entrepreneurs such as Couture, Akanegbu, and Eder acknowledge the supporting roles that their families have played in promoting their activism or even providing seed money to help establish their work as activists. Researchers who study political participation have long known that political participation levels are strongly correlated with higher measures of socioeconomic status, and most of the Gen Z entrepreneurs and activists that I interviewed for this book come from higher socioeconomic backgrounds or are in college—or will be soon.[2]

PREFACE

Gen Z men are not absent from leadership in progressive political spaces. The first Gen Zer elected to Congress in 2022 was Maxwell Frost from Orlando, Florida, who became active in the gun violence prevention movement after the Parkland shooting. Frost is also the nation's first Afro-Cuban elected to Congress. Parkland shooting survivor David Hogg, who cofounded March for Our Lives, has been among the most recognizable champions for gun violence prevention and other progressive causes that many members of his generation prioritize; in 2023, he helped launch the grassroots organization Leaders We Deserve to recruit young progressive candidates to run for state legislature. I talked with many politically active Gen Z men for this book as well.

You will also meet Gen Z Americans from the political right, both women and men. I also spoke with transgender and nonbinary Zoomer political activists. Many of my Gen Z women and men interviewees identify as LGBTQ.

My findings are also informed by fifteen focus group conversations I conducted with Gen Z Americans across the country. These focus groups were designed to capture a range of ideological viewpoints, including female, male, and LGBTQ college students, as well as interviews with participants from IGNITE, a nationally recognized political training organization for young women.

I also employ statistical analyses of surveys to make the case that gender and LGBTQ status is essential to understanding the politics of Generation Z. Using the survey firm Qualtrics, I administered original, national surveys of Gen Z Americans in 2019 and 2022. Although not based on random probability samples—Qualtrics maintains a panel of respondents, which it builds through a variety of websites using incentives—the samples were designed and weighted to be representative of the adult Gen Z population in the United States.[3] The surveys provide a deeper analysis of the political behaviors of a wide swath of the members of Generation Z—not just those from the activist class or those in college—and show that class remains an important factor in understanding which Americans are more likely to participate in politics and which are not.

PREFACE

I am also privileged to serve as the CEO of one of the nation's leading nonpartisan research institutes, Public Religion Research Institute (PRRI), which tracks Americans' attitudes about many of the issues that animate Generation Z politically, as well as their broader political leanings, using gold standard, random probability samples. Where appropriate, I use PRRI data as well as other well-known surveys based on probability samples when considering how gender and LGBTQ status influence the political behavior of Generation Z.

Using this mixed-method approach, here's what I've found: most Gen Zers—particularly Gen Z women and those who identify as LGBTQ—trend in the politically progressive direction, with little enthusiasm for far-right politics. While Zoomers are far more likely than older Americans to reject identifying with the current incarnation of the Republican Party, this tendency is especially pronounced among Gen Z women and LGBTQ Zoomers.

I developed a Gen Z political engagement model that analyzes the factors behind the historic Trump-era development of Gen Z women participating in more political activities than Gen Z men. The model shows that they are driven to such engagement by their deep commitment to progressive values, their identities as Democrats, and their belief that the political system is not responsive to their concerns (see chapter 2 for a full description.) Those concerns continue to drive higher levels of political activism among Gen Z women as does support for a variety of progressive causes, including support for abortion rights (explored in detail in chapter 4); commitments to racial and LGBTQ rights (chapter 5); and concern for climate change and gun violence prevention (chapter 6). While Gen Z women's overall levels of political engagement persisted into the Biden presidency, by 2022, I found the Gen Z men had begun to close the overall *gap* with women in terms of numbers of political acts undertaken—although evidence from 2023, after the *Dobbs* decision that overturned the constitutional right to an abortion, suggests that this reverse gender gap is present again. Although not the case in 2019, by 2022 and 2023, I also show that political activism among LGBTQ Zoomers surged significantly compared with their straight counterparts.

In short, the gendered political revolution is underway. Its roots are deep, and it is heading, for now, in a clear direction.

USING A GENERATIONAL LENS

Social scientists have spent decades studying individual-level characteristics that drive some to participate in politics more than others. We know higher socioeconomic status is linked to higher political participation. In addition, some people simply have more interest in politics or are more likely to think that their activism has the potential to make a difference, so they are more inclined to be politically engaged.

The political habits and values of individuals can also be shaped by the shared experiences of their youth. Unlike their parents or grandparents, members of Generation Z have grown up in a world in which mass shootings have become far more prevalent, including at their schools. This has led some to label Gen Z as the lockdown generation. Gen Zers have come of age as the Earth's temperature is warming dramatically, and they possess an acute sense of how they will suffer the impacts of climate change. Gen Z is the first generation of young people to witness a presidential candidate's refusal to concede his defeat in a free and fair election, leading to the almost unimaginable events of January 6, 2021. Debates about the rights of marginalized groups, whether people of color or LGBTQ Americans, have taken a central role in their political lives. Unlike their parents, Zoomers face a world in which some long-assumed rights, such as access to abortion, are not guaranteed.

Such shared experiences have the potential to impart what generational scholars call a cohort effect on the outlooks and habits of Gen Z well into the future. Scholars have found that major political, cultural, or economic events can impart a form of generational consciousness that have a deep impact on the political orientations of adults for decades.[4] Those shared experiences also involve major advances in technology, including television, computers, the internet, and social media. Not only

PREFACE

do such advances profoundly shape daily lives, generational expert Jean Twenge argues; they also produce "downstream" consequences that help explain why generational cohort effects—including political orientations and habits—tend to linger.[5]

Many commentators who discuss Gen Z today often assume that behavioral characteristics of a generation are immutable. That is not necessarily true; Gen Z's political views could change as they age through what is known as the life-cycle effect. In other words, their views may turn more conservative as they age. For instance, we know that members of Generation Z currently want a more activist government and are more satisfied with current taxation levels compared with other generational cohorts.[6] But as they mature and their earnings grow, they may desire lower taxes and less government. So the large generational political differences we are currently seeing may be indicative of youth, and cross-sectional surveys cannot statistically disentangle age from generation.[7] The reliance on cross-sectional survey data in the book largely prevents me from tackling the statistically thorny age, time period, and cohort (APC) problem—although in some cases I do speak to cohort effects where possible by comparing Gen Z's political behavior with earlier generations of young Americans when longitudinal survey data allow.

A deeper dive into Generation Z is warranted, however, because decades of research find that the political values and attitudes shaped in early life and in young adulthood, when individuals are most impressionable to political influence, tend to persist as they grow older.[8] Generation Z differs significantly from older generations in ways that will likely have important political ramifications in the decades to come.

First, Gen Z is the most racially and ethnically diverse generation in U.S. history, with non-Hispanic white Zoomers constituting what some call a "bare" majority (around 52 percent.).[9] Second, Gen Z is also far more likely to identify as LGBTQ than members of older generations. My organization PRRI finds in its 2022 American Values Atlas that roughly one in four Zoomers identify as part of the LGBTQ community. By comparison, just 8 percent of Americans older than Gen Z identify as LGBTQ. Third, Gen Z is also more likely than older Americans to be religiously unaffiliated.

PREFACE

PRRI's 2022 Census of American Religion finds that 38 percent of younger Americans, those aged eighteen to twenty-nine, identify as a religious "none" at rates much higher than younger Americans in the past.[10] While about one in four younger adults in this age group identify as a Christian of color, only 23 percent of Zoomers identify as white Christians, compared with 58 percent of Americans aged sixty-five and older. These demographic features of Generation Z help explain why the Republican Party, whose base is far more likely to be white, Christian, and straight, is struggling to attract younger voters.

It will become clear in the pages ahead why the Republican Party will continue to struggle in its bid for the votes of Generation Z women and LGBTQ Zoomers in particular. Gen Z women have come of age amid a renewal of the women's movement after Trump's election; have borne witness to the Me Too movement; and have seen the political rise of younger, more diverse political role models, such as Alexandria Ocasio-Cortez. Progressive Gen Z women are also driven by a strong desire for a more inclusive politics that promotes and celebrates the voices of marginalized communities.

Many of the progressive Gen Z women and LGBTQ activists I interviewed are also keenly aware that women of color, poorer women, LGBTQ women, and nonbinary individuals are subject to a unique set of intersectional pressures. Kimberlé Crenshaw, the legal scholar who coined the term "intersectionality,"[11] describes it as "a lens through which you can see where power comes and collides, where it interlocks and intersects. It's not simply that there's a race problem here, a gender problem here, and a class or LBGTQ problem there."[12] Progressive Gen Z activists remain undaunted, however, by intersectional challenges—and believe the organizations that they are creating for themselves offer a new avenue for diverse leaders to emerge. As Katie Eder, the founder of Future Coalition who identifies as LGBTQ, told me, the diverse groups she partners with are drawn to more "super non-traditional [and] super non-hierarchical" styles of activism. Progressive political entrepreneurs such as Eder are actively building the sorts of inclusive groups that reflect their diversity and desire for change, with their fellow Zoomers becoming more involved in the political process.

PREFACE

PROMISE AND PERILS OF GENDER, GEN Z, AND POLITICS

While predicting the political future is risky, I believe that Gen Z activists, largely led by Gen Z women and LGBTQ Zoomers, are in the process of moving the nation and its politics in a more progressive direction. When their political rights are on the line or when they face events that disproportionately affect their generation, Gen Z has shown a remarkable willingness to fight back. The mass shooting in Parkland, Florida, many experts agree, ignited a desire to vote among young people, leading to record turnout in 2018 among younger Americans aged eighteen to twenty-four; the 2020 elections also saw record youth voter turnout.[13] While the midterm voter turnout among Generation Z was slightly lower in 2022 than it was in 2018, it was still the second highest level of youth voter turnout in the past three decades—and even higher in key battleground states, where the youth vote was critical in helping Democrats win Senate elections in Pennsylvania, Arizona, and Georgia.[14] All three elections saw a distinct gender divide among Generation Z. Gen Z women's voter turnout was roughly 5 percentage points higher than that of men their age in 2018 and 2020; young women voters continued to outvote younger men in 2022, although by slightly smaller margins.

In each of these cases, Gen Z women voted for Democratic candidates at much higher levels than their male counterparts. Although Gen Z men were more likely than older men to vote for Democrats in the past three elections, the Democratic-Republican vote margin (which subtracts the percentage of all voters who voted for Democratic candidates minus the percentage of all voters who voted for Republican candidates) for young women aged eighteen to twenty-nine was staggering in 2022—a whopping 46 percentage points, no doubt a reflection of the *Dobbs* decision.[15] In 2022, PRRI found that Gen Z women were significantly more likely than Gen Z men or Americans more generally to say that they will vote only for a candidate who shares their position on abortion.[16] William Frey of the Brookings Institution found in his analysis of the 2022 midterms that

PREFACE

among the 47 percent of young female voters who were angry about the *Dobbs* decision, 83 percent voted for a Democratic candidate, fueling a Democratic resistance to the red wave that was expected to be far bigger than what emerged.[17]

Paying attention to these patterns is important because Gen Z is becoming a bigger part of the electorate. In the 2020 election, Gen Z represented 10 percent of eligible voters, but by 2036, that figure will grow to nearly 30 percent, according to the Democracy Fund Study group.[18] While historical analysis of the LGBTQ vote is hard to discern because pollsters only recently began systematically asking about the sexual orientation and gender identity of respondents, estimates suggest that LGBTQ voters are also poised to become a bigger bloc of the electorate in the years ahead.[19]

It remains to be seen if antidemocratic efforts, which appear to be gaining momentum, will dampen this progressive Gen Z trend. Red states are making it more difficult to vote in the name of securing "free and fair elections," and the Supreme Court took a dramatic right turn during its 2021–22 session. Not only did the Court overturn a constitutional right to abortion in its 2022 *Dobbs* decision, but it has also begun to limit the federal government's regulatory power in other areas of policy that have motivated and driven much Zoomer political advocacy these past few years, such as climate change and gun violence prevention.

We also cannot predict future life and world events that may alter the political thinking and trajectory of this generation. Who knows what analog to January 6 or Parkland lies ahead? While Generation Z is already "chronically online"—we know that the social media habits of this generation have shaped their lives in myriad ways, unlike their parents and grandparents—new technical advances, such as the rapid growth of artificial intelligence, will no doubt alter the lives of Gen Z and other Americans in unpredictable ways.

It is always possible that a backlash effect among some Zoomers—particularly young men—may take root if there is a sense that Gen Z's current political leaders become so ideologically strident as to prevent compromise in the political arena—or if they exclude the voices of younger men. (Whether Gen Z men are becoming more conservative on gendered issues or more Republican as a response to the political left's embrace of identity politics is discussed more in chapter 7 and in the book's conclusion.) If the progressive orientations hold among many Zoomers—particularly Gen Z women and Zoomers who are LGBTQ—some may also wonder if the incremental nature of American politics will lead younger progressive activists to leave politics out of frustration or burnout.

Nonetheless, Gen Z's explosive growth as a voting bloc in the coming years will leave candidates and parties scrambling to appeal to this cohort. As Republican leaders in Congress and in state legislatures take extreme and unpopular policy actions, whether banning abortion, stopping environmental protections, or limiting the rights of LGBTQ Americans, these policies will likely inspire Generation Z to become more involved in the political process.

It seems likely that Generation Z will be the one to offer solutions to crucial national priorities, from safeguarding democracy to protecting the rights of women, LGBTQ Americans, and racial and ethnic minorities. My book shows why Gen Z women and LGBTQ Zoomers are leaning hard into progressive political activism—and why many of those activists, such as Rosie Couture, Zikhora Akanegbu, and Katie Eder—can build a more equitable and inclusive world.

ACKNOWLEDGMENTS

I am extremely grateful to the more than two hundred Generation Z Americans (also known as Gen Zers or Zoomers) who took the time to be interviewed for my book or to participate in one of my fifteen focus groups. Many of these passionate, inspirational Zoomers are strongly invested in making their communities, states, and nation a better place. I appreciate their candor and their willingness to share their stories and perspectives. I've tried to remain faithful to what they have told me.

I'd like to thank IGNITE for underwriting the costs of the focus groups and for contributing funds for the two surveys of Gen Z Americans that I use throughout the book. I am extremely grateful for the strong support and wise counsel of Dr. Anne Moses, IGNITE's founder and former president, and its current CEO, Sara Guillermo, who was in the trenches with me for many of the in-person focus groups. I am also indebted to Shauna Shames of Rutgers University for initially introducing me to Anne, Sara, and the amazing work that IGNITE is doing in training the next generation of women leaders. I am also grateful to Susannah Wellford of Running Start, Karin Lipps of the Network of Enlightened Women, and

ACKNOWLEDGMENTS

Melissa Kilby of Girl Up for connecting me with several dynamic young women who are active in politics today.

Coordinating a diverse set of focus groups across three college campuses and later on Zoom, is no joke. I am grateful to Janet Box-Steffensmeier of Ohio State University; Sarah Gershon of Georgia State University; and Stella Rouse, formerly of the University of Maryland and now director of the Center of Hispanic Studies at Arizona State University, for their help in finding student participants and facilities on campus. Eric McDaniel helped me connect with students at the University of Texas-Austin who participated in my Zoom focus groups.

I have been fortunate to work with some wonderful political scientists as part of the research for this project. I can't say enough great things about Jared McDonald, of Mary Washington University, whose advice has made all the work in these pages infinitively better—and his humor, good spirits, and statistical advice have been very much appreciated. I have been so very fortunate to work on several ongoing projects with the outstanding Steve Greene, Laurel Elder and Mary-Kate Lizotte on gender and public opinion on abortion and gun attitudes. In addition to being enthusiastic supporters of my book project, they helped me to design parts of the second survey and, in Mary-Kate's case, helped to fund it as well.

I am grateful as well for the advice and support from Mileah Kromer, one of the most talented pollsters I know. I'll mention Stella Rouse here a second time because she not only helped with my focus groups; she also provided her expertise and encouragement at different stages of the project. I am sure that I am omitting some folks here, but the advice and support for this project from the following individuals was especially appreciated: Kelly Dittmar, Julie Dolan, Michele Swers, Christina Wolbrecht, Erin Cassese, Mirya Holman, and Paul Djupe. The anonymous reviewers of the book manuscript also provided helpful suggestions for improving the work.

I started the research and writing for this book while I was a full-time professor of political science at Washington College, and I am grateful for the support from my former departmental colleagues, including Christine Wade, Andrew Oros, Tahir Shad, Joseph Prud'homme, Carrie Reiling,

ACKNOWLEDGMENTS

and Flavio Hickel. I am also grateful to Michael Harvey, former interim provost of Washington College, who was also very enthusiastic about the work. The college provided generous underwriting for some of the costs of my survey research. During the early data collection of the work, students in my courses at Washington College provided great and unfiltered advice about the project, too!

I completed the book while serving as CEO of the Public Religion Research Institute (PRRI), an amazing job that I started in summer 2022. I am so very grateful for the encouragement of my good friend, Dr. Robert P. Jones, founder and president of PRRI, whose own research, writing, and prophetic public voice have been a source of personal inspiration for many years; it's been a pleasure working him to colead PRRI, and I'm excited about the new directions we are taking the organization. I'm also very fortunate every day to be working with PRRI's incomparable chief of staff, Sean Sands, and our talented research director, Dr. Diana Orcés, in addition to an extraordinary team at PRRI. I thank Sean, Diana, Ian Huff, Maddie Snodgrass, Jack Shanley, Colleen Ross, Jessica Royce, Belén Bonilla, and Toni Baptiste for their assistance and encouragement while completing the book. Thanks also go out to the team at Avōq, especially Colleen Frerichs and Kent Holland, for their help in promoting the book and my work on Gen Z more broadly.

The writing of this book has been tremendously improved by Jennifer Thompson, from Nordelyset Literary Agency, who was an early champion of this work and who gave me wonderful and concrete suggestions for honing my arguments while boosting my confidence. Her partner Isabelle Bleeker also graciously read several chapter drafts and provided helpful feedback. I am also very grateful to not one—but two—very talented developmental editors for their help in polishing the final version of the manuscript: David Nitkin and Karen Nitkin. They helped to streamline the prose, honed my arguments, and forced this sometimes long-winded academic to adopt shorter paragraphs! I'd hire both again in a heartbeat.

A special thank you goes out to my editor, Stephen Wesley, at Columbia University Press, for his unwavering support for the project and his advice on how to make the manuscript better. Copyediting by Marianne L'Abbate

ACKNOWLEDGMENTS

and Ben Kolstad was fantastic. Three anonymous reviewers also provided helpful feedback on the book.

I'd also like to thank my friends and family for their encouragement of my work. I am grateful to my parents, Lloyd and Diann Deckman, for a lifetime of love and pride. I am especially grateful for my loving, encouraging husband, Sean Fallon, who has always supported my work, believed in my abilities, and served as an important sounding board. He consistently challenges my assumptions and encourages me to think about my work and ideas from different angles. But most important, Sean makes my life far more fun and helps me to put things in perspective.

Last, I thank my two favorite Gen Zers, my sons Mason and Gavin, to whom I dedicate this book. They have never shied away from sharing their many, *many* thoughts about this book and my research in general. It is a privilege to be their mother and to watch them grow into fine young men. My hope is that they, along with the rest of their generation, will find meaningful ways to safeguard our democracy and build stronger communities. I have no doubt they will be up for the challenge!

THE POLITICS OF GEN Z

1

GEN Z AND THE ROLE OF GENDER AND SEXUALITY IN THEIR POLITICS

Katie Eder started her political organizing days as a fourth-grader in Milwaukee, Wisconsin. Upset that a teacher required boys and girls to play separately in gym class and noting that the boys had far more fun, Eder organized a sit-in to persuade the instructor to change the rules. "We all walked in the class and sat down and, after a lot of pleading and some negotiation, our gym teacher eventually gave in," Eder recalled. "And, yeah, we all got to play together." Two years later, after reading former U.S. vice president Al Gore's *An Inconvenient Truth*, which chronicles the dangers of global warming, Eder worked with school administrators on an environmental pep rally, during which she handed out reusable straws. "Way ahead of the trend," she told me. In high school, she began organizing creative writing workshops for underserved youth, which led to the development of a nonprofit group, Kids Tales. Through Kids Tales, older teens led workshops for middle school students, with the resulting anthologies later sold online.

Flourishing as an increasingly sophisticated political activist toward the end of high school, Eder organized several school walkouts in 2018 to protest gun violence as part of a coordinated national effort known as the

National School Walkout, which followed the horrific shooting at Marjorie Stoneman Douglas High School in Parkland, Florida. Eder's gun violence prevention work snowballed into the creation of 50 Miles More in Milwaukee, a youth-led gun violence awareness march modeled after the historic Civil Rights March in Selma, Alabama. She then connected with leaders from March On, a national nonprofit group of women-led and grassroots organizers that grew out of the historic Women's March in Washington held soon after Donald Trump's inauguration in January 2017. With the help of March On, Eder cofounded Future Coalition, which connects progressive, youth-led organizations under one umbrella. Eder spent two years full-time as Future Coalition's executive director before enrolling at Stanford University in fall 2020.

Eder's passion for political organizing is clear as she told me about Future Coalition, which "acts as a connective tissue between youth activists and organizers and provides resources that traditionally have only been available to adult-led organizing." She describes Future Coalition as playing a more supportive role for young activists rather than a directional one:

> Before Future Coalition existed, there was really nowhere a youth organizer or activist could go and find resources like funding and connections to adults that know how to do things, such as web designing or a very long list of things that [makes organizing] more easily accessible. So our goal is really to lower the accessibility barrier to youth activism so that more young people can engage in the work and engage in it in more depth.

Among other initiatives, Future Coalition provides grant money and in-kind support for new youth-led groups, and links nascent groups with political mentors and training through its Future Accelerator program. More than one hundred organizations—most of them connected to climate change, civic engagement, gun violence prevention, or gender equality—have participated with Future Coalition, with many relying heavily on social media as a strategy to connect young activists.

Eder is truly remarkable in many respects. Relatively few Americans participate in politics so actively, let alone create several successful political organizations that amass thousands of followers online, bring together legions of young people to march in the streets, or build coalitions that have real impact on the political process. Eder, who is also part of the LGBTQ community, is emblematic of the next generation of political activists in the United States, who are young; diverse with respect to race, ethnicity, and LGBTQ status; unabashedly progressive; and, more often than not, female.

Future Coalition's own leadership team has been staffed mostly by LGBTQ Gen Z people; most are also people of color. Eder, who is white, told me that this very diversity with respect to gender and race has been key to the success of Future Coalition and other youth-led groups because many of the Gen Z activists Eder works with want a different brand of inclusive politics that is willing to confront their issue priorities in new ways. "We have to innovate, we have to be radical, we have to take risks," she said. A generation or two ago, the face of young political activism in this country would typically have been white, straight, and male. With Generation Z, we are seeing a sea change because Gen Z women and LGBTQ people are participating in politics at higher levels than their male and straight counterparts, respectively. While Gen Z is not politically monolithic, and young men are certainly active across political spaces today, the movers and shakers in terms of progressive political activism are young women like Eder.

GEN Z AMERICANS ARE THE MOST DIVERSE AND LEAST RELIGIOUS GENERATION

In assessing Gen Z's political priorities, it is essential to recognize that it is the most diverse generation in American history in terms of race, ethnicity, and LGBTQ status.[1] According to U.S. Census Bureau data, barely half of Gen Z Americans are white, 14 percent are African American, 25 percent are Latinx (i.e., Hispanic or Latino/Latina of any racial category),[2] 6 percent are Asian American, and 5 percent are multiracial or fall into some other category.[3]

Many of the Gen Z women political entrepreneurs that I spoke with note that their diverse identities have directly shaped their decisions to become politically active and to strive for a more inclusive political arena. Mariah Cooley is one example. Cooley, who is Black, grew up in Peoria, Illinois, and had always been politically engaged. The 2012 death of Trayvon Martin, the unarmed Black teenager who was shot and killed by a Community Watch member in Miami Gardens, Florida, profoundly shaped Cooley's social conscience. Then Trump triumphed in the 2016 election—"a racist, narcissistic person," she said, "yet America voted for him to win." Cooley responded by organizing a new group in her high school to create space for discussing controversial political topics. Hoping for a political career, Cooley attended Howard University in Washington, DC. She soon realized there was no campus chapter for March for Our Lives, the gun violence prevention group, so she started one.

After police killed Breonna Taylor and George Floyd, Cooley organized Black Lives Matter (BLM) protests in her hometown of Peoria and helped create a social justice organization there called Young Revolution that is dedicated to police reform. A prolific writer, she has penned op-eds on gun violence and the BLM movement for numerous online publications, including BET.com and Seventeen.com.

Cooley was not surprised to learn that young women of color like her are leading many of Gen Z's progressive political movements. "The most oppressed group in the world is Black women," she told me. "We are dealing with so many different systemic issues." Marginalized groups must lead the way to systemic changes in American politics, she continued. "I will say to any college student, any minority group, be it Black people, Indigenous, Hispanic, LGBTQ—we are the ones who need to be engaged the most because there are a group of people in this country that are trying to take us back fifty or sixty years. And if we sit and let that happen, the world as we know it will not be the same." She called on all young people to support leaders who are trying "to make it a more just and equal America."

Part of creating a "just and equal America" for many Gen Z women activists involves advancing gender equality and the rights and recognition of LGBTQ Americans. Ina Bhoopalam started DREAM EQUAL in 2018 as a sixteen-year-old in Lincoln, Nebraska. The daughter of Indian immigrants, Bhoopalam was the only girl on her high school debate team and promptly began winning competitions. Her male teammates, who had been middle school friends, began teasing and harassing her, calling her "bitchy."

Bhoopalam remembered reading an article explaining that gender stereotypes begin around the age of six, when "girls start to think they are not as smart as boys or that boys can't start to show their emotions." She looked into the gender equality movement and found a "huge gap" because it focused primarily on "teen girls and older and only cis girls. And it was truly completely taking out this entire population that needed to be included in the conversation.[4]"

Working with gender study experts, parents, and teachers, Bhoopalam lobbied school administrators to organize a voluntary after-school program in her former elementary school that would reach young people of all genders, not just cis girls, and that would promote gender equality and gender sensitivity training. Although her first efforts resulted in just a handful of students attending, by the time she graduated high school, her program had spread to eighteen elementary schools in Nebraska. Bhoopalam told me that the fight for gender equality and LGBTQ rights is especially important to young female and nonbinary activists of color. "We feel that the issues that are affecting us aren't being talked about, and I think as a woman of color, you start thinking about all of the other marginalized communities that don't fit that heterosexual, patriarchal norm, and you start to bring more people in. You start realizing that 'I didn't fit in, but that I wasn't the only one not fitting into the movement.'"

So many Gen Z women activists engaging in the work of LGBTQ rights is unsurprising: Gen Zers as a whole are more likely to identify as part of the LGBTQ community than older Americans are, and Gen Z women are even more likely to do so than Gen Z men.[5] My 2019 and 2022 Qualtrics surveys of Gen Z Americans, for instance, find that the percentage of cisgender men who identify as LGBTQ ranges from 12 to 15 percent; for cisgender women, it ranges from 24 to 30 percent. Other random probability studies also find that cisgender Gen Z women are far more likely to identify as LGBTQ than cisgender Gen Z men.[6]

Compared with most older Americans, Gen Z Americans are also more religiously unaffiliated, which may help to explain their leftward drift politically. While no generation is immune from religious disaffiliation—that is, leaving the religious tradition in which one was raised and not becoming affiliated with another religious tradition—the Public Religion Research Institute's (PRRI) 2022 Census of American Religion finds Gen Z is disaffiliating at higher numbers than older Americans (save for millennials).[7] They are also more likely to have been raised without a religious affiliation to begin with. Gen Z is more than twice as likely (38 percent) as baby boomers (18 percent) to claim no religious affiliation, and more Gen Z women identify as unaffiliated (41 percent) compared with Gen Z men (36 percent).

The religious disaffiliation gap between LGBTQ and straight Zoomers is huge. The PRRI 2022 Census of American Religion finds that 60 percent of LGBTQ Zoomers are unaffiliated compared with 32 percent of their straight Gen Z counterparts. While a majority of Zoomers continue to claim some sort of religious identity, far fewer Zoomers are white and Christian (25 percent) compared with Americans aged sixty-five and older (58 percent).

These religious patterns have important partisan implications. PRRI's 2022 Census of American Religion finds that the Democratic Party's religious makeup more closely resembles the demographics of younger Americans, who skew more religiously unaffiliated and who also have higher rates of non-white Christians and religious groups. Meanwhile, more than two-thirds of Republicans are white Christians (68 percent), and there are far fewer religiously unaffiliated Republicans or Republicans who are religious and non-white. Efforts by Republicans in many red states to ban abortion, remove discussion of African American history or LGBTQ themes in classrooms and books, and restrict access to health care for transgender people are driven in part by the conservative Christian base of the party. Such policies will face headwinds with Generation Z, however, given its

GENDER, SEXUALITY, AND GEN Z'S POLITICS

diversity in terms of race, ethnicity, LGBTQ status, and its greater propensity to be religiously unaffiliated.

GEN Z AMERICANS DIFFER FROM OLDER AMERICANS IN THEIR PARTISANSHIP

One reason that Gen Z women and LGBTQ Zoomers are poised to lead our politics in a more leftward direction is that they are far less likely to be Republicans. Given the strong pull of partisanship on how people vote and the issues they care about,[8] Gen Z's greater reluctance to identify as Republican will have important ripple effects on who wins elections and which policies those candidates will support. Figure 1.1 contains a breakdown of American women and men overall in terms of partisanship, featuring data from my May 2022 Qualtrics survey.[9] I also included partisanship data for LGBTQ and straight Gen Zers. Independent "leaners" are coded as partisans.

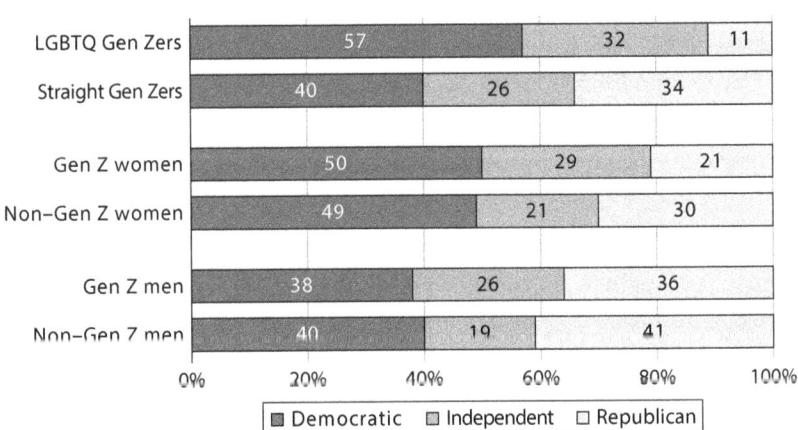

FIGURE 1.1 Partisanship, by gender, LGBTQ status, and generation. Among members of Generation Z, women and LGBTQ people are more likely to identify as Democrats than men and straight people are. Qualtrics survey conducted by the author in May 2022, with a sample of 1,600 Americans aged eighteen to twenty-four and 1,600 Americans aged twenty-five or older.

7

While Gen Z women in my survey are just as likely to identify with the Democratic Party compared with older American women, they are significantly less likely to identify as Republican—and more likely to be "truly" independent because, when pressed, they don't say that they prefer any party (meaning that they are not what political scientists call "independent leaners").[10] While Gen Z men in my survey are significantly less likely to identify as Republican than older men, they are more Republican and less Democratic than Gen Z women. LGBTQ Gen Zers are by far the most Democratic—and least Republican—of any group.

My Qualtrics findings were generally consistent with random probability-based national surveys, including PRRI's 2022 American Values Atlas (AVA), which found that 57 percent of Gen Z women identified as or leaned Democratic and at higher levels than older women. The AVA also found that roughly just one in four Gen Z women identified as or leaned Republican, at rates lower than non–Gen Z women. Like my Qualtrics survey, PRRI's AVA showed that just around one in ten LGBTQ Zoomers identified as or leaned Republican.[11] The 2022 AVA also found that among Gen Z men, 45 percent identified as or leaned Democrat, 14 percent identified as independent, and 35 percent identified as or leaned Republican.

The longitudinal General Social Survey (GSS) suggests that Gen Z women are unique from other generations of women at their age in terms of partisanship, at least compared with millennials and my generation, Gen X, at similar ages. The 2022 GSS found that 55 percent of Gen Z women aged eighteen to twenty-four identified as or leaned Democratic. Millennial women aged eighteen to twenty-four in the 2006 GSS, the equivalent year for when the millennial generation was the same age group, were less likely to identify as, or lean, Democratic, at 38 percent. Similarly, in 1990, 37 percent of young Gen X women aged eighteen to twenty-four identified or leaned as Democrats.[12] But looking back one more generation, baby boomer women aged twenty to twenty-four in 1972 (the year the GSS began collecting data) identified with the Democratic Party in higher numbers—63 percent—than the current eighteen to twenty-four cohort of Gen Z women. These women were coming of age, however during the Richard

GENDER, SEXUALITY, AND GEN Z'S POLITICS

Nixon presidency, and other research shows older baby boomers—both women and men—trended more Democratic.[13]

These data might be encouraging to Democratic leaders, but many Gen Z progressive activists I spoke with expressed much ambivalence about the state of the party. Antoilyn Nyugen, as a high school senior, helped form the California Menstrual Justice Network, a network of students who provide menstrual products for domestic violence shelters and advocate for related legislation. She liked to think of the Democratic Party as "a platform for future progress." But at the same time, she worried about alienating the political center.

Other progressive Gen Z women expressed outright frustration with the Democratic Party. One was a woman from my University of Texas at Austin focus group: "In certain aspects, the Democratic Party just kind of feels like the Republican Party with different labels. They are extremely similar to each other in so many aspects." While she acknowledged that Democrats tend to talk about issues that young women care about, such as the BLM movement or health-care accessibility, when party leaders have the "power and the ability, they end up just trying to keep the status quo or making very minimal changes. And I find that very frustrating because it seems like they only talk about change when they are trying to persuade us to vote for them."

Mai Do, a nonbinary activist with the Democratic Party who helped charter Santa Clarita's Young Democratic Club as a teenager in 2017 and who is currently a doctoral student at the University of California, Riverside, said that they know plenty of young progressive activists who "won't register as Democrat because the Democrats are failing on housing, on wages, on immigration." While they say that this decision may not be limited to just Gen Z activists, "it is likely amplified with this group."

My conservations with the progressive Gen Z women and LGBTQ activists showed, however, that the Republican Party in its current form held no appeal for them. Republican Party policies "seem to be really out of touch with what's happening in today's world," said one focus group member at Ohio State University, who, like others, raised climate change as a driving issue. "Our planet is dying and people in power don't really seem to be doing all that much about it. And when we look at the Republican Party's policies and their focus, it's in an entirely different direction."

Other Gen Z female Democrats expressed alarm at the Republican Party's stance on LGBTQ rights. "The consensus is that marriage equality is good and Republicans are still saying that that should be a state's issue and they should revisit it," said a Democratic woman from one of the IGNITE focus groups. (IGNITE is a nonpartisan organization that trains young women to run for office.) "[T]hose kinds of issues are the things that are pushing away younger Americans who are pretty pro-LGBTQ." This participant also indicated that she had once identified as a Republican but left the party when Trump was nominated; she came out as gay a year later.

Roughly 20 percent of Gen Z women, however, still identify as Republicans. Ophelie Jacobson was a leader with the Florida Federation of College Republicans and was president of the University of Florida chapter of Network of Enlightened Women (NeW), which organizes college conservative women. She said that she is active in the GOP because of policies that are "putting America at the forefront of our priorities, and definitely being proud of our heritage. I mean, obviously recognizing that every single country has its dark past and dark moments in history but realizing that we are the greatest nation in the world and that we should be proud of that as Americans." Republicans, she added, do "a really good job" at addressing free speech "because that is something that's very much under attack, especially on college campuses."

Many Gen Z women choose to stay Republicans because of their attitudes about abortion, including an Ohio State student, who told me, "I am pro-life, hands down. I feel like if you're pro-life and you really stick to it, it's impossible to be a Democrat at this point." Another Ohio State Republican woman said her decision to identify with the party was rooted in economics, adding: "I cannot subscribe to the idea of socialism, and capitalism is something that I strongly support. I'm all for free markets." A female Republican from the University of Maryland also said that her party identification stemmed from "reading up on politics and realizing that I am very fiscally conservative." Although she identified as more socially liberal, this student took issue with the economic policies advocated by Democrats because "they're going to spend too much money." Chloe Sparwath, who headed the University of Virginia chapter of the NeW, identified as a Republican because of her libertarian outlook: "I think my philosophy is as uninvolved as government can be in people's lives is the better way to go." She also counted herself as a strong defender of Second Amendment gun rights. Other Gen Z women choose to identify with neither party and remain "pure" independents, meaning that, unlike independent "leaners," they don't tend to vote regularly with one party. While older Americans are beginning to identify as pure independents in growing numbers, Zoomers still remain more likely than older Americans to identify as independents. My research corresponds to other work showing that Gen Z is the least partisan generation.[14]

THE POLICY PRIORITIES OF GEN Z AMERICANS

Gen Z women and LGBTQ Zoomers embrace more concerns about progressive causes overall. To get a better sense of which issues Gen Zers care about most, I asked respondents whether a wide range of political issues were critically important to them personally, whether each issue was one among many important issues, or whether each issue was not that important to them. Figure 1.2 shows that in my May 2022 survey, the issues that rose to the top included health care, mass shootings, abortion, mental health, and racial inequality, with responses broken out by gender. Figure 1.3 poses the same questions broken out by LGBTQ status. The findings from the May 2022 survey didn't change that much compared to the July Qualtrics 2019 survey—except that health care becomes a more salient issue for Zoomers after the COVID-19 pandemic.

Two details are particularly notable from my surveys. First, Gen Z women expressed much more concern about almost all these issues than Gen Z men.[15] Second, LGBTQ Gen Zers were similar to Gen Z women overall in terms of issue priorities. Generation Z identified health care,

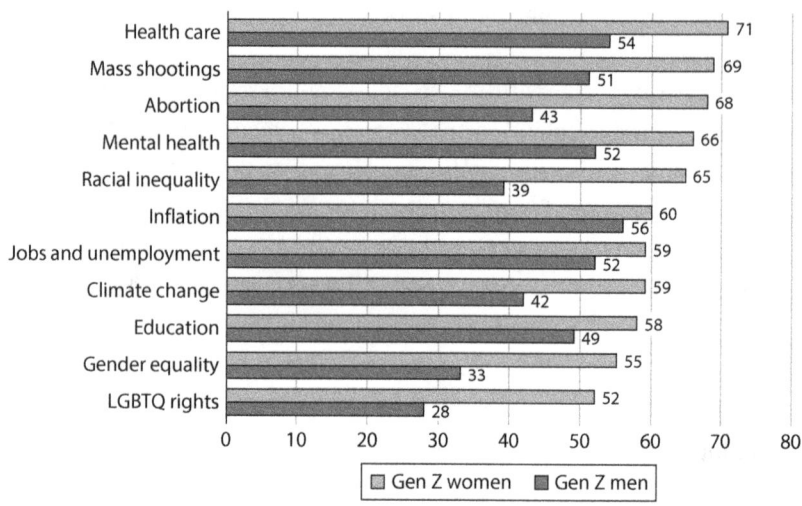

FIGURE 1.2 Percentage of issues of critical importance, by gender. Among members of Generation Z, women prioritize progressive issues more than men. Qualtrics survey conducted by the author in May 2022, with a sample of 1,600 Americans aged eighteen to twenty-four.

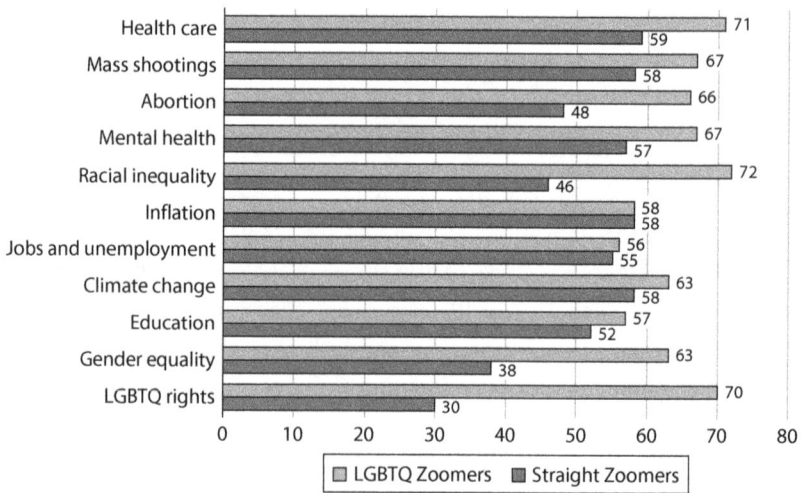

FIGURE 1.3 Percentage of issues of critical importance, by LGBTQ status. Among members of Generation Z, LGBTQ people prioritize progressive issues more than straight people. Qualtrics survey conducted by the author in May 2022, with a sample of 1,600 Americans aged eighteen to twenty-four.

mass shootings, climate change, jobs, and education among their most pressing concerns. My findings that Gen Z women and LGBTQ Zoomers were more likely to name health care and mental health as critical issues compared with Gen Z men and their straight counterparts were consistent with other research showing that the pandemic affected the mental health of women and LGBTQ Americans more than men and straight Americans, respectively.[16]

Gun violence remained a more critical issue concern among Gen Z women and LGBTQ Zoomers than among Gen Z men and straight Zoomers in my survey. Most progressive Zoomer women activists I interviewed named a March for Our Lives protest as their first political action, including Chloe Moore, who founded the group's local chapter in Ithaca, New York, while in high school. "I've been in school shooter drills since third grade," she said. "I don't know how to explain the feeling of being ten and locked in the bathroom with your classmates for an hour, because this is something you might have to deal with later."

Another issue closely linked to the politics of Generation Z was climate change. The survey again showed a gender and LGBTQ divide in terms of the salience of the issues among respondents. Like the issue of mass shootings, many Gen Zers saw climate change as an existential threat.

Neha Desaraju is a Gen Z female climate activist from Texas who served as a decentralized communications coordinator with the Sunrise Movement, a youth-led organization dedicated to stopping climate change. She said that the environment was by far the most important issue facing young people: "If we don't have a planet in ten years, then, you know, there's no pointing fighting for all these other issues."

Gen Z women and queer Zoomers also stood apart from Gen Z men and their straight counterparts, respectively, when it came to prioritizing racial equality, women's rights, and the rights of LGBTQ citizens.

Originally from Chicago, Lauren Williams, who is Black, started the civic engagement platform The Young Vote (theyoungvote.org) during the pandemic lockdown in 2020 while attending Yale University. The group collaborated with twelve college campuses to help college students register to vote and locate their polling places. Williams said that Gen Z Black women are particularly compelled to participate in politics today because they clearly see how people of color bear a disproportionate impact of societal problems. "[Black women] know that if they don't have good economic policy, since they're the group who is most likely have low-wage jobs, that's going to affect them. They know that with tough on crime policies, even though data shows that all races of women are using and selling drugs at the same rate, they're the most likely to be in prison. And so that relates with a lot of other things, whether it's health care, climate change, and on and on," Williams said. "So I think we just see how it's going to affect our lives more."

Gen Z women and LGBTQ Zoomers in my surveys were also far more interested in gender equality and LGBTQ rights. Maddie Proctor was active with High School Democrats of America in her native Colorado before entering Harvard in 2022. She said that Gen Z women have been engaged in these spaces because "we have to be our own advocates." She identifies as LGBTQ and believes that many women and LGBTQ Gen Z folks were more likely to participate in politics and prioritize such concerns because, "if you feel like you're someone who has been excluded or someone who feels like the system isn't working for you, then you are inherently more motivated to go change it."

The May 2022 survey showed a twenty-five-point gap between Gen Z women and Gen Z men on the issue of abortion as being critically important to them personally—which is likely to be more salient for Gen Z women in wake of the *Roe* reversal. The organization I colead, PRRI, conducted polling immediately after the *Dobbs* decision in late June 2022 and found that 71 percent of Gen Z women thought abortion should be legal in all or most cases, compared with 59 percent of Gen Z men.[17] Even before *Dobbs*, it was clear that abortion was top of mind for many progressive Gen Z women I spoke with, who cited the direct impact that access to reproductive rights had on their future choices. "I don't want to be pregnant anytime soon," one Democratic woman from the University of Maryland told me. "I would assume that the majority of us don't want to have a kid while we're in school."

Other Democratic women in my college focus groups agreed, noting that challenges to abortion's legality in many conservative state legislatures have made reproductive rights a more pressing concern for their generation—even before the *Roe* reversal. One Ohio State female student said, "I think that the salience of this issue [has] increased tenfold on both sides. That's why a lot of young women might be even more engaged, because they're responding to an equally heavy attack from Republican legislators."

Future chapters will take a closer look at the importance of abortion, gun violence and climate change for members of Gen Z. It is worth repeating, however, that majorities of Zoomer women and queer Zoomers—but not necessarily Gen Z men or their straight counterparts—appear to prioritize these progressive issues.

GEN Z WOMEN AND LGBTQ ZOOMERS ARE OUTPERFORMING GEN Z MEN AND STRAIGHT COUNTERPARTS IN POLITICAL ENGAGEMENT

In 2017, PRRI partnered with MTV to study the political attitudes and habits of Americans aged fifteen to twenty-four.[18] We found notable gender gaps with respect to political and civic engagement, with young women being significantly more likely than young men to report following a campaign or organization online, posting about politics on social media, volunteering, donating money to political causes, or attending a rally. The participation gap between teen girls and boys aged fifteen to seventeen was especially pronounced.[19] It was this study that sparked my investigation of the "reverse" gender gap because women historically have been less likely to participate in politics than men, or they had reached parity on most forms of political participation in the last decade or so. The PRRI-MTV study had some limitations because we did not ask respondents about their LGBTQ status, and we were unable to ask respondents about a wider

GENDER, SEXUALITY, AND GEN Z'S POLITICS

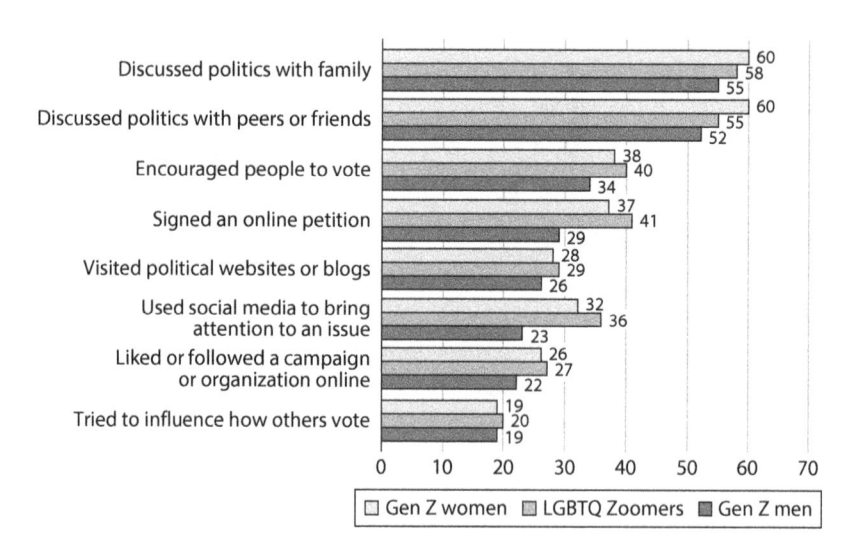

Activity	Gen Z women	LGBTQ Zoomers	Gen Z men
Discussed politics with family	60	58	55
Discussed politics with peers or friends	60	55	52
Encouraged people to vote	38	40	34
Signed an online petition	37	41	29
Visited political websites or blogs	28	29	26
Used social media to bring attention to an issue	32	36	23
Liked or followed a campaign or organization online	26	27	22
Tried to influence how others vote	19	20	19

FIGURE 1.4A Percentage of Gen Zers engaged in passive politics, by gender and LGBTQ status, as of 2019. Among members of Generation Z, women and LGBTQ people participate in most forms of passive politics at higher rates than men or straight people. Qualtrics survey conducted by the author in July 2019, with a sample of 2,200 Americans aged eighteen to twenty-two.

range of political participation habits. But I was curious about whether young women coming of age during the Trump presidency were different than their male counterparts in terms of orientation toward politics and willingness to engage in the political system.

My 2019 and 2022 Qualtrics surveys set out to determine if this reverse gender gap, first identified in the 2017 PRRI survey, was still present and whether it applied to a wider range of political activities, including both passive forms of politics (such as using social media to follow or post about politics, or discussing politics with friends and family) and active forms (like attending a protest rally or showing up for government meetings).[20] Relatively few Americans participate in these active forms of politics, and this was true of Generation Z in my surveys as well.

Figures 1.4A and 1.4B show the levels of engagement for Gen Z women, Gen Z men, and LGBTQ Zoomers on eight different passive forms of

GENDER, SEXUALITY, AND GEN Z'S POLITICS

Activity	Gen Z women	LGBTQ Zoomers	Gen Z men
Discussed politics with family	62	63	57
Discussed politics with peers or friends	53	63	58
Encouraged people to vote	33	38	32
Signed an online petition	35	48	31
Visited political websites or blogs	24	32	24
Used social media to bring attention to an issue	37	44	26
Liked or followed a campaign or organization online	29	33	24
Tried to influence how others vote	17	21	19

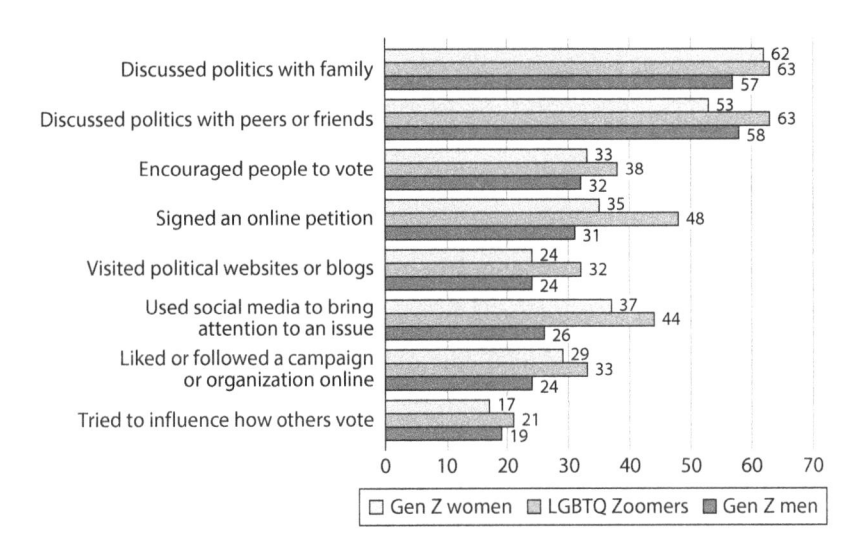

FIGURE 1.4B Percentage of Gen Zers engaged in passive politics, by gender and LGBTQ status, as of 2022. Among members of Generation Z, women and LGBTQ people participate in most forms of passive politics at higher rates than men or straight people. Qualtrics survey conducted by the author in May 2022, with a sample of 1,600 Americans aged eighteen to twenty-four.

politics in 2019 and 2022. Participation levels for straight Zoomers can be found in the appendix to this book. (See Figures A.1 and A.2.)

While most Zoomers discussed politics with their family or peers, Gen Z women in my survey were significantly more likely to engage in such discussions in both years. In 2019, Gen Z women were also more likely than Gen Z men to have discussed politics with their friends, but these positions reversed in 2022, with Gen Z men more likely to say that they discussed politics with their friends; this is the only measure on both surveys in which Gen Z men reported significantly higher levels of engagement. LGBTQ Zoomers discussed politics with friends and family at similar levels compared to their straight counterparts in 2019 but, by 2022, LGBTQ Zoomers reported much higher levels of discussing politics than their straight counterparts.

GENDER, SEXUALITY, AND GEN Z'S POLITICS

THE ROLE OF SOCIAL MEDIA IN SHAPING GEN Z'S POLITICAL VIEWS

When it comes to digital forms of engagement, the 2019 survey found that Gen Z women were significantly more likely than Gen Z men to encourage people to vote and to use social media for political purposes. While Gen Z men began to close the participation gap with Gen Z women on several of these digital indicators by 2022, Gen Z women continued to report that they followed politics or a campaign online, used social media to bring attention to a political issue, and signed an online petition at significantly higher rates than Gen Z men.

I cannot overstate the importance of social media to the story of Gen Z women's political activism. They use social media to educate themselves about political issues, find and build platforms to share their thoughts, and organize more effectively. This digital approach is unique to young women of this generation.

Melissa Kilby spent the last decade working with Girl Up, an advocacy group sponsored by the United Nations that provides programming in leadership development for adolescent girls both in the United States and abroad. Now the executive director of Girl Up, Kilby said that the surge of Gen Z female engagement is linked to social media:

> When we launched Girl Up, there was no Instagram. It didn't exist even ten years ago. I remember celebrating a hundred thousand followers on Facebook, right? . . . And the fact that there is now Instagram, Tik Tok, Snapchat, and all of these platforms, young people every year have more and more access to information. So I can see the difference . . . this sort of power of information and power of the knowledge . . . has opened up Gen Z to a different reality. . . . It's actually resulting in this sort of being compelled to do something with new information, which is the biggest shift I've seen over the ten years.

Kilby added that these young women have yet to endure the challenges faced by previous generations of women activists. "When you're young, you have that sort of belief that you can do all the things, right? You haven't come up against all the 'nos'. . . . You still have that sort of spirit, combined with the power of the social media platform," she said. Kilby told me that her perusal of Gen Z social media space showed that they were populated far more frequently by women than by men, adding, "Gen Z women are taking advantage of the shift of the knowledge, of the community, of these platforms and of this moment in a really strategic and smart and calculated way."

As political scientist Kevin Munger noted in his book *Generation Gap*, Zoomers get news and information very differently than older Americans. They have never known a world without internet access, and they were raised by parents whose more restrictive parenting style often resulted in Zoomers playing outside less and hanging out inside more. Thus, Generation Z is "chronically" online.[21] Gen Z is largely bypassing the traditional legacy media sources that informed their parents and grandparents, instead relying on content about news and culture that they produce themselves.[22] Platforms like Tik Tok and YouTube have, in Munger's words, "brought about the true democratization of the creating of video media, encouraging everyone to participate."[23] Gen Z is the first generation that crowdsources and produces its own news and content, thus establishing its own priorities organically. "More Gen Zers are actively engaged in storytelling, singing, dancing or debating with their peers through these formats, shifting the way that political organizing is done and raising awareness about issues that older generations do not always prioritize in the same ways," wrote Munger.

Social media is the lifeblood of the Gen Z women political entrepreneurs I interviewed, and many started their own online political organizations. Pranjal Jain, for example, founded Global Girlhood, which is dedicated to sharing stories about women of color who are social justice activists and pathbreakers. While in high school, Jain wrote about social justice for *Brown Girl Magazine*, an online publication created by and for South Asian women. She was also an associate director with the Gen Z Girl Gang, an online organization that connects Gen Z women activists and organizers. Jain said that Generation Z was especially poised to capitalize on social media to advocate for political change and social progress, building on lessons from the past generation. While millennials, she said, "would post pictures of themselves, looking pretty," Gen Z, by contrast, has been able to "take [social media] to the next step and realize the power behind it. We're able to use social media in a more purpose-driven way."

SOCIAL MEDIA AND THE *DOBBS* DECISION ON ABORTION RIGHTS

The extraordinary power of social media was on full display in the summer of 2022, after the Supreme Court overturned *Roe v. Wade*. Many young pro-choice Gen Z activists, largely women, took to Twitter, Instagram, TikTok, and other platforms to express outrage but also to encourage their friends to become more engaged in politics, including registering to vote.

That activism paid off in several states, most notably Kansas, where voters had the opportunity in early August, in the first political test of abortion politics after *Dobbs*, to change their state's constitution as a step toward banning the procedure. Not only did voters reject the ballot measure by a landslide—59 to 41 percent—it was women voters who were critical to that effort. Tom Bonier, who runs the Democratic-leaning data and polling firm TargetSmart, noted that voter registration spiked in Kansas after the decision, and 69 percent of the new registrants were women. Other states also saw a significant gender gap in voter registration in the wake of the *Roe* reversal, although nationally data also show that voter registration is growing after *Dobbs* among Gen Z men as well.[24]

Social media also allows activists to raise enormous amounts of money in a post-*Roe* world. Olivia Julianna, a political strategist with Gen Z for Change, a youth-led organization that promotes political engagement among Gen Zers, took to Twitter soon after conservative Florida Republican Representative Matt Gaetz body-shamed and targeted Julianna's work on behalf of reproductive rights in July 2022 on Twitter. She turned his tirade into a fundraising gold mine, and her more than 300,000 Twitter followers donated $2.2 million for abortion care and spread information on voter registration—an overwhelming and rapid rebuke to the online misogyny she faced.[25]

For many progressive and largely female-led Gen Z digital organizations, social media offers a way to shift passions from computer and phone screens and onto the streets. Through instant text messages and technologies such as Linktree that gathers various sources of information and links in one place, followers and supporters have easy access to "actionables," such as prepopulated form emails to send to elected officials and information about upcoming in-person events.

For example, the Linktree of Generation Ratify (now known as the Young Feminist Party), the youth-led gender equality organization founded to lobby for the ratification of the Equal Rights Amendment (ERA), allows followers, in one step, to send emails to Congress to defend and expand abortion access, fund community organizing for abortion access, write Congress about removing the deadline for ratification of the ERA, and organize activists in states to pass constitutional amendments that would enshrine gender equality in state constitutions.

GEN Z WOMEN AND LGBTQ ZOOMERS PARTICIPATE IN OFFLINE ACTIVITIES MORE

Any political organization that seeks to effect real change must adjust its technology to meet an increasingly mobile and tech-savvy world. However, the use of social media for political and social justice causes may hold special appeal for Gen Z women compared with Gen Z men. For instance, an April 2021 Pew Research Center report shows that American women overall are much more likely than men to use the social media platforms that are popular with Gen Z women, including Instagram, TikTok, and Snapchat.[26] My analysis of Pew's 2018 study of Gen Z teens shows similar trends. For instance, 75 percent of Gen Z girls reported using Instagram, compared with 69 percent of Gen Z boys.[27] (One exception is that Gen Z boys report using YouTube more than Gen Z girls—a finding that tracks with my own experience with two teenage sons.) While almost all Gen Zers use social media in their daily lives, social media use for political purposes among LGBTQ Gen Zers has grown precipitously during the past several years, with LGBTQ Zoomers outpacing their straight counterparts in terms

GENDER, SEXUALITY, AND GEN Z'S POLITICS

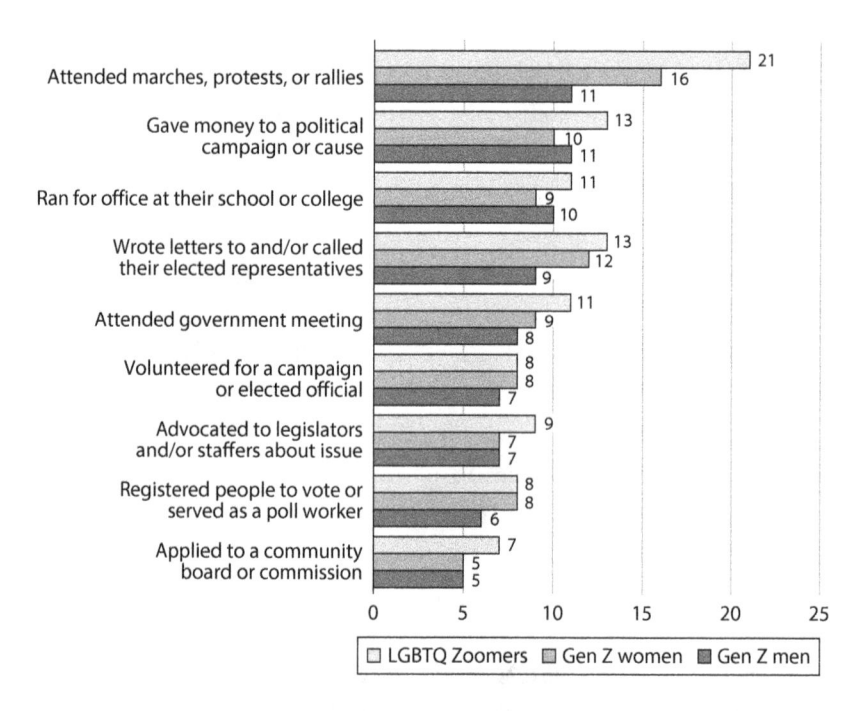

Activity	LGBTQ Zoomers	Gen Z women	Gen Z men
Attended marches, protests, or rallies	21	16	11
Gave money to a political campaign or cause	13	10	11
Ran for office at their school or college	11	9	10
Wrote letters to and/or called their elected representatives	13	12	9
Attended government meeting	11	9	8
Volunteered for a campaign or elected official	8	8	7
Advocated to legislators and/or staffers about issue	9	7	7
Registered people to vote or served as a poll worker	8	8	6
Applied to a community board or commission	7	5	5

FIGURE 1.5A Percentage of Gen Zers engaged in active politics, by gender and LGBTQ status, as of 2019. Among members of Generation Z, women and LGBTQ people participate in most forms of active politics at higher rates than men or straight people. Qualtrics survey conducted by the author in July 2019, with a sample of 2,200 Americans aged eighteen to twenty-two.

of online political participation according to my 2022 survey. Studies show that LGBTQ youth rely heavily on social media to develop their identities and engage with others in a safe space, and that access to social media was especially critical during the pandemic.[28]

While digital political activism is by far the most popular form of political engagement with Zoomers overall, studies show that individuals who engage in political discourse through social media are also significantly more likely to participate in the sorts of active politics showcased in figures 1.5A and 1.5B. (See Figures A.3 and A.4 for data on straight Zoomers.)[29]

GENDER, SEXUALITY, AND GEN Z'S POLITICS

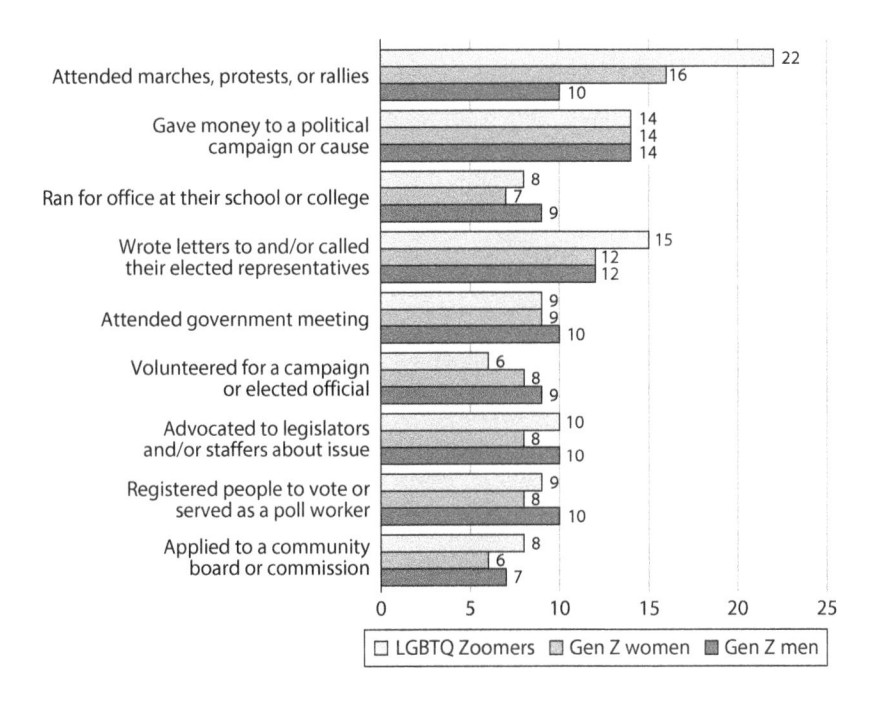

Activity	LGBTQ Zoomers	Gen Z women	Gen Z men
Attended marches, protests, or rallies	22	16	10
Gave money to a political campaign or cause	14	14	14
Ran for office at their school or college	8	7	9
Wrote letters to and/or called their elected representatives	15	12	12
Attended government meeting	9	9	10
Volunteered for a campaign or elected official	6	8	9
Advocated to legislators and/or staffers about issue	10	8	10
Registered people to vote or served as a poll worker	9	8	10
Applied to a community board or commission	8	6	7

FIGURE 1.5B Percentage of Gen Zers engaged in active politics, by gender and LGBTQ status, as of 2022. Among members of Generation Z, LGBTQ people participate in most forms of active politics at higher rates than straight people; Gen Z women and men participate at largely similar rates. Qualtrics survey conducted by the author in May 2022, with a sample of 1,600 Americans aged eighteen to twenty-four.

Social media makes political organizing much easier and more accessible. Many progressive Gen Z women activists I spoke with attended the January 2017 Women's March in Washington and other cities. As one female focus group participant at Ohio State said, social media became a "connector for activism" on a national scale.

Mass protest was the most popular form of offline political participation, with Gen Z women far more likely to march in the streets than Gen Z men in both my 2019 and 2022 surveys (see figures 1.5A and 1.5B). LGBTQ Zoomers also outpaced their straight counterparts in terms of attending marches, protests, and rallies in both years. Other studies found that younger Americans were far more likely to have participated in marches sponsored by climate change, racial justice, and gun violence prevention activists than older Americans.[30]

The other political activities listed in figure 1.5 were less popular forms of involvement in either 2019 or 2022—and most did not elicit any gender differences, except that Gen Z women reported being somewhat more likely to contact government officials about an issue than Gen Z men in 2019. Compared with their straight counterparts, LGBTQ Zoomers in 2019 and 2022 were more likely to contact their government officials.

DEMOCRATIC GEN Z WOMEN, LGBTQ ZOOMERS PARTICIPATE MORE

The specific forms of political engagement matter less, however, to the story of gender and LGBTQ status and politics than overall levels of political participation. When combining all the forms of political activities, Gen Z women in the 2019 survey reported engaging in 3.82 activities, on average, compared with 3.34 reported by Gen Z men, a statistically significant difference.[31] In 2019, LGBTQ Zoomers participated in an average of 4.05 political acts compared with 3.46 reported by their straight counterparts, also a statistically significant difference.[32]

When I asked Gen Zers about their levels of participation in May 2022, Gen Z men had largely caught up with Gen Z women, engaging in 3.61 activities on average compared with 3.78 political activities of Gen Z women. However, this difference is not statistically significant. While Gen Z women have held steady in terms of their levels of political engagement since 2019, and Gen Z men are increasing their political activities, political engagement among LGBTQ Zoomers moved ahead at a rapid pace. By May 2022, LGBTQ Gen Zers reported engaging in a statistically higher average of 4.43 political activities compared with 3.46 activities reported by their straight counterparts.[33]

The intersection of gender, LGBTQ status, and partisanship gives us a glimpse into the political future. Figure 1.6 shows the average number of political activities reported in the past year from the 2019 and 2022 Gen Z

GENDER, SEXUALITY, AND GEN Z'S POLITICS

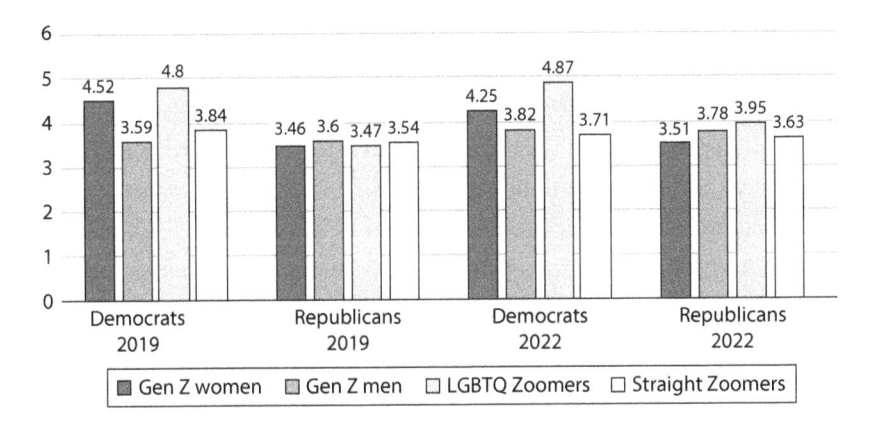

FIGURE 1.6 Average number of political activities in 2019 and 2022, by gender, LGTBQ status, and party. Generation Z women and LGBTQ people participate in more political activities than others. Qualtrics survey conducted by the author in July 2019, with a sample of 2,200 Americans aged eighteen to twenty-two; Qualtrics survey conducted by the author in May 2022, with a sample of 1,600 Americans aged eighteen to twenty-four.

surveys for gender, LGBTQ status, and partisanship. I omitted Gen Zers who do not affiliate with a political party because in both years, overall levels of activities among pure independents were low among both Gen Z women and men, which corresponds to other studies that find that independents are historically less likely to participate in politics.][34]

As figure 1.6 shows, Democratic women reported the highest level of political engagement by far compared with Gen Z Republican women or Gen Z men of either party. In 2019, that was 4.52 political activities—almost a *full* activity more than Gen Z Americans of other partisan and gender types. Democratic Gen Z women not only outperformed both female and male Republican Gen Zers when it came to numbers of political activities that year, but their average number of actions was also higher than Gen Z men who identified as Democrats.[35] Although reported activity levels among Gen Z Democratic men rose in 2022, they still participated in fewer political actions overall than their Gen Z Democratic female peers. The fact that Democratic Gen Z women appear to be leading the charge politically is reinforced by other studies that analyzed youth political engagement since Trump's election in 2016, which showed that Democratic teen girls were much more interested in political protest than other teens.[36]

With respect to LGTBQ Gen Zers, there were fewer than one hundred cases of Republicans in each of the surveys, so those figures should be interpreted with some caution. Nonetheless, LGBTQ Democrats reported participating in more political activities than LGBTQ Republicans in both 2019 (4.80 political activities versus 3.47) and 2022 (4.87 political activities versus 3.95).[37] If these participation levels among Generation Z hold, Gen Z women and LGBTQ Zoomers will undoubtedly shift our politics in a leftward direction in the coming decades.

THE HISTORIC NATURE OF GEN Z WOMEN'S POLITICAL SURGE: THE REVERSE GENDER GAP

Gen Z women participated at higher levels in politics than Gen Z men during the Trump administration, which represents a historic *reverse* gender gap in political participation—at least among the nation's youngest generation. Throughout U.S. history, politics has been the province of men. Strict social codes in the nineteenth century even mandated "separate spheres" for men and women—with home considered the woman's domain and men generally deemed best suited for politics and public life. Breaking these societal norms was difficult. Early women's rights advocates such as Elizabeth Cady Stanton and Lucretia Mott called for ballot access and other rights at what is considered the first women's rights convention in Seneca Falls, New York, in 1848, but it would take more than seventy years for women's universal suffrage to be ratified in the Constitution—and longer still for African American women to win the right to vote in many Southern states. Yet even after women won that hard-fought battle, the expectation that politics was a man's world lingered for decades. As political scientists Christina Wolbrecht and Kevin Corder meticulously documented in their book *A Century of Votes*, it took women until the late 1960s to vote regularly at the same rates as men in American elections.[38]

The norms that kept many women (at least middle-class and wealthier women) at home began to dissolve with the onset of the women's rights movement in the 1970s, when economic conditions led more mothers to work outside the home to maintain a middle class lifestyle. Men still continued to dominate political life well into the early twenty-first century (aside from voting).

Data from the American National Election Studies (ANES) show this trend clearly.[39] From the 1970s through the early 2000s, men continued to hold anywhere from a seven- to thirteen-point advantage over women in terms of engaging in any sort of campaign-related activities, such as volunteering for a campaign, attending a rally, or making a political donation (see the appendix, Table A.3, for more specifics.) That gap began to narrow at about 2005, when women's level of engagement in campaign-related events began to even out.

Why did men have this advantage in political participation for so long? American men historically had higher levels of education that made the political process and policies easier to understand, and they enjoyed higher levels of income that helped to facilitate greater donations to political causes and were more likely to work in professions or jobs that fostered the sorts of organizational skills or development of personal networks that made political activity more likely.[40]

More recent studies showed that women, as they made huge advances in education and careers, have largely leveled the playing field for political engagement beginning around 2010—although women remain still far less likely to run for political office.[41] But it is possible that generational data showing that women participated at lower levels before 2010 or at comparable rates after 2010 obscure a pattern in which *young* women were more likely to get involved in politics in previous generations than young men. If that is true, the gender gap that both PRRI's 2018 survey and my 2019 Qualtrics survey show would be less remarkable if we expand our lens to include younger Americans from earlier generations.

One caveat is that, in addition to voting, the most consistent forms of political participation data the ANES collects are data centered around elections, such as volunteering with a campaign, attending a campaign event, donating to a political campaign, and trying to influence someone's vote.

If I isolate my analysis to American women and men aged eighteen to twenty-four from ANES from 1972 through 2020, young women were not more engaged in those activities than young men. In several presidential election cycles, young men outperformed their female counterparts, but there were no discernible patterns showing young women were participating more than young men. (There is no systematic data collection during those years with respect to LGBTQ status.)

But what about *other* forms of participation that aren't related to campaigns? For example, perhaps the reverse gender gap that I documented during Trump's presidency also showed up among the millennial generation if we move outside *campaign*-related political events. In 2012, the Pew Research Center undertook one of the most comprehensive studies ever about the civic engagement habits of all Americans, asking them whether they had participated in a large range of political and civic activities. Turning to eleven different offline activities, such as attending government meetings and protest rallies as well as working in campaigns, my analysis of the 2012 Pew data showed that *both* young women and men aged eighteen to twenty-four reported in engaging in an average of 1.6 offline activities in the past year. (Like ANES, there were no questions about LGBTQ status on this survey.)

The 2012 Pew study also asked Americans about the extent to which they engaged in twelve different forms of digital activism, including signing an online petition, using social media to encourage action on a political or social issue or post about such issues, and following political groups or candidates online (see the appendix, Figures A.5 and A.6, for specifics on both offline and online forms of political engagement). Again, I found no systematic gender differences in online political engagement among young millennial women and men. Like Americans overall, young millennial women by 2012 had caught up with men their age in terms of engaging in politics—but they had not surpassed them, which suggests that the gender gap that appeared during Trump's presidency, in which Gen Z women became more involved in politics than Gen Z men, was historically distinct.

The fact that young women of Generation Z have become the more pronounced, recognized leaders of burgeoning progressive movements addressing climate change: gun violence prevention: the fight for gender, racial, and LGBTQ rights: and more is a notable departure from other eras. When baby boomers were coming of age and calling for civil rights reforms or fighting against U.S. involvement in the Vietnam War, young women were often excluded from leadership within those movements or faced other forms of sexual discrimination which thus dampened or masked their contributions. The trivialization of such concerns by some male leaders in both the civil rights and antiwar causes helped light the fire under the second wave women's movement by the early 1970s, which sought to eradicate sexism through legal channels, advocate for women's reproductive rights, and champion the ERA.[42]

Progressive Gen Z women are not just championing greater rights for women today, which have grown more uncertain after the *Dobbs* decision. They have emerged as leaders across the progressive political space. Unlike the second wave women's movement, which did not always prioritize the needs of women of color, working-class women, or LGBTQ women in their fight for gender equality,[43] progressive Gen Z women leaders are more deliberately intersectional and inclusive in their approach to political organizing. This reflects their greater racial, ethnic, and LGBTQ diversity than other generations in U.S. history.

This book will address factors that have led to these monumental shifts in the progressive leadership ranks and in political engagement levels overall among Generation Z women and LGBTQ Zoomers. These young leaders are shaping a political world that is more inclusive and is upending our notions of what politics in the United States will look like.

2

POLITICAL CONTEXT, GENDER, AND SEXUALITY IN SHAPING THE POLITICAL ENGAGEMENT OF GEN Z

At her Ann Arbor, Michigan middle school, Naina Agrawal-Hardin would don plastic gloves to pull plastic juice bottles out of the lunchroom trash and set them aside for recycling, a move that made her "*really* popular" with her classmates," she noted sarcastically. She was later devastated to learn that her efforts were for naught: "The cafeteria recycling actually just got thrown in the trash at the end of every day. That was sort of the first switch that flipped about the scale of the problem that we faced."

Agrawal-Hardin was thirteen in 2016 when Donald Trump won the presidency, an event she believes "has had a massive impact on my generation." Several environmental disasters shortly thereafter also raised Agrawal-Hardin's concern about climate change, including a forest fire in East Tennessee that nearly engulfed her grandparents' home and significant flooding in her father's hometown in northern India. Trump administration reversals of Barack Obama's environmental policies, including withdrawal from the UN Paris Agreement on climate, also motivated Agrawal-Hardin to become more active in climate justice.

Agrawal-Hardin joined Sunrise Movement, a popular grassroots organization of young people that seeks to stop climate change. "It was really the first time that I felt like that balance between politics and protests was there," she said. "And I think that balance is so critical, especially when it comes to combating the climate crisis." Initially, Sunrise largely targeted college-age activists; Agrawal-Hardin expanded it to high schools and middle schools as founder of its National Middle and High School Support Team. "I wanted to see more fourteen- to eighteen-year-olds . . . working with an organization that is not just about recycling plastic bottles or saving the animals but that also stresses equality and justice and systematic solutions," she said.

Agrawal-Hardin smiled ruefully when I told her that Gen Z women were more engaged in politics than their male counterparts during Trump's presidency. She believes that many young women like her have been inspired by diverse, powerful young women leaders such as U.S. Representative Alexandria Ocasio-Cortez and her fellow Squad members. "The political icons that my generation has latched onto and gravitated toward have activist roots," she said. "If politics and activism are so connected for people, that means that to meaningfully engage with politics for Gen Z requires you to talk about and demonstrate what you are about and what you're passionate about." By comparison, she said, "straight, cisgender [Gen Z] men are not socialized to express what makes them feel scared or hopeful. A lot of these emotions that are so central to activism are emotions that men are told not to express or not to feel."

Agrawal-Hardin is just one example of the young women who were pulled into progressive political activism during the Trump era, in which she and others witnessed millions of women in pink hats flooding the streets the day after Trump's inauguration, the rise of the Me Too Movement, and a record number of women running for political office in 2018. Agrawal-Hardin was not alone in citing the emotional pull of activism in the Trump era. "I think, simply, young women have more to worry about than young men do regarding the political atmosphere," said one participant of the focus groups at IGNITE, the nation's largest and most diverse young women's political leadership program. "They don't have to think about the things that we have to think about, and it's just always been like that. It's a systematic thing. So we're here doing this thing because we have to be the voices because we're drastically underrepresented."

In this chapter and the next, I take a closer look at how gender and sexuality contribute to the political engagement of Gen Z—in particular which factors help explain the historically unique gender gap that emerged during Trump's presidency and how such factors continue to drive political activism among Gen Z women and LGBTQ Zoomers. Put together, these elements reveal why gender and LGBTQ status will likely continue to play a profound role in building a more inclusive political future, despite (or perhaps even because of) growing political threats to the rights of marginalized groups in the United States.

MY GEN Z POLITICAL ENGAGEMENT MODEL

An entire political science subindustry has evolved to illuminate the factors that lead some Americans to political activity. We don't yet know, however, whether such factors shape the political participation habits of this nascent generation and, if they do, whether they apply differently to Gen Z women, Gen Z men, and LGBTQ Zoomers.

A statistical technique known as multiple regression can help us untangle these knots. Kristen Soltis Anderson, a well-known pollster, compares such statistical models to recipes, "a bunch of different ingredients [that] are included in different amounts to create something useful in the end."[1] I am interested in understanding why Gen Z Americans participate in politics and whether such factors work differently for Gen Z women than Gen Z men, as well as the impact of LGBTQ status on political engagement; thus, the "ingredients" of my Gen Z political engagement model include elements that have long been linked to higher levels of political participation.

Using my July 2019 and May 2022 Qualtrics surveys, I first take a closer look at some of the individual factors that might explain why Gen Z women surged ahead politically during Trump's presidency and why LGBTQ Zoomers participate at higher rates than straight Zoomers. As a first cut, I report relationships at the bivariate level of analysis, which means that

I take a closer look at how factors such as socioeconomic status, race/ethnicity, or past involvement in high school activities shape Gen Z women and men's mean levels of political engagement *one factor at a time*. I do the same to compare LGBTQ Zoomers with their straight counterparts. Then I consider whether such relationships, if they exist at this level of analysis, hold up once I control for other factors in my multivariate models. The initial relationships we are seeing between such factors and levels of engagement might in fact be explained by a third factor that is driving variation for both variables. For instance, although high school involvement could lead to higher levels of political engagement among the members of Gen Z, perhaps Zoomers who come from families of means are more likely to be active in high school activities, so socioeconomic status is really the driving force that explains the apparent link between political engagement and high school participation that we are initially seeing in the bivariate relationship. To return to the recipe analogy, which ingredients are really flavoring the food that captures political participation rates among Gen Z and which ingredients drown in the mix?

I also talked to members of Generation Z and leaders of organizations that seek to cultivate political leadership in young women and girls about their perspectives on why this historic reverse gender gap in political participation emerged in the Trump Era and about their thoughts on why we are seeing the activist class on the political left among Gen Z dominated by Gen Z women and LGBTQ Zoomers.

HOW SOCIOECONOMIC STATUS AND RACE/ETHNICITY SHAPE GEN Z POLITICAL ENGAGEMENT

People who are active in politics tend to be better educated, have higher incomes, and are more likely to work in professional jobs compared with those who are less active.[2] Studies based on data from the 1990s and earlier suggest that if women had had the same levels of socioeconomic resources as men, they would have participated in politics at largely the same rates across several eras.³ More recent work from the early 2000s bore that prediction out—as women became better educated, earned more, and gained more professional work experience, they largely closed the participatory gap—save running for office—by the 2010s.⁴

In focus groups, some participants said educational advances might explain why Gen Z women were more politically involved than Gen Z men during the Trump presidency. "I know that more women are in university, more women are in law school. And maybe even I think doctors as well, might be overtaken by women," said a Republican man from the University of Maryland. He's exactly right—Gen Z men are far less likely to attend college than Gen Z women; experts who study education trends know that women have been more likely to earn college degrees than men since the mid-1980s.⁵ In the past several years, the female-male gap in higher education reached an all-time high, a trend accelerated by the COVID-19 pandemic.⁶

Examining the impact of education on Gen Z Americans' political participation is tricky because the individuals were between the ages of eighteen and twenty-two in my 2019 Generation Z survey. Although that age range expanded when I conducted my 2022 survey, there were still a lot of respondents who had just graduated from high school or were still in college. My surveys in both years generally found, however, that current educational status is positively related to political engagement for *all* Zoomers, regardless of gender or LGBTQ status.⁷ The starkest differences emerge between Zoomers who possess only a high school degree (or less) and those who have at least some college education.

Turning to other demographic measures, we know that white Americans, often as a function of having higher levels of education and income, tend to participate more in politics than other racial and ethnic groups.⁸ The findings with respect to Gen Z are mixed at first glance: Gen Z women report similar levels of political engagement in both 2019 and 2022 regardless of race and ethnicity. In both years, white Gen Z men have higher rates of engagement than Black Gen Z men, but they have comparable rates of engagement compared with Zoomer men who are Latinx, Asian, or multiracial. There are no statistically distinct racial/ethnic political participation patterns among LGBTQ Zoomers in either year.⁹

POLITICAL CONTEXT, GENDER, AND SEXUALITY

HOW CIVIC SKILLS ARE SHAPING GEN Z'S POLITICAL ENGAGEMENT

Individuals who develop civic skills through community participation tend to be more politically active, and Gen Z Americans have had such opportunities through involvement in numerous school organizations, community groups such as Girl Scouts or Boy Scouts or through taking a civics or public affairs class in high school. In the past decade or so, numerous organizations have emerged to train young women in broader leadership and organizational skills, and to foster political ambition among girls.[10] One such organization is Girl Up, started in 2010 as an outgrowth of the UN Commission on the Status of Women. Melissa Kilby, Girl Up's executive director, told me that her organization and similar groups remain vital for "overcoming so many distortions of the perception of the value of girls."

"I think girls themselves are still battling their own internal value of their voice and their potential," Kilby said. "[Y]ou are still surrounded by parents, teachers, adults, peers, who don't get it and don't see it and don't understand why it's necessary to build up the young women in their lives."

Several of the Gen Z female activists I spoke with participated in Girl Up programs, including Riya Goel, a civic engagement and voter registration activist with Do Something and cofounder of Asians Lead, a youth-based organization in West Orange, New Jersey, that empowers Gen Z Asian American and Pacific Islander leaders to confront Asian stereotypes. Although she had participated in school events and clubs in high school before, Goel said her political activism "picked up and went on another scale when I got to go to the Girl Up Leadership Summit." Goel counts networking experiences she had through Girl Up as vital to her political growth, including meeting Ibtihaj Muhammed, an Olympic fencer who was the first Muslim American woman to wear a hijab at the Olympics while competing. Goel later started the first fencing club at her own high school.

In addition to her involvement with Girl Up, Goel was a delegate to the UN Commission on the Status of Women in 2019 representing Girl

Scouts, another group that she credits with developing her leadership skills. Studies commissioned by the Girl Scout Research Institute show that former Girl Scouts are more likely to think it is important to make a positive impact on society through their work and are more involved in civic engagement and politics later in life compared with women who did not participate in scouting.[11]

Under the leadership of Sylvia Acevedo, Girl Scout CEO from 2016 to 2020, the organization developed badges for leadership and civic engagement. Scouts don't merely learn about such topics; they are rewarded for action. Acevedo told me about Ana De Almeida Amaral, a 2018 National Gold Award Girl Scout, who designed and taught an ethnic studies course in her Chula Vista, California, high school after lobbying school officials about the need for such a curriculum in the majority-minority school district. "[Ana] didn't do a parade. She didn't protest. She had taken the badges and learned how to shape policy. She went to the school board; she had to develop a curriculum. They implemented the curriculum. . . . To me, that is a great example."

During her time as CEO, Acevedo said, Girl Scouts influenced a wide array of policies at the state and local levels, including curriculum development, plastic straw bans, and the establishment of bees' habitats. The Girl Scouts' approach has always been nonpartisan, she added, with the most important goal being that "Girl Scouts use their voices."

Other nonprofits that seek to empower young women to run for political office have emerged in the past decade or so. Anne Moses started IGNITE in 2010 after stints with EMILYs List and Emerge America, political organizations that raise funds for and train older women to run for political office. A nonprofit, nonpartisan organization, IGNITE has become a preeminent political leadership program, training more than thirty thousand high school and college women. Moses noted that Gen Z women have been particularly receptive to IGNITE's work since the election of Trump, which, she said, "changed the dynamics about the volume of women who were interested in this kind of thing, who I think understood the urgency and actually woke up to the fact that sexism, it's not a thing of the past."

POLITICAL CONTEXT, GENDER, AND SEXUALITY

Many teens are also heavily involved in social and political clubs in their high schools. Studies find that involvement in such school activities can boost political participation among young adults.[12] The first political experiences of most of the progressive Gen Z political entrepreneurs I interviewed involved organizing their fellow classmates around gun violence prevention, climate change, and racial and gender justice issues in middle school or high school or as part of after-school programming.

Goel, the New Jersey Girl Up alum and cofounder of Asians Lead, launched a Meatless Mondays program and a women's leadership group in her high school. "I think the importance of starting your own organizations or initiatives, whether that be in a school or community setting, is powerful in terms of realizing the potential that one has as a changemaker, and really understanding that change is possible," she said.

The cultivation of civic skills is not limited to progressives. Chloe Sparwatch, a Republican Gen Z activist from Georgia, served as the University of Virginia's chapter president of the Network of Enlightened Women (NeW), a leading conservative organization for college women. Sparwatch's passion for politics began in high school when she participated in a mock Georgia State government program run by the YMCA. She told me that this program shaped her political views, fostering what she describes as a minor obsession with the first constitutional amendments ("I have a Bill of Rights T-shirt and everything."), shaping her libertarian-leaning views, and leading her to believe that having government as "uninvolved in people's lives is the better way to go." Through her involvement with the mock legislative program, Sparwatch began volunteering on the campaigns of local Republican candidates.

My Gen Z surveys in 2019 and 2022 asked respondents whether they participated in one of eight organization or club opportunities while in high school, whether they took a civics class, or whether they participated in Girl Scout or Boy Scouts. The vast majority reported participating in at least one of these activities during their high school years—roughly 96 percent of Gen Z men and 97 percent of Gen Z women, in both 2019 and 2022, with 97 percent of LGBTQ Zoomers in both 2019 and 2022 reporting that they participated in at least one high school organization or group. Collectively, however, in 2019, Gen Z women reported significantly higher mean numbers of high school participation (3.22 activities) then Gen Z men (2.94 activities) in my survey.[13] In my 2022 survey, the differences evened out, with 3.04 activities for women versus 2.89 for men, which is no longer statistically significant.

The average number of high school activities reported by LGBTQ Zoomers in 2019 was 3.21, which was significantly higher than straight Zoomers, who participated in an average of 3.02 activities.[14] As with Gen Z women and men, however, differences in rates of high school activities diminished in 2022, with LGBTQ students reporting an average of 3.01 activities compared with 2.95 activities for straight Zoomers. In both years, the more Zoomers participated in high school or civic activities, the more they engaged with politics.[15]

It's hard to tell from one data point whether this participation helps explain the reverse gender gap in political involvement. It's plausible that in 2019, in a political context in which gender mattered, those higher levels of school engagement on the part of Gen Z girls were a unique contributor to the gender gap in political engagement for that year. By May 2022, with Trump no longer in the White House and Americans continuing to cope with the aftermath of the global pandemic, participation in high school activities, while still a significant predictor of political engagement levels overall, may no longer have mattered uniquely to Gen Z women.

One thing that sets Generation Z teen girls apart is widespread attention to building self-esteem and leadership skills through K–12 curriculum and other efforts, such as Girl Scouts and books designed to promote science, technology, engineering, and mathematics (STEM) careers. These may have helped overcome the sorts of psychological barriers that women have often faced in becoming interested in politics or feeling as though their participation matters. By May 2022, those same programs may have lost some punch because they moved online in 2020 and 2021 due to the COVID-19 pandemic.

Virtual connections, which rose during the pandemic lockdown, may have boosted the political engagement levels of LGBTQ Zoomers. Studies show that online resources can provide critical communities for LGBTQ teens, who may not have sufficient support in schools or in their face-to-face communities, and that online communities can also propel LGBTQ teens toward involvement in civic and political causes as they become more knowledgeable about issues that affect their communities.[16]

HOW PSYCHOLOGICAL RESOURCES SHAPE GEN Z'S POLITICAL ENGAGEMENT

When people express more interest in politics, believe that their participation can lead to change, and identify strongly with a political party, they are more likely to participate in politics.[17] Charlotte Kerpen, a New York Zoomer who served as the national chair of the High School Democrats during the 2020–2021 school year, embodies all these elements. With parents active in the Democratic Party, Kerpen sent her first tweet at age ten in support of President Obama's reelection campaign when she learned that Mitt Romney wanted to stop federal funding for public broadcasting (she was a big Sesame Street fan growing up).

Too young to vote, Kerpen volunteered for Hillary Clinton's presidential campaign in 2016, hoping to witness the election of the nation's first female president. Clinton's loss was devastating to Kerpen, who found solace and political inspiration while attending the Women's March in Washington, DC:

> It just felt like a real sense of community . . . it was less about anti-Trump. It was more pro-women. I wanted to advocate for making sure that women were represented and making sure that women were being heard, because what I saw was a candidate who I thought was so fit to win and I thought was going to win, you know, not just win the election, but win the election by a landslide.

While Kerpen is far more active in politics than a typical young person (or most older Americans, for that matter), the idea that Gen Z women care more about politics than their male counterparts is a theme that came up in several of my focus groups. "I don't understand *where* men are being politically engaged," said one Georgia State student who rarely discusses politics with male friends. "Women will talk about it . . . I feel like I talk about politics a lot with my friends. And my friends will post on social media, but where are guys doing that?"

My 2019 national survey finds, however, that Zoomers hold similar levels of political interest, regardless of gender or LGBTQ status. Among all adults in nationally representative studies, American women, despite reaching parity levels of political participation with men in the last decade or so, continue to show less interest in politics than men.[18] Thus, the finding that Gen Z women had political interest levels on par with Gen Z men in 2019 is notable. By May 2022, my Qualtrics survey found, however, that Gen Z men reported following politics at slightly higher levels (69 percent) compared with Gen Z women (63 percent).[19] Differences between LGBTQ and straight Zoomers with respect to political interest remain statistically indistinguishable in 2022 among survey respondents. Younger women may have been following politics more closely in 2019 relative to previous generations because of factors like the women's movement, the Me Too movement, and record numbers of women running for office.

When I conducted my national Qualtrics survey of Gen Z respondents in May 2022, these gendered elements were not as heightened, but the *Dobbs* decision in late June no doubt prompted more attention to politics among Gen Z women. Indeed, my organization, Public Religion Research Institute (PRRI), conducted a survey shortly after the Supreme Court's *Dobbs* decision overturned the constitutional right to an abortion in which we asked Americans how much attention they pay to politics.[20] We found that the gender gap in political interest among Zoomers was statistically indistinguishable by July 2022, with 59 percent of Gen Z men reporting that they pay attention to politics a lot or some of the time, compared with 56 percent of Gen Z women. Our same July 2022 survey found, however, that American men *overall* still reported paying attention to politics and current affairs more than American women, 72 percent versus 63 percent, respectively.[21] In other words, the historical trend that men pay more attention to politics in the United States after *Dobbs* was alive and well—except among Generation Z.

Political scientist Jennifer Wolak argues that self-confidence plays a key mediating role in political interest among Americans and operates differently for men and women.[22] While both confident men and women express more interest and engagement in politics, Wolak's research found that women's lower levels of confidence compared to men contributes to women being less interested in politics, regardless of age. Yet Wolak's data are drawn from surveys more than a decade old—so Zoomers were not part of her analysis. That Gen Z women generally appear to have closed the gender gap in political interest with Zoomer men indicates how unique these younger women are. While neither my surveys nor PRRI surveys control for self-confidence, Gen Z women's exposure to programming in schools and elsewhere that fosters leadership skills and self-esteem may be chipping away at what used to be young women's comparative lack of interest in politics.

In both my 2019 and 2022 Qualtrics surveys, interest in politics is linked to higher levels of political participation among Gen Z more broadly: both Gen Z women and men who hardly follow politics report engaging in fewer than 2.5 political activities annually. Those numbers more than doubled, however, among Zoomers who said that they followed politics most of the time. LGBTQ Zoomers in both years who did not closely follow politics at all reported engaging in fewer than three activities, while those who followed politics closely engaged in 4.5 political activities in 2019 and 5.49 activities in 2022.

Another way to capture political interest is to consider the number of political issues that Americans care about, a concept referred to as "issue publics" by political scientist Hahrie Han.[23] In both years of my Qualtrics surveys, the more critical issues that Gen Z respondents cared about, the more they engaged in politics; this relationship exists, however, regardless of gender or LGBTQ status.[24] Yet Gen Z women listed a significantly higher number of critical issues about which they care compared with Gen Z men: in 2019, 6.68 versus 5.79 critical issues,[25] and in 2022, 8.59 versus 6.48,[26] respectively. (The 2022 survey also asked about mental health as a critical issue in addition to the original fourteen issues, raising the overall averages for both groups.) LGBTQ Zoomers also listed more issues as being critically important to them personally compared with straight Zoomers: in 2019, 6.99 versus 6.11 issues; in 2022, 8.82 versus 7.11 issues, respectively.[27]

INTERNAL AND EXTERNAL POLITICAL EFFICACY AS PSYCHOLOGICAL RESOURCES

Internal political efficacy is a concept that taps into Americans' belief that individuals understand how government works so they can influence its decision making; external political efficacy considers how well the government is responding to the wishes of its citizenry. Having low levels of either form of political efficacy typically results in lowers levels of political engagement,[28] particularly among women historically.[29] Some focus group participants acknowledged that they or their friends are not heavily involved in politics because they doubt that political engagement results in meaningful political change, such as this Democratic woman from Georgia State University:

> I know, personally, I feel a lot of helplessness, like, "Oh, I want to do something, but I don't know what to do." Or the options presented to me, are like, "Oh, you can vote," but I have a feeling of like, "I will vote, but . . . how much does my vote matter?"

Other participants said that many of their Gen Z peers avoid politics because they believe the system is fraudulent or ineffectual. "I feel like a lot of people are in the mindset that politics is such a corrupted, polarizing thing that they just don't want to be involved at all, and they don't really see it as something that they should invest themselves in," said a Democratic man from the University of Maryland.

My Gen Z surveys considered internal efficacy by asking respondents the extent to which they personally understood how government works, a measure linked to political engagement.[30] Gen Z men were more likely in 2019 to say that they strongly agreed (29.9 percent) that they understood how government works compared with Gen Z women (24.9 percent)[31]—so it is not likely that expressing greater confidence about understanding how government works among Generation Z explains the reverse gender gap in political participation that year.

That internal efficacy gap widened in 2022, with 27 percent of Gen Z men and 20 percent of Gen Z women indicating they strongly agreed with this measure.[32] LGBTQ Zoomers were not distinct from straight Zoomers with respect to scores on internal efficacy for either year; higher levels of internal political efficacy were linked to higher levels of political participation for Generation Z regardless of LGBTQ status.[33]

External political efficacy, which taps into Americans' belief that government is responsive to the needs of the people, was a stronger contributor to Gen Z's reverse gender gap in my 2019 survey. For Gen Z women, anger about the government's lack of response to their issues and concerns fueled their political fire.

Riley Reed, the founder of Pride in Running, which organized young people to volunteer for LGBTQ candidates in 2020 and 2021, tapped into that sentiment when asked why she thought Gen Z women were more involved in politics during Trump's presidency than Gen Z men. "From my experience, [Gen Z men] are a lot more conservative in terms of issues," she said. "I grew up around a bunch of white men and they think that nothing affects them. So that's why they don't really want anything to change. You're not going to change the system that benefits you."

My 2019 national survey data supports Reed's thesis that it is the *lack* of response from government that drove higher levels of political involvement from young women while Trump was president. I asked Zoomers if they agreed that the political system in this country helps the public with their genuine needs.[34] As figure 2.1 shows, in 2019, Gen Z women who *disagree* that the government is meeting the public's needs reported participating in more political activities (4.41 activities) than Gen Z women who were more satisfied with government's responsiveness (3.95).[35] In contrast, Gen Z men reported statistically similar levels of political engagement whether they agreed or disagreed with that sentiment. Although LGBTQ Zoomers who disagreed with this sentiment participate in more activities than those LGBTQ Zoomers who thought government was responsive, this difference was not statistically significant in 2019. When I surveyed Gen Z Americans in May 2022, dissatisfaction with the political system continued to drive Gen Z women toward more political engagement (see figure 2.2). Like 2019, Gen Z men's political participation habits were not affected by views of government responsiveness.

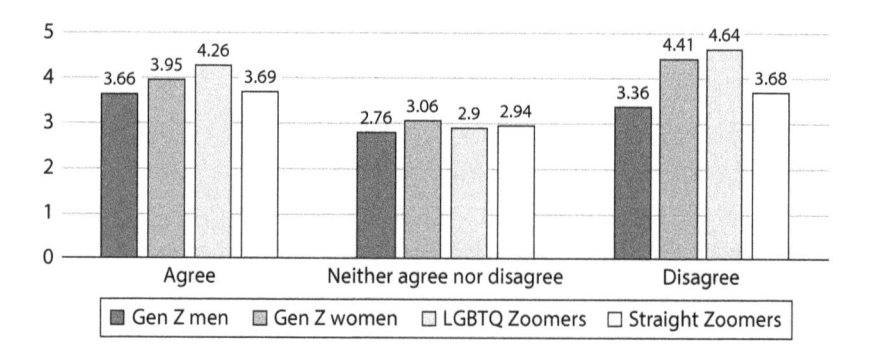

FIGURE 2.1 Average number of political activities, by gender, LGBTQ status, and belief that the government meets the needs of the public, as of 2019. Gen Z women and LGBTQ Americans who disagree that the government meets the needs of the public participate in more political activities than others. Qualtrics survey conducted by the author in July 2019, with a sample of 2,200 Americans aged eighteen to twenty-two.

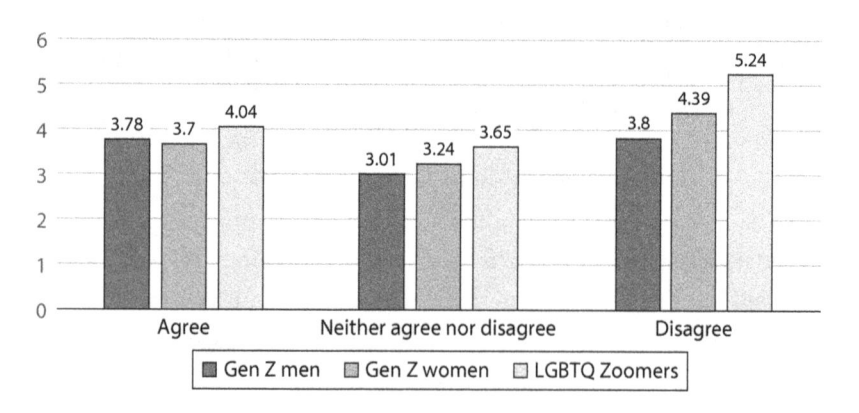

FIGURE 2.2 Average number of political activities, by gender, LGBTQ status, and belief that the government meets the needs of the public, as of 2022. Gen Z women and LGBTQ Americans who disagree that the government meets the needs of the public have higher mean levels of political participation than others. Qualtrics survey conducted by the author in May 2022, with a sample of 1,600 Americans aged eighteen to twenty-four.

In my 2022 Qualtrics survey, LGBTQ Zoomers were motivated to participate in more political activities because of dissatisfaction with government and at much higher levels than their straight counterparts.[36] Rising political and legal threats faced by LGBTQ Americans since Trump left office, Reed said, have driven engagement by her fellow LGBTQ Gen Zers. "A lot of queer people are feeling activated to do stuff and are a lot more engaged, resulting in the [participation] gap between queer people and straight people," she said. "You have to fight harder if *your* rights are on the line, which is really unfortunate, but yeah, it needs to happen."

PARTISANSHIP AND IDEOLOGY AS PSYCHOLOGICAL RESOURCES

Studies show that partisan intensity, regardless of party, drives political engagement among Americans and is a particularly important factor to consider given the increasing rise of polarization facing the nation. Americans who are "pure" independents are the most disaffected group in American politics and tend to tune out what is happening with government—and this is true for Generation Z as well.[37]

For Gen Z men, however, strength of partisanship did not drive more political participation according to my 2019 Qualtrics survey. The real story here involves Gen Z women who were strong Democrats (see figure 2.3); they made up about 25 percent of Gen Z American women overall in my 2019 survey, and they reported engaging in an average of five political activities, far higher than all other Gen Z women and Gen Z men.[38] Party strength, which denotes the extent to which someone strongly affiliates with a party, was not a significant predictor of levels of political participation for LGBTQ or straight Zoomers in 2019.[39]

Strong Democratic Gen Z women in my May 2022 survey engaged in 4.3 political activities compared with 5.05 activities in the July 2019 survey, and strong Democratic women still reported statistically higher levels of engagement compared with strong Republican women (3.59 activities). Unlike Gen Z women, strong partisanship among both Democratic and Republican Gen Z men led to similar levels of political actions, 4.14 political

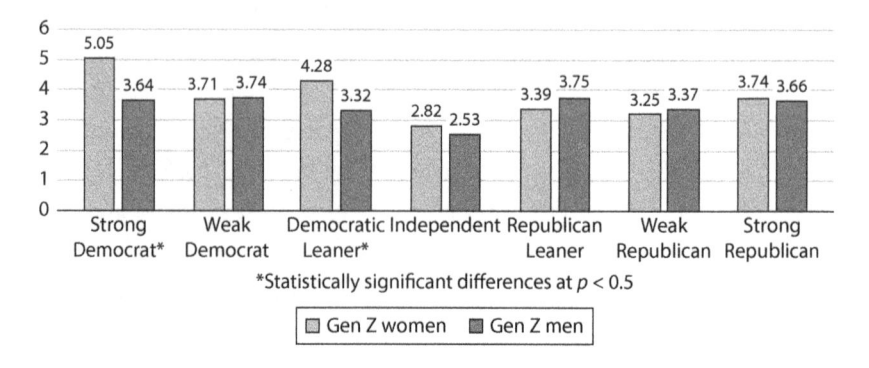

```
6
5   5.05
4        3.64  3.71 3.74   4.28                    3.75         3.74 3.66
                                3.32          3.39      3.25 3.37
3                                    2.82 2.53
2
1
0
    Strong      Weak      Democratic Independent Republican  Weak       Strong
    Democrat*   Democrat  Leaner*                 Leaner    Republican  Republican
              *Statistically significant differences at p < 0.5
                    ☐ Gen Z women   ■ Gen Z men
```

FIGURE 2.3 Average number of political activities, by gender and party strength. Gen Z women who identify as strong Democrats report the highest levels of political engagement. Qualtrics survey conducted by the author in July 2019, with a sample of 2,200 Americans aged eighteen to twenty-two.

actions versus 4.08 political actions, respectively. Zoomers who are pure independents—female or male, LGBTQ or straight—engaged in fewer activities in 2022 than Zoomers who identified as partisans overall; but for both LGBTQ and straight Zoomers, strength of partisanship was not significantly related to their political engagement levels in 2022.[40]

As for ideological dynamics, my 2019 survey found liberal Gen Z women participated in more activities (4.69) than conservative Gen Z women (3.64).[41] The same cannot be said of Gen Z men—liberal and conservative Zoomer men reported participating in about 3.5 political activities on average. By May 2022, liberal Gen Z women continued participating at significantly higher rates (4.36 activities) compared to conservative Gen Z women (3.78 activities).[42] Ideological differences in political engagement remained minimal among Gen Z men in 2022.

Not surprisingly, LGBTQ Zoomers were almost twice as likely to self-identify as politically liberal than conservative. In my 2022 survey, for instance, 49 percent of LGBTQ Zoomers choose to describe themselves as liberal—and they were more likely to do so than their straight counterparts (29 percent). While straight Zoomers who are liberal participated at higher levels than straight conservatives in 2019,[43] ideology was statistically unrelated to political participation in 2022 among this cohort. Unlike their straight counterparts, liberal LGBTQ Zoomers participated in politics at

POLITICAL CONTEXT, GENDER, AND SEXUALITY

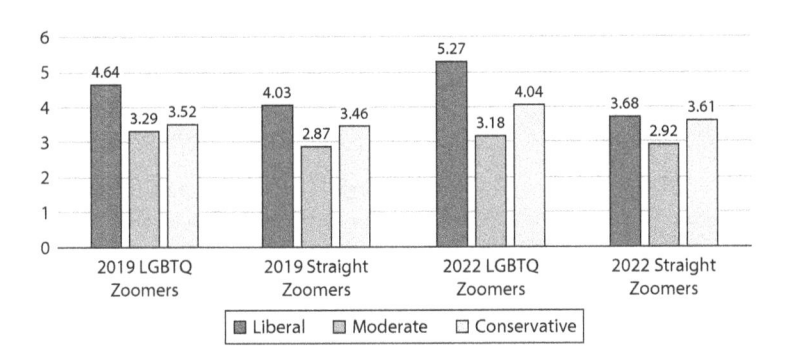

FIGURE 2.4 Average number of political activities, by LGBTQ status and ideology. Among members of Generation Z, liberal ideology drives higher mean levels of political engagement for LGBTQ and straight people in 2019 but just for LGBTQ people in 2022. Qualtrics survey conducted by the author in July 2019, with a sample of 2,200 Americans aged eighteen to twenty-two; Qualtrics survey conducted by the author in May 2022, with a sample of 1,600 Americans aged eighteen to twenty-four.

much higher rates than those who identify as conservative or moderate, for both years (see figure 2.4).[44]

POLITICAL MOBILIZATION AND POLITICAL ENGAGEMENT AMONG GEN Z

Being asked to participate in politics by groups such as parties, campaigns, or other nonprofit organizations raises the chances that individuals will in fact do so. Many college focus group participants noted that their campuses held get out the vote (GOTV) efforts or that they were targeted by such initiatives via social media. Others said that women's leadership organizations encouraged their political engagement, "We've seen a lot more organizations like IGNITE that give young women an avenue to finally be politically active," said a Democratic woman from Ohio State. "Those organizations may not exist for young men primarily because they don't really need them. A huge part of why I'm so active is because there are so many organizations that I am able to be a part of."

POLITICAL CONTEXT, GENDER, AND SEXUALITY

Alise Maxie, a Black lesbian who graduated in 2022 from Prairie View A&M University in Houston, Texas, first became politically aware as a thirteen-year-old, when she learned about the police killing of Michael Brown in Ferguson, Missouri, and began participating in Black Lives Matter (BLM) marches. In college, she became active with the Human Rights Campaign (HRC), an LGBTQ rights organization that flew Maxie to Washington, DC, for a summit of young Black LGBTQ Americans:

> It was the first time I felt like a whole bunch of queer, Black individuals were educated all in one space, doing great things. There were parties, lawmakers. And it just really sparked me, like, I can be like this one day. It was really about teaching us and educating us about diversity and, LGBTQIA training, and trying to bring that back to our campuses [so] that we could make our campuses more inclusive. So that was kind of like the start of my LGBTQIA activism.

After the summit, Maxie learned about HRC's Time to Thrive campaign on Instagram and became an HRC Foundation Youth Ambassador, sharing stories and raising awareness about the most pressing issues facing LGBTQ youth. After the training, Maxie led her first BLM March in Houston after Breonna Taylor's death and continues to advocate for the rights of racial minorities and LGBTQ Americans.

My Gen Z surveys asked young Americans whether they were encouraged to participate in politics by a political party, a campaign organization, or a national political group to determine if such interactions boost their political engagement. Zoomers nationally in both surveys reported participating in more political activities when they were contacted by such groups, regardless of their gender or LGBTQ status.[45]

Unlike many of the Gen Z political entrepreneurs I interviewed, however, relatively few Zoomers nationwide reported being contacted by such groups—roughly one in five. Therefore, the reverse gender gap in 2019 among Gen Z Americans nationally was not a function necessarily of Gen Z women being more likely to be contacted by political groups and campaigns.

POLITICAL CONTEXT, GENDER, AND SEXUALITY

EMOTIONS AND POLITICAL ENGAGEMENT

Scholars have increasingly focused attention on the role of emotions[46] or fears about external threats[47] in motivating political participation. This pull was dramatically evident among progressive Gen Z women when I asked them what prompted their first engagement with politics. "Trump winning just kind of scared us all to our cores," said a Democratic woman from the University of Maryland. "My rights are being threatened and just walking down the street, I am being threatened and I need to do something."

One Ohio State Democratic woman said that Trump's victory over Clinton inspired her to attend several protest marches, noting that Clinton's loss was particularly jarring because, in her mind, Trump is "not a normal Republican, so that made me more angry than . . . if a woman had simply lost to another contender."

Other focus group participants expressed alarm at Trump's treatment of immigrants, including this IGNITE participant: "At first, [Trump's election] enacted fear, a lot of fear in me, my family and lots of immigrants that I know. But as time passed by . . . I channeled the fear into energy to empower myself, and just to make sure that I would have the right representation, or I could fight for it at least."

I asked Zoomers to rank the extent of their feelings, both negative (anger, fear, nervousness, and disgust) and positive (enthusiasm, hopefulness, pride, and happiness), about the country as a lot, somewhat, a little, or not at all. Gen Z women were significantly more likely to say they were experiencing all the negative emotions *a lot* compared with Gen Z men in both 2019 and 2022—and were correspondingly less positive about the state of the nation. The same is even more true for LGBTQ Zoomers compared with their straight Zoomer counterparts.[48] Those negative emotions are linked to higher levels of engagement among both Gen Z women and LGBTQ Zoomers than Gen Z men and straight Zoomers, respectively, in both the 2019 and 2022 surveys.

Figure 2.5 shows the political engagement levels by Zoomers in my survey for 2022, but the trends are similar for both years. Generally speaking, holding positive views about the state of Americans drove Zoomers overall to be less engaged in politics. Although relatively very few LGBTQ Zoomers looked at the state of affairs in 2022 with pride or enthusiasm, those who did so participated in politics at higher rates than their straight counterparts. Gen Z women who felt negative emotions about the state of their country reported participating in more political activities; Gen Z men reported similar levels of engagement regardless of whether they indicated they felt positively or negatively about how things were going in the country.

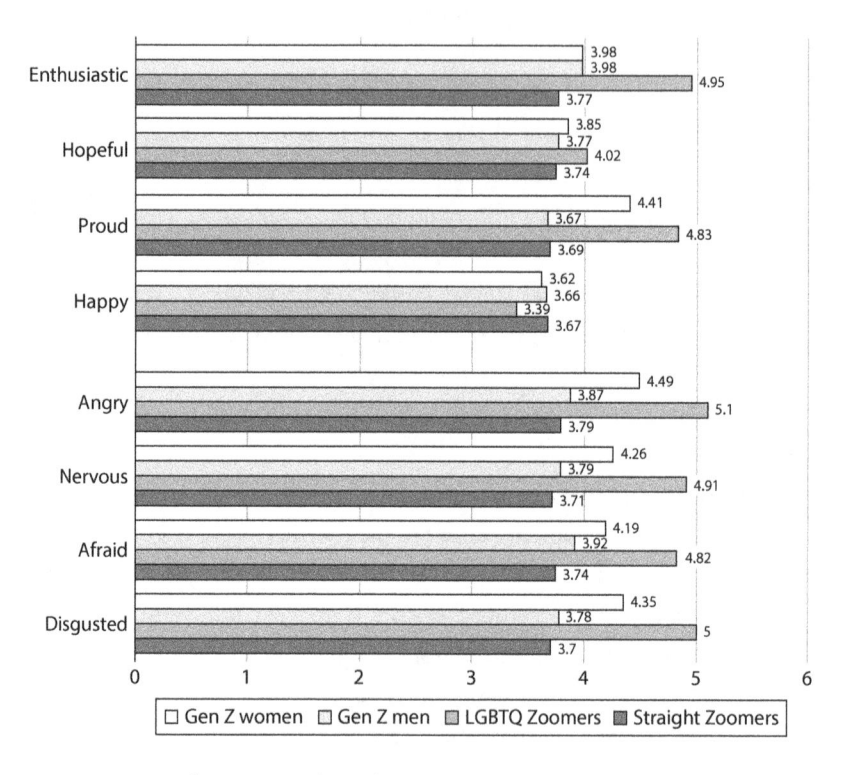

Emotion	Gen Z women	Gen Z men	LGBTQ Zoomers	Straight Zoomers
Enthusiastic	3.98	3.98	4.95	3.77
Hopeful	3.85	3.77	4.02	3.74
Proud	4.41	3.67	4.83	3.69
Happy	3.62	3.66	3.39	3.67
Angry	4.49	3.87	5.1	3.79
Nervous	4.26	3.79	4.91	3.71
Afraid	4.19	3.92	4.82	3.74
Disgusted	4.35	3.78	5	3.7

FIGURE 2.5 Average number of political activities, by gender, LGBTQ status, and those feeling emotions "a lot." Among members of Generation Z, women and LGBTQ people who feel negative emotions about the state of their country report higher levels of engagement than men and straight people; LGBTQ people who feel enthusiastic or proud about the state of their country report higher levels of engagement than straight people. Qualtrics survey conducted by the author in May 2022, with a sample of 1600 Americans aged eighteen to twenty-four.

THE GEN Z POLITICAL ENGAGEMENT MODEL: THE IMPORTANCE OF POLITICAL CONTEXT

Many factors that drive political participation among older Americans appear to work similarly for members of Generation Z, often regardless of gender or LGBTQ status—but not always. So which of the potential ingredients of my political engagement recipe really contribute to the finished product? And do these ingredients differ for Gen Z women, Gen Z men, and LGBTQ Zoomers?

Figure 2.6 is a dot plot that shows the coefficients of my political engagement model for 2019 for all Zoomers in my surveys. It allows for

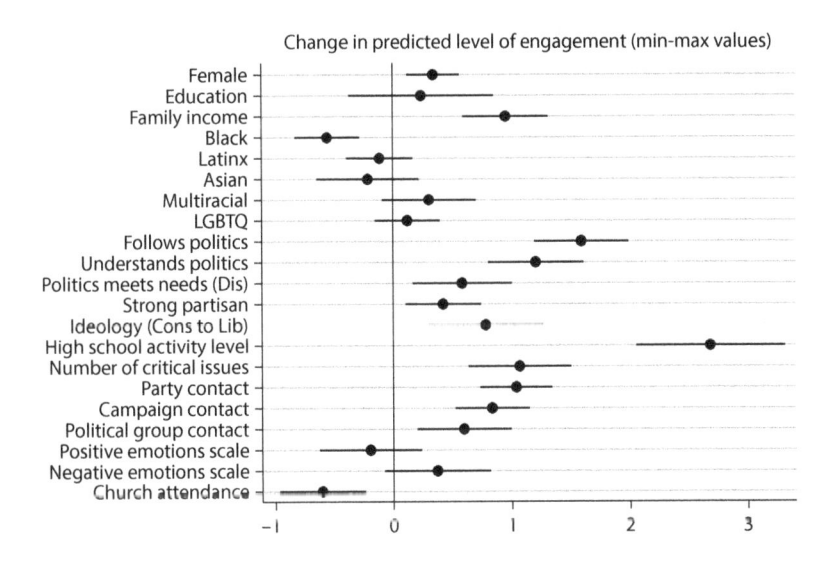

FIGURE 2.6 The 2019 Gen Z political engagement model. High family income; interest and understanding of politics; disagreement that politics is meeting people's needs; strength of partisanship; liberal ideology; high school activities; care for critical issues; and contact from parties, campaigns, and political groups predict higher levels of political engagement among all members of Generation Z. Qualtrics survey conducted by the author in July 2019, with a sample of 2,200 Americans aged eighteen to twenty-two.

Note: All variables are coded to range from 0 to 1.

a more intuitive understanding of which variables statistically contribute to explaining levels of political engagement, which do not, and which may matter more than others. (See the appendix for the full model results.)

The dots for each of the variables represent the coefficients that have been calculated in the statistical analysis. The coding for each of these factors has been normalized, which means that the lowest score a respondent has on a measure is 0 and the highest score a respondent has is 1.[49] Thus, the dot represents the impact of going from the minimum to maximum value of a variable (i.e., family income level, interest in politics, etc.) on the average number of political activities undertaken by Gen Z Americans. Surrounding each dot is the solid line that statisticians call the 95 percent confidence interval, which basically means the range of values that are likely to encompass the true value of the measure.[50]

Look at the vertical line that emanates from the score of 0 on the *x*-axis. If the straight line passes through the 0 line, it means that the variable does not contribute in any meaningful way to the average number of political activities undertaken by Gen Z Americans in my survey. If the straight line falls to the right of the 0 line, then that variable has a statistically significant *positive* effect on political engagement among Gen Z Americans. If the confidence interval falls to the left of the 0 line, it has a statistically significant *negative* effect on political engagement.

We see in the plot graph that being female has a significant, positive effect on the average number of political activities undertaken among Zoomers in my 2019 Qualtrics survey. Being a woman boosts the average number of political activities that a Zoomer participates in by about .3 points while controlling for the other factors listed. Thus, the Gen Z political engagement model affirms the historic reverse gender gap among the members of this generation during the Trump presidency. Gen Z women *were* more engaged in politics than Gen Z men in my survey, even after I accounted for all the ingredients that contribute to political participation. Notice that the line for LGBTQ Zoomers passes through the zero mark, meaning that, although LGBTQ Zoomers reported engaging in more activities than straight Zoomers, once we consider other factors at the same

POLITICAL CONTEXT, GENDER, AND SEXUALITY

time, their levels of engagement are essentially the same as their straight counterparts in my 2019 Qualtrics survey.

Figure 2.6 also shows that neither education nor the emotions scales are statistically related to Gen Z's participation levels overall. Black Zoomers in my survey participated in lower rates than their white peers (the reference category), but otherwise there are no racial/ethnic differences related to Zoomer political engagement. Clearly, the most influential factor in understanding what drives political activity among members of Gen Z is their participation levels in high school. Almost all the Gen Z activists I interviewed cut their teeth in politics through high school activism. The skills fostered in such organizations have clear spillover effects for participating in politics among Gen Z Americans, even after they leave high school.

Closely following politics and having a good sense of how politics works also contribute to significantly higher levels of political engagement among Gen Z; however, *disagreeing* that the political system meets the needs of the public also results in higher levels of political activity. Being contacted by political organizations raises participation overall among members of Gen Z.[51] Coming from a family with resources also drives political participation, as does caring about lots of issues. Identifying as a strong partisan[52] is also significantly and positively linked to political engagement; even more important is ideology: moving from very conservative to very liberal results in nearly one additional political action being performed by Gen Z Americans in 2019. Attending church, however, has a negative impact on political engagement for Gen Z Americans.[53]

My graph in figure 2.6 shows which ingredients help us understand the political participation recipe for Gen Z Americans writ large among respondents in my Qualtrics survey in 2019. Figure 2.7 shows how each of these individual factors connect to the decision of the members of Gen Z to participate in politics, disaggregated by women and men. To simplify the presentation, I omit variables on the graph that are not significant for either Gen Z women or Gen Z men in terms of their participation levels in politics. Many of the variables that have long explained greater participation in politics historically continued to matter for both Gen Z women and Gen Z men.

POLITICAL CONTEXT, GENDER, AND SEXUALITY

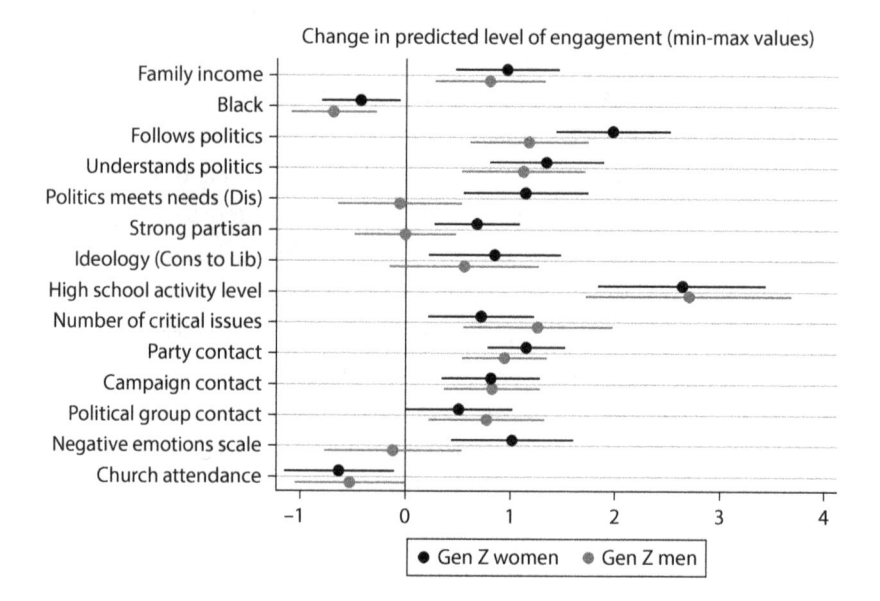

FIGURE 2.7 The 2019 Gen Z political engagement model by gender. Unique contributors to Gen Z women's political engagement include disagreement that politics is meeting people's needs, strength of partisanship, liberal ideology, and negative emotions about the state of the country. Qualtrics survey conducted by the author in July 2019, with a sample of 2,200 Americans aged eighteen to twenty-two.

Note: All variables are coded to range from 0 to 1.

The factors that drove Gen Z women's engagement compared to men in 2019 are more revealing. Women who were strong partisans (especially Democrats) and who were very liberal participated in more political activities.[54] Anger at the political system also drove Gen Z female political engagement, and disagreement that the political system is meeting the needs of the public is positively linked to higher levels of participation. Holding negative emotions about the state of the country also fueled Zoomer women's engagement. Attending church depressed Gen Z women's political engagement. None of those factors, however, contributed to participation levels among Gen Z men in my 2019 Qualtrics survey.

POLITICAL CONTEXT, GENDER, AND SEXUALITY

What emerges in the comparison of these two models for Gen Z women and Gen Z men in 2019 is a story about the role that progressive ideology, strong partisanship, and anger at the political world played in defining Gen Z women's engagement—concerns that did not shape Gen Z men's political participation levels. Women's higher levels of engagement compared with men were thus likely a product of the political context in which they found themselves in a post-2016 political world, as illustrated by many Democratic women in my focus groups and among the progressive activists I interviewed. While many Gen Z women have been the beneficiary of programs designed to boost their political leadership skills and have honed such skills in high school, their desire to participate in politics was also driven by their progressive views. Rather than retreat from a political system that appeared unresponsive to their needs, Gen Z women in 2019 harnessed their anger and frustration into higher levels of political engagement. Those forces did not work in similar ways that year, however, among Gen Z men, who, as a group, appear less unhappy with the political status quo.

Figure 2.8 shows that, by 2022, however, a somewhat different story emerged among Generation Z. Gender was no longer a statistically significant factor in predicting levels of engagement among Generation Z by May 2022, when my second Qualtrics survey was conducted. Yet many of the same factors that explained overall levels of political engagement among Generation Z in 2019 remained the same.

If I break down the model to consider only Gen Z women and only Gen Z men, most variables did not change. (You can see the full model results in the appendix.) Historic political participation drivers—financial resources, interest in and understanding of politics, past organizational history, caring about issues, and being mobilized by political organizations—continued to matter to Generation Z in my spring 2022 survey, regardless of gender. For Gen Z women, ideology and partisanship no longer mattered statistically as they did in 2019, and they continued to explain little about the participation habits of Gen Z men in 2022.

POLITICAL CONTEXT, GENDER, AND SEXUALITY

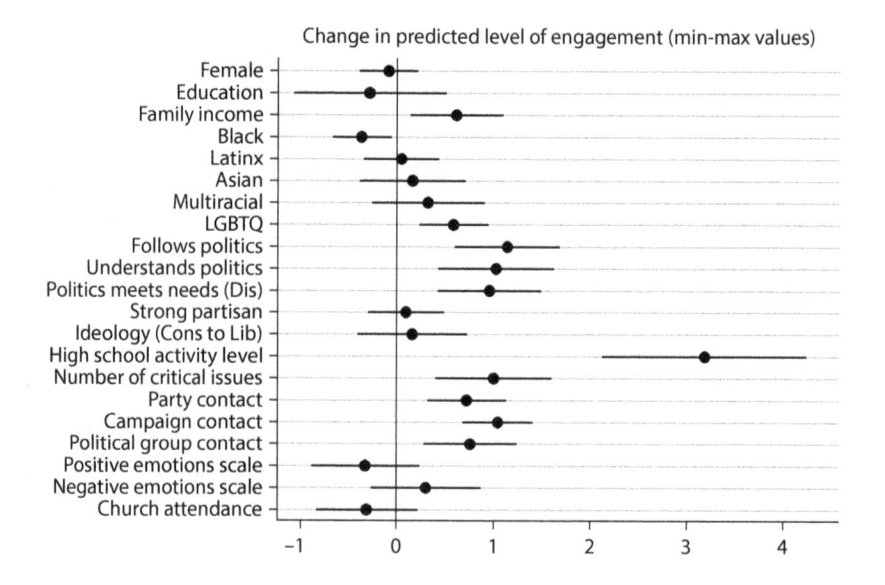

Change in predicted level of engagement (min-max values)

[Dot-and-whisker plot showing coefficients for variables: Female, Education, Family income, Black, Latinx, Asian, Multiracial, LGBTQ, Follows politics, Understands politics, Politics meets needs (Dis), Strong partisan, Ideology (Cons to Lib), High school activity level, Number of critical issues, Party contact, Campaign contact, Political group contact, Positive emotions scale, Negative emotions scale, Church attendance. X-axis from -1 to 4.]

FIGURE 2.8 The 2022 Gen Z political engagement model. High family income; identifying as LGBTQ; interest and understanding of politics; disagreement that politics is meeting people's needs; high school activities; care for critical issues; and contact from political parties, campaigns, and activist groups predict higher levels of political engagement among all members of Generation Z. Qualtrics survey conducted by the author in May 2022, with a sample of 1,600 Americans aged eighteen to twenty-four.

Note: All variables are coded to range from 0 to 1.

Gen Z women remained distinct in that negative emotions continued to drive their engagement in my 2022 survey; but emotional factors, again, remained unimportant to Gen Z men in 2022. In spring 2022, however, Gen Z men's participation was more rooted, like their female counterparts, in dissatisfaction with the political system. Compared with Gen Z men who strongly agreed that the political system was responsive to their needs, Gen Z men who disagreed strongly participated in about .775 more political activities on average among survey respondents. The impact was even stronger among Gen Z women. Those who strongly disagreed that the system was meeting their needs participated in, on average, 1.15 activities more than those Gen Z women who believed the system was responsive.

Statistical models, of course, don't capture every driver of political behavior. But perhaps the changes in understanding participation habits among Gen Z women and men in my May 2022 survey compared with my July 2019 was that gender was a less salient issue at that time than at the height of the Trump presidency. With Joe Biden in the White House and the Democrats controlling both houses of Congress, in spring 2022, the need to engage in higher levels of political activities may not have been top of mind for many Zoomer women. (Of course, it is important to remember that my 2022 survey was in the field before the Supreme Court handed down the *Dobbs* decision, overturning the constitutional right to abortion.) Moreover, in spring of 2022, both Gen Z women and Gen Z men were continuing to deal with the aftermath of the global pandemic, as were many Americans. Very few gave the government high marks in its handling of this health crisis.

The political context in spring 2022 may help to explain, however, why LGBTQ status emerges as a significant factor in the 2022 Qualtrics survey. As figure 2.8 shows, compared with their straight counterparts, LGBTQ Zoomers engaged in .58 more political activities in 2022, even while controlling for other factors. This finding came as no surprise to Alise Maxie, the young LGBTQ activist from Houston. She said that young LGBTQ activists are responding to efforts by state legislates and conservative governors to restrict the rights of LGBTQ young people, most notably governor of Florida, Ron DeSantis. DeSantis signed the so-called Don't Say Gay bill in spring 2022, forbidding Florida public school teachers from instructing or discussing sexual orientation or gender identity in grades K–3. She told me, "I honestly feel that some people don't pay attention to politics until it directly affects them. A lot of my concerns that I face daily as a queer person are not ones shared by my straight counterparts, who have the luxury of living every day without having to think about these things. Natural rights for them are a struggle for us to even obtain."

Katie Eder, the LGBTQ activist who founded Future Coalition, believes that threats for LGBTQ Americans became more heightened in 2022 and that the spike in political activity among LGBTQ Zoomers was linked to the pandemic. Eder took two years off before starting Stanford in 2021 to run Future Coalition, so she is slightly older than most of her college peers. She credits the role of TikTok and other social media outlets for increasing LGBTQ people's knowledge about politics and bolstering their identity as LGBTQ folks. "If TikTok and these [other] online spaces existed when I was a junior in high school, which is right around the time I was coming out, it would have made such a difference in making me way more confident. And so, yeah, I think that this element of exposure to queerness over COVID extended to many [young] people who were in these pockets that wouldn't have gotten [exposure to] it."

The common element that drove a spike in political engagement among Gen Z women in 2019 and LGBTQ Zoomers in May 2022 was the direct threats to their rights. In 2019, my survey collected data on Zoomers aged eighteen to twenty-two. Their formative years politically took place during the Trump years, in which they witnessed a sea of pink hats marching in unity to express women's solidarity the day after Trump's inauguration. While not all Gen Z women are progressive, holding such views propelled young women to participate in higher numbers than Gen Z men.

By May 2022, those immediate threats for women's rights perhaps seemed less dire—although it is important to remember, again, that this survey was conducted before the *Dobbs* decision was handed down. The impact of the *Dobbs* decision appears to be influencing political engagement levels once again among Gen Z women, at least according to a survey conducted by PRRI in August 2023, more than a year after *Roe* was overturned. Although PRRI did not replicate each of the seventeen self-reported measures of political engagement from my own Qualtrics survey, the PRRI survey asks Gen Zers whether, in the past year, they had engaged in nine comparable forms of political activities, including what I term more "passive forms" of politics online (such as signing petitions, following political groups or campaigns, posting on social media about politics, and encouraging others to be active on social media) and "active forms" of politics (such as attending rallies, volunteering for political groups, contacting an elected official, attending local meetings, or boycotting certain brands for political purposes.) See the appendix Table A.12, for more specifics on the gender breaks for each measure.

Most Zoomers in the PRRI survey are not that involved in politics; on average, they report participating in just 1.88 activities in the past year (out of nine). Yet Gen Z females reported engaging in 2.07 activities compared with 1.69 activities by Gen Z males, a difference that is statistically significant.[55] One unique aspect of the PRRI study is that we surveyed teen Zoomers aged thirteen to seventeen as well as older Zoomers. The gender gap was largest among teens, with Gen Z teen girls reporting that they engaged in an average of 1.54 activities compared with 1.06 activities reported by Gen Z teen boys.[56] Gen Z women aged eighteen to twenty-five still reported participating in more activities than Gen Z men, 2.43 versus 2.16, respectively, but this difference is no longer statistically significant. The gap with respect to LGBTQ activism among the members of Gen Z is also alive and well in the 2023 PRRI study. LGBTQ Zoomers engaged in an average of 2.80 activities, compared with 1.41 activities among straight Zoomers.[57]

In total, the story of Gen Z political engagement is linked to many of the traditional factors that drive political participation levels among adults more broadly, but it is also linked to the role of women's issues and LGBTQ issues, respectively, for Gen Z women and LGBTQ Zoomers at different points in time. Political context matters. It provides the potential to alter and shape the long-standing political habits of young people in ways that distinguish them generationally from their parents and grandparents.

The historic reverse gender gap in 2019 that we witnessed during Trump's presidency for this generation also appeared at a time when the number of women running for political office skyrocketed in 2018. The next chapter considers the effect that political role models may have played in shaping the political decisions of Gen Z women shortly after those historic elections.

3

NO MORE OLD WHITE MEN

How Role Models Shape the Political Engagement of Gen Z Women

As a fifth-grader in Philadelphia, Sabirah Mahmud traveled to Bangladesh in 2014 to visit family. She was stunned by waterways overrun with algae and the tragedy of a massive flood that displaced thousands during the last days of her trip. The effects of human-induced global warming were hitting her parents' homeland hard. A few years later, Mahmud was scrolling through Instagram and came across the work of climate activist Greta Thunberg. Thunberg's mobilizations in Europe felt similar to the anti–gun violence efforts that Mahmud had helped lead locally but "pertain to an issue that I also care about." She was motived and inspired.

That spring, Mahmud organized her own school walkout to raise awareness about climate justice. She later became executive director of the Pennsylvania Youth Climate Strike and worked for a time as national logistics director of the U.S. Youth Strike for Climate.[1] Both groups were known for collective action through student mass protests. In high school, Mahmud also established the Philly Earth Alliance, concentrating her climate justice energy closer to home. The group sponsored clothing swaps, held livestream events and webinars to educate young people about fossil fuel divestment, and lobbied local elected officials to try to reduce Philadelphia's carbon footprint.

Mahmud credits her family for introducing her to politics. "When I was growing up, there were a lot of democracy protests for Bangladesh at the embassy [in Washington DC]. My parents took me and we would ride the bus. I didn't understand what we were doing, like the signs and the yelling," she recalled. "For me, it was like, 'No school!'" But the formative events gave her "first-hand experience" in political organizing and helped her find a voice. Mahmud's political leadership activities may be exceptional, but they illustrate a common characteristic of active Gen Z women: political participation that is often shaped and inspired by parents and political role models—from candidates to elected officials, to prominent movement leaders such as Thunberg.

Several young women of color have inspired Mahmud's political journey, and the importance of seeing women who look like them in organizing spaces is critical to explaining why some Gen Z women have been so involved in politics. Mahmud met Xiye Bastida, dubbed by some as America's Greta Thunberg, through involvement with the U.S. Youth Strike for Climate. Bastida hails from the Otomi-Toltec region of Mexico, and her family immigrated to New York after prolonged droughts and flooding in her hometown. Bastida's firsthand experience with extreme weather and climate change propelled her to become a leader in Fridays for Future (FFF), a group inspired by Thunberg. Mahmud praised Bastida as someone who has "broken barriers," noting that both have engaged in climate activism after seeing their family's homelands affected by extreme weather.

Many Gen Z women that I spoke with said that their political engagement has been inspired by other female leaders. One Democratic woman from Georgia State University told me in a focus group that she got involved in politics during the first gubernatorial campaign of Stacey Abrams in 2018. "I was knocking on doors for her and I just knew she was the better candidate," this woman said. "Seeing us get so close [to winning] with her made me . . . both optimistic and pessimistic at the same time. It felt like Georgia didn't want to change, but also that in reality we're on the cusp of a real shift. All of that made me hopeful that I could be a part of that shift."

We have seen through my earlier analysis that young Gen Z women participated in politics at higher levels than Gen Z young men in 2019, creating an historic reverse gender gap in political engagement among young Americans. Gen Z women have also come of age during a time of unprecedented visibility of female political role models. In 2018, women set records in terms of running for political office—in direct response to Donald Trump's election—and were historically diverse in terms of race and ethnicity, sexual orientation, and age.[2] For instance, Congress welcomed thirty-two new women in 2019, including Alexandria Ocasio-Cortez (popularly known as AOC), who, at twenty-nine, was the youngest woman ever elected to the House and was its most visible new star. It is hard to overstate the impact that AOC has had on active and aware Gen Z Democratic women, as we will see. The 2018 election also saw the first two Muslim American women, first two Native American women, and first bisexual female senator elected to Congress.[3] And while Abrams of Georgia narrowly lost her bid to become the nation's first black female governor, she won national acclaim, and her efforts at mobilizing voters after her defeat have been credited with helping flip Georgia blue in the 2020 presidential election.

THE IMPORTANCE OF ROLE MODELS IN SHAPING WOMEN'S POLITICAL CHOICES

Political scientists have long considered whether seeing more women as visible political leaders increases women's interest and engagement in politics. Research finds that exposure to women who seek elected positions or who serve as appointed political leaders often spurs other women to run for office, talk more openly about politics, and participate more frequently in politics[4]—not just in the United States but also in other nations.[5] Living in areas where more women serve in elected and appointed positions also makes women more confident in the ability of other women to govern[6] and promotes higher values of faith in democracy's ability to meet the needs of its citizenry among women.[7] The idea that those serving in or running for political office should closely match its citizenry in terms of gender, race/ethnicity, or other traits, is a concept political scientists refer to as descriptive representation, and it is a powerful reason that the role model effect works.[8]

Historically lower levels of political engagement among women and racial minorities[9] can be linked to lower levels of faith in government responsiveness,[10] in part because such groups perceive that white male politicians are less likely to take the concerns of disadvantaged groups seriously.[11] In contrast, when citizens are exposed to government bodies that are gender-balanced, democratic legitimacy is enhanced among both women *and* men, reinforcing the importance of descriptive representation.[12]

Political habits are often developed in late adolescence and early adulthood, making young adults particularly susceptible to a role model effect.[13] A growing body of research finds that the role model effect for women is understandably greatest on adolescent girls and young women.[14] In their study of the impact of female political candidates on the political discussion patterns of men and women, Notre Dame political scientists Christina Wolbrecht and David Campbell find that young women residing in districts in which there is a new, viable female candidate are more likely to discuss politics than other young women from other districts. Older women were not as susceptible, however, to the presence of newer female candidates. After the 2018 elections, in which a record number of Democratic women sought office, often running on platforms that promoted the inclusion of more women in politics, Wolbrecht and Campbell also found that the presence of Democratic women candidates in their districts led to a more positive perception of U.S. democracy among teenage girls.[15]

In a separate study, Campbell and Wolbrecht noted that Democratic girls after 2016 expressed more interest in participating in future political protest—particularly those whose parents engaged in such activities. These findings corresponded with other research suggesting that teenage girls were more likely than their male counterparts to be politically socialized at home. The role model effect for young women is therefore not limited to women running for or serving in office. It also includes parents.[16]

ROLE MODELS: A VIEW FROM
THE ACTIVISTS AND FOCUS GROUPS

In interviews with activists and focus groups, I asked Gen Z women who they considered to be their political role models. About 95 percent of Gen Z women activists that I interviewed cited at least one political role model. Close to eight in ten Gen Z women (78 percent) cited nationally prominent political women, such as women elected to Congress, female presidential candidates, women who work in the White House, and the late Supreme Court Justice Ruth Bader Ginsburg. About one in five (17 percent) Gen Z women cited elected female officials or candidates whom they admired or knew personally at the state and local level, while a similar number (17 percent) cited political activists working in specific policy areas, pathbreaking women leaders historically (such as notable suffragists), and current ideological thought leaders.

The role models cited by Gen Z women were not exclusively women—about 17 percent cited male political figures as inspiring their political activism, with U.S. Senator Bernie Sanders being the top male choice among progressive Gen Z women activists. Several Gen Z women said that their parents or grandparents served as important political role models or noted the importance of their parents in helping shape their political trajectory.

THE AOC EFFECT

One name came up above all others when it comes to *specific* role models who serve as inspiration: U.S. Representative Alexandria Ocasio-Cortez (AOC) of New York. Her name was volunteered by almost half (45 percent) of the Gen Z women I interviewed who lean to the political left. Ocasio-Cortez was also mentioned frequently in my focus groups of Democratic college students.

AOC shocked the political world in 2018 when she defeated Democratic caucus chair Joe Crawley in a primary in one of the most liberal congressional districts in New York City. She immediately shot to national prominence because of her youth, her unlikely path to elected office, her media savvy, and her unabashed progressive political values. Each characteristic has inspired many Gen Z women with whom I spoke, including Aarushi Pant, a Gen Z gender rights activist from Houston, Texas, and founder of Women Inspiring Social Harmony (WISH), a youth-led community organization that focused on women's rights and empowerment:

> I try not to, like, idolize politicians, but I'm a huge fan of AOC because I feel like she's very *for* the people. And I usually understand what she's saying. She usually makes it easy to understand what's going on. . . . I love the fact that she's answering questions on Instagram, you know, tweeting things out and just letting people know what she's doing. She does a lot of videos of, like, "This is what I'm doing today. This is my dog. Like, I'm a human, you know, I'm just like you, I can be very relatable."

That relatability, youth, and use of social media, added Stella Heflin, a Gen Z climate change activist from the University of Arizona, was why AOC was so influential as a role model for Gen Z women: "I'm really impressed with AOC, [and how] she posts things, like Q and As, on her social stories and really tries to engage with voters and engage them with politics," Heflin said. "I think single-handedly, she's doing a lot for an entire generation in a way that it's hard for other people even, Bernie Sanders, to do, just because of her age."

Malavika Kannon is an author; podcaster; and cofounder of the Homegirl Project, a youth-led collective that trained girls of color in political organization from 2018 through 2022. She says that AOC's appeal was important to young women because "she is able to vocalize what a lot of people are feeling. . . . She's so articulate and so intentional about the way she uses social media, not just for her congressional duties, but the way that she articulates the need, for example, to abolish the police. It's super exciting. I think she gives Gen Z a voice, almost like a proxy or someone who is thinking for us."

Others lauded AOC's relatable background, which included a stint as a bartender while also working as a community organizer. One Democratic woman from Georgia State University said that she admired AOC because "she was doing an everyday person job kind of thing and she made a change. She got up there. She did what she needed to and she's putting her voice into the world." Added another Democratic woman at the same focus group in Atlanta, Georgia, "I also feel like it's important that she's young. She has a worldview and political views that are closer to what I think."

Gen Z progressive women activists often cited three other women of color first elected to the U.S. House of Representatives in 2018 along with AOC as important roles models as well: representatives Ayanna Pressly of Massachusetts, Rashida Tlaib of Michigan, and Ilhan Omar of Minnesota. These three representatives and Representative Ocasio-Cortez famously formed a tight-knit group they dubbed the Squad, and they routinely defended and promoted each other's policies.

Several Gen Z women singled out Omar as an important influence for them because of shared histories. Said Teya Khalil, a climate change activist and writer for Women Republic, an online feminist blog: "I like Ilhan Omar because her background is most similar to mine, [being] from an immigrant family and also Muslim." Perri Easly, a Yale student and voting rights activist who is African American, said she looked up to all four original Squad members because they are "so outspoken, so progressive, and really, a representation of what America looks like and will continue to look like."

A number of Gen Z women said they were inspired by Abrams of Georgia. Resisting appeals to run for the U.S Senate in 2020, Abrams focused her efforts on voter registration, forming a national voting rights organization, Fair Fight. She was later unsuccessful in a second bid for governor in a 2022 rematch against Brian Kemp. One of my IGNITE focus group participants, a Georgia native, said working on Abrams's campaign was a pivotal experience. "Seeing Stacey lose really wasn't really a loss because she opened the door for so many other people," this woman said. "I feel like she's encouraged other women to run for office."

Several Gen Z women I interviewed who identified as LGBTQ considered Senator Kyrsten Sinema, the first openly bisexual U.S. legislator, as well as several LGBTQ women candidates and officeholders, as sources of inspiration. In addition to looking up to Sinema, Maddie Proctor, a Colorado Democrat Zoomer who was active in education policy advocacy, also admired Leslie Herod, the first gay African American woman elected to the Colorado House of Representatives. "I like [Herod] and saw her speak at a protest once. The intersectionality there is amazing, and she's gotten some serious work done in Colorado politics," said Proctor. "It's amazing to see how people have started to respect her."

Sophie Clinton, a Girl Up alum who has worked with The Greater Good Initiative, a youth-led think tank, said that in addition to Sinema, she also admires Sabrina Haake, a gay woman who unsuccessfully sought a U.S. House seat in Indiana. "Just having that kind of role model or somebody to identify with is really just something that I look up to," Clinton said, adding that she hopes to one day run for office as well. "They're gay, I'm gay. I can move forward. And you know, not having to be afraid to be fully who I am wanting to run for office [is inspiring]."

Nationally known political leaders are undoubtedly inspiring, but Susannah Wellford, the founder of Running Start, an organization that trains young women to run for political office, said that in her program, it is just as important that young women meet local and state officials who are closer to their age. Inspirational talks by Delaware state senator Sarah McBride, the nation's first openly transgender state senator, and Abrar Omeish, one of the first Muslim woman elected to political office in Virginia to serve on the Fairfax County school board, have made lasting impacts. "Yes, those big national stories are exciting, but when they meet people who are their own age and can actually ask them questions, this is the best thing we do," Wellford said.

A new generation of younger female political leaders is making its mark on many Democratic women. "You wanna see yourself in those places, so it makes it more believable, that like, 'Oh, I can do this, or my kids can do this,'" said one Georgia State University student. For women of color or LGBTQ women who know the importance of having government officials look like them, that power is enhanced and inspires more political engagement. "I think it's really good to see minorities, people like me, reflected in our elected officials, [and] to know it's not just old white men governing the country and telling everybody else that these are our laws and policies," said one Ohio State focus group member.

ROLE MODELS FOR REPUBLICAN WOMEN

Republican political leaders also inspire Gen Z women who lean to the political right. Gen Z GOP women frequently mentioned former governor of South Carolina and 2024 Republican presidential candidate Nikki Haley, who served as Trump's first ambassador to the United Nations, as a source of inspiration. One Republican woman from the University of Maryland said her dream was for Haley to become the first woman president, adding that if "we could say the first woman president was a female Republican and woman of color, I think that would. . . . Oh my gosh, the Democrats would be so mad."

Others cited Kayleigh McEnany, former press secretary for Trump, as a woman they admired in politics. They include Ophelie Jacobson, former president of the University of Florida's chapter of Network of Enlightened Women (NeW), a leading conservative organization for college women. Jacobson worked as a reporter with Campus Reform, a conservative watchdog news site that covers liberal media bias on college campuses:

> My biggest political role model is Kayleigh McEnany. I just think the way that she carries herself, the way that she presents herself with the podium, when she was press secretary and the way she handled the media was just super inspiring. Not to mention she has an adorable baby girl. She's in a good marriage and is a Christian conservative, really true to her beliefs. And she's so strong and powerful. I really strive to have that same type of mentality and that same type of conviction when I'm talking about politics and when I'm presenting my side of the story.

Emily Fehsenfeld, a Gen Z Republican Party activist who works on Capitol Hill, also cited McEnany as "someone I really look up to" because she is "a strong mother, a strong woman, and an unabashed conservative." Fehsenfeld also admired Dana Perino, a former White House press secretary from the George W. Bush administration who now serves as a Fox News anchor.

Other GOP women I spoke with often cited conservative women activists with an outsized presence in conservative media as their role models. These included Candace Owens, an African American conservative commentator and cofounder of Blexit, an organization that encourages Black Americans to leave the Democratic Party. Owens previously served as the communications director for Turning Point USA, an organization that promotes conservative activism among college and high school students. Gabby Reichardt, an activist with Turning Point at the University of Colorado who now works full time for the organization, loves Owens because she "completely shatters the idea that you have to vote a certain way because of who you are, how you look." A Republican woman from my focus group at the University of Texas at Austin added that she admired Owens as well, adding "it just shows how women can be so empowering and so strong. Even while being a conservative, despite all the backlash."

Other role models cited by GOP women in my study were elected or appointed officials at the state or local level. Several praised conservative women who were active in efforts to restrict abortion rights, including Governor Kay Ivey of Alabama, who signed one of the nation's most restrictive abortion bills. One Republican focus group member from Ohio State said that she was criticized, however, for her support of Ivey's leadership in this area. "I got a lot of crap on Facebook for that, just people telling me like, 'How can you support women and then support this woman?' Like she's a disgusting example of a woman. A lot of really insulting things."

Another participant in the same focus group cited former Ohio Supreme Court Justice Judi French as her role model. "I met her a bunch of times since I've been here," she said. "I just wish I had more access to her at an earlier stage because seeing people like that in office makes me think that's something that I could possibly do." She added that French's success as a Republican woman was particularly important in thinking about her own interest in one day running for office. "If I just see all of these Republican men in office, it's like, something I could do, but it's a lot less likely because you don't see anybody like you." Along the same lines, another participant at the GOP focus group added that, if more "really strong, Republican women would run for office, that would be a very good role model for young people."

POLITICIANS ARE NOT IDOLS

A few Gen Z activist women stood out as exceptions, saying that they didn't have role models. Aurora Yuan, a climate activist at the University of Pennsylvania who served as the international press coordinator with FFF (Fridays for Future) while in high school, said that she makes a point of not having role models because she does not want to "idolize" politicians. Afiya Rahman, a Harvard student who cofounded a Black Lives Matter (BLM) group in her native Syracuse, New York, agrees. Politicians, she said, "shouldn't be like celebrities because they are here to serve the people." Yasmeen Metullus, an IGNITE fellow and gender equality activist from Miami, Florida, added that she did not want to make elected leaders "seem like superheroes." Despite these views, it was clear in my interviews that younger, social-media-savvy elected officials were inspiring Gen Z women leaders to become more involved in politics and chart a future for themselves.

INSPIRATION AT HOME

Many Zoomer women from both sides of the political aisle acknowledged the important role that families played in shaping their political journeys. Katie Eder, the founder of Future Coalition, said that she owed much of her own political success to her mother, who helped her develop many of the organizational skills necessary to start her first nonprofit, Kids Tales, which taught lower-income students how to create and publish their own works of fiction.

Norah Rami, a gun violence prevention activist, campaign intern, and writer from Sugarland, Texas, also said that her mother had a strong role in shaping her political views. Rami's mother often took her to gun violence prevention protests as a child. Both Rami's mother and grandmother were strong supporters of women's rights, she said. Growing up in a "women-powered household," she said, "something that was always driven into me was that, as a woman, you are very powerful." That upbringing, she said, shaped "how I presented myself to the world."

Many focus group participants recounted how their mothers, grandmothers, and extended family inspired them to become involved in politics. Said one University of Maryland participant, whose mother had actively campaigned for many state Democratic candidates and worked in local government: "I've been really plugged into all of that, just from my birth, I have wanted to be [like] my mom in every way. Whenever she would go to events or they would have rallies, I went with her and I was like, 'I wanna be in it. I wanted to learn more.'"

Another Democratic woman from Ohio State University said that she became far more politically active after the 2016 election, in part because her family attended the Woman's March after Trump's inauguration in Washington, DC. "It was really empowering," she said. "I went with all of my female extended family members. Not only were we politically making our voices heard but we were also bonding together over something that we all believed in, which is something that with family doesn't often happen."

It is important to remember that for the many Gen Z women political entrepreneurs I interviewed, the pivotal role of their families in supporting their political activism was linked to socioeconomic status. Parents with means are more likely to develop a parenting style that sociologist Annette Laureau describes as "concerted cultivation."[17] These parents have both the resources and inclination to spend more time investing in their children's education and providing them with opportunities such as sports leagues and arts classes that in turn enhance their ability to navigate higher education or build organizational skills that can complement political organizing.

National survey data show that parents also have a strong impact on the political orientation of their children. Young adults often choose to identify with the same political party as their parents—particularly if they come from families who are highly engaged in politics and frequently discuss politics.[18] The impact of parental engagement in politics on the participation habits of their children also extends to Gen Z Americans overall—at least when it comes to discussion of political issues in the home. In my 2019 Qualtrics survey, I asked respondents how frequently they talked with their parents about politics while growing up. Figure 3.1 shows that Gen Z Americans in my survey who grew up discussing politics frequently with

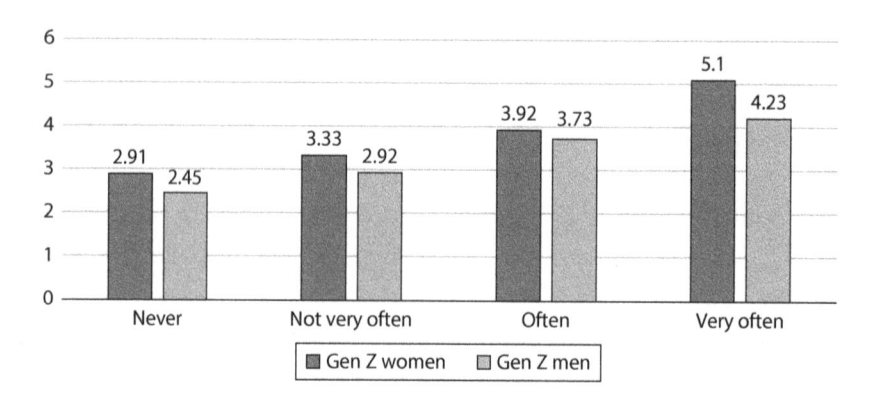

[Bar chart data:
- Never: Gen Z women 2.91, Gen Z men 2.45
- Not very often: Gen Z women 3.33, Gen Z men 2.92
- Often: Gen Z women 3.92, Gen Z men 3.73
- Very often: Gen Z women 5.1, Gen Z men 4.23]

FIGURE 3.1 Average number of political activities, by gender and by how often parents talk about politics. Among members of Generation Z, women whose parents talk with them frequently about politics engage in more activities on average than men. Qualtrics survey conducted by the author in July 2019, with a sample of 2,200 Americans aged eighteen to twenty-two.

their parents also reported engaging in higher levels of political activity—a positive relationship that extended to both Gen Z women and Gen Z men. However, Gen Z women who reported discussing politics "very often" with their parents while growing up reported significantly higher levels of engagement in the past year (5.1 activities) than Gen Z men (4.23 activities) who discussed politics very often in their households.[19] Although not reported in the figure, LGBTQ Zoomers who discussed politics very often also reported much higher levels of political engagement (5.27 activities) than those who never discussed politics (3.06. activities). This same relationship exists among straight Zoomers, too.

Recall my Gen Z political engagement model from chapter 2, which identified the factors that are linked to the decision for members of Gen Z to participate in politics. When I add frequency of parental discussion to that model, it should come as no surprise that the more that Gen Zers discuss politics with their parents, the more they participate in politics. (See the appendix for the full results.) Controlling for all other factors, Gen Z women in my 2019 survey who discuss politics very often with their parents engaged in an average of 4.34 political activities compared with the 3.30 political activities reported among Gen Z women who never have political discussions with their parents. A similar parental discussion impact also exists for Gen Z men, but the impact is not as pronounced. The parental effect was even higher for LGBTQ Zoomers; those LGBTQ Zoomers in my survey who discussed politics with their parents frequently engaged in 4.64 political activities in 2019, compared with just 3.21 activities among those LGBTQ Zoomers who never discussed politics with their parents, again controlling for other factors in the models.

FEMALE CANDIDATES AND A SURVEY EXPERIMENT

In addition to their parents, the Gen Z women I spoke with said that they were inspired to become more involved in politics because of their exposure to younger, more diverse political role models. The Gen Z female political activists I spoke with were already heavily engaged in politics, so it wasn't clear whether exposure to female political role models, particularly those who were younger and more diverse, would have a similar influence among Gen Z American women nationally. Most Americans, including Gen Zers, are not likely to start political or community organizations, but I wanted to know whether exposure to female role models among Gen Z Americans lead Gen Z women to want to engage in politics at higher levels. To address that question, I turned to an imbedded survey experiment in my 2019 Gen Z Qualtrics survey. Social scientists often use survey experiments to isolate a causal effect in a population of individuals because they can randomly assign respondents to treatment and control groups and measure outcomes immediately after exposure.

I worked with another political scientist, Jared McDonald of the University of Mary Washington, to develop an experiment in which Gen Z survey respondents were randomly exposed to candidates running for the state legislature via a fictionalized news story that provided background information.[20] We changed the age and race of the fictional candidates to analyze whether exposure to younger white women, younger women of color, older white women, and older women of color running for office encouraged young women to be more inclined to participate in politics compared with a similar group of male candidates.

This survey experiment allowed us to determine whether (1) an "AOC effect" was happening among Gen Z women during the Trump era, (2) broader exposure to women candidates also affected the decision of Gen Z women to want to become more engaged in politics compared with Gen Z women who were exposed to male candidates, and (3) any of these impacts also filtered into the political decisions of Gen Z men. There were simply not enough LGBTQ Gen Z Americans in the 2019 survey to run a separate experiment testing the role model effect using LGBTQ candidates.

To assess the possibility of a role model effect among Generation Z, we randomized the age of the politician (twenty-two or sixty-eight), the race of the politician (white or Black[21]), and the gender of the politician (man or woman).[22] More details about the experiment can be found in the appendix, but in all eight conditions, respondents read the following fictional news account and saw photos of prospective candidates:

> [MICHAEL/MEGAN] Williams announced [HIS/HER] candidacy as a Democrat for the state legislature Friday. A recent [COLLEGE GRADUATE/RETIREE] and [twenty-two/sixty-eight] years old, Williams decided to run for office after successfully organizing a voter registration drive in [HIS/HER] community. After years of low voter engagement in [HIS/HER] town, [HIS/HER] efforts were widely credited for the surge of voting that helped make up the gap in turnout with other parts of the state. Williams told reporters, "I knew that if I did that as a citizen of my town, what could I do as a state rep?"

Because some Gen Zers would infer the partisanship of a politician based on age, race, or gender, we labeled the politician as a Democrat. The remaining text in the story was intended to show that the politician was engaged and hopeful about the future of politics but not controversial in any meaningful way, which is why we decided to provide a backstory on promoting a voter registration drive as a precursor to a campaign. After the treatments, Gen Z survey participants were asked a series of questions designed to measure their future willingness to engage in politics by considering if they intended in the next year to undertake one of eight forms of political engagement, which We later developed into a scale.[23] Differences between groups based on which candidate they read about in the survey experiment could be interpreted as the percentage change across the response scale.[24]

We also wanted to see if a strong sense of attachment to one's gender, known as gender social identity, influenced the role model effect, particularly for Gen Z women. Social scientists have long recognized that Americans often sort themselves along a variety of identifiable groups that may signify a subjective sense of belonging, which may have spillover effects on political and social behavior. Gender social identity potentially connects with the role model effect because individuals who do not feel a subjective sense of belonging to their gender should be unlikely to care if a politician they are evaluating is a member of the in-group or out-group.

Women who seek to advance the interests of those in their group should be more motivated to engage in the political system when the slate of candidates reflects a greater gender diversity than normal. This theoretical process is played out in several of the passages discussed from the interviews and focus groups earlier in this chapter—many of those Gen Z women recounted how seeing women run for office, particularly more women with more diverse backgrounds, inspired them to become more engaged in politics themselves because of their shared identities. To gauge gender social identity among Zoomers, we asked them how important being a woman or a man was to them and how often they used "we" instead of "they" when talking about gender groups.[25] These questions were averaged together to form a measure of gender social identity, which we used as a moderator for the treatment effects.[26]

First, we consider whether Gen Z Americans overall, regardless of whether they were women or men or whether they strongly identified with their gender, were motivated to participate in politics at higher levels if they were exposed to one of the younger or more diverse candidates in my experiment. We chose the white male sixty-eight-year-old candidate as the baseline or comparison category because this description of a politician fits most closely with the average visible politician in the United States.[27]

Overall, Zoomers who were shown a younger candidate in the survey experiment expressed no more desire to participate in politics than those who were shown the older white man. None of the conditions were significantly different from one another, and it did not appear that the four conditions featuring a twenty-two-year-old performed any better on average than the four conditions featuring a sixty-eight-year-old. (See figure A.7 in the appendix for full results.) But once we consider the impact of gender social identity among Zoomers, we find important results—at least with respect to Gen Z women. The graph in figure 3.2 shows that Gen Z women who have a strong sense of attachment to their gender and who were exposed to a female candidate (young or old, white or Black), represented by the gray lines, showed significantly more interest in future political activities compared to those Gen Z women who read about the older white male candidate and who were low identifiers in terms of gender identity. Reading about young women candidates had the strongest effects for Gen Z women in terms of thinking about future political engagement, suggesting that a female role model effect for Gen Z women existed in 2019, at least among those Gen Z women with a strong sense of gender social identity. However, these same Gen Z women also had a similar response to the younger male candidates, and a marginal response to the older Black male candidate, too, in terms of future willingness to become involved in politics. Figure 3.2 shows a clear trend toward greater engagement among highly identified Gen Z women in all seven of the conditions not featuring an older white male as the politician.[28]

The type of candidate that women with a weak sense of gender social identity, represented by the bolder, black lines in figure 3.2, were exposed to in the experiment made no difference to their willingness to engage in politics. Those women who did not feel strongly attached to a social group defined by womanhood experienced, on average, a slight decrease in future interest in political engagement when exposed to a politician who did not

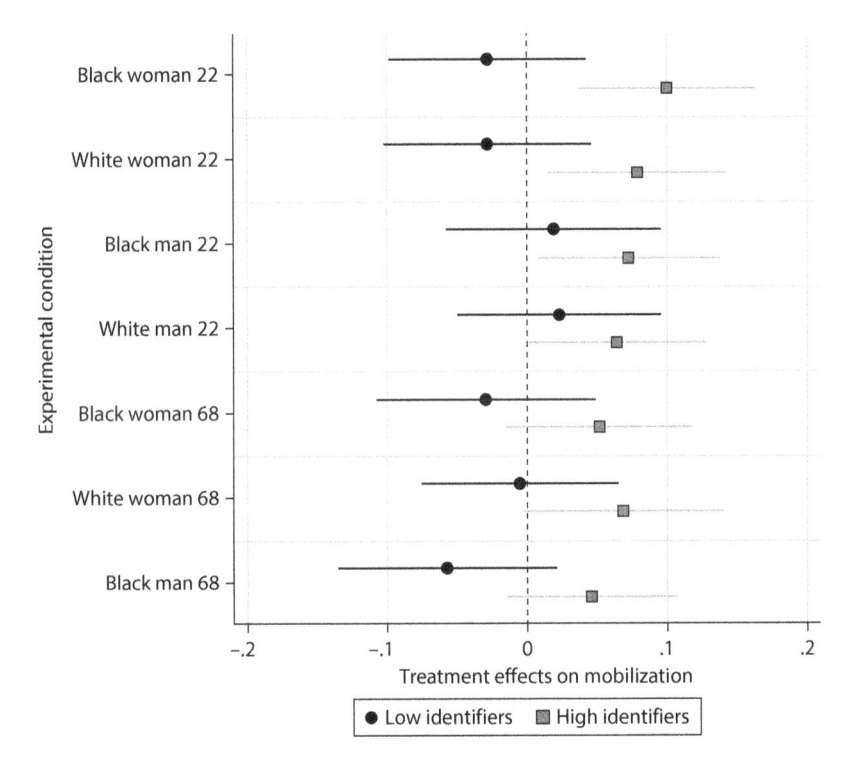

FIGURE 3.2 Effect of treatment among Gen Z women by gender social identity (older white male candidate is the comparison category). Generation Z women with a strong sense of gender social identity express more future willingness to engage in politics when they are exposed to candidates who are not white men; there is no effect among Generation Z women with a weak sense of gender social identity. Qualtrics survey conducted by the author in July 2019, with a sample of 2,200 Americans aged eighteen to twenty-two.

fit the classic description of a politician, although these decreases were statistically insignificant.

Shifting the focus just to Gen Z men, there was little indication that exposure to younger candidates or those who had more diverse backgrounds led them to think about participating more in politics. If anything, there was slightly suggestive evidence that seeing minority or female candidates depressed their motivation for getting involved, but these effects were statistically insignificant. Gender social identity among men—that is, whether being a man is important to them—appeared to play little role in determining whether they were motivated to engage in future political activity. (See figure A.8 in the appendix for full results.)

It wasn't surprising that Gen Z women with a strong sense of gender social identity responded more positively to women seeking public office, but given past studies about the role model effect and young women, the fact that this effect extends to younger male and older Black male candidate treatments is notable and likely because these three male candidates, along with all the female candidates, represented individuals in historically marginalized groups in terms of elected office.

According to group empathy theory, individuals who belong to one historically marginalized group will feel a stronger sense of connection to individuals who belong to a different historically marginalized group.[29] While we saw that young women who had a strong sense of attachment to their gender were inclined to be more active in politics when they saw other young women running for office, they were also motivated by the presence of candidates in other marginalized groups.

Together, these results suggest that diverse fields of candidates can motivate young women who have a strong sense of gender social identity to engage in the political system—particularly when the political context is one that is ripe with gendered themes, which was the case in 2019, during Trump's presidency.

CONCLUSION: ROLE MODELS AND PARENTS AS POLITICAL MOTIVATORS

The role model effect helps explain in part why young women in Generation Z were more engaged in politics than young men during the Trump era. Interviews with Gen Z female political entrepreneurs such as Sabirah Mahmoud, the environmental activist we met earlier in the chapter, shows the important role that parents and female political leaders, especially other young women and women with more diverse backgrounds, played in shaping the political choices of Gen Z women.

The 2019 Gen Z survey experiment also demonstrates that exposure to women running for office raised interest in political participation among Gen Z women who experience a strong sense of group identity as women. Political figures outside the traditional white male stereotype also raised interest in political participation among Gen Z women for whom being a woman was important, at least in 2019. Women and minority candidates are still far from achieving political parity in elected office, but in the past several years, women, including women of color, have made large gains in running and winning seats. Therefore, the context in which Gen Z women were being socialized might help explain why our experimental treatments had such significant effects on Gen Z women who had a strong gender social identity during the Trump presidency.[30]

My survey experiment also provides evidence that group identities—in this case, a powerful sense of group identity defined by one's gender—can have a profound impact on political engagement. Recall the Ohio State University student who said that it was important to know that it is "not just old white men governing the country." Exposure to more diverse, younger, and female leadership mattered to the political choices of young women and helped to explain the historic reverse gender gap that we witnessed among Generation Z in 2019.

4

"GROWING THEIR FEMINIST THING"

How Women's Rights and Reproductive Rights Are Propelling Activism Among Gen Z

ROSIE COUTURE'S STORY

Rosie Couture turned thirteen the day that Donald Trump was sworn in as president of the United States. That evening, she boarded a bus in her hometown of Decatur, Georgia, and arrived in Washington, DC, the next day to participate in the historic Women's March on the Mall—her first act of political participation and one she describes as "very empowering."

The next year, after the shooting in Parkland, Florida, Couture organized a walkout in her middle school to protest gun violence and became active with March for Our Lives, the national organization founded by the Parkland school shooting survivors. Having moved to Arlington, Virginia, with her family, Couture—a self-described nerd—began researching proposed legislation in the Virginia General Assembly and stumbled upon a resolution to ratify the Equal Rights Amendment (ERA) to the U.S. Constitution. She had never heard of the ERA nor could she believe that it was controversial.

Couture sent an email to Jennifer Carroll Foy, the resolution's lead sponsor in the Virginia House of Delegates, asking how she could help raise awareness about the resolution. The lawmaker pointed her to a state organization dedicated to ratifying the ERA in Virginia. While fully supporting the cause and volunteering with the group, Couture grew concerned that its leadership was not reflective of all women: "I just kept on getting really frustrated, being, like, the only person under the age of fifty ever going to meetings or being involved with anything."

Couture, who identifies as LGBTQ, told me that as she read more about the failed history of the ERA, she was struck by similarities with that first effort to pass the amendment in the 1970s, namely, that the activism and strategy were "centered around straight white women." So, in the summer of 2019, Couture and her high school classmate Belan Yeshigeta, a first-generation Ethiopian immigrant, cofounded Generation Ratify, a youth-led political organization seeking to ratify the ERA and to, in its own words, "correct the historical exclusion of women and people beyond the binary from the Constitution."

Generation Ratify worked to elect more Democrats to the Virginia State Senate in 2019. Democrats took control of both legislative chambers following that election, and Virginia became the thirty-eighth state to ratify the ERA in February 2020. After the Virginia vote, attention turned to Congress to extend a ratification deadline it set in the 1970s. Couture, Yeshigeta, and other Generation Ratify members partnered with Representative Cori Bush of Missouri who, in March 2023, helped create a congressional ERA caucus and cosponsored a bill that would make the ERA the Twenty-eighth Amendment, seeking to work through the office of the U.S. Archivist to certify it.[1]

Generation Ratify advocated for other gender equality legislation, such as pay equity and better maternal health care for Black mothers, who are disproportionately more likely to die in childbirth than white women. After the Supreme Court's June 2022 *Dobbs* decision, which overturned the right to abortion established in *Roe v. Wade*, Generation Ratify became more involved in abortion rights, educating its members through digital forums and social media posts, and providing both resources and "actionables" for members. In late 2023, Generation Ratify changed its name to the Young Feminist Party.

The Young Feminist Party's work centers around recruiting, training, and mobilizing young people to advance feminist policies at all levels of government, including "having women and people beyond the binary have a more equitable future." Rosie said that after the 2020 presidential election, her organization focused more on finding female candidates and those who identify as nonbinary, gender nonconforming, and femme to support in local and state races. It would be a mistake to underestimate Couture. She organized an occupation of Constitution Avenue outside the National Archives in late August 2023 to demand action on the ERA—and was promptly arrested after she and her fellow activists failed to disband. (Charges were later dropped.) In October 2023, she was recognized by *Teen Vogue* and Gay and Lesbian Alliance Against Defamation (GLAAD) as one of their and twenty under twenty political activists to watch.

FEMINIST MOTIVATIONS FOR GEN Z ACTIVISM

As is becoming clear, ideologically progressive Gen Z women and LGBTQ Zoomers are driving much of this generation's political actions. Angry about the state of U.S. politics, many Gen Z women were also motivated by seeing a more diverse set of actors engaged in politics and running for political office. Their motivation also stemmed from the renewed women's rights movement that emerged after Trump's election as well as the Me Too movement. Interest in IGNITE, which trains young women to run for office, skyrocketed during Trump's presidency, said founder Anne Moses. "I think many young women actually woke up to the fact that sexism is not a thing of the past and then they began naming their experience," Moses said, adding that Trump made it "more comfortable for younger women to identify with the feminist movement."

These Progressive Gen Z activists have led efforts to change policies regarding other gender equality issues and have worked to combat gender stereotypes and promote more trans and nonbinary inclusion in school curricula, such as Ina Bhoopalam's youth-led organization DREAM EQUAL.

"GROWING THEIR FEMINIST THING"

Menstrual justice is another cause championed by many Gen Z women activists, including Nadya Okamoto, who at age sixteen cofounded PERIOD., an organization dedicated to ending the state sales tax on period products. "A huge part of my focus was around seeking systemic change mainly around taking down the tampon tax that still today exists in thirty states and fighting for free period products in schools, shelters, and prisons," she said. PERIOD. has registered hundreds of volunteer chapters in the United States and abroad that work to repeal such taxes on period products, destigmatize menstruation, and donate menstrual products to those in need.

Other Gen Z women have begun programs that are more intersectional in their approach or aim to reach young women in rural areas. LOUDwomen, for example, is a nonprofit that targets gender inequity in education through debate preparation, mentorship, and leadership development. Anna Dean started the organization with Priya Thelapurith after their experiences in their home state of Arkansas, where they participated in their high school debate team competitions. Dean felt that these competitions unequally treated girls compared with boys. "We'd get ballots back after the debate, and I was in a lot of notes about how I'm really aggressive," said Dean. "There were never notes about that about my male counterparts. Or I would get comments about how there's a hole in my tie or my skirt is too short or you should do your hair like this from now on. And I was like, 'You're focusing a lot more on what I look like and how I'm presenting myself rather than the contents of my arguments.'"

In addition to reaching more than 2,500 girls in Arkansas through its debate preparation program, LOUDwomen lobbied for more equitable education policies for girls and rural students and promoted reproductive rights. After *Roe* was overturned, LOUDwomen helped organize a "Bans Off Our Bodies" protest in Bentonville, Arkansas, on July 4, 2022, which drew Gen Z activists who spoke against the restrictive abortion policies in their state.[2]

Gen Z women have come of age when access to abortion has become scarcer. By the start of 2024, 15 states had banned or nearly banned all abortion; according to the Guttmacher Institute, which tracks abortion policy, an additional 6 states have very restrictive policies, such as bans at

6 weeks of a pregnancy or later.³ For many Gen Z women, greater access to reproductive health is giving them greater incentive to become engaged in politics with the backdrop of abortion politics playing out on the national and state stages.

DO YOU CONSIDER YOURSELF A FEMINIST?

Not all Gen Z women prioritize gender equality or support abortion rights. As we'll see, even some Democratic Gen Z women struggle with calling themselves feminist, a term that continues to carry negative connotations long after conservative leaders in the 1970s argued that feminists hated men, burned their bras, and sought to annihilate the traditional nuclear family. My Qualtrics surveys in 2019 and 2022 found, however, that about nine in ten Gen Z female respondents identified as a feminist in some way, said that gender equality was at least somewhat important to them politically, or believed that abortion should be legal under at least some circumstances. Gen Z feminists and strong abortion rights advocates were more engaged in politics today than other Gen Z Americans. One of the progressive participants from my IGNITE focus groups explained it like this:

> I see it as a liberation type of thing. We now have an opportunity and we have a stage open for us to be more vocal about issues that are really affecting us. For years, it's been white men basically making the decisions over women's bodies, women's rights, everything. Now we can finally take over and speak up for ourselves.

FEMINISM THEN AND NOW AS A MOTIVATOR FOR ACTIVISM

Throughout U.S. history, the struggle for women's rights has been far from smooth. While today we celebrate the work of suffragists who secured women's right to vote, the movement of women who fought for the franchise dissipated after the Nineteenth Amendment's ratification in 1920. Some reformers at the time hoped that newly enfranchised female voters would unite around policies that helped women and children, but this was not to be. It would take decades before women would turn out to vote in high numbers, and there was no consensus among women voters (or men, for that matter) about the need to extend women's rights further.[4] The original ERA, penned by suffragist Alice Paul in 1923 to eradicate sex as a discriminatory category in the Constitution, languished for more than four decades.

Yet the ERA would become a clarion call that brought together a new generation of women as part of the second-wave feminism propelled by two important publications in 1963: *The Peterson Report*, written by President John F. Kennedy's Commission on the Status of Women, which documented the widespread discrimination many women faced in employment and economic opportunities, and *The Feminine Mystique*, Betty Friedan's classic work that identified "a problem with no name" among well-educated housewives who found domestic life unfulfilling and sought a greater role in public life.

By the end of the 1960s, women's rights advocates had borrowed from the civil rights movement and turned to the courts to try to strike down state laws and policies that discriminated against women.[5] This piecemeal approach was largely viewed as insufficient by women's rights advocates. Instead, the National Organization for Women (NOW), formed in 1968 by Friedan and forty-eight other feminists, strongly promoted the ERA as the way to make women the legal equals of men. Although it seems impossible to believe in today's era of tense party polarization, the ERA passed both houses in Congress with strong bipartisan support in 1972. Within a year, thirty of the necessary thirty-eight state legislatures had voted for ratification.

Then came the backlash, led most visibly by long-time Republican activist and abortion foe Phyllis Schlafly, who launched a successful campaign to stop ratification of the ERA. Painting ERA supporters as radical "women libbers" intent on waging "a total assault on the family, on marriage and on children," Schlafly convinced millions of Americans—and state legislators who had yet to ratify the ERA—that its passage would lead to women being drafted in the military, women losing alimony and custody of their children in cases of divorce, and the removal of all sex-specific bathrooms.[6] Schlafly famously marshaled her female supporters to lavish baked goods on undecided legislators in states that had yet to ratify the ERA, convincing them that the amendment would threaten the homemakers' way of life. The movement to ratify the ERA ultimately fell three states short.

The longer legacy of Schlafly's STOP ERA movement is that it helped to channel thousands of social conservatives into more direct political activism at the federal, state, and local levels. They fought back against a range of women's rights policies, such as legal abortion, Title IX sports equity, universal paid maternity leave, affirmative action for women (and racial minorities), and sex education—often portraying feminists as unfulfilled, unhappy women who saw themselves as victims in a male-dominated world and whose real goal was to promote a sexually promiscuous society while demoting men to second-class citizenship.

Schlafly's views were reinforced by a growing right-wing media ecosystem. Rush Limbaugh, the late right-wing radio personality, coined the term "feminazi" in the early 1990s to describe women who supported women's rights. Throughout his career, Limbaugh routinely chastised supporters of women's rights with that term, including, perhaps most infamously, Georgetown University law student Sandra Fluke, who testified before Congress in 2012 in favor of insurance companies including comprehensive birth control as part of routine coverage for its customers.[7] (Limbaugh went further, labeling her a slut and prostitute on his show, even though the majority of Americans supported the policy.)

Decades of bashing have resulted in a hesitancy among Americans to describe themselves as feminists, even while broadly accepting the basic principles for which both many suffragists and women's activists in the second wave women's movement fought. For instance, in a 2019 *Washington Post* survey, 94 percent of Americans said that men and women should be social, political, and economic equals,[8] yet a national poll conducted by Ipsos in the fall of 2019 found that just 29 percent of American women identified as feminists.[9]

There may be reason to believe that Gen Z women are different with respect to embracing feminism. Icons of popular culture have begun to refurbish and repopularize the term "feminist." Beyoncé famously performed on an MTV stage in 2016 with the giant word emblazoned in the background. Taylor Swift, who distanced herself from the word early in her career, turned in her later albums to anthems that called into question male privilege. Some argue that Gen Z women, unlike their mothers' generation, are especially attuned to a feminist movement that is more inclusive. Today, the feminist movement is described by the feminist website Bustle as "queer, sex-positive, trans-inclusive, anti-misandrist, body-positive and digitally-driven."[10]

In the past decade, a rash of books and programs have been developed that are aimed at building self-esteem among girls more broadly, or at helping girls develop and hone specific skills that allow them to become political and community leaders or to pursue careers in traditionally male-dominated fields, such as science, technology, engineering, and mathematics (STEM).[11] One need look no further than popular organizations such as Girls Who Code, Girl Scouts, Girl Up, or a host of similar groups founded in local communities around the country that have developed programming to train girls to become leaders in politics, business, or science-related fields. A communal sense has developed in the larger public discourse that girls and women continue to face certain disadvantages in U.S. society—a belief that many of the progressive Gen Z women activists I spoke with discussed at length.

THE ROLE OF SOCIAL MEDIA FOR YOUNG FEMINISTS

Social media has been instrumental in raising awareness about feminism and gender inequality among Gen Z women and increasing their willingness to get involved. "With the Me Too movement and [what's] happening now in the White House, it's really disturbing to feel like we're never going to get away from this unless we actively participate in its destruction," said one IGNITE participant when Trump was president. "The fact that we are all on our phones and on the Internet and we can see it so often, that really disturbs us now."

Social media also provides a sense of community, letting Gen Z women "really amplify our voices and say what we need to say and advocate for what we think," said Riya Goel, cofounder of Asians Lead, a nonprofit that promotes social activism for Asian and Pacific Island young people. "Although boys have a lot of different things they also need to advocate for, it's not nearly comparable to the injustices that women and girls have." Social media can provide valuable support to young women experiencing sexual harassment, Goel added, "when they are kind of isolated by their own communities" and can find a place to speak out and connect.

Malavika Kannon of Seminole, Florida, and cofounder of the Homegirl Project, a political group for Gen Z women of color that was active from 2018 through 2022, said that social media was pivotal to her own decision to become active in fighting for women's rights. "Especially if you go to a school where being politically active is not the norm, it's really punishing for girls who speak out," she said. "They will be branded as crazy or as bitches, that's a legitimate thing. But I think that being able to have your validation come from other people online, being able to find that community of people online who share your beliefs. . . . I guess the solidarity and community helps a lot of girls."

As Isabella D'Alacio, an IGNITE fellow and gun violence prevention activist from South Florida said, young women are learning much more about women's rights than ever before. "We find community in social media and in our spaces in general. We're hearing more people tell their stories and how they're affected, especially with sexual assault, giving more women courage to speak up. I think that that's been very pivotal in Gen Z women, stepping up and doing our own thing. Seeing how other women have had to suffer for so long just to get a seat at the table, now we're like, 'Let's make our own table.'"

"GROWING THEIR FEMINIST THING"

FEMINISM AND POLITICAL ACTIVISM

If past is prologue, Gen Z women who identify as feminists should be more likely to participate in politics than Gen Z women who do not. Scholars have shown that women who strongly believe that gender inequality is a problem are both more interested in and more likely to participate in politics.[12] One study of college feminists who were active in the second wave women's movement found that women who had been heavily engaged in feminist and antiwar movements while in college in the late 1960s and early 1970s continued to participate in politics at much higher levels decades later compared with other women. As one participant told the authors of that study, "It was a thrilling time to come of age, to be a female, to find out that it was okay to be bright, successful and independent. I found my confidence through my participation in the movement."[13]

In my conversations with progressive Gen Z women, many expressed similar thoughts, linking their decisions to participate in politics to their own self-identity as feminists, their frustrations with the political status quo brought to light by Trump's presidency and his sexist behavior, and the larger Me Too movement. Trump's election in particular lit a political fire in many Gen Z women, many of whom who had been relatively unengaged in politics before. "Just the fact that Trump has stated so many derogatory things about woman and he's won, it's kind of like society's accepting it at some level," said a female Gen Z Democrat from the University of Maryland. "We have elected this man and we might do it again. It just really pushes me personally to want to get people rallied up and want to do something to stop this from happening."

An IGNITE participant I spoke with linked her engagement in politics to what she called the "heartbreaking" election of Trump:

> It was like, "What the hell do we do now?" How many things that women have experienced, because a lot of us have probably experienced sexual assault, tackled sexual harassment, and he emboldened those things. So, it's like coming into a room after this man gets elected, and saying, "Wow, the man that attacked me probably thinks that what he

did is okay." Young boys across this country probably think it's okay to grab women by the ass or say stuff like that. That was the most heartbreaking to me.

Others said that Trump's election propelled them to attend the Woman's March, either in Washington, DC, or closer to home, where they saw "all of those women of all different colors and shapes," in the words of one Democratic Zoomer from Ohio State. One Georgia State Democratic woman said that young women are more engaged because "they are getting more educated, realizing that there's feminism going on and they are growing their feminist thing." Like earlier incarnations of women's rights activists, these Zoomers drew a clear line between their own decisions to become politically active and their concerns about gender inequality—concerns that were heightened after Trump's election and the Women's March.

My Gen Z surveys asked respondents whether they identified as feminists, didn't identify as a traditional feminist but supported women's equality and rights, or didn't identify as feminists in any way. As figure 4.1 shows, in July 2019, there was still some hesitation to use the term "feminist" among Gen Z women, with just one in three identifying as feminists in my survey, only slightly above other national surveys conducted in that year, such as the Ipsos poll cited earlier. Yet by May 2022, far more Gen Z women embraced the term—48 percent. By contrast, relatively few Zoomer men identified as feminists in either year. The feminist mantel is also far more popular with LGBTQ Zoomers than straight Zoomers.

Conservative Gen Z women were reluctant, however, to embrace the feminist moniker because they believed it represented a brand of politics that was too radical. Emily Fehsenfeld, a Maryland Gen Z Republican who has worked on Capitol Hill, told me that she would call herself a feminist and "fight for equality in all capacities" if this were the early 1900s. But she thinks equality has largely been achieved for women. "I don't think there's any room for conservative women in the modern feminist movement," she said. "It's not any longer about equal pay for equal work or just equality in general; it's strictly a liberal policy platform

"GROWING THEIR FEMINIST THING"

[Bar chart showing percentages for Gen Z women 2019, Gen Z men 2019, LGBTQ Zoomers 2019, Straight Zoomers 2019, Gen Z women 2022, Gen Z men 2022, LGBTQ Zoomers 2022, Straight Zoomers 2022. Values: Gen Z women 2019: 33, 53, 14; Gen Z men 2019: 11, 56, 32; LGBTQ Zoomers 2019: 36, 51, 14; Straight Zoomers 2019: 19, 55, 25; Gen Z women 2022: 48, 47, 5; Gen Z men 2022: 16, 54, 30; LGBTQ Zoomers 2022: 49, 44, 7; Straight Zoomers 2022: 26, 53, 21.

Legend: I'm a feminist; I'm not a feminist, but I support women's equality; I don't identify as a feminist in any way]

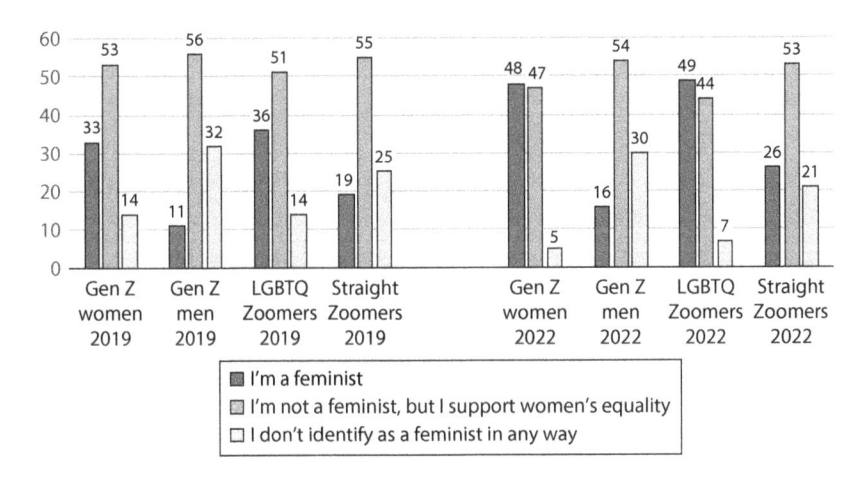

FIGURE 4.1 Percentage identifying as feminist among Gen Z, by gender and LGBTQ status, as of 2019 and 2022. Among members of Generation Z, women and LGBTQ people are more likely to identify as feminists in 2022 than are women and LGBTQ people in 2019. Qualtrics survey conducted by the author in July 2019, with a sample of 2,200 Americans aged eighteen to twenty-two; Qualtrics survey conducted by the author in May 2022, with a sample of 1,600 Americans aged eighteen to twenty-four.

with social issues, like transgenderism." Another GOP Republican woman from my Ohio State University focus group also lamented that the current feminist movement was not welcoming for young Republican or conservative women. "Republican women don't feel the love from other women," she said.

Not all Democratic Gen Z women embrace the term "feminist" either, although I found that they were more likely to do so than GOP Gen Z women.[14] "A lot of people just don't want to identify with the term because it makes you look silly," said a Democratic woman from my focus group at the University of Texas at Austin. "I guess sometimes people make fun of me for it. Personally, I'm sensitive. I do hold progressive beliefs, but I don't outright say that [I'm a feminist] because I don't like the connotations that come with it." When pressed to explain those connotations, she added: "That you are dramatic or you hate men or you're a lesbian."

"GROWING THEIR FEMINIST THING"

Some progressive Gen Z women I spoke with rejected the term "feminist" because they believed it was too closely aligned with white women's causes. "As a Black woman, I can never outright say I am a feminist, because the history of feminism doesn't really cater to women who look like me," said a University of Texas at Austin Democratic woman. "It's not intersectional enough for me. When we speak about feminism, I think we are speaking for white women or cisgendered women. That's not me, not my friends. I can't very much get down with it, although I have some of the same principles." (My national Qualtrics survey data showed, however, that among Zoomers, white women and women of color identified as feminists at similar rates in both 2019 and 2022.)

Still, feminist identification among Gen Z women is clearly linked with higher political engagement levels among survey respondents. Figure 4.2 shows that the average levels of engagement among both Gen Z women *and* Gen Z men were highest among self-proclaimed feminists, far more than those who merely expressed support for women's equality more generally; levels of participation among Gen Z women feminists were highest overall in 2019.[15] Although not shown graphically, LGBTQ Zoomers who were feminists also recorded higher levels of political activity than LGBTQ Zoomers who did not use the term; the same was true for straight Zoomer feminists, at least in 2019.[16]

When I added the question about calling oneself feminist to my Gen Z political engagement model for 2019, it had a positive and significant effect in explaining Generation Z levels of political engagement. (See the appendix, Table A.18, for the full model results.) During the Trump era, Zoomers who identified as feminists scored higher on the political engagement scale (3.98) than those who did not (3.49), even while controlling for other factors.[17] However, this relationship only held for Gen Z women in 2019; the initial relationship between feminist identity and political engagement among Gen Z men failed to remain significant once other controls were considered.

With respect to the historic reverse gender gap that we witnessed during the Trump years, feminist identity is an important part of the equation. Yet the political engagement model found that feminism is not a significant

"GROWING THEIR FEMINIST THING"

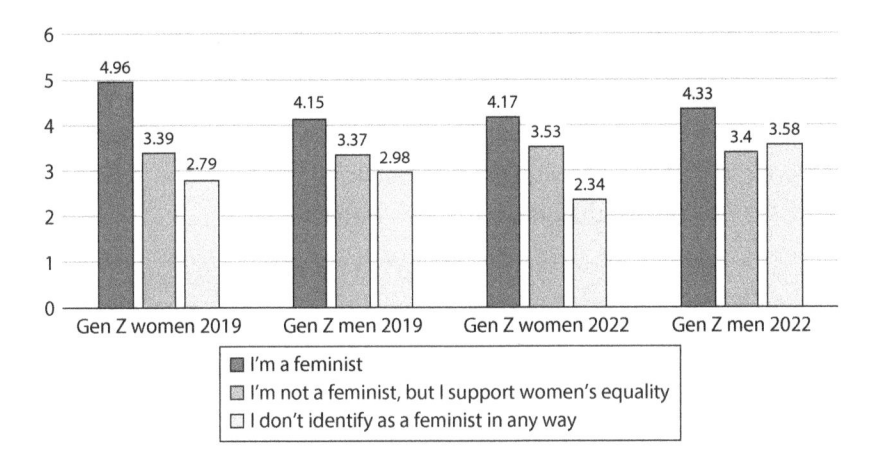

	Gen Z women 2019	Gen Z men 2019	Gen Z women 2022	Gen Z men 2022
I'm a feminist	4.96	4.15	4.17	4.33
I'm not a feminist, but I support women's equality	3.39	3.37	3.53	3.4
I don't identify as a feminist in any way	2.79	2.98	2.34	3.58

FIGURE 4.2 Average number of political activities, by gender and feminist identification, as of 2019 and 2022. Both women and men in Generation Z who identify as feminists engage in more political activities than those who do not identify as feminists. Qualtrics survey conducted by the author in July 2019, with a sample of 2,200 Americans aged eighteen to twenty-two; Qualtrics survey conducted by the author in May 2022, with a sample of 1,600 Americans aged eighteen to twenty-four.

factor for LGBTQ Zoomers.[18] By May 2022, however, identifying as a feminist had no statistically significant impact on the number of political acts undertaken by Zoomers, regardless of gender or LGBTQ status. While members of Generation Z, particularly Gen Z women and LGBTQ Zoomers, have begun to express more willingness to embrace the feminist label, other factors better explained what drove Gen Z women and queer Zoomers to participate in politics in this year, such as holding a strong interest in politics and possessing a strong sense of internal political efficacy, having a history of high school activism, and being contacted by political groups. Like the respondents in my 2019 survey, a strong belief that the political system is unresponsive to their political views also drove higher levels of political engagement among both Gen Z women and LGBTQ Zoomers in 2022; for Gen Z women, negative emotions also fueled more participation in politics in 2022, but not for their LGBTQ counterparts.

An important takeaway here is that feminism can provide an important frame of meaning for many Gen Z women, inspiring more political action, especially related to feminist issues. The same cannot be said for Gen Z men, so the historic reverse gender gap among the members of Generation Z during the Trump presidency can be explained partly by Gen Z women who were connecting their feminist ideals with politics.

A FEMINIST FUTURE?

There is good reason to believe that feminism will be embraced at higher levels among Gen Z women and girls in the years ahead. A Democratic woman in my Georgia State focus group said that Trump's election opened the eyes of a lot of young women and girls to gender discrimination. Even a cousin in second grade, she said, wanted to know if Trump didn't like women. "With social media, kids are getting more knowledge than I ever did," she said. "I didn't even know what feminism was until seventh grade." Added another participant, "I also feel like we're moving into a more well-rounded phase of feminism. Younger generations in middle school and high school are not just learning about mainstream feminism; they're learning more about intersectional feminism, more than I did in middle school or high school."

As we saw in figure 4.1, it is notable that Gen Z women increased feminist self-identification from 33 percent in July 2019 to 48 percent in 2022. My 2022 survey also contained data for Americans older than Gen Z, which showed how distinct Gen Z women were from older American women, as demonstrated in figure 4.3. At 48 percent, Gen Z women were significantly more likely to identify as feminist compared with women in older generations.

That the salience of feminism matters more to Gen Z women compared with older American women is also supported by Public Religion Research Institute's (PRRI) Politics of Gender Survey, conducted in March 2023. In this random probability sample, we asked more than five thousand Americans (both women and men) whether the term "feminist" described them and whether it was very important to them. Gen Z women stood apart

"GROWING THEIR FEMINIST THING"

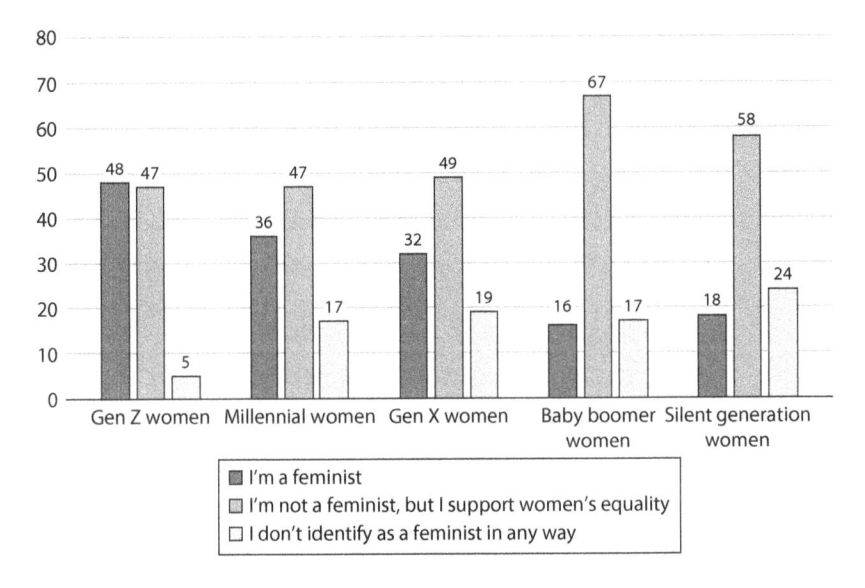

```
80
70                          67
60                                58
50  48 47      47     49
40        36
          32
30                                24
20     17     19  16 17  18
10  5
 0
   Gen Z women  Millennial women  Gen X women  Baby boomer  Silent generation
                                                women         women
```
■ I'm a feminist
▨ I'm not a feminist, but I support women's equality
□ I don't identify as a feminist in any way

FIGURE 4.3 Percentage of women by feminism categories and generations. Gen Z women are more likely to identify as feminists than women in other generations. Qualtrics survey conducted by the author in May 2022, with a sample of 1,600 Americans aged eighteen to twenty-four and 1,600 Americans aged twenty-five or older.

from older generations of American women, with 32 percent saying that they were feminists and the term was important to them; an additional 29 percent said that they would call themselves feminist but indicated it was not all that important to them, meaning that roughly six in ten Gen Z women said the term feminist describes them. For older generations of women, those falling in the first category as committed feminists ranged from 20 percent of boomer women to 22 percent of millennial women.[19]

Data on feminist identification among younger women, as a generational cohort, are hard to come by historically, but the 1996 General Social Survey (GSS) asked Americans whether they thought of themselves as feminists, with a simple yes or no response (the only year in which it did so). Isolating the cases to women aged eighteen to twenty-four years, which included two years of the "oldest" Gen Xers, as well as some millennials,

30 percent of young women identified as feminist. (Among women older than twenty-four, feminist identification dropped slightly, to 27 percent.) The GSS data suggests that, roughly three decades ago, younger women were less likely to embrace the feminist term compared with Zoomer women today. If that proportion endures, we could witness a future in which this generation of women will prioritize the fight for women's equality.

THE FIGHT FOR ABORTION RIGHTS AND GEN Z'S POLITICAL ENGAGEMENT

Before the *Dobbs* decision in 2022, many of the progressive Gen Z women activists I spoke with recognized that legal access to abortion was in real jeopardy. "Every female that I've talked to is aware that reproductive rights are being restricted in America right now," said a Democratic woman from the University of Maryland. These concerns were even more pressing for prochoice women in states with Republican legislatures, who at the time were passing more stringent laws. Said one Democratic female student from Ohio State University: "One of the most frustrating things about all of these abortion bills being passed . . . is seeing who is legislating these policies. You see pictures and it's, like, ten old white men and maybe one woman. It's just the fact that people who do not have those same reproductive systems as us, they won't ever be in a position to have to deal with those topics."

Not all Gen Z women (or men) support abortion rights. Several Republican young women I spoke with were quite outspoken in their opposition to abortion. "I am prolife, hands down," said a Republican woman from Ohio State. "I feel like if you're prolife and you really stick to it, it's impossible to be a Democrat at this point." Another Republican woman from Ohio State praised both Alabama governor Kay Ivey for signing what was, at the time, the most restrictive abortion law in the nation, which makes performing abortions a felony in virtually all cases, and her own state senator from Ohio, a Republican woman who led the effort to the pass Ohio's heartbeat bill, which prevents abortion after six weeks.

But Republican Gen Z women were far from monolithic in their take on abortion. One Republican from Ohio State, describing herself as a "small c" conservative who generally opposes government intervention in personal decisions, said that having a friend become pregnant after being sexually assaulted made her hesitant to support very strict abortion laws. "It's a very complicated issue," she said. "I cannot say that if I was raped and I got pregnant off of it that I would be able to keep that because that's just such an emotional burden and that's not a decision that I should ever have to make."

Another Republican woman at the University of Maryland said that she also opposed legislation that bans abortion at all stages. "My personal view, a mother's life always comes first," she said. "If the mother's life is in danger and an abortion is necessary to save the mother, then it's sad, but that's what has to happen. I think there is no conclusive research on when actually life begins. I think that's the big disagreement between Democrats and Republicans on this issue." She believed, however, that liberal women who were prochoice were more engaged politically because of attempts to regulate abortion heavily. "I definitely think that it's gotten, especially a lot of liberal women, more active in politics," she said. "In general, it is an issue that is targeted toward women, so that's not surprising to me."

My Gen Z surveys asked respondents to place themselves in one of four categories when it came to abortion attitudes; this wording was modeled after language used by the American National Election Studies. Figure 4.4 shows the categories and results of both the July 2019 and May 2022 surveys for Gen Z women and Gen Z men. Two things are apparent: Gen Z women were far more supportive of abortion rights than Gen Z men, and support for legalization in all cases grew in those three years among all Zoomers, but particularly among Gen Z women. Seventy-eight percent of Zoomer women fell into the broader abortion rights category (combining the two choices of legally allowing women to obtain an abortion always, and permitting the procedure for reasons other than rape, incest, or danger to the mother's health) by May 2022, compared with 60 percent of Zoomer men.

Similar disparities existed among LGBTQ and straight Zoomers. In my 2019 Qualtrics survey, 58 percent of LGTBQ Zoomers adopted the most liberal position for legality compared with 39 percent of straight Zoomers.

"GROWING THEIR FEMINIST THING"

[Bar chart showing abortion attitudes by gender in 2019 and 2022]

	Gen Z women 2019	Gen Z men 2019	Gen Z women 2022	Gen Z men 2022
By law, women should always be able to obtain an abortion	48	36	62	39
The law should permit abortion for reasons other than rape, incest, health	14	16	16	21
The law should permit abortion only in cases involving rape, incest, health of the mother	25	31	14	23
By law, abortion should never be permitted	14	17	8	18

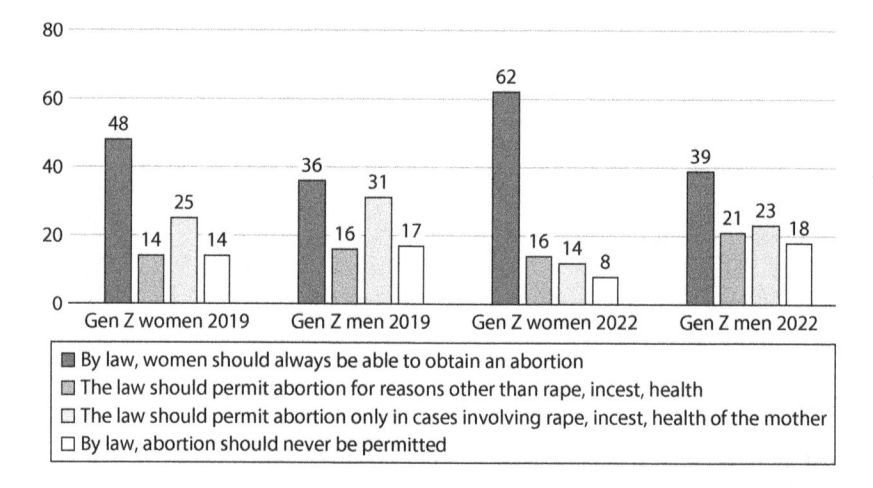

FIGURE 4.4 Abortion attitudes, by gender, percentages as of 2019 and 2022. Among members of Generation Z, women express higher levels of support for abortion legality than men; support for abortion legality also rose for Gen Z women in 2022. Qualtrics survey conducted by the author in July 2019, with a sample of 2,200 Americans aged eighteen to twenty-two; Qualtrics survey conducted by the author in May 2022, with a sample of 1,600 Americans aged eighteen to twenty-four.

That gap grew by May 2022, with 69 percent of LGBTQ Zoomers adopting the most liberal position compared with 44 percent of straight Zoomers.[20]

Gen Z women were also significantly more likely to support abortion rights compared with other generations of American women. Sixty-two percent of Gen Z women supported abortion legality in all cases, according to my May 2022 Qualtrics survey, but support for this most liberal position ranged from 44 to 53 percent among millennial women, Gen X women, and baby boomers. Among women born in the silent generation, support dropped to 34 percent.[21] Our surveys at PRRI also find that Gen Z women are far more supportive of abortion rights compared with both older women and Gen Z men.[22]

Evidence suggests that Gen Z women, as a generation, may be unique in their overwhelming support for abortion rights. Turning to the American

National Election Studies (ANES), in 1990, 44 percent of Gen X women aged eighteen to twenty-four—the first year Gen Xers made up an entire cohort of voters that age—agreed that abortion, by law, should be legal in all cases. While the ANES did not ask about abortion in its 2006 survey—when millennials began to make up an entire cohort of young voters aged eighteen to twenty-four—the 2008 ANES found that 49 percent of young women in that age category supported abortion's legality in all cases.

In contrast, Gen Z women ages eighteen to twenty-four in my May 2022 Qualtrics survey expressed higher levels of support for abortion's legality in all cases. Although the question wording is slightly different in PRRI's survey, our 2023 Politics of Gender Survey found that roughly three in four Gen Z women believed abortion should be legal in all or most cases. These are much higher rates than Gen Z men and at higher rates than women in other generational cohorts.[23]

This trend toward greater acceptance of abortion rights among Generation Z women and queer Zoomers is also linked to higher levels of political engagement. Figure 4.5 shows that, in my 2019 and 2022 Qualtrics surveys, Gen Z women in *either* abortion rights category reported engaging in more political acts in the past year than Gen Z women who opposed abortion rights, while those who were the most liberal on this measure undertook more political acts.[24]

Gen Z men's engagement in politics did not appear to be linked to their abortion attitudes in the 2019 survey, but Gen Z men who were the most supportive of abortion rights in 2022 did show significantly higher levels of political engagement than those who were the most opposed to such rights. (Although not shown in the chart, both LGBTQ Zoomers and straight Zoomers who adopted the most liberal position engaged in statistically higher levels of politics than those who were the least liberal).[25]

Support for abortion rights attitudes had a positive impact on political engagement levels for Gen Z women in both 2019 and 2022 once I add views on abortion into my political engagement model. In 2019, Gen Z women who were the most supportive of abortion undertook 4.12 activities, almost one entire political activity more than Gen Z women who believed abortion should not be legal (3.21 activities), even controlling for ideology,

"GROWING THEIR FEMINIST THING"

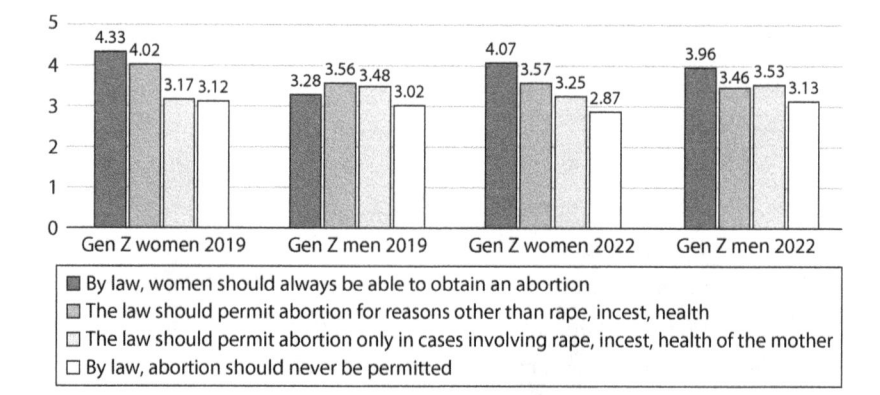

	Gen Z women 2019	Gen Z men 2019	Gen Z women 2022	Gen Z men 2022
By law, women should always be able to obtain an abortion	4.33	3.28	4.07	3.96
The law should permit abortion for reasons other than rape, incest, health	4.02	3.56	3.57	3.46
The law should permit abortion only in cases involving rape, incest, health of the mother	3.17	3.48	3.25	3.53
By law, abortion should never be permitted	3.12	3.02	2.87	3.13

FIGURE 4.5 Average number of political activities, by gender and abortion views, from the 2019 and 2022 Qualtrics surveys. Support for abortion rights drives higher levels of political activities among Gen Z women in both 2019 and 2022 but just for Gen Z men in 2022. Qualtrics survey conducted by the author in July 2019, with a sample of 2,200 Americans aged eighteen to twenty-two; Qualtrics survey conducted by the author in May 2022, with a sample of 1,600 Americans aged eighteen to twenty-four.

party strength, and other factors.[26] In contrast, abortion attitudes were not significantly related to Gen Z men's political engagement in 2019, although they did drive LGBTQ and straight Zoomers to engage at higher levels that year.[27] (See Appendix, Table A.20, for full model results.)

While not as pronounced an effect on the overall levels of participation among Gen Z women in 2019, concerns about reproductive health still had an impact on the decisions of Gen Z women to participate in politics several years into Biden's presidency when I conducted my 2022 survey in May—even before *Dobbs* was handed down. My 2022 Qualtrics survey shows that abortion attitudes *maintained* their significance in terms of propelling Gen Z women to engage in politics at higher levels, with Gen Z women most supportive of abortion rights engaged in 3.95 activities compared with those who are most opposed (3.32 activities).[28] Abortion views continued to remain statistically less important to the political participation levels of Gen Z men in May 2022, but they also failed to emerge as significant in understanding the participation levels of LGBTQ Zoomers. In 2022, support for abortion rights was linked to higher levels of political engagement among straight Zoomers.[29] (See Appendix, Table A21, for full model results.)

WHAT FEMINISM AND REPRODUCTIVE RIGHTS MEAN FOR THE FUTURE OF AMERICAN POLITICS

Generation Z has been socialized politically in an environment in which a renewed women's movement has taken shape in response to Trump's election and the Me Too cause. These young people also now face a landscape in which the constitutional right to abortion no longer exists nationally. For Gen Z women who identify as feminists and who support abortion rights, as well as LGBTQ Zoomers, these important events have resulted in significantly higher levels of political engagement. Views on feminism and abortion, however, are largely not linked to Gen Z men's decision to participate in politics. Anger about the state of reproductive rights and gender equality in the United States helped to drive the historic reverse gender gap that saw Gen Z women outperforming Gen Z men in terms of political acts in 2019 and continues to fuel their political behavior as the fight over access to legal abortion rages on in many states.

Because abortion attitudes drive Gen Z women to engage at higher levels in politics, the *Dobbs* decision will likely kick their engagement into overdrive—and we have already begun to these trends play out. In summer 2022, after *Dobbs*, abortion was on the ballot in Kansas after a referendum campaign. A record number of off-year voters turned out to reject overwhelmingly a proposed state constitutional amendment that would have allowed lawmakers to say that there is no right to an abortion in Kansas. Democratic strategist Tom Bonier of TargetSmart noted that, in the week after the *Dobbs* decision, voter registration among women in Kansas surged by more than 70 percent.[30] Many analysts credit Gen Z—particularly Gen Z women—with helping Democrats keep the U.S. Senate blue in the

2022 midterms and staving off what were originally expected to be large losses by Democrats in the U.S. House. Center for Information & Research on Civic Learning and Engagement (CIRCLE), the organization at Tufts University that studies young voters, found in its analysis of exit polls in 2022 that that 44 percent of U.S. voters ages eighteen to twenty-nine years listed abortion as their top issue in deciding their vote—far more than any other generation, with four in five younger abortion rights supporters casting their ballot for House Democrats.

History repeated itself in what would normally be a sleepy race for a seat on the Wisconsin Supreme Court in April 2023, when liberal judge Janet Protasiewicz easily defeated a conservative rival. Running on a platform of protecting abortion rights, her election shifted the balance of the Wisconsin court from a four-to-three conservative majority, providing a new check on the GOP-controlled state legislature. Commentators were quick to note that savvy political organizing efforts by progressive political groups, such as NextGen America and Gen Z for Change, used TikTok, dating apps, and voter registration drives on college campuses to spur turnout.[31]

Gen Zer Tatiana Washington was one of those organizers. The former director of the gun violence prevention organization 50 Miles More in Milwaukee, Wisconsin, and employee of March for Our Lives, Washington took a full-time position with NARAL Pro-Choice America (now known as Reproductive Freedom for All) as a Midwest regional organizer in February 2022 when she began reading about how vulnerable reproductive rights would be if *Roe* were overturned in her home state. Knocking on doors during the judicial campaign, she was struck by the extent to which the abortion issue was galvanizing young people, especially woman. She told me that many young women she canvassed hadn't been paying attention to politics, but "right after the decision happened, people I know were impacted by *Roe* being overturned, saying, 'That's really what's making me go out and vote and like get my friends to vote.' So I think this decision is lighting a fire under Gen Z voters, to get out and vote and vote for people who are reproductive freedom champions."

Anna Dean, the founder of LOUDwomen, agreed that the impact of *Roe's* reversal will be profound among young women in the years ahead:

"GROWING THEIR FEMINIST THING"

"There was a huge shock factor [with *Dobbs*] that we didn't think would happen. There's just no way we could conceptualize those rights being taken away, and then they were. . . . This is now a very slippery slope and this isn't the end to our rights being taken away."

The restrictive reproductive rights measures that the GOP passed in many states enjoyed very little public support with Generation Z, particularly Gen Z women and LGBTQ Zoomers. As the political contests in the wake of *Dobbs* are demonstrating, progressive Zoomers are not willing to face the loss of reproductive rights without a fight—and instead they are mobilizing in record numbers.

5

HOW GEN Z WOMEN AND LGBTQ ZOOMERS FIGHT FOR RACIAL AND LGBTQ EQUALITY

During the early days of the COVID-19 pandemic, Zikora Akanegbu, the daughter of Nigerian immigrants and a high school sophomore from suburban Baltimore, Maryland, had some free time and a desire to explore the voices and concerns of young women from the perspective of people of color. So she began building GenZHER—first as an Instagram account and later as an online magazine publishing stories about social and political activism written by girls of her generation. Akanegbu told me that, because the COVID-19 lockdown prevented attendance at protests and gatherings—like the March for Our Lives rally in Washington, DC, that helped inspire her activism—another outlet was needed. "People are still fighting for change," she said. "And that's why I started GenZHER."

With the encouragement of her parents, who provided Akanegbu with seed money for professional website development, GenZHER grew into a leading online resource for Gen Z activists who care about intersectional gendered advocacy. Within three years of its founding, the digital magazine published more than 120 teen female authors from across the United States and ten other nations, many of them racially or ethnically diverse or queer. They wrote on climate change; mental health; and gender, racial, and

LGBGQ+ rights. GenZHER has also developed a mentorship program matching more than 150 Gen Z teens with female college students.

Akanegbu was also tapped to be part of a local government task force devoted to racial equity—the youngest member of a panel that developed policy recommendations in public safety, policing, and the prevention of gender-based violence. She was an advocacy director for her local chapter of Girl Up, the UN organization that fosters leadership in girls and lobbied her state representative to consider a bill to extend the reach of advanced placement classes to more students of color. The bill was adopted by the Maryland General Assembly in 2020.

Akanegbu's political activism stemmed in many ways from her identity as a young woman of color. Noting that "Gen Z is the most diverse and socially conscious generation to date," Akanegbu said "having all these different perspectives is really what sets us apart, because for Gen Z, when it comes to politics, it's also related to identity politics." Like many other Gen Z women of color that I interviewed, Akanegbu's deep commitment to politics was driven by a desire to see a more intersectional approach, one that promoted and celebrated marginalized communities.

HOW RACE AND ETHNICITY SHAPE PRIORITIES AND POLITICS AMONG GEN Z WOMEN

Many nonwhite Gen Z women activists I spoke with discussed how their intersectional identities—overlapping characteristics, with each subject to their own form of discrimination[1]—inspired them to become more engaged in politics, and particularly to fight for racial equality and women's rights. Malavika Kannan, a gender rights activist from Sanford, Florida, became involved in both the gun violence prevention cause and the women's movement, but she saw that more was needed to help young women of color learn to become more effective political advocates. "I saw definitely a need for training for girls of color," said Kannan, who is Indian American. "I noticed that a lot of people, my friends included, knew what had to be done, but there weren't any resources; there wasn't a space for us to work together and grow together."

Connecting with like-minded Gen Z women of color through Instagram, Kannan founded the Homegirl Project in 2018 as a blog for young women of color to interview and share stories of inspiring women of color in their communities. Kannan had served as part of the national youth cohort for the national Women's March in 2019, and she relied on its leaders to help the Homegirl Project build a digital political training program for young women and nonbinary youth of color to become leaders in their own communities. (The group disbanded in 2022.)

For many Gen Z women of color, the fight for racial equality has been central to their decision to participate in politics. For instance, a Black Democratic student at Ohio State University said that she first got involved in racial equality issues during the height of the Black Lives Matter (BLM) movement. "I felt like there was momentum amongst Black people," she said. "We felt like we had an opportunity to remedy that situation." The murder of George Floyd by a white Minneapolis, Minnesota, police officer spawned massive protests in the summer of 2020, during the pandemic. Another Black Democratic woman from a University of Texas at Austin focus group said that the Floyd killing and the massive response from young people "woke up a lot of feelings" for her and her friends, who realized that "this is an issue that you need to care about. And then, the intersectionality between women and Black women, trans women—all of those kinds of things that have really taken a spotlight this summer as they should." The death of Breonna Taylor, a Black woman killed in March 2020 by Louisville, Kentucky, police officers who entered the wrong home using a controversial no-knock warrant, was also a galvanizing event.

Alise Maxie, who served as a youth ambassador with the Human Rights Campaign (HRC) and is active in promoting LGBTQ+ rights, helped organize her first protest march in their native Houston, Texas, to commemorate and bring awareness to the death of Taylor that summer:

> We really noticed that when things happened in the Black community, like a Black death happens, we noticed that a lot of times, if it's in the

spotlight, it's a male, like Mike Brown or Trayvon Martin. It's usually a guy's face plastered [on media], when in reality, it's not just Black men who are going through this. There are also Black women who are getting killed by police. . . . It is so easy to think about how close these incidents are to yourself. So my friends and I . . . just really wanted to be active for that Black woman. To be a voice for Black women.

More than three hundred people attended the rally at Hermann Park in downtown Houston, and Maxie and her friends collected contact information and sent instructions on how to reach local officials to address racial equity issues.

Maxie was clear that her identity as a Black, LGBTQ woman shaped her activism. "The Black woman is the most disrespected person in America," she said, noting that, despite often being on the front lines of social justice causes, Black women are often not credited with that work. "People never see what I am doing most of this time because I'm not a man, I'm not white, and I'm not straight in any type of way," Maxie said. "And I just feel like it really curves my thinking [about politics]."

Like Maxie, Aalayah Eastmond said that the killings of Taylor and Floyd were drivers of her fights for police reform and racial justice. A survivor of the shooting at Marjory Stoneman Douglas High School in Parkland, Florida, Eastmond worked full-time with Team ENOUGH, the youth-led offshoot of the Brady: United Against Gun Violence. Founded after the Parkland shootings, Team ENOUGH supports the political engagement of Brown and Black youth—an acknowledgment that young people of color are disproportionately more likely to be affected by gun violence than young white people.[2]

Eastmond acknowledged feeling tokenized by her early involvement in March for Our Lives, which was founded by several of the largely white survivors of the Parkland shooting, but her experience with Team ENOUGH has been different. "Its entire foundational basis is based off intersectionality," she said. "Our entire executive council are students from various backgrounds, whether they are from different racial backgrounds, religious backgrounds, LGBTQ. The organization was founded on diversity."

Eastmond has spent more than five years lobbying on behalf of Team ENOUGH, but it was the resurgence of the BLM movement in 2020 that pushed her to cofound Concerned Citizens DC, which is focused specifically on racial justice. The group helped organize BLM protests, has fought for police reform, and has demanded voting rights and statehood for citizens living in Washington, DC. The killing of Taylor and the larger racial justice movement, as Eastmond put it, "poked me into really formulating my voice because it is just exhausting being silenced or shunned." She added:

> There's just a lot of things that I have to think about as a young woman of color in this country. I have to think about, you know, when I want to have children, whether or not I'm going to leave the hospital alive because Black women are disproportionately impacted by that issue when it comes to giving birth. I have to think about dying from gun violence. I have to think about police officers. . . . Just being from very early on in this space of activism and being involved with politics—because I was a Black woman, I wasn't allowed into certain spaces.

Recognizing the challenges, Eastmond was nonetheless excited about the ways that members of Generation Z were using a collective voice to raise awareness about racial and gender equality and gun violence prevention.

AN INTERSECTIONAL APPROACH TO CLIMATE CHANGE

Many Gen Z women of color also bring an intersectional lens to other causes, such as climate change. Amy Quichiz was completing her bachelor's degree in women's studies and sociology at Syracuse University in 2017 when she started an Instagram page aimed at sharing easy vegan recipes that young people could make in dorm rooms. A first-generation American from Queens, New York, whose parents hail from Columbia and Peru,

FIGHTING FOR RACIAL AND LGBTQ EQUALITY

Quichiz said that she turned to veganism after a friend at college lent her the book *Sistah Vegan*, by A. Breeze Harper, which links food culture in the United States with environmental racism and ecological devastation from the perspective of Black women.

Quichiz's recipe posts grew in popularity, leading to the formation of the nonprofit Veggie Mijas, which she describes as a "folks of color collective where we get together to speak about our plant-based lifestyles and how they intersect with our marginal identities . . . but also [where we] can create action for food and climate and environmental justice kind of work." (Quichiz, born in 1995, technically misses the Gen Z window, but most of the members of Veggie Mijas is in this generation.) Veggie Mijas grew through word of mouth, building multiple chapters in cities around the country. Members cooked together in vegan potlucks, developed community gardens and fridges, and engaged in political activism around food and climate issues.

Veggie Mijas emphasizes how marginalized groups are often hit harder by lack of healthy food options. "We have to address food inequality and everything that has been constructed around food for people of color," Quichiz said. "That includes emotions, too, such as feeling shame that you can't feed yourself healthy foods, due to income or due to what's around you." By providing resources so that members can adopt a vegan lifestyle at least part of the time, "what Veggie Mijas does really well is not shaming people about what they eat," Quichiz said, "but we also look the health disparities in Black and Brown communities because of the fast-food places near us."

PRIORITIZATION OF RACIAL EQUALITY AMONG MEMBERS OF GEN Z IN THE UNITED STATES

For many Gen Z women activists of color, their multiple identities—or intersectionality—shape their approach to political and community activism. My May 2022 Qualtrics survey found that a solid majority—

66 percent—of Gen Z women of color, which includes Black women, Latinas, Asian American women, and those who are multiracial, said that racial inequality was a critical issue to them personally, while more than the 62 percent of white Gen Z women said that the issue was critically important to them personally.[3] Commitment to racial inequality issues increased among Gen Z women from my July 2019 Qualtrics survey, among both Gen Z women of color (from 60 percent) and white Gen Z women (52 percent), likely the result of renewed visibility of the BLM movement in wake of Floyd's murder.

Gen Z men in my May 2022 survey were less likely than Gen Z women to report that racial inequality was critically important to them personally—just 39 percent overall, although Gen Z men of color were more likely to report that racial inequality was a critical issue to them (45 percent) compared with white Gen Z men (36 percent);[4] half of Zoomer Black men (52 percent) prioritized racial inequality, however. (Those numbers were largely comparable to findings from my July 2019 survey.) LGBTQ Zoomers were the group most likely, by far, to prioritize racial inequality in 2022, at 72 percent, which rose from 60 percent in July 2019. In contrast, around 45 percent of straight Zoomers in both years indicated that racial inequality was critically important to them.[5]

The prioritization of racial equality among Zoomers in my May 2022 survey was linked to higher levels of political engagement for Gen Z women regardless of gender or racial status—but not for Gen Z men.[6] For LGBTQ Zoomers, a commitment to racial inequality issues also drove higher levels of political engagement, but not for straight Zoomers (see figure 5.1).[7] Although not reported in the figure, LGBTQ Zoomers of color reported similar levels of political engagement compared with white LGBTQ Zoomers when considering the importance of racial inequality.[8] These trends were similar to findings from my 2019 Qualtrics Gen Z survey. (See the appendix, Figure A.12, for more details.)

Using my Gen Z political engagement model, I identified racial inequality as a critically important issue that fueled higher levels of political participation among Generation Z, while controlling for other factors. (See the appendix, Table A.23, for full model results). In both July 2019 and

FIGHTING FOR RACIAL AND LGBTQ EQUALITY

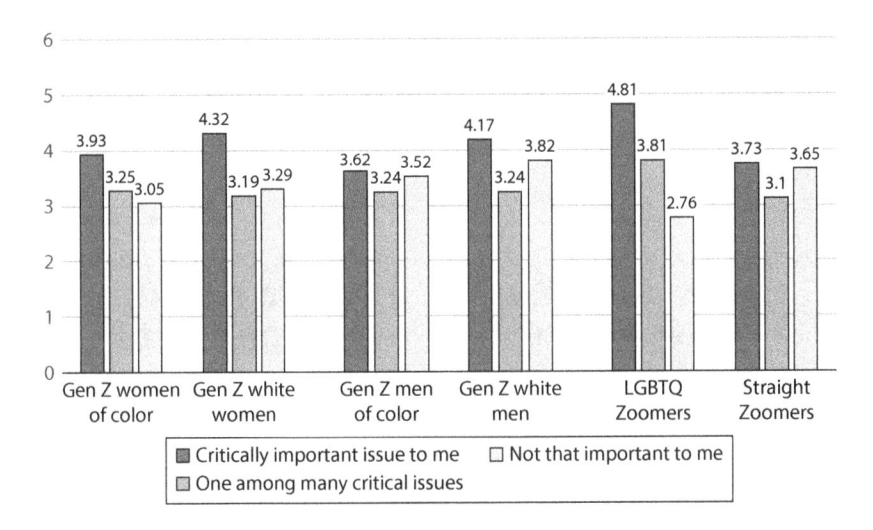

FIGURE 5.1 Average number of political activities, by the importance of racial equality, gender, race, and LGBTQ status. Members of Generation Z who identify racial equality as a critical issue engage in more activities on average than those who do not. Qualtrics survey conducted by the author in May 2022, with a sample of 1,600 Americans aged eighteen to twenty-four.

May 2022, Zoomers who embraced racial equality, on average, participated in roughly .5 or one-half more activities than those who did not.

In both years that I conducted the survey, a commitment to racial inequality issues had positive impact overall on political engagement levels among Gen Z women and Gen Z men; racial equality attitudes significantly drove higher political participation among LGBTQ Zoomers in 2019. When isolating the analyses by groups based on race and gender, however, white Zoomer men were the only group for whom attitudes about racial equality were not significantly linked to higher levels of political engagement. (For both years, there were too few cases to break down the analysis by race and LGBTQ status in the full regression model, see appendix, Tables A.24-A.26, for full model results.)

Combined with the powerful personal narratives of the Gen Z women activists of color I spoke with, my surveys show the incredible importance of intersectional identities in shaping political views and involvement of Gen Z women, especially those who are racially and ethnically diverse. Many Gen Z white women also care deeply about racial equality, and this concern drove them to engage in politics at higher levels as well.

HOW CONCERNS ABOUT LGBTQ RIGHTS DRIVE POLITICAL ACTIVISM FOR GEN Z

Riley Reed arrived at DePaul University in 2018 with a wealth of political organizing experience. As a high school student in Milwaukee, Wisconsin, she was involved with Junior State of America, a nonpartisan national training organization that helps high school students build civic and leadership skills. Too young to vote, she volunteered for Hillary Clinton's 2016 presidential campaign. Like many other Gen Z teens, the shooting in Parkland, Florida, galvanized her to become involved in gun violence prevention, ultimately becoming a college coordinator with March for Our Lives in Chicago. While at DePaul, Reed became active in women's rights issues, becoming president of the Women's March chapter on campus. She helped lead a DePaul rally protesting the confirmation of Brett Kavanaugh to the U.S. Supreme Court in the wake of sexual assault allegations.

Reed, a gay white woman, began spending more time in LGBTQ activism, including stints as a campus ambassador for Gay and Lesbian Alliance Against Defamation (GLAAD), the gay rights organization. There, she developed social campaign videos to increase awareness about LGBTQ concerns. She did the same as a political assistant with the LGBTQ Victory Fund, a political action committee that backs LGBTQ candidates for political office nationally. Reed was struck, however, by a lack of political organizing groups expressly devoted to LGBTQ young people. As a gay woman "coming into my own identity and being more comfortable with myself," she founded Pride in Running, a nonprofit, youth-led organization to help LGBTQ young people gain political skills, advocate for progressive policies to improve the lives of queer young people, and support candidates committed to LGBTQ rights. Reed disbanded Pride in Running after graduating from DePaul, but continued to work in LGBTQ advocacy. Recognizing the resilience of Generation Z, whose formative years have been marked by school lockdown drills, climate change, economic uncertainty, and a global pandemic, Reed said Gen Z is uniquely situated to deal with these problems from an intersectional perspective as "one of the most accepting generations." She added:

> [G]rowing up, hearing that all of these different groups of people were marginalized and discriminated against, and many of those are us or our peers, our friends. We don't want our Black friends to be systematically oppressed. We don't want our immigrant friends to be deported. We don't want people to be forced into the closet and forced to live a life if it's not authentic to themselves. . . . There are definitely people that aren't as accepting in my generation; I will say that. But, yeah, I think [overall] we really want to push for that change and we are the right people to do it.

The process of navigating their own gender identity and sexual orientation has prompted many LGBTQ Gen Z youth to take political action, such as Aarushi Pant, an Indian American woman who uses they/them pronouns. While in high school in Houston, Pant founded spectrum, an online forum for LGBTQ youth. They said:

> At the time, I was kind of exploring my identity, figuring out who I was and in the process, I kind of felt that I didn't really have people to talk to about it. . . . So, kind of just using my experiences, I thought, for other people who are also questioning, it would be really great if they would have a platform that answered their questions and that told them more about this community and all the resources that they have. That's what made me start spectrum, as a way to write about my experiences to make sure that other people who are going through the same things don't feel alone.

Pant's digital blog, while it was active, provided links and resources to Gen Z teens who wanted to learn more about LGBTQ issues. Many entries helped young people understand the political stakes involved for members of the LGBTQ community and informed younger Americans about what they could do to advocate for change. Pant told me, "A lot of young people may identify as queer but won't really know what's going on in terms of politics. It's, you know, a bunch of really long bills and legislation; people don't know what's going on. So the goal is to simplify that and make it clear what's going on, make it clear what you can do, to contact your representatives, to make your voice heard and to just know what's going on."

Many young queer political activists said that larger movements do not always recognize the intersectional concerns of LGBTQ people of color. "I have a bone to pick with the face of queerness being a white, well-off gay man," said Adam Neville, a mixed race climate justice activist with Future Coalition who is from New York City. "I don't think it is a coincidence that the face of gayness is most often depicted as such." Neville identifies as queer and has not yet settled on a gender identity, saying that "nonbinary is probably like the most accessible label" to describe themself.

Other LGBTQ Gen Zers that I spoke with discussed racial and class inequities within the LGBTQ community at length, including this focus group participant: "[M]e and some of my friends who are queers, trans and people of color, kind of talk about how cis gay white men; they have this kind of level of privilege that a lot of other people in the community don't have. . . . Sometimes [I wonder whether] they're even part of the community or have the elevated themselves above us? Because they can be very exclusionary and very hurtful."

The combined intersectional pressures facing queer Gen Zers of color has hardened the resolve of many of the activists I spoke with, who feel passionate about making sure their voices are included in the larger queer rights movement. Luke Chacko, whose father is Indian American, is a talented teen singer and musician from Arlington, Texas. When they were eleven years old, Chacko was brought on stage at an Idina Menzel concert and belted out her hit song "Let It Go." The performance went viral, and they were invited on the *Ellen* show, where they used the platform to shine a light on bullying and LGBTQ youth. In 2021, while in high school, Chacko came out as nonbinary. While Chacko continues to pursue a music career, their advocacy on behalf of the mental health of young queer Americans has led to them becoming a youth ambassador for HRC, where they regularly speak out on issues of concern for kids like them.

Noting that their background as nonbinary and Asian has directly shaped their political approach, Chacko's main advocacy platform concerns education in public schools: "There's not a lot of education going on about that kind of stuff, about being gay, about being nonbinary. . . . I think LGBTQ history is really, really important, and I think it should be taught in schools."

Chacko's education policy advocacy, they told me, was geared at young people who are LGBTQ and "who haven't come out or who are struggling to come out, who are hiding in the closet or who are out and struggling."

Many youth-led progressive organizations are working to recognize the challenges faced by LGBTQ+ Americans of color and to be more inclusive in their activism and organizing. Rosie Couture, who we met in chapter 4, founded the gender equality organization Generation Ratify (now Young Feminist Party), which describes itself as an intersectional feminist organization seeking to advance the rights of young women *and*, according to its website, "non-conforming, non-binary, femme and queer folx." Her group members have lobbied Congress to pass the Equality Act, which seeks to extend federal civil rights protections to LGBTQ Americans by amending the Civil Rights Act of 1964. While job discrimination based on sexual orientation and gender identity have been ruled unconstitutional by the Supreme Court, LGBTQ Americans in 2023 still don't have public accommodation protections in most states and face discrimination in other areas of life, including medical treatment.

Couture is deliberate in building an organization that is inclusive. "I [use] my privilege as a white woman to bring other people in [to Generation Ratify] who are not white and who may not be cisgender. I think my privilege within the gender equality space is much greater than the marginalization that I face as a queer person." Couture also believes what sets

Generation Z apart from older Americans is that they have a much better understanding of what it means to have these different intersectional identities—an understanding that is shaping their desire to fight for a more equitable world for all Americans, white or nonwhite, gay or straight, cisgender or transgender.

ARE GEN Z AMERICANS PRIORITIZING LGBTQ RIGHTS? DOES IT DRIVE THEIR POLITICAL ENGAGEMENT?

It is not surprising that many Gen Z progressive activists care passionately about LGBTQ rights because Generation Z is the generation most likely to identify as LGBTQ. Roughly one in four Gen Z Americans identify as part of the LGBTQ community, compared with just one in ten Americans overall, according to 2022 national data collected by my organization Public Religion Research Institute (PRRI) as part of our American Values Atlas (AVA). In contrast, just 15 percent of millennials, 7 percent of Generation Z, and 4 percent of baby boomers identify as LGBTQ.[9]

Generation Z has come of age at a time when Americans have become largely more accepting of LGBTQ Americans. In 2022, PRRI found that more than two-thirds of Americans (68 percent) fully embraced the rights of Americans to marry someone of the same sex. In contrast, at the start of Bill Clinton's second term in office in 1996, Gallup found that just 27 percent believed that gay marriage should be legal.[10] PRRI also found in 2022 that eight in ten Americans favored laws protecting against LGBTQ discrimination in jobs, public accommodations, and housing—up from 71 percent in 2015.[11] PRRI finds that younger Americans are more consistently supportive of both same-sex marriage rights and non-discrimination laws than older Americans are. For instance, while 80 percent of Zoomers also supported discrimination protections—comparable to the national average—they were more likely to *strongly* favor support (54 percent) of such protections compared to all Americans (48 percent).

The salience of support for same-sex marriage and LGBTQ discrimination protections was higher for Gen Z women: 63 percent of Gen Z women *strongly* favored same-sex marriage protections compared with 45 percent of Gen Z men; 60 percent of Gen Z women *strongly* favored discrimination protections for LGBTQ Americans compared with 46 percent of Gen Z men.

Americans' support for transgender rights has not been as high, however, and even showed some backsliding in the past few years. PRRI recorded an increase in the percentage of Americans who favored requiring transgender people to use the bathroom of their sex assigned at birth rather than their current gender identity—52 percent of Americans in 2022, up from 35 percent in 2016, when we first asked that question. This change was driven, no doubt, by right-wing hammering on this culture war issue, as evidenced by shifting views among Republicans, whose support for that restrictive policy grew from 44 percent in 2016 to 74 percent in 2022.[12] Many conservative lawmakers have recently sought to limit the rights of transgender Americans in high-profile moves such as banning drag shows in public.[13]

Of particular concern to LGBTQ Zoomers and their progressive Gen Z allies is that many anti-trans proposals in red states have targeted the young. An analysis by the *Washington Post* found that, as of late 2022, twenty-two states had passed twenty-seven laws barring trans athletes from high school sports or from using school facilities that matched their gender identities.[14] States are also outlawing gender-affirming care for minors under the guise of child protection,[15] even though medical groups such as the American Academy of Pediatrics endorse such care in some cases for gender dysphoria.[16]

Activists in my LGBTQ focus group shared that many young queer people, particularly trans and nonbinary youth, continued to struggle to get access to basic medical care, including hormones and birth control. Other legislatures were considering banning discussion about LGBTQ issues in schools. Perhaps the most well-known law, Florida's Don't Say Gay bill, signed by Governor Ron DeSantis in 2022, placed limitations on instruction about LGBTQ issues in kindergarten through third grade.

The following year, the Florida Department of Education extended that ban to all grades.[17]

These Republican legislators know that Generation Z Americans are not just more likely to identify as LGBTQ; they are also the generation most tolerant of LGBTQ rights. Former Wisconsin governor Scott Walker, who now heads Young America's Foundation, a group dedicated to advancing conservative causes on college campuses, wrote on X (formerly known as Twitter) that the progressive attitudes of Gen Z Americans come from "years of radical indoctrination—in campus, in school, with social media, and throughout culture. We have to counter it or conservatives will never win battleground states again."[18]

As documented by Adam Nagourney and Jeremy W. Peters at the *New York Times*, conservative organizations have used trans issues to galvanize social conservatives at all levels of government in the past few years. Having lost the battle on same-sex marriage, these organizations and politicians have gravitated toward trans issues because, here, public opinion is far more divided.[19]

PRRI highlights the fact that younger Americans are far more comfortable with changing gender norms and are more accepting of trans and nonbinary Americans. In spring 2023, PRRI asked Americans the extent to which they would be comfortable with a close friend telling them that they are in same-gender relationships, are transgender, or wish to be referred to with gender-neutral pronouns (see figure 5.2). Most Americans remained less comfortable with gender-neutral pronouns and transgender identity—a wedge that many conservative activists seem eager to exploit. Yet members of Generation Z, especially Gen Z women, expressed far more comfort with these ideas.

While I did not specifically ask about transgender issues in my national Gen Z surveys, I did ask about the extent to which LGBTQ rights were critically important to Gen Z Americans. In the July 2019 Qualtrics survey, that figure was 39 percent. It rose slightly to 42 percent by May 2022. Recall that my 2022 survey had comparable data on all Americans, showing that 22 percent of American adults said that LGBTQ rights were critically important to them personally, almost half the percentage of Generation Z.

FIGHTING FOR RACIAL AND LGBTQ EQUALITY

```
                    65
                         58              
        48          54        54
                                      46
              41                 42
        35
  All Americans  Gen Z women   Gen Z men
```

■ ...they are in a same-gender relationship. □ ...are transgender.
▨ ...use gender-neutral pronouns.

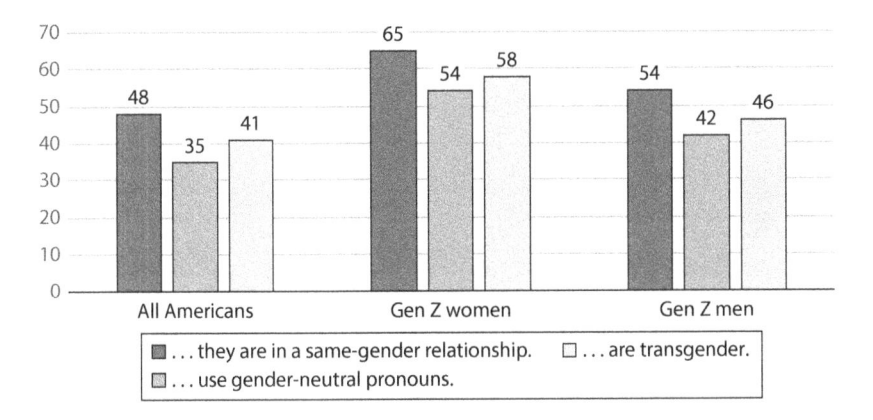

FIGURE 5.2 Percentage of those who feel comfortable with a friend telling them that they are in a same-gender relationship, they use gender-neutral pronouns, and/or they are transgender. Among members of Generation Z, women are more comfortable than men with a friend telling them that they are in a same-gender relationship, use gender-neutral pronouns, and/or are transgender. Public Religion Research Institute (PRRI), Politics of Gender Survey, 2023.

But once again, Gen Z women were almost twice as likely as Gen Z men to say that LGBTQ rights were critically important to them, 53 percent to 26 percent, respectively. The divide between LGBTQ Zoomers and their straight counterparts was even more striking, with 70 percent of LGBTQ Zoomers prioritizing LGBTQ rights compared with 30 percent of straight Zoomers.[20]

Does that concern for LGBTQ rights drive higher levels of political engagement among Gen Z Americans in my surveys? For Gen Z women and LGBTQ Zoomers, the answer was a resounding yes (see figure 5.3).[21] Gen Z women who said that LGBTQ rights were critically important to them engaged in an average of 4.21 political activities in 2022, significantly more than those Gen Z women who said such rights were either one of many important issues or not as important to them.[22] Gen Z men who prioritized LGBTQ rights also participated at higher levels, but the effect was less pronounced. LGBTQ Zoomers who prioritized LGBTQ issues reported engaging in the highest numbers of political acts in the past year;

FIGHTING FOR RACIAL AND LGBTQ EQUALITY

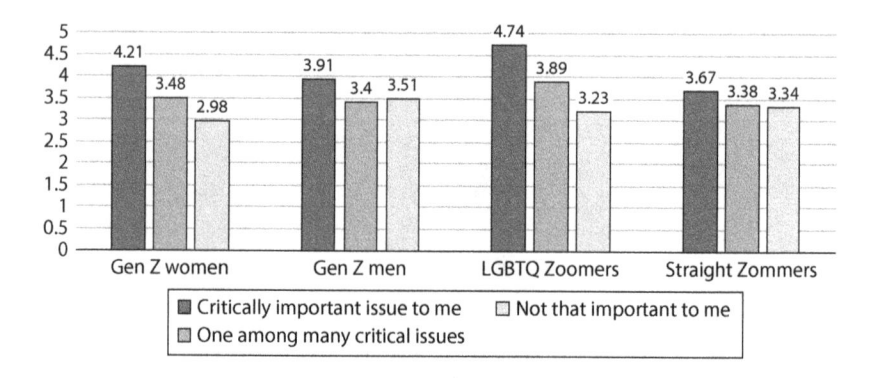

	Critically important issue to me	One among many critical issues	Not that important to me
Gen Z women	4.21	3.48	2.98
Gen Z men	3.91	3.4	3.51
LGBTQ Zoomers	4.74	3.89	3.23
Straight Zommers	3.67	3.38	3.34

FIGURE 5.3 Average number of political activities, by gender, queer status, and the importance of LGBTQ equality. Generation Z women and LGBTQ people who identify LGBTQ equality as a critical issue engage in more political activities than Generation Z men or straight people. Qualtrics survey conducted by the author in May 2022, with a sample of 1,600 Americans aged eighteen to twenty-four.

like Gen Z men, there was a less pronounced but positive effect on political engagement levels for straight Zoomers.[23] Similar trends were found in 2019 (see the appendix, see Figure A.13), with the embrace of such rights mattering more in terms of overall levels of participation among Generation Z women and LGBTQ Zoomers once again.

When I added whether Zoomers personally identified LGBTQ rights as being a critically important issue to them in my full political engagement model, it was significantly linked to higher levels of overall engagement for Gen Z Americans in 2019, even while controlling for all the other factors introduced in chapter 2. Concern for LGBTQ rights dropped in significance for Zoomers overall in 2022 in terms of explaining political engagement. Passion for LGBTQ rights nonetheless drove both Gen Z women and LGBTQ Zoomers to participate in higher levels of political activities in both years (see the appendix, see Tables A.27 and A.28, for more details.). In contrast, attitudes about LGBTQ rights were not significantly linked to political engagement levels for either Gen Z men or straight Zoomers once I controlled for other factors in either year.

FIGHTING FOR RACIAL AND LGBTQ EQUALITY

IDENTITY POLITICS DOES NOT MATTER FOR ALL ZOOMERS

While Gen Z is by far the most accepting and diverse generation when it comes to race, ethnicity, and LGBTQ politics, my conversations with some young Republicans show that not all Gen Zers embrace identity politics. They often report enormous pressure to conform to political views held by a majority of young people, particularly on college campuses, and there was a palpable sense among many conservative Gen Z women that "intersectionality" as a term only applied if you were politically progressive. For instance, a white bisexual Republican woman from Ohio State, described herself as a staunch libertarian who, in her own words, "hate[s] intersectionality in every aspect. Like. It's terrible." As a member of the university's rugby team, she often felt ostracized by her teammates and other classmates who had hard a time reconciling her support for Donald Trump with the fact that she is not straight. "The fact that I am bi should have nothing to do at all with my actual political opinions," she said.

Another white woman in the same focus group recognized that LGBTQ individuals have faced adversity and, as a libertarian, she supported gay marriage and gay rights broadly. "I don't think that the government should be able to tell me what I identify as or who I should be able to marry," she said. As the same time, she described many LGBTQ Gen Zers that she knows as "liberal snowflakes," and described walking into a room and using the expression "hey guys," only to learn that LGBTQ students were offended by the greeting. "If you want equality and you want me to treat you equally, that's just how I talk," she said. "If I have to tiptoe around you every time I'm around you and think consciously about what I'm saying every second, then that's not equality."

Another member of the same focus group agreed that "people are too sensitive," adding, "We all want equality, that's the ultimate goal—but you can't be equal if you're going to get offended every single time that I say something that's not 100 percent politically correct or not 100 percent what you believe in." Other participants from Republican focus groups at Ohio

State University who are women of color recounted hostile treatment from more liberal classmates. One Black woman said that when she tells people she is a Republican, she is often told "you are being a hypocrite to your race." Her response: "I was breaking it down, telling them, 'Do you know that Republicans are the ones who worked to get slaves to be free?' or 'Did you know Democrats helped make mass incarceration?'" A Latina at the same focus group shared that her identity as both Hispanic and Republican often compelled her to explain her views and "defend myself sometimes because *they* think I should."

At the same time, there were signs that young Republicans were recognizing a need for greater inclusivity, particularly if the GOP were to remain a viable alternative for Gen Z voters. A white Republican female student at Georgia State University told me that if the GOP would "appeal to more LGBTQ stuff" and "talked more and were more open about that issue," the messaging shift would attract more Gen Zers to their party.

A Black Georgia State Republican student would like to see more women candidates, particularly women of color, in the GOP. "It would definitely change the party and the way people see the party," she said. "I know Democrats are all like, 'Yeah, we're for everyone.' Well, Republicans are for everyone, too." An Indian American participant in the Georgia State Republican focus group added: "I guess if there were more diversity within the [Republican] party . . . it'd give a wider perspective for the people, and I guess [Gen Z] would be more supportive of it."

As a student at Binghamton University, Alexandria Chun served for several years as vice chair of communications with Gen Z Grow Our Platform (GOP), a youth-led, nonprofit group that was dedicated to encouraging the Republican Party to address the most pressing needs of Generation Z, which they defined as the environment, entrepreneurship, education, and equality. Started in 2020, the group disbanded in 2022. Recognizing that Gen Z is the most diverse generation in U.S. history, Chun said that the Republican Party needed to do far more to recruit and appeal to voters in her generation. "I don't think that Republicans are doing enough outreach to young women," she said. "I think that people on the left are promoting this aura of inclusivity. I do think the Republican Party has that [too], but is just not as open as it should be about that." Chun is Asian American and believes the Republican Party should do more outreach to this demographic; many Asians she believes hold traditional social attitudes and conservative economic views that have been the foundation of the Republican Party historically.

The need for the Republican Party to recruit more diverse, qualified candidates was echoed by an African American male student in my focus group of Republican men at the University of Maryland. When the United States becomes a majority-minority country, he said, "Republicans will not win unless they're able to appeal to more diverse groups of people. They won't be able to win elections on a widespread scale until they do that. So I think that's something that they should focus on."

But other Republican men in the same focus group raised concerns about tokenism. "I don't want to insult people just like, 'Oh, we have a black guy running. Black people vote for my guy,'" said one white Republican male. "That seems stupid. I think our message of freedom, dignity of life, free speech, the right to bear arms—those are values that transcend race, they transcend tribe or culture or religion, and I think we should stick to that message."

These last comments are a good reminder that Gen Z is far from monolithic with respect to its political views. Yet, a blind adherence to these more right-leaning issues, without a nod to diversity and inclusion, will likely fail to resonate with most younger Americans, who, my data show, are largely embracing a more progressive political future that is more inclusive of marginalized groups.

While they see challenges ahead, many Zoomers that I spoke with were cautiously optimistic, having "entered a time in our lives where we feel more entitled to speak our truth," as one activist from the LGBTQ focus group put it. This optimism extended to young women of color. In the words of one Black woman from Ohio State, who was delighted to see a record number of candidates of color elected in 2018: "I think it's really easy, as a Black woman, to feel like there's no one really fighting for you and for issues that you care about. And so seeing more candidates, especially women of color, out here and winning and representing me, it means a lot."

6

HOW THE FIGHTS AGAINST GUN VIOLENCE, CLIMATE CHANGE, AND INCOME INEQUALITY HAVE BECOME GENDERED SPACES

Jaclyn Corin was a high school junior at Marjory Stoneman Douglas High School in Parkland, Florida, when a young man opened gunfire on her classmates on Valentine's Day in 2018, killing seventeen students and staff members. Hunkered down in a classroom for more than three hours, Corin went home later that evening, and remembers, above all else, before the sadness kicked in, before she knew how many and which people had been lost that day, that she was angry. "I remember getting into a little tiff with my Dad, because he was like, you know, this [shooting] was a one off. This is just one person and you need to calm down. I just felt really shocked by that comment. And angry."

As she sat at her computer later that night of the shooting, her social media feed was filled with prayer requests and messages of strength and solidarity for the Parkland community. Corin decided to post a more pointed plea on Facebook and Instagram. Prayers were obvious, she wrote "but also let's do something on the local and state level to fix this problem." She said, "And that was kind of a unique post at that point in time." A friend of Corin's family who had previously served as a county commissioner then contacted her, noting that she had connections in Tallahassee,

Florida's state capital, and could help set up some meetings. One month earlier, Corin had completed a class research project on gun control, becoming well versed in systemic issues that lead to gun violence and the stranglehold that the National Rifle Association (NRA) held on gun control politics. She had also watched a documentary about the 1999 Columbine school shooting that shocked the nation.

By the next day, Corin had spoken with her state senator, Kristin Jacobs, who told her any legislative efforts would have to come quickly because it was late in the legislative session, which meets for just eight weeks annually. Corin and Jacobs decided to bring one hundred Parkland students to the state capital. "Over the next few days," Corin told me, "the state senator's office began organizing meetings with other legislators while I did a lot of the logistics . . . finding buses, working with the Red Cross to get cots in a civic center that we could stay in overnight." Although not active in politics previously, Corin mobilized one hundred students, with parents signing permission slips, and got Uber Eats and others to donate meals. She also worked to compile rotating groups of students to connect with individual lawmakers in the statehouse as well as with Governor Rick Scott, a Republican with an A rating from the NRA.

The lobbying efforts paid off because the Florida General Assembly passed and Governor Scott signed a law that banned bump stocks, raised the minimum age for buying a gun to twenty-one and added a three-day waiting period before gun purchases—the first tangible gun control measures to pass in a red state in decades. "That was really what made me recognize the power that I could have in, you know, changing the course of gun laws in my state, at least," said Corin.

Shortly after the lobbying trip, Corin became an official cofounder of March for Our Lives, after her friend Cameron Kasky told her he was organizing a protest march for students. Kasky said to Corin, "I need you to be part of this because it's not going to happen without you." March for Our Lives eventually organized what was likely the largest youth-led protest march in U.S. history on March 24, 2018, in Washington, DC. Notable celebrities and corporations donated millions of dollars to underwrite the event. More than eight hundred companion marches were also held that day around the country. March for Our Lives has evolved to mobilize young people to vote, rate candidates in key races on their gun violence prevention views, and lobby state and national lawmakers to pass common-sense gun reform.

When asked about the gender dynamics of the organization, Corin said that most of the companion marches and chapters created in its first year were headed and organized by young women. She also said that some of the initial cofounders were young men who took charge and "would not take the women's ideas as seriously" in the group, often claiming credit for the work of their female colleagues—including her own. When some of those male leaders eventually stepped away, Corin and other young women "really started to . . . take those leadership positions," she said. "I honestly remember, a lot of the women would come up to me and be like, 'You're the only person in a leadership capacity that I like feel totally comfortable talking to.'"

She also noted that as the organization grew and hired paid staff in Washington, DC, most of the hires at the national level were women. There were certainly young men involved with March for Our Lives as volunteers and in prominent leadership positions. One notable example is David Hogg, a Parkland survivor, March for our Lives cofounder, and one of the nation's most effective and compelling advocates for gun violence prevention. Yet most of the full-time staff and youth advisers remained women.

In the first year of March for Our Lives, while she was a senior in high school, Corin acted as director of outreach and helped create more than two hundred chapters in high schools and colleges across the country. She took a step back during her first year at Harvard University, where she graduated with a degree in public policy at the university's Kennedy School in 2023, but she continued as an adviser and spokesperson, ultimately joining the board of the organization.

Asked about the legacy of March for Our Lives and Generation Z, Corin said that the organization represented one of the first political experiences for many young people. Looking back, Corin acknowledged the enormous impact that March for Our Lives had on many Gen Z youth.

"I think young people really saw themselves in us and said, 'If they're doing it, I can do that, too.'" Indeed, most of the progressive women and LGBTQ activists that I interviewed said that they participated in or helped organize one of the companion gun violence prevention marches after the Parkland shooting. The passion and organizational skills they built soon found other causes, too, such as climate change and broader equality issues.

GUNS, CLIMATE CONCERNS, AND ECONOMIC ISSUES DIFFERENTIATE GEN Z

Many Gen Z activists first began marching in the streets after the Parkland shooting in 2018 or after Greta Thunberg created the climate advocacy organization Fridays For Future (FFF), which inspired more than a million young people worldwide to ditch their classes in March 2019 (and more in subsequent protests) to demand political action to prevent climate change. The concerns that found outlets after the Parkland shooting or in the international climate strikes show no signs of abating soon—and help set Generation Z apart politically from older Americans.

Zoomers are far more likely than older Americans to worry about mass shooting, support stricter gun control, and prioritize climate change concerns on a regular basis.[1] My May 2022 survey, which has comparable data on Gen Z and older Americans, finds that 62 percent of Gen Z Americans say that mass shootings are an issue that is critically important to them personally compared with 50 percent of survey participants not from Gen Z. Gen Z Americans are also more likely to say that climate change is a critically important issue compared with older Americans, 53 percent to 42 percent, respectively.[2]

Gen Z also differs from older generations in their attitudes about economic issues. Compared to Americans overall, for example, polling from Axios and Survey Monkey finds that Gen Z is more likely to believe the federal government should pursue policies to reduce the gap between wealthy and less-well-off Americans, 80 percent versus 66 percent, respectively.[3] This isn't surprising for a cohort of young people who came of age during an era of unprecedented income inequality, compiled massive amounts of student debt, and were hit hard by the economic fallout of the COVID-19 pandemic.

THE LOCKDOWN GENERATION

It is difficult to understand the politics of Gen Z today without understanding the indelible mark left by growing up with school mass shootings. While the 2018 shooting in Parkland, Florida, was the catalyst for many Gen Z teens, such as Corin, lots of Zoomers recalled that the December 2012 shooting at Sandy Hook Elementary School in Newtown, Connecticut, which claimed the lives of six adults and twenty children, changed forever their perceptions about safety and schools.

"After Sandy Hook, you would expect things to get better, but it ushered in a new era where school shootings are kind of normal and you just have school shooter drills," said Claire Chang, who was a sixth grader in Connecticut at the time. "Then Parkland happened, which kind of scared us because we were like Parkland's school district, safe and relatively affluent, and nobody ever thought something bad was going to happen." Chang organized a walkout and cofounded a gun control organization, Violence to Voices, in her hometown after Parkland.

Isabella D'Alacio, from Pembroke Pines, Florida, also felt compelled to become politically engaged after the shootings at Marjory Stoneman Douglas High School, which was in the same county where she grew up. "Our entire school came out in the courtyard," she said. "I never thought that my school [was] that engaged, but they were so engaged and we were just chanting, 'We want change.' And then we all just stormed out the doors and over to the administration, and essentially, I thought change is really possible." After college, D'Alacio joined Team ENOUGH, a youth-led organization that mobilizes and educates young people about gun violence prevention, particularly in Black and Brown communities.

THE GENDER DIVIDE ON ATTITUDES TOWARD GUN VIOLENCE

While many Gen Z men have marched and advocated against gun violence, my research has found important gender differences with respect to gun policy attitudes. As we saw in chapter 1, Gen Z women in my Qualtrics surveys were more likely to prioritize mass shootings as a critically important issue than Gen Z men. The same was true for LGBTQ Zoomers compared with their straight counterparts.

Gen Z women and LGBTQ Zoomers are also more likely to want to ban the sale of semiautomatic weapons. The Supreme Court has recently moved to shore up Second Amendment rights, including in its 2022 *Bruen* decision, which ruled that Americans have a right to carry concealed firearms in public for self-defense. The Court has yet to rule, however, on whether states have the right to ban the sale, possession, and use of semiautomatic guns, which are the type used in many mass shootings. Many blue states have begun to pass laws that ban semiautomatic weapons, although those restrictions have faced legal challenges.[4] Youth-led organizations such as March for Our Lives and Team ENOUGH routinely lobby for the ban of such weapons and of high-capacity magazines.

Figure 6.1 shows that three in four Gen Z women from my May 2022 Qualtrics survey supported banning semiautomatic weapons, with 42 percent expressing strong support for a ban. Gen Z men, however, are equally like to support or oppose such bans.[5] Gen Z men are more than three times as likely to *strongly* oppose such bans compared with their female counterparts. The levels of support among LGBTQ Zoomers for such bans mirrored Gen Z women nationally, while LGBTQ Zoomers were significantly more likely to support the ban of semiautomatic weapons than straight Zoomers.[6]

It is not surprising that Gen Z women supported stricter gun control than Gen Z men considering that American women have historically been more likely to support strong gun control measures compared with men, and they are less likely to be gun owners.[7] Women are more likely to believe

GUNS, CLIMATE CHANGE, AND INCOME INEQUALITY

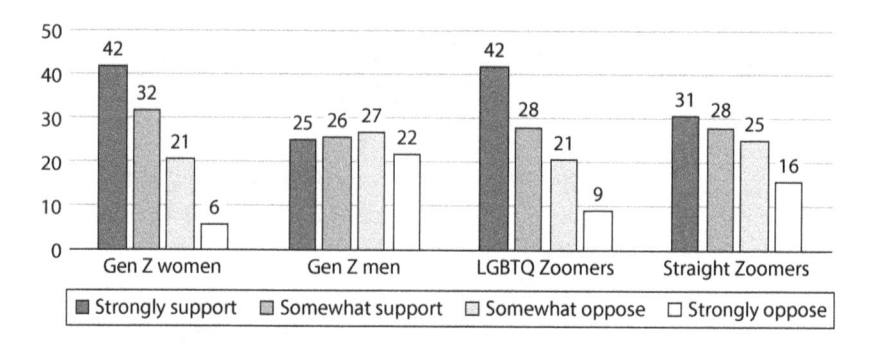

FIGURE 6.1 Support for semiautomatic weapons bans, by gender and LGBTQ status. Generation Z men are distinct in showing less support for semiautomatic weapons bans than other members of Generation Z. Qualtrics survey conducted by the author in May 2022, with a sample of 1,600 Americans aged eighteen to twenty-four.

gun control measures ensure greater safety and security in their communities, while men are more likely to believe that greater access to guns ensures their own safety.[8]

The fact that LGBTQ Zoomers held more liberal positions on gun control than straight Zoomers also corresponds with other studies.[9] The LGBTQ community has recently been the target of several high-profile mass shootings, including the November 2022 shooting at the Club Q gay bar in Colorado and the June 2016 massacre at the popular Pulse gay nightclub in Orlando, Florida, where forty-nine were killed and fifty-three were wounded, one of the worst mass shootings in American history. LGBTQ people are also disproportionately more likely to be victims of gun violence than their straight and cisgender counterparts[10] and LGBTQ youth, particularly transgender youth, are far more likely to be threatened with a weapon on school property.[11]

Some Gen Z women I spoke with said that their gun violence prevention advocacy stemmed from a desire to protect women from domestic violence. Tatiana Washington is a past leader of the gun violence prevention and civil rights organization 50 Miles More, based in Milwaukee, Wisconsin. She has also worked as a political organizer for (NARAL)

Pro-choice America (now known as Reproductive Freedom for All). Washington told me that her involvement in political activism stemmed directly from her aunt's death, whose estranged husband shot her while Washington's two younger cousins were present in the home. "No family should go through what my family has been going through," she said. "No one should see their parents die in a horrific way." In addition to leading school walkouts and organizing politically at the state level with 50 Miles More, Washington volunteered with her community's local domestic violence shelter. March for Our Lives cofounder Jackie Corin agreed that the surge of Gen Z women in this movement stems from a growing recognition that, "in the gun violence prevention space, domestic gun violence is very much a thing."

Kathryn Fleischer founded Not My Generation, a leading national youth-led gun violence prevention organization in late 2018. She agreed that gun violence prevention has strong gendered dimensions. "I see my gun violence prevention work, specifically how it intersects with domestic violence and interpersonal violence, as being an issue of equity," said Fleischer, who started the nationally recognized program while in college in her native Pittsburgh, Pennsylvania. Her organization builds coalitions with other young activists across the country, and Fleischer noted that relatively few of the activists serving in leadership roles in her group are single, straight, white cisgender men:

> All of us who are drawn to this work have understood some slice of injustice for longer than we can name what it's been. Whether it's people of color on our board who for a long time understood that because of the color of their skin, they are treated differently by individuals and systems. And for those of us who identify as women that, you know, since forever, we've been expected to act a certain way because our bodies aren't built in a certain way and because certain gender roles are pushed onto us. And differently abled communities have grown up having to be aware of how they're forced to navigate the world differently because the systems aren't set up for them. . . . I, as a white Jewish cisgender woman who does identify as part of the disabled community, I will never know what racial

injustice truly feels like. I will never know what being physically disabled is truly like, I will never know those things, but I know my own intersections. And I think it makes me more compassionate and aware of what other people are going through, too.

Most white men, Fleischer believes, "don't have to come against those systems of oppression or don't have to walk around every day fearing for their safety or wondering if, you know, what's meant to protect them is actually going to harm them."

Not all Gen Z women support more gun control, however. Several Republican women activists I spoke with care passionately about protecting gun rights, in part because they believe that greater access to guns may *better* protect them and their families. Chloe Sparwath was the president of the University of Virginia chapter of the conservative young women's organization Network of Enlightened Women (NeW) before she began working full-time for the organization. She argued that most gun violence prevention activists were misguided and that young women should fully support gun rights as a matter of safety:

> Guns were a huge thing that got a lot of young people involved [in politics] and therefore a lot of young women involved. But I think a lot of times it's just framed incorrectly and just depends on how you look at it. For me, guns are a women's issue because they're the great equalizer. If I'm in my house or on the street and a man who most likely is going to be larger than me, we're not equal, if he's trying to rob or rape or assault me in some way, if I have a gun to protect myself, then we're equal, if not more than equal.

My Qualtrics surveys found strong partisan differences emerge among Gen Z women, with 81 percent of Gen Z Democratic women supporting semiautomatic bans compared with 59 percent of Republican women.[12] Statistically significant differences exist between Democratic and Republican men in my survey, too, but both sets of Zoomer men are less supportive of semiautomatic weapon bans, 60 percent versus 43 percent, respectively.[13]

GUNS, CLIMATE CHANGE, AND INCOME INEQUALITY

(There were not enough cases of Republicans who identify as LGBTQ to report partisan differences among LGBTQ Zoomers.)

Partisanship also colored how Gen Z women and Gen Z men view mass shootings. Gen Z Democratic women in the survey were the most likely to indicate that mass shootings are critically important to them (74 percent) compared with 61 percent of Republican Gen Z women. Gen Z Democratic men were similar to Republican Gen Z women in terms of issue prioritization (59 percent); however, fewer than half of Republican Gen Z men said that mass shootings were critically important to them (46 percent).

Identifying mass shootings as a critically important issue is linked to higher levels of political engagement among Democratic women and Democratic men for the respondents in my 2022 survey—but levels of average numbers of political activities are still higher overall among Gen Z Democratic women who view the issue as critically important (4.5 activities) compared to Democratic men (3.99 activities) (see figure 6.2). Attitudes on the importance of mass shootings appear to have little impact on the political engagement of Gen Z Republican women—although it has the opposite impact on Republican Gen Z men.

In my Gen Z political engagement model, identifying mass shootings as a critically important issue fueled significantly higher levels of political engagement among members of Generation Z in both my 2019 and 2022 Qualtrics surveys when controlling for other factors (see the appendix, Tables A.29 and A.30, for full model results). All other things considered, deep concern about mass shootings results in Zoomers reporting about .5 more activities, on average, for both years. Concerns about mass shootings increases political engagement for all members of Generation Z, however, whether female, male, LGBTQ, or straight. Although this relationship in figure 6.2 appears muted for Gen Z Republican women or even works in the reverse direction for Gen Z Republican men, the net effect of caring about mass shootings is to propel members of Generation Z to participate more in politics.

Shortly after the mass shooting at a religious school in Nashville, Tennessee, in 2023 that killed three elementary school students and three teachers, I asked Jackie Corin for her sense of how the gun violence prevention movement was doing five years after the shootings at Parkland.

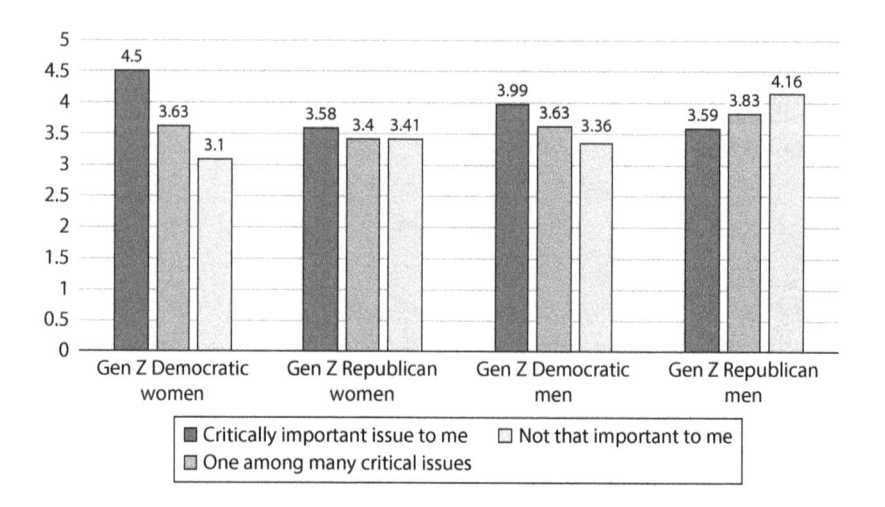

[Bar chart showing values:
- Gen Z Democratic women: 4.5, 3.63, 3.1
- Gen Z Republican women: 3.58, 3.4, 3.41
- Gen Z Democratic men: 3.99, 3.63, 3.36
- Gen Z Republican men: 3.59, 3.83, 4.16

Legend: Critically important issue to me / One among many critical issues / Not that important to me]

FIGURE 6.2 Average number of political activities, by gender, party, and the prevalence of mass shootings. Members of Generation Z who are Democrats and who identify the prevalence of mass shootings as a critical issue engage in more political activities than those who do not. Qualtrics survey conducted by the author in May 2022, with a sample of 1,600 Americans aged eighteen to twenty-four.

While she understood that many Zoomers could feel hopeless, she also said that many members of her generation remained active in the cause, including more than seven thousand young people who were organized by March for Our Lives and who showed up at the Tennessee State House shortly after the shooting to lobby for more gun violence prevention legislation. She said:

> We know what the solutions are; we just need to wait for older elected officials to move out so we can move in and solve all these problems. Hopelessness is never a good thing to lean on in politics. The challenge of our generation is that the group of people who are more politically and civically engaged, who are channeling their frustrations into anger and action, really need to persuade these [young] people who have fallen victim to hopelessness and show them through education and encouragement that there is a vehicle for change. Truly I think the thing that pushes me forward is knowing that we have been able to move the needle since 2018.

Corin noted that the first federal law on gun safety in thirty years, the Bipartisan Safer Communities Act, was passed by Congress in June 2022 after the Uvalde, Texas, mass shooting, in which nineteen students and two teachers lost their lives. The law enhanced background checks for gun purchasers between the ages of eighteen and twenty-one; increased resources for youth mental health; and incentivized states to pass red flag laws, which seek to keep guns away from people who may be viewed as a threat to themselves or others.[14] She also noted that more than two hundred state-level gun safety laws have been passed since 2019. Corin predicted that gun violence prevention would remain a top concern for Gen Z voters because it is the leading cause of death for children in this country and is part of the reason that her generation is trending Democratic.

THE GENDERED DIMENSIONS OF CLIMATE CHANGE

Along with gun violence prevention, perhaps no other issue sets Gen Z apart from other generations than climate change. A 2021 Pew Research Center study found that Zoomers were far more likely than older Americans to discuss the need for climate change, to view social media content about the need for climate action, and to have personally acted themselves to address climate change.[15] "Most young people would echo me that climate change is the number one issue on every one's mind right now," said Ina Bhoopalam, who, in addition to starting the youth-led gender equality group Dream EQUAL (first discussed in chapter 1), was a cofounder of OneUpAction, a leading climate rights advocacy group led by and for marginalized young people. "Gen Z cares because we are going to be the ones most affected, even though we did literally nothing to deserve this life." Bhoopalam rejected the idea that her generation is inspiring when it comes to their leadership on climate issues; instead, she said, "we are just fighting for our right to live on a breathable planet. We deserve that, too."

Devishi Jha, a student at Harvard, served as partnerships director with Zero Hour while in high school. Zero Hour, a leading youth-led climate advocacy group, was founded in 2017 after Seattle, Washington, native Jamie Margolin connected with Nadia Nazar of Baltimore, Maryland, via Instagram to look for young people interested in forming a climate march modeled after the historic March on Washington led by Dr. Martin Luther King, Jr. Two of Margolin's friends, Madelaine Tew and Zanagee Artis, also joined the group as cofounders.[16] Today, Zero Hour continues to lead climate marches across the nation, use social media campaigns to draw awareness to the cause, and file lawsuits at the state and national levels to advocate for environmental change. Jha told me that Gen Zers are drawn to climate advocacy because they have been taught about the potential catastrophic impact on inaction. "Climate change affects us directly in the future." she said. "Hearing about it in class, and just watching how if the Earth rises this many degrees, our well-being is greatly affected."

While political efforts are important, said Jha, Zoomers also need to put pressure on the private sector to adopt greener programs. Working with another climate activist and high school student, Isabel LoDuca, Jha started Voyagers, a youth-led platform that worked with businesses to adopt more sustainable practices that ran for several years starting in 2020. Jha, LoDuca, and their staff of high school and college activists worked with an advisory group of adults from businesses such as Sephora, IKEA, and Clif Bar & Company to share their perspectives on the importance of sustainability as young consumers through different forums sponsored by the retailers.[17] In 2023, Jha founded and became CEO of LeafPress, which helps businesses navigate carbon management and disclosures.

As with gun violence prevention, Gen Z women are more likely to prioritize climate change as a critical issue compared with their male counterparts. In my May 2022 Qualtrics survey, for instance, 59 percent of Gen Z women said that climate change was an issue of critical importance to them personally compared with just 42 percent of Gen Z men.[18]

Jha said that women are more active in the fight about climate change because "women are definitely affected more by the climate crisis than men." She pointed to studies by the United Nations indicating that women around the world will be far more vulnerable to drastic changes in climate, particularly women living in poverty, who are more likely to work in food production and who are more responsible for the household water supply and food security.[19] Jha said that another reason for the preponderance of Gen Z female leadership on climate change was that young women were seizing the opportunity to be part of large political progressive movements. "The origin of this whole activism [in climate and other progressive causes] was spurred by the need for more people to have a voice in politics that weren't given the channels before," she said. "There's a historical element that definitely plays into why it's so majority [Gen Z] women right now."

Another reason for the gender divide in climate activism may be linked to empathy—the notion that women are conditioned to take the community's needs at heart more than men, to hold more of what political scientist Mary-Kate Lizotte calls "pro-social values." In other words, women, on average, support more government involvement in regulating the environment (and other issues) than men because of their greater conditioning to care about others' well-being.[20] This point was echoed by Stella Heflin, who graduated from the University of Arizona in 2023 with a degree in atmospheric sciences and led a push for her school to divest its endowment from fossil fuel corporations. She relayed that, in her experience in climate activism, "young women are more engaged than young men." After classroom discussions, her colleagues concluded that "women tend to either be forced to, or just naturally care more, about the community as a whole, whereas men tend to think more individualistically."

My May 2022 Qualtrics survey found that Gen Z women who prioritized climate change engaged in a higher number of actions than those who didn't, but this was not the case for Gen Z men (see figure 6.3). Prioritization of climate change among both LGBTQ and straight Zoomers was also related to higher levels of political engagement, although the effect was more pronounced for LGBTQ Zoomers.

When attitudes about the salience of climate change were added to my larger 2022 Gen Z political engagement model, they continued to have an impact on the political decisions of Gen Z women in a positive direction (see the appendix, see Tables A.31 and A.32, for more details). If we control for other factors, we see that identifying climate change as a critical issue led Gen Z women to engage in .621 more political activities that Gen Z

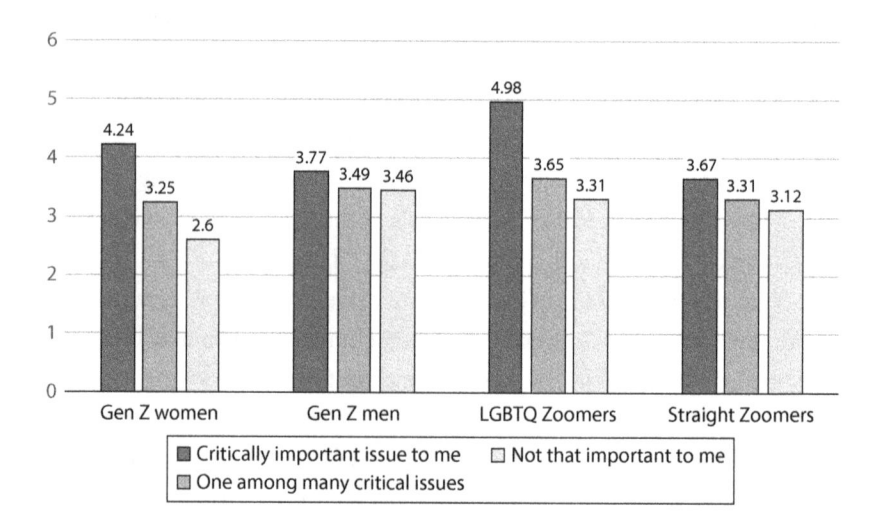

Bar chart showing average political activities by group and climate change concern level (Critically important issue to me / One among many critical issues / Not that important to me):

- Gen Z women: 4.24, 3.25, 2.6
- Gen Z men: 3.77, 3.49, 3.46
- LGBTQ Zoomers: 4.98, 3.65, 3.31
- Straight Zoomers: 3.67, 3.31, 3.12

FIGURE 6.3 Average number of political activities, by gender, LGBTQ status, and concern about climate change. Generation Z women and LGBTQ people who identify climate change as a critical issue engage in more political activities than Generation Z men or straight people. Qualtrics survey conducted by the author in May 2022, with a sample of 1,600 Americans aged eighteen to twenty-four.

women who did not. The impact of climate change attitudes was even higher for LGBTQ Zoomers, who engaged in .737 more activities than LGBTQ Zoomers who do not identify climate change as being as personally salient. For Gen Z men, attitudes about the saliency of climate change were not significantly related to their levels of political engagement, at least as found in my May 2022 survey.

In 2019, I found that identifying climate change as a critical issue in my model was also statistically linked to higher levels of engagement among Gen Z women, LGBTQ Zoomers, and straight Zoomers (see the appendix). Yet climate change *also* drove more political engagement among Gen Z men that year. While it's hard to speculate why climate change failed to result in more engagement among Gen Z men in 2022 compared with 2019, it does serve as a reminder that deep concern for the planet has the potential to galvanize young people to become more involved in the political process.

INCOME INEQUALITY, THE ECONOMY, AND GEN Z

Gen Z is the generation that is most critical of capitalism. Gallup reported that, among young adults aged eighteen to twenty-nine, positive views of capitalism had dropped from 66 percent in 2010 to 51 percent in 2019. In contrast, positive views on capitalism had increased among older Americans during that time frame, with 61 percent of Gen Xers and 68 percent of baby boomers and older Americans holding positive views of capitalism in 2019.[21] Such views are strongly shaped by partisanship. The Pew Research Center found in 2022 that just 29 percent of younger Democrats aged eighteen to twenty-nine viewed capitalism positively compared with 60 percent of younger Republicans aged eighteen to twenty-nine. These partisan divides were alive and well among the Gen Z activists I interviewed.[22]

Many progressive activists and Gen Z Democrats I spoke with were very critical of the capitalist system today, believing that it offered bleaker prospects for them than it did for their parents. Left-leaning Zoomers pointed to overwhelming student debt and a lack of affordable health care, good-paying jobs, and housing—issues exacerbated by the COVID-19 pandemic—as driving their grave doubts about capitalism. A Democratic woman from Ohio State perhaps summed up her generation's feelings about the economy and linked them to other existential threats that her peers will face as they age: "I think something that kind of brings this all together, at least in my head, is the fading American Dream. It's a concept that has been talked about a lot in my life and in my classes. And how, because of climate change, because baby boomers are getting older and [there's] a lack of class mobility—that that is now a reality for a lot of people in our generation."

Teya Khalil is a former political science student at the University of Michigan who has been active in climate change politics and has written articles about human rights for the feminist online magazine *Women's Republic*. She said that income inequality is her largest political concern today. "I see it interwoven in every other problem. [Gen Z has] seen it a lot with the pandemic, how some people have had their lives completely turned upside down by losing their jobs and other people have just kind of floated by comfortably."

GUNS, CLIMATE CHANGE, AND INCOME INEQUALITY

Lu Lu is a Chinese American Gen Z woman and past leader with the Homegirl Project, a youth-led political organization for teenage girls and nonbinary youth of color that operated from 2018 to 2022. She said that government should "start with more accountability for corporations because there's a lot of problems." She added:

> With climate change, corporations have a big hand in causing that, and there's also the wealth gap, as you can see with all those billionaires who, during COVID, earned even more money, while others were starving and not having any income. So I think making corporations take accountability will provide relief on multiple fronts.

A finance and data science major, Lu plans a career in impact investing, which explores how social and environmental issues can be better addressed by more responsible financial strategies.

Sam Dobson is a nonbinary college student originally from South Carolina who attended Columbia University and held a national leadership position with High School Democrats of America. They said that capitalism and income inequality are the most pressing issues facing their generation. Like many other progressive activists I interviewed, Dobson observed strong links between capitalism and gender and racial inequality. They told me, "You can always trace things back to capitalism and whiteness and white supremacy, really. . . . Like mass incarceration, drug colonization, and stuff like that. There's a lot of economic inequality; the [gender] wage gap is one of the worst in the world here in America."

Norah Rami, who majored in political science and cognitive science at the University of Pennsylvania, was active with Everytown for Gun Safety and interned for several congressional campaigns while a high school student in Sugarland, Texas. "Unhindered capitalism does play a large part in many of the problems we see in our society," Rami said. "Most of our problems right now—whether they be racial, gender based, climate change based—all can be traced back to the capitalism that allows for the exploitation of workers and allows them to be exploitative of [different] races and women and the environment."

GUNS, CLIMATE CHANGE, AND INCOME INEQUALITY

In 2019, I asked Zoomers nationally whether they had largely positive views of capitalism, socialism, and other aspects of economic systems, questions that unfortunately were not included in my 2022 survey. I found that just 44 percent of Gen Z women held positive views of capitalism compared with 58 percent of Gen Z men (see figure 6.4).[23] Although fewer than half of Gen Z Americans hold positive views of socialism (48 percent), Gen Z women were more likely to do so than their male counterparts.[24] LGBTQ Zoomers were even more skeptical of capitalism, although their attitudes in general mirrored those of Gen Z women overall. Gen Z women were also less supportive of free enterprise and big business compared with their male counterparts. Yet most Zoomers held largely *positive* views of important elements of a free market system, including free enterprise, small business, and entrepreneurs.

Riya Goel, author of *The Gen Z Book* and founder of Asians Lead, the youth-led organization promoting activism among Asian Americans, acknowledged that Gen Z was more drawn to socialism than older generations. "We feel everyone should be treated the same, no matter how

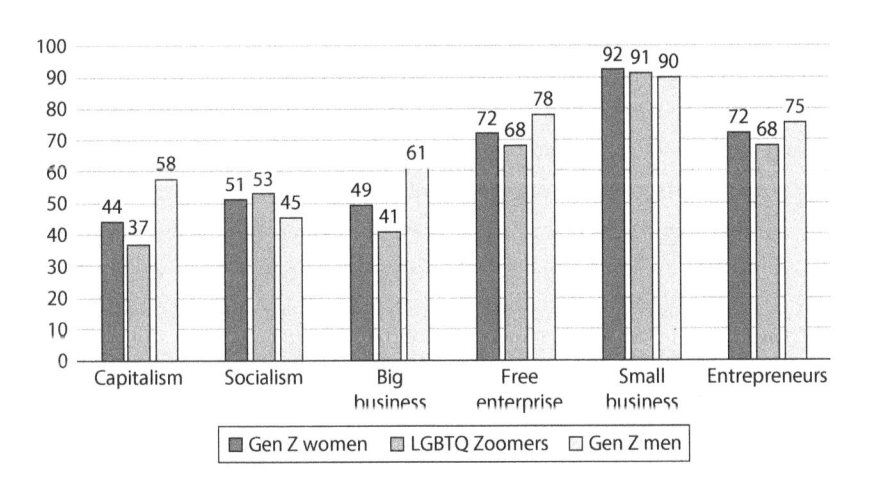

FIGURE 6.4 Percentage of Gen Z members holding positive views of economic terms, by gender and LGBTQ status. Members of Generation Z hold positive views about free enterprise, entrepreneurs, and small businesses; there is less support, but along gender divides, on support for capitalism, socialism, and big business. Qualtrics survey conducted by the author in July 2019, with a sample of 2,200 Americans aged eighteen to twenty-two.

you identify, no matter your circumstances. Some of these barriers that kind of create societal buckets, if you will, should be broken down as they perpetuate injustices throughout centuries, really. That's something that we've experienced firsthand. I think socialism is definitely an issue that is more accepted in the Gen Z generation." At the same time, Goel recognized that Gen Z was by far the most entrepreneurial generation, adding that social media and the gig economy provided "so many resources at our fingertips, so now more than ever, we're able to actually make money off of things that we would like to be doing." Indeed, as a Barnard College student, she began an investing group for young women to promote informed financial decisions and careers in finance.

Many Gen Z Republicans I spoke with, however, drew a clear line on economic policy. "I cannot subscribe to the idea of socialism," said a Republican woman from my Ohio State University focus group. "Capitalism is something that I strongly support. I'm all for free markets. I think with proper economic knowledge, most people would fall into the capitalist sphere. Because I don't think socialism is sustainable." Added another Republican Ohio State woman student, "I definitely fall into the Republicans' sphere a lot because of my beliefs as a capitalist."

Although born in 1995, which misses the Gen Z cutoff by two years, Maria Sofia worked closely with Gen Z Republicans in her prior role as chair of the Maryland Young Republicans. She later went on to work in the administration of Maryland's popular former Republican governor, Larry Hogan. Sofia said that her biggest political concerns surrounded the national debt and the direction of the economy, particularly its impact on small businesses. From her perspective, she worries also about what she views as Gen Z's lack of engagement in the workforce. "I'm also really concerned about the amount of people in the Gen Z generation who don't want to work anymore," she said. "Long-term, that's going to really influence our economy."

While Gen Z may have mixed feelings about whether socialism or capitalism offers the best approach to our economy, I found that Gen Z women who had positive views of socialism participated in politics at significantly higher rates than Gen Z women who did not, 4.1 average activities compared with 3.5 average activities, respectively, in my July 2019 Qualtrics survey. When I added attitudes about socialism to my Gen Z political engagement model, it remained statistically significant for Gen Z women once controlling for other factors—a bump of about 0.25 activities overall. In contrast, Gen Z men who held *negative* views of socialism participated in more political activities (3.5 activities) than Gen Z men who held positive views of socialism (3.1 activities).[25] This relationship between socialism attitudes and levels of political engagement for Gen Z men also held up when I controlled for other factors in my model (see the appendix, Table A.33).

Although initially LGBTQ Zoomer who held positive views of socialism participated at higher rates (4.35 activities) than LGBTQ Zoomers who did not (3.71 activities),[26] once such views were added to the larger Gen Z political engagement model, they were no longer statistically significant. In other words, views about socialism did not have an impact on the political engagement levels of LGBTQ Zoomers overall in my 2019 survey—nor did such views impact political engagement among straight Zoomers.

GENDER, GEN Z, AND CREATING A MORE CARING, EQUITABLE WORLD

Comparable to concerns about gender and racial inequality, progressive views about climate, gun violence prevention, and creating an equitable economy were leading Gen Z women in my surveys to engage in politics at higher levels compared with their male counterparts. Gen Z women were certainly not monolithic about all these concerns—the Republican Gen Z women I interviewed showed that to be the case—however, the embrace of a progressive political agenda resulted in many young women showing up at the polls, marching in the streets, and organizing in their communities and states to advocate for policy change at higher levels than Gen Z women who were not politically progressive. LGBTQ Zoomers were more likely to prioritize all three issues (climate, gun violence prevention, and creating an equitable economy) compared with their straight counterparts, but the prioritization

GUNS, CLIMATE CHANGE, AND INCOME INEQUALITY

of mass shootings and climate change worked to boost the number of political activities for both LGBTQ and straight Zoomers.

Many Gen Z men *did* express concerns about both mass shootings and climate change. My model for Gen Z men in both years of my survey showed that caring deeply about gun violence propelled them to engage in more political activities than Gen Z men who did not prioritize mass shootings as a personally salient issue. Yet Gen Z men were far less likely than Gen Z women to see the need for regulating semiautomatic weapons. Although concern about climate change was linked to Gen Z men engaging in more political activities in 2019 in my survey, it failed to remain a significant driver of their political engagement in 2022.

In my conversations with Gen Z women political activists, it was telling just how personally they felt invested in these concerns and how they believed that multiple issues were intrinsically linked to being a young woman today. Compared with Gen Z men, many Gen Z women said that women's greater capability to empathize or to have the socially sanctioned space to show that empathy was part of what they believed ultimately explained the reverse gender gap in American politics among their cohorts.

This theme was perfectly captured by Gen Z climate activist and University of Pennsylvania student Aurora Yuan, who served as the international press coordinator with Thunberg's Fridays for Future (FFF) digital organization. "I feel like it's almost seen as a weakness if [Gen Z men] care really deeply about things like gun violence or climate change, when it really shouldn't be," she said. In contrast, Yuan and other women in her generation have grown up at a time when their leadership in these activist spaces was encouraged, whether in their schools, on college campuses, or on social media platforms.

This encouragement reinforces a need and expectation for many that their voices are necessary to make substantive political change happen. Yet Gen Z men are failing to heed such calls at similar levels. Chapter 7 considers how norms of masculinity and the rapid feminization of the politics of Generation Z are affecting the political choices of Gen Z men from their own perspective—and whether the state of Gen Z politics is perhaps making extremist, far right politics more appealing for at least some Zoomer men today.

7

GEN Z MEN AND POLITICS

Thanasi Dilos grew up in Queens, New York, and struggled with mental health issues, spending time in and out of hospitals and missing school. As a result, he spent hours alone online, playing video games. As the 2016 election cycle ramped up, Dilos was confused. Without his own community to sort through politics, Dilos sought answers to his political questions on the internet:

> I found myself instantly pulled as a young guy into the radical conservative circles. . . . [A]ll the algorithms, all of the Instagram, whatever, pulled people [like me] into those communities . . . the algorithms would naturally funnel you toward a community and then your brain would be like, "Oh, I'm very happy to be with people of any ideology. Let me stay here." I was, like, this is horrible.

Dilos shared those experiences in short articles posted on Instagram and amassed close to sixty thousand followers. For several years, he ran a nonpartisan news service for Gen Z on social media. Learning and writing about politics gave Dilos what he described as an "authentic purpose" for the first time in his life, connecting him with caring people and building confidence for him to return to high school and become more active in politics.

Dilos talks quickly and with passion about his work in civic engagement, telling me about Civics Unplugged, an organization he cofounded in May 2019. It provides seed money to Gen Z activists through its Civic Innovators Fellowship to foster the development of programs promoting democracy, sustainability, and more. Since its inception, Civics Unplugged has worked with more than 1,500 fellows in all fifty states and forty-seven countries, roughly 75 percent female. Thinking about that gender imbalance, he posited that young men are "not really incentivized to look for political communities because they have all these microcosms of community, of a home in video games, in sports with their friends." Dilos believes that young women, in contrast, were more likely to participate in digital communities centered around social causes or political issues, partly because their mothers and other women were fighting for gender equality.

As discussed in chapter 1, Gen Z men have largely caught up with Gen Z women in terms of *overall* levels of political engagement when I compare my May 2022 Qualtrics survey to my 2019 Qualtrics survey—although newer data from the Public Religion Research Institute (PRRI) shows that, once again, a year after the *Dobbs* decision, Gen Z women (especially teen girls) began participating in politics at higher levels than their male counterparts. But if we consider what I'd call the activist class—young people who are forming or serving as leaders or highly engaged participants in progressive political organizations—it is Gen Z women and queer Zoomers who are most often at the forefront of social justice groups. While there are certainly cisgender, straight progressive men who serve in leadership capacities, Gen Z women have often been dominant, representing a new development in U.S. political history. Many Zoomers who are the most active in these youth-led groups are also people of color and/or LGBTQ. At least on the political left, Generation Z has been building a more inclusive political space.

The idea that Gen Z women were are at the forefront of progressive political spaces was shared in my focus groups of partisan Gen Z men and in interviews with more than a dozen highly engaged male Gen Z political activists from both sides of the political aisle. Most—though not all—of these Gen Z men believed that their female counterparts were more invested in politics because issues of equality mattered more to women. Some Gen Z men also said that many political groups today do a better job of mobilizing and welcoming young women's political involvement and that the importance of political activism among Gen Z women, particularly in left-leaning spaces, was amplified through social media. But this leadership shift in youth-led politics—and the historic reverse gender gap I have identified—could have major impacts on Gen Z men.

This chapter explores the status of Gen Z men in today's political climate. I examine the potential for backlash in response to the increasing participation of young women and LGBTQ Americans in our political system—or if Gen Z men feel that the political climate is one that pressures them to stifle or suppress their political views. I also consider how members of Gen Z are considering broader conversations about masculinity in society, and I review evidence about whether Gen Z men are becoming more conservative—or even violent—in the Trump era, particularly in response to the political left's emphasis on gender equality, LGBTQ rights, and racial justice.

THE POLITICAL ASCENDENCE OF GEN Z WOMEN IN THE TRUMP ERA: A MALE PERSPECTIVE

Many of the Gen Z men I spoke with noted that, in their own circles, women of their generation have been more engaged in politics. Abdullah Memon, as a high school teen, led the California chapter of State of the Students, a nonpartisan youth-led organization that encourages civic participation by connecting teens with elected officials. Memon said that young women are facing greater threats. Men, he said, "are not, you know, facing a wage gap; their reproductive rights aren't being targeted." As a result, he said, young men feel, "I don't really need to be part of this conversation. I can spend my time doing something else."

Other Gen Z men noted that the sexism displayed by political leaders, particularly Trump, inspired Gen Z women they know to become more involved. "With Trump's election and other politicians' sexist remarks, and tweets that are all out in the news now . . . it doesn't hit the same personal note for me that it's gotta hit [for] so many young women," said one young man from University of Maryland, College Park.

Several Democratic men that I interviewed believed that some progressively minded Gen Z men intentionally reduced their political activity to allow women, people of color, and LGBTQ Americans to take ownership of issues important to them. Jack Siegel, a white Gen Zer active in racial justice initiatives in his hometown of Collierville, Tennessee, praised "a culture [on the political left] about allowing marginalized groups of peoples to have their own voices and their own space and to be able to dominate the discussion." Women and marginalized communities and people of color, he said, "should be the ones leading the discussion. . . . That could be why some Gen Z men don't get as active or at least don't get into leadership roles."

Alvin Lee, the son of Chinese immigrants, in 2017 started Generation Up, an education equality advocacy group with more than four thousand student members. Lee noted that Zoomers involved in his organization disproportionately come from marginalized groups:

> I think historically, [white] men have benefitted from privilege, or the system of patriarchy. Actually, if you look at the sort of activists within the male [progressive] community, a lot of them tend to be people that aren't white. And so I think a lot of it really just has to do with the fact that if you come from an identity [in which] your background has been historically oppressed or marginalized in some way, that gives us a compelling reason for why we go and advocate.

Lee added that, in his experience, young men of color were far more compelled to build diverse coalitions with progressive women in order to advocate for political power, often around common themes of identity and inclusion.

Some Gen Z male activists—particularly those on the right—disagreed that their female friends were engaging in politics more than their male friends. Ben Kelley, who cochaired his chapter of College Republicans while at Catholic University, said that Gen Z women didn't outnumber Gen Z men in his political circles. And one man from my University of Maryland focus group, who was active with College Republicans, said that, in his experience, young women were *less* involved than men. (Recall from chapter 1 that Republican women, in both years of my survey, reported less engagement in politics than Gen Z Republican men.) He said:

> There's sort of different levels of participation in politics. There's the people who are [social media] activists; they post stuff on their Twitter about veganism and they may go out and vote and they may have a Bernie Sanders sticker on their laptop . . . and then there's the type of political involvement that's showing up to committee hearings, volunteering on campaigns and doing tons of hours. So, I'd be curious to see if the increase that we're seeing in women being involved in politics is sort of like those soft activities that it's really easy to do, it's really easy to talk about things, it's really easy to post . . . because from my perspective, . . . I'm involved in a lot of heavy stuff; I really haven't seen it. And it's unfortunate, but it's the case that probably three out of every four young volunteers for a [Republican] campaign are men, and a lot of the staffers are men.

Ryan Doucette, a cofounder of Gen Z GOP, a political group that encouraged the Republican Party to address climate, education, and equity issues better to appeal to younger voters that was active from 2018 through 2022, also saw fewer young women than young men in Republican Party activism. It was a problem, he believed, the Republican Party needed to work on, citing this gender imbalance as "an indictment that we haven't provided as many opportunities" for women. Doucette also said, however, that Democrats have a built-in advantage with young women voters, so it wasn't surprising that Gen Z women who were Democrats often participated at higher levels. "I suspect that young left women would be more highly engaged than young left men from the party structure because the Democrats want to see more young women involved," he said.

CANCEL CULTURE AND PEER PRESSURE

In recent years, right-wing media groups have routinely claimed that college campuses are populated by so-called woke professors and activists bent on indoctrinating young Americans into adopting far left positions. In his 2018 book *Campus Battlefield: How Conservatives Can WIN the Battle on Campus and Why It Matters*,[1] Charlie Kirk, who at age nineteen cofounded Turning Point USA to train young conservative activists, described college campuses as "leftist echo chambers that reinforce an anti-American, anti-freedom, pro-Marxist worldview." In 2022, Kirk called for most young people to skip college entirely in his book *The College Scam*, encouraging younger Americans to start businesses or develop other life skills.[2]

In February 2021, the Conservative Political Action Conference (CPAC) named its annual gathering of right-wing activists America Uncanceled to emphasize its concern that political progressive leaders, tech companies, and media corporations are trying to silence conservative viewpoints.[3] To support their claims, they pointed to examples of liberal activists calling for bans on public figures such as comedian Dave Chappelle, country singer Morgan Wallen, and author J. K. Rowling. But the message of cancel culture may be finding greatest appeal for outspoken young Republican leaders on college campuses. Many Americans may not have a clear understanding of what cancel culture entails,[4] but one 2021 study found that about 25 percent of Republicans between the ages of eighteen and forty-four listed cancel culture as a top political concern compared with just 1 percent of similarly aged Democrats.[5]

Many young college-age Republicans I spoke with agreed that their campuses were not welcoming of conservative viewpoints, including Gen Z Republican women such as a Georgia State University student who told me that identifying as liberal was "trending among young women right now." She added, "I feel like if it's not what everyone else is doing like, okay, then I'm not gonna talk about being conservative as a young woman." A Republican female student from the University of Texas at Austin told me that when she has "come out" as a Republican to more progressive female students that she meets on that heavily Democratic campus, they say, "I don't want to be your friend anymore or I don't want to associate with you because you're conservative."

These concerns were echoed by Republican Gen Z men that I spoke with, including a University of Maryland student who said, "Around here, if you're a Trump person, you gotta keep it quiet; you don't really want to tell anyone." At that same focus group, another man who regularly attended Trump rallies said that he enjoyed those events compared with the atmosphere at college and living in a blue state. At Trump rallies, he said, "you don't have to be ashamed of anything; you don't have to hide anything; you're like, 'Oh, we agree on this issue, that's awesome.'"

Doucette, the former Gen Z GOP leader, said that the political climate could be an unforgiving space for those who might make a mistake. He said that young people need the space to speak with others with whom they disagree politically. He continued:

> I worry that if we are so concerned with the content of what people are saying, there is no room for growth. I worry about that as a young American who wants to see more civil discourse in the future. It is especially difficult with the rise of social media. For young conservatives on campus, there is less incentive to become involved when you could blow up on social media as being xenophobic, etc.

Patton Byars, a former University of South Carolina student who was active with Gen Z GOP, told me that he knew a lot of men his age who were scared to share their views on politics, particularly if those views were conservative. "A lot of people, are like, 'I'm dating this girl; she's a Democrat. If I say this, it's going to mess up this whole thing. I don't want to repost this controversial Republican post because I don't want what this generation calls the social justice warrior to come at us at school or get canceled.'" This hesitancy, he added, could help explain why Trump was an appealing candidate for some young men who might otherwise have felt silenced.

Having grown up in a small Southern town where many popular young white conservative men would rail against politically correct culture, Siegel, the University of Virginia student active in racial justice causes, wondered whether social dynamics may push "some guys with left-leaning political beliefs to hide them in order to fit in with this kind of dominant, non-PC [politically correct] front."

Alabama native Jeremiah Lowther, a Black Zoomer whose parents are active in Democratic politics in Tuscaloosa, Alabama, expressed a similar sentiment. "Many of the white, straight, liberal boys that I have noticed in the Deep South feel that they don't belong because there is no space for them," said Lowther, who served as the Alabama chair for State of the Students while in high school and participated in Jack and Jill of America, a nationally recognized civic and political engagement organization founded in the late 1930s to provide social and cultural opportunities for young Black students. "And because many of them don't align with being either an ethnic minority, a woman, or LGBTQ, they feel that they cannot speak out because they really don't belong. In my opinion . . . a lot of the boys feel that if they speak about relevant Democratic issues, they will be ostracized by the other progressives because it isn't their fight."

Societal pressure from male peers, said Dilos, the Civics Unplugged cofounder, creates silence in some young men who might otherwise overtly share progressive positions. He said that he has seen young men "get bullied as a guy caring about issues that are traditionally Democratic issues. If you care about abortion and a women's right to choose, if you care about gender equality, if you care about racial equity; you're like, 'Oh my God, what a fucking loser! Like what, are you like, a pussy?'"

SURVEY RESULTS: THE ROLE OF THE POLITICAL CLIMATE

In my July 2019 Qualtrics survey, I asked Gen Z Americans the extent to which they agreed that "the political climate prevents me from saying things I believe" to get a greater sense of whether cancel culture was a big

GEN Z MEN AND POLITICS

concern among Zoomers, particularly Gen Z men. Attitudes were mixed among Gen Z overall because 56 percent either somewhat or strongly agreed with that sentiment—although only about one in four (27 percent) *strongly* agreed. Yet Gen Z men were significantly more likely than Gen Z women to strongly agree, 30 percent compared with 24 percent, respectively.[6] Twenty-nine percent of straight Zoomers strongly agreed that they faced a chillier political climate that stifles their willingness to say things about politics compared with 20 percent of LGBTQ Zoomers.[7]

The pressure to avoid speaking about politics was clearly felt more strongly by Republicans, however, particularly Gen Z men (see figure 7.1).[8] Fewer Gen Z Democrats strongly agreed that the political climate prevented them from saying things they believe, although Gen Z Democratic men were significantly more likely to say so that than their female counterparts.[9] LGBTQ Zoomers who were Democrats were the least likely to agree that the climate prevented them from speaking in 2019. (Because there were fewer than one hundred cases of LGBTQ Zoomers who identified as Republican, they were omitted from the figure.)

	Gen Z women	Gen Z men	LGBTQ Zoomers	Straight Zoomers
Democrats	19	27	16	26
Independents	24	23	23	25
Republicans	32	39		36

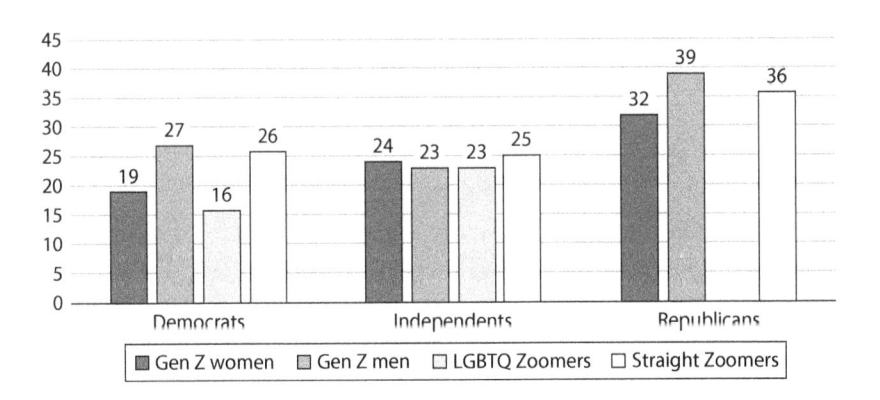

FIGURE 7.1 Percentage of Gen Z members who strongly agree that political climate prevents them from saying things they believe, by gender, LGBTQ status, and party. Among members of Generation Z, Republicans are more likely to say that the political climate prevents them from saying what they believe. Qualtrics survey conducted by the author in July 2019, with a sample of 2,200 Americans aged eighteen to twenty-two.

Yet attitudes about a chilly political climate did not appear to affect political participation among Zoomer men: in my survey: Gen Z men who agreed that the political culture prevented them from saying things they believe engaged in roughly the same number of political activities (3.52) than those who did not (3.72); this lack of significance held when controlling for party (see the appendix). Levels of political engagement among LGBTQ Zoomers who agreed and disagreed about the political climate were largely similar. Gen Z women who agreed that the political climate was stifling participated in fewer activities (3.94) than those who did not (4.67);[10] straight Zoomers who agreed reported engaging in fewer political activities (3.63) compared with those who disagreed (4.21).[11] When I included this political climate measure in the 2019 Gen Z political engagement model, however, it dropped in significance in all cases.[12]

Despite complaints in some circles that cancel culture dampens the political activism of younger Americans, particularly among young men, there was no evidence in my July 2019 Qualtrics survey that this was happening among Gen Z nationally.

A CRISIS OF MASCULINITY?

Conservative political leaders have raised the alarm about the status of masculinity in U.S. society, including Republican senator Josh Hawley, who argues that the "crisis of American men is a crisis for the American Republic."[13] Noting statistics that show American men are working less, getting married in fewer numbers, and using drugs at higher rates, Hawley asked in a keynote address to the National Conservatism Conference in November 2021: "[C]an we be surprised that after years of being told they are the problem, that their manhood is the problem, more and more men are withdrawing into the enclave of idleness, and pornography, and video games?" Hawley elaborated on these themes in his book *Manhood: The Masculine Virtues America Needs*,[14] in which he argues that the left's "disdain for masculinity" has pushed liberals' more traditional concerns with liberty "into nihilism, defining it as a right to live free from biological sex, family, tradition and God—free from reality."[15] Hawley's solution to this problem is to look for renewal in the Bible, which he argues provides man his "sacred duty, and his purpose in life."

Such themes are hardly new on the political right. As historian Kristin Du Mez chronicles in *Jesus and John Wayne*, appeals in recent years to a more "muscular Christianity" among the Christian right that fiercely defends a patriarchal worldview have arisen in response to women's larger gains in society and have also become central to today's Republican Party because conservative Christians make up a disproportionate number of its base of voters and activists.[16] PRRI's research shows patriarchal views rooted in a conservative theology, such as the belief that women must submit to a man's leadership in the home, are linked to holding more traditionally hierarchical views of society.[17]

Concerns about masculinity also emerge from more secular sources, such as Jordan Peterson, a once well-regarded clinical psychologist who morphed into a more controversial self-help guru when he released a series of YouTube videos beginning in 2016 railing against a Canadian bill that would ban discrimination based on gender identity or expression. The bill would violate his free speech, Peterson said, because he did not want to refer to transgender students by their preferred pronouns. Now with more than 4 million Twitter followers, a popular podcast, and sold-out international talks, Peterson continued in 2024 to speak out against transgender activism, intersectionality, and what he viewed as the broader rise of political correctness and cancel culture.

Several young Republican men that I spoke with referenced Peterson's work, including a student in my 2020 University of Maryland focus group who said that he was not surprised to learn that Gen Z women were more politically engaged than Gen Z men during the Trump era:

[With Gen Z Men] and political engagement, there's less force, less drive, I don't know, less responsibility being taken or something, I don't know. The whole Jordan Peterson phenomenon has kinda . . . that's what went into my mind when you brought this up because what he does a lot of the time is he talks to an audience that's like 80 percent men and he tells them to get their life together, basically, and that you can be the architect of your own destiny, that you can change things for the better. And I don't know how this message got away from men, I don't know what the reasons are for that, maybe it's just how the culture has changed in the last fifty, one hundred years. But whatever that change is, it definitely happened and so I'm not really surprised to hear about the effects culminating now.

Peterson's writing, particularly his best-selling book *Twelve Rules for Life*,[18] holds special appeal to many young men, whom he encourages to take more responsibility for themselves in the face of evidence that they are struggling to succeed compared with young women.

Of course, whether men today are less masculine than older generations of American men—and if so, whether that denotes a crisis—is a hugely debatable point. Many Republican Party leaders—including Trump—argue, however, that part of what ails U.S. society and politics is a notion that, as a nation, we have become less tough, less responsible, and less "manly." And there is evidence that Republicans nationally largely agree with this sentiment. For the past few years, PRRI has asked Americans the extent to which they believe that the United States has become "too soft and feminine." Our data showed that, in 2023, a clear majority of Republicans—65 percent—agreed, compared with just 18 percent of Democrats.[19]

Endorsing this viewpoint can have important political implications. In earlier work I conducted with Erin Cassese, we found that individuals who think that the United States has become too soft and feminine were far more likely to have voted for Trump in 2016, even after controlling for party.[20] When I asked Gen Zers this question in my July 2019 survey, 38 percent of Generation Z agreed. The 2019 PRRI American Values Survey (AVS), conducted around the same time, found that 42 percent of all Americans agreed that the United States has become too soft and feminine.[21] The same PRRI AVS survey found that 38 percent of Americans aged eighteen to twenty-nine agreed; there were too few respondents to consider the perspectives of Zoomers, who were aged eighteen to twenty-two in 2019.

Yet my 2019 Qualtrics survey showed that Gen Z men were significantly more likely than Gen Z women to agree that the United States has become too soft and feminine—49 percent to 29 percent, respectively.[22] Just over one in four LGBTQ Zoomers (26 percent) believed that the United States has become too soft and feminine. In 2019, PRRI also found a gender gap among all Americans about whether the United States has become too soft and feminine, although it was more muted compared with the gender difference among the members of Gen Z in my Qualtrics survey: 48 percent of American men compared with 35 percent of American women.[23]

Partisanship strongly shaped the attitudes of Gen Z on this measure, with more than two in three Gen Z Republican men in my July 2019 Qualtrics survey agreeing that the United States had become too soft and feminine (see figure 7.2). Gen Z women and LGBTQ Zoomers who were Democrats were the least likely to agree with this sentiment. (To save space, I omitted straight Zoomers from the figure, but 43 percent agreed that the United States had become too soft and feminine while 29 percent disagreed.)

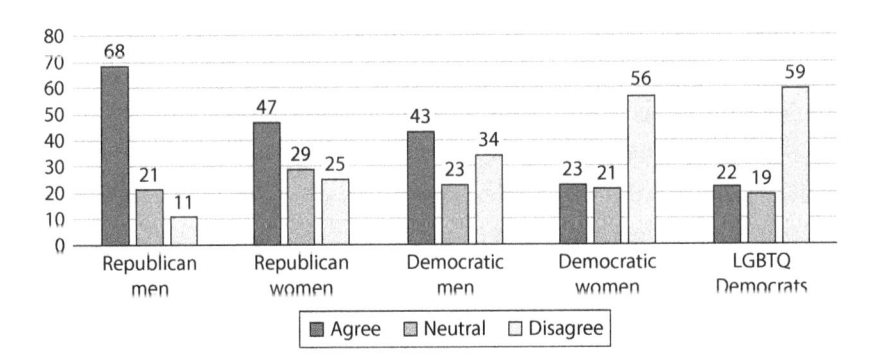

	Republican men	Republican women	Democratic men	Democratic women	LGBTQ Democrats
Agree	68	47	43	23	22
Neutral	21	29	23	21	19
Disagree	11	25	34	56	59

FIGURE 7.2 Percentage of Gen Z Americans who agree/disagree that America is too soft and feminine, by gender, LGBTQ status, and party. Among members of Generation Z, Republican men most likely to agree that America is too soft and feminine. Qualtrics survey conducted by the author in July 2019, with a sample of 2,200 Americans aged eighteen to twenty-two.

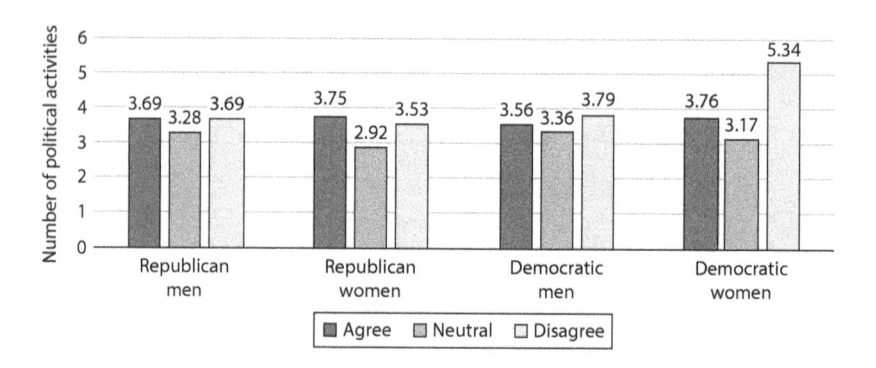

FIGURE 7.3 Average number of political activities, by gender, party, and agreement or disagreement with the idea that America is too soft and feminine. Among members of Generation Z, Democratic women who disagree that America has become too soft and feminine engage in more political activities. Qualtrics survey conducted by the author in July 2019, with a sample of 2,200 Americans aged eighteen to twenty-two.

As figure 7.3 shows, however, attitudes about whether the United States was too soft and feminine did relatively little to explain differences among either Republican men or Democratic men when it came to political participation in 2019. Both Republican and Democratic Gen Z men reported participating in roughly the same levels of political activities regardless of their views about the perceived masculinity of the United States.[24]

The highest levels of political engagement, by far, were among Gen Z Democratic women and LGBTQ Gen Z Zoomers who *disagreed* that the United States was too soft and feminine. Although not shown in the figure, straight Gen Z Democrats who disagreed that the United States was too soft and feminine also engaged in more activities annually (5.1) compared with those who did not (3.77). When this measure was included in my Gen Z political engagement model, women, LGBTQ Zoomers, and straight Zoomers who disagreed that the United States was too soft and feminine participated in politics at higher rates, even after controlling for other measures (see the appendix, Table A.34). For Gen Z men, however, attitudes about the state of masculinity in the United States did not drive their political engagement, at least not in 2019.

My 2022 survey did not ask Zoomers about their attitudes on whether the United States has become too soft and feminine; however, a December 2022 PRRI survey found that 49 percent of Gen Z men and 31 percent of Gen Z women indicated that they agree that the United States had become too soft and feminine, which is comparable to my July 2019 Qualtrics Gen Z survey results. However, in PRRI's 2023 AVS, conducted in early September 2023, that number had crept up to 60 percent of Gen Z men—although it was just 19 percent who *completely* agreed compared with 41 percent who somewhat agreed. Gen Z women's attitudes on that measure remained the same.[25] Overall, the percentage of Americans nationally who indicated that the United States had become too soft and feminine increased from our 2022 AVS survey from 42 percent to 48 percent.

The Gen Z men I spoke with, however, largely rejected the notion that a masculinity crisis explained the reverse gender gap in political engagement that arose during the Trump era. "I [just] think generations are different from one another," said Doucette. "In terms of young men getting involved, I don't think it is because they are less masculine than previous generations; I just think it is a generational shift in politics." Later in our conversation, he said, "I do think we have a lot of issues to address socially, but I don't think it is because we have ganged up against men for all of these years." Siegel also disagreed with Hawley's assessment that a crisis in masculinity stemmed from pressure from the political left to diminish manhood: "Obviously this is a political talking point, but I don't think the left has a worldview that men should be excluded from political conversations, or any of these radical things that Republicans [such as Hawley] suggest."

The fixation on toxic masculinity among some on the political right as an excuse to explain Gen Z men's retreat from public life may really be a cynical attempt to rationalize the fact that growing numbers of women, people of color, and LGBTQ Gen Zers are finally using their voices politically, at least according to Finn Pollard, a transgender male student at University of Virginia: "I think that there's finally equal representation in politics and other things. And a lot of cis heterosexual men are not taking that well. Like, 'Oh, well we used to have this space. And now we have to share this space, [so] then we are basically not welcome.' And that's not the case. I think it is ridiculous to say that men aren't welcome in those spaces. I think they are being oversensitive and overreacting because they see something that they used to dominate so completely."

A MOVE TOWARD EXTREMISM: GEN Z MEN, MISOGYNY, AND VIOLENCE

What happens to some younger men, who may feel less than welcome among their activist Gen Z peers and who thus cede politics largely to women and other Gen Z activists from historically marginalized groups? Make no mistake—there are certainly many dynamic, politically active young men involved in politics today on both sides of the political aisle who happily work with Gen Z women, people of color, and LGBTQ activists on a variety of political causes. But for those young men who feel unwelcome in those spaces, perhaps even a sense of rejection, could the seeds be planted for something darker to emerge for those young men today? As partisan polarization continues to grip American culture, and growing levels of political extremism in American politics rises, particularly on the political right, could the perception that the political role of Gen Z men is diminished lead to not merely less political engagement but something worse?

A discussion on the political views of Gen Z men must thus note those at the fringes. There are too many examples of young males who have taken to violence after participating in far-right rallies and protests or who have become consumed by misogynistic anger stoked by the right. Look no further than the Unite the Right rally that took place in Charlottesville, Virginia, in 2017 to protest the removal of a Confederate memorial. Although its organizers were older, the image left in the minds of most Americans of that horrible event involve young white men carrying tiki torches and spewing hateful, anti-Semitic rhetoric on the storied campus of the University of Virginia. Those extremists, mostly younger white men, took to the streets the following day when a counter-protestor and two police officers were killed.

In Kenosha, Wisconsin, in the summer of 2020, many young, armed conservative white men showed up as self-anointed vigilantes during civil unrest after police officers fatally shot a Black man, Jacob Blake. Among them was seventeen-year-old Kyle Rittenhouse, who drove from neighboring Illinois with a semiautomatic rifle and ultimately killed two protestors and injured a third during a confrontation. Rittenhouse was acquitted of several counts of homicide after claiming he was scared for his life and acting in self-defense, and he has become a conservative cause célèbre, with pundits on the right lionizing his actions.

The far-right media today not only celebrates these extremists. It also propagates a misogynistic worldview as women are either seeking or preserving political rights, which is not a new development in our political history. In her 1991 book *Backlash*, Susan Faludi chronicled conservative political responses to the success of second-wave feminists in the 1970s, from the Christian right's ascent in Republican politics during the Ronald Reagan years to media stories that depicted single and working women as miserable and disdainful of traditional family life.

In the years since, social media has created a particularly hostile and accessible outlet for promoting and normalizing such views. Lucina di Meco, a gender equality expert and cofounder of #ShePersisted, an organization that tracks online attacks against women in politics globally, found that women political leaders were increasingly facing online abuse. In her analysis of the 2020 presidential Democratic primary, women candidates were far more likely to be attacked than male candidates on social media.[26] Other studies found that women running for Congress in 2020 faced higher numbers of personal attacks than men on Twitter and Facebook.[27] Such amplified attacks on women political leaders pose grave threats to our democracy, according to Di Meco, because it's "not only the women who are the direct targets of these attacks that are weakened, but what these women stand for and in many ways embody: women's equal rights, particularly sexual and reproductive rights, LGBTQ rights, liberal values and inclusive diverse democracies."[28]

Other women's rights activists are alarmed at the popularity of social media influencers who spread misogynistic views, including Andrew Tate, the former champion kickboxer of British American ancestry who became notorious in the United Kingdom after being kicked off the reality show *Big Brother* because he appeared to attack a female contestant physically. Young men have been drawn to the flashy, outlandish self-made Tate because he offers exercise and financial tips and promotes self-empowerment for young men. One study found that Tate's videos on TikTok have garnered more than 11 billion views.[29] But it is his statements about women, from calling them "intrinsically lazy;" saying that they belong in the home; and, in one case, tweeting that women "bear some responsibility for being raped," that have alarmed many critics and have led him to be banned on numerous social media platforms. The nonpartisan Center for Countering Digital Hate (CCDH), a research organization that monitors online hate and misinformation, identified more than forty videos of Tate promoting what they termed "extreme misogyny."[30] In 2023, he was facing charges of sexual assault in Romania, where he lived.

The fact that a figure as polarizing as Tate continues to find a large and growing audience, particularly among many Gen Z men, speaks to a cultural moment that finds many young men and boys struggling. As Richard Reeves chronicled in *Of Boys and Men*, young men are falling behind their female counterparts in educational achievement, are losing ground in the labor market, and are less present in their children's lives. Men are also more than three times as likely to commit suicide than women[31] and they are far more likely to commit violent crimes. The Violence Project, which collects data on U.S. mass public shooters, found that 97 percent of mass shooters were men.[32] Several of the deadliest shootings in the United States since 2018 were committed by *young* men under the age of twenty-one, including the murders at Marjory Stoneman Douglas High School in Parkland, Florida; the killing of Black patrons at a Buffalo, New York, grocery store by a white supremacist gunman; and the shooting of Hispanic schoolchildren in Uvalde, Texas.[33]

Those who study far-right extremism note that white grievance and misogynist themes are often used to appeal to disgruntled young men on social media. CCDH studies the "Incelosphere:" social media forums that cater to young men who are involuntarily celibate (incel) and who blame women for their lack of romantic relationships and other failings. This term came to broader public light in 2014, after twenty-two-year-old Elliot Rodger killed six people and injured an additional fourteen before taking his own life in Isla Vista, California. Immediately before the killings, he posted a YouTube video blaming women for his sexual failings and his turn toward violence. In recent years, self-proclaimed incels have also been responsible for numerous mass killings.[34] In a 2022 report, CCDH analyzed more than 1 million posts on the world's leading incel forum and found disturbing upticks between 2000 and 2022 in posts that supported rape and pedophilia.[35] The report noted that the content on the forum was driven by a relatively small group of roughly four thousand active members, but it still garnered millions of visits each month.[36]

CCHD also found that extremist rhetoric and misinformation about members of the LGBTQ community have been on the rise on more mainstream social media platforms such as Twitter and Facebook. Falsehoods about LGBTQ people "grooming" children, CCHD noted, has driven some offline hate crimes,[37] including the storming of a drag queen story hour at a library in California by the white nationalist group Proud Boys[38] and an attempted white supremacist attack on a gay pride parade in Idaho by the white nationalist group Patriot Front.[39]

Scholars who study white supremacy note that hostility toward women is a view often shared in tandem with racism. The Anti-Defamation League (ADL) argues that "there is a robust symbiosis between misogyny and white supremacy; the two ideologies are powerfully intertwined. While not all misogynists are racists, and not every white supremacist is a misogynist, a deep-seated loathing of women acts as a connective tissue between many White supremacists, especially those in the alt-right." In *Healing from Hate: How Young Men Get into—and out of—Violent Extremism*, sociologist Michael Kimmel interviews former and current American neo-Nazis, white supremacists, jihadists, and anti-immigration skinheads, and argues that part of the draw of such movements for these young men centers around what he calls "aggrieved entitlement." He wrote:

> These young men feel entitled to a sense of belonging and community, of holding unchallenged moral authority over women and children, and of feeling that they count in the world and that their lives matter. Experiencing threats to the lives they feel they deserve leads these young men to feel ashamed and humiliated. And it is this aggrieved entitlement—entitlement thwarted and frustrated—that leads some men to search for a way to redeem themselves as men, to restore and retrieve that sense of manhood that has been lost.[40]

As our society become increasingly multiracial and multiethnic, and young women and members of the LGBTQ community are more prominent as leaders and activists, it is worth considering whether a small minority of younger men—especially younger white men—who feel disenchanted with these developments begin to find political extremism more appealing.

Recall Dilos's experiences as a teen who found social media leading him down the path of extremist websites. He told me: "I think it's really smart that the conservative side of politics has built these funnels for young men in spaces [online] that young men are traditionally inhabiting anyways." He points to cryptocurrency websites, which disproportionately draw views from younger men than younger women. While lots of young men who are interested in making money quickly inhabit these sites, Dilos does not believe many of them come with any preconceived political ideology. He argues, however, that "conservative idealists go into those spaces and recognize that [young men] are more malleable and don't really have a political identity yet. And therefore those groups are able to imprint their political identity." From Dilos's perspective at least, social media algorithms combined with societal pressure have pushed some Gen Z men into radicalized spaces online or to be "extremely apathetic about politics in general."

THE COSTS OF POLITICAL POLARIZATION

The vast majority of Americans, including young men, are not committing acts of political violence. But the appeal of misogynist figures such as Tate and the popularity of extremist forums among young men—and the ease with which misogynist, homophobic, and racist messages are available online—does raise serious concerns about whether exposure to such materials leads some younger Americans to support political policies that aim to remove rights for women and LGBTQ Americans, stifle conversations about racial progress, and possibly bolster support for political violence. As young men fall further behind economically and socially on several fronts compared with young women, scapegoating women and minorities and members of the LGBTQ community may hold appeal for some of them—as does attacking liberal young men who support progressive causes as being insufficiently masculine. But do these trends also shape attitudes among Gen Z men that the use of political violence is becoming more acceptable?

These concerns have taken on greater urgency in the wake of January 6, 2021, when thousands of Trump supporters sought to overturn the free and fair election of Joe Biden by assaulting Capitol Hill police and forcibly breaking into the Capitol building, sending members of Congress, staffers, and Vice President Mike Pence fleeing for their lives. The bipartisan congressional committee that examined the causes of that horrible day found that far-right militia groups such as the Proud Boys and the Oath Keepers plotted for weeks to stop the peaceful transfer of power; members of both groups were found guilty of seditious conspiracy and obstruction in federal court.[41]

To get a sense of where Americans stand with respect to political violence, PRRI asked Americans whether they think that because things have gotten so far off track, "true American patriots" may have to resort to violence to save our country. In December 2022, just 16 percent agreed, with no meaningful gender differences. Gen Z supported this idea at somewhat higher levels, with 21 percent in agreement, but there were no overall gender differences there either: 20 percent of Gen Z men and 21 percent of Gen Z women agreed. PRRI did find, however, that 10 percent of Gen Z men *completely* agreed with this sentiment compared with 4 percent of Gen Z women—so perhaps an appetite for political violence was bit higher for Gen Z men. But that's still a relatively small percentage of Gen Z American men.

When we step back and consider the full picture, there appears to be little evidence that attitudes about the fragile state of masculinity or concerns about cancel culture are leading many Gen Z men to become engaged in politics as a sort of backlash effect to the progress of women, racial minorities, or LGBTQ Americans. There is also little evidence to suggest that Gen Z men (or Gen Z women, for that matter) in the United States believe political violence is necessary. It is a *rejection* of the notion that the United States has become too soft and feminine that has led Zoomers to be more involved in politics, at least among Gen Z women and LGBTQ Gen Zers. Many Gen Z men from all racial, ethnic, and LGBTQ backgrounds—and from both parties—recognize that the growing diversity of their generation is not merely inevitable but brings positive changes to our society and our political system.

Another, more beneficial scenario for Gen Z men may emerge as growing numbers of Gen Z women take the lead politically. As one Democratic young man who participated in my University of Maryland focus group said, the ascendence of women into visible advocacy positions "is going to have a good effect in terms of respecting and then eventually accepting women as political leaders, too." That's perhaps one hopeful message to consider. At the same time, the appeal of gendered extremism, a topic that is far too accessible on online platforms, remains an important issue to monitor as the United States strives to become a more inclusive democracy—and young men continue to fall behind on many educational and economic measures.

CONCLUSION

The Possibilities of a More Inclusive Political Future

At twenty-three, Selena Torres became the youngest woman and the youngest Latina person ever elected to the Nevada legislature in 2018. Torres grew up in Las Vegas with parents who were active in community and political organizing. Both her mother and grandmother advocated for safe and legal abortions and other women's rights for decades, and she was inspired to volunteer for political campaigns and lead the Hispanic student union. A high school English teacher by profession, Torres is passionate about education equity, immigration, justice reform, and protecting worker's rights. Having a father from El Salvador, Torres grew up understanding "how systems and structures impacted communities like mine."

Her decision to run for office in 2018 was difficult. For one thing, most state legislators looked nothing like her, she told me. But a male lawmaker asked her to take on the race to keep Latinx representation in the seat, which was being vacated by a young man who also has Salvadoran parents. At first, Torres said no. "I was a first-year teacher, driving my 1997 Honda Accord; it didn't even have heating or AC," she recalled. But her mentor was persistent, so she talked it over with her family, jumped in the race, and won. Since then, Torres has fought for criminal justice, education reform, and collective bargaining rights—all the things, she believes, "impact Nevada workers and impacts, quite honestly, families like mine."

After the 2018 election, women held thirty-two of Nevada's sixty-three legislative seats, making it the first state ever to have elected a majority of women to state legislative office.[1] By 2023, the number grew to thirty-nine, meaning that 62 percent of Nevada's seats in its upper and lower chambers were held by women. In contrast, women held 33 percent of state legislative seats nationally in 2023, according to data from Rutgers University's Center for American Women and Politics (CAWP).[2]

Torres told me that a majority-female legislative body changes the nature and focus of decision making. "I think we have a lot more conversations about how women are impacted by policy because women are there," she said. A case in point was a menstrual justice bill that Torres helped adopt. The idea came from a Gen Z high school activist, Samantha Glover, who cofounded the youth-led nonprofit group Red Equity, which works on decreasing period poverty.

Studies show that women legislators are more likely to prioritize women's issues and to sponsor legislation that is related to women, children, and families—both in Congress and in state legislatures.[3] Female legislators have historically voted more often for pay equity, abortion access, and greater economic assistance to women and children compared to their male counterparts, although that tendency has diminished recently with more conservative Republican women being elected. Republican women now are far more likely to vote the party line than to cross over to support women's rights legislation or more expansive social welfare programs.[4]

Women lawmakers today remain far more likely to be Democrats: among women serving in Congress in 2023, just 28 percent were Republican.[5] At the state level, two-thirds of female legislators were Democrats. In Nevada, the female-led legislature expanded protections for pregnant workers, improved paid sick leave, increased abortion access, and made it harder for businesses to discriminate on pay. The state also toughened domestic violence and sex trafficking penalties.[6] While passage of these progressive policies was also a function of the Democratic majority in the Nevada assembly and senate, it showcased the policy gains that can result when women hold powerful political roles. Nevada also represents the sort of future that could be possible if more younger progressive women are elected to political office and could breathe life into the policies endorsed by many progressive Gen Z women and LGBTQ Zoomers.

A NEW VANGUARD OF GEN Z WOMEN AND LGBTQ CANDIDATES?

Getting more women to run for political office remains a challenge in U.S. politics. Even in 2018, which saw a record number of women candidates, only about one in four candidates for the U.S. House were women; just 21 percent of candidates running for U.S. Senate were women. Women made more gains as candidates in 2020. However, men still made up about 72 percent of all candidates running for Congress; at the state legislative level, men made up two-thirds of all nominees.[7] Women's political candidate numbers stayed relatively stagnant in 2022.

Studies point to myriad reasons why women are reluctant to run for office. Often primary caregivers, women are more likely to express concerns about how political candidacies would affect their work/family balance as well as about the emotional toll that campaigns could have on their families.[8] Others point to the gatekeeping function of political parties, which have historically been less likely to recruit women than men, although there have been more efforts recently by some party leaders, particularly Democrats, to train women to run for office.[9]

Above all, however, women are less likely to express interest in running for office and are less confident in their qualifications, characteristics that political scientists have labeled as "political ambition." Studies show that women are less likely to *consider* such positions in the first place—even among those with backgrounds (attorneys, business leaders, or other political experience) that would make them strong contenders.[10]

This political ambition gap has been noted among millennial college students. In 2012, political scientists Jennifer Lawless and Richard Fox asked college students whether they had thought about running for office when they got older many times, whether it had crossed their minds, or whether they had never thought about it. They found that that 63 percent of millennial college women, compared with just 43 percent of college men, had never thought about it. In contrast, college men were twice as likely as college women—20 percent compared to 10 percent—to have thought about running for office many times.[11] Their study also found that college women in 2012 were less likely than college men to be encouraged by their parents to run for office in the future, less likely to participate in student government, and less likely to discuss politics in class or with friends.

Given that progressive Gen Z women and LGBTQ Zoomers are participating in politics overall at higher levels than other members of Gen Z, I wanted to see if there were unique gendered patterns when it came to rising political ambition among Generation Z. In both of my national Qualtrics surveys, I asked Zoomers whether running for office was something they would never do, had no interest in doing now but had not ruled it out forever, might do if the opportunity presented itself, or something they would "definitely" do in the future. While the question wording options were different than the Lawless and Fox study of millennial college students and considered the views of all Zoomers (not just those in college), I found *no* significant gender differences. In 2019, just 8 percent of Gen Z women and Gen Z men indicated that running for office was something they would definitely do in the future; in contrast, 75 percent of Gen Z women and 72 percent of Gen Z men reported either never wanting to run for office or having no interest in running for office now (but might do so if the opportunity presented itself). By 2022, just 4 percent of Gen Z women and 6 percent of Gen Z men said that they definitely would run for office in the future, but that difference was not significant. Both groups expressed more disinterest in running for office than in 2019, with about 80 percent saying that they never wanted to run or had no interest in running for office now. Yet this *lack* of gender difference among Zoomers in my Qualtrics surveys may actually represent genuine progress because most American women remain less likely to run for office compared with men.

Why are we seeing these apparent changes from earlier studies on political ambition and the gender gap? Unlike previous generations, Gen Z women see more women who look like them in political office. As chapter 3 detailed, visible female role models who are younger and more diverse signal to younger women that there is room for them at the political table. Gen Z women are likely reaping the benefits of programs designed by well-known girls' organizations, such as Girl Scouts or the UN program Girl Up, that work on developing political and organizational skills, leading them to shift their thinking about holding office. And many Gen Z women with serious political ambitions now have access to programs, such as IGNITE, designed specifically for them.

Founded in 2010, IGNITE has trained more than thirty thousand high school and college-age women in political leadership.[12] Sara Guillermo, who has worked with IGNITE since its inception and became CEO in 2021, said that Gen Z women are different in important ways from those who came before them—and they stand ready to become political candidates at much higher levels than millennial women. When IGNITE began, Guillermo said, the organization spent lots of time explaining the basics of policymaking to their participants; Gen Z women, in contrast, come to their organization already well versed in the political process:

> [O]ur primary job was to connect the dots for people. Like, you care about gun violence. Do you understand how it's created in terms of policy? Do you understand who makes the policy? I feel like for most of Gen Z women right now, it's less about having to connect the dots, which I think is driving them closer to political leadership faster.

Guillermo also observed that Gen Z women were less likely to be caught up in the gender norms that pressure young women especially to please others. Rebecca Yanez, an IGNITE fellow from Oklahoma City, Oklahoma, who has been active in Democratic Party politics, shared similar thoughts with me, while also discussing Gen Z women's concerns about the need for a more diverse set of lawmakers: "I really want to push for giving people a voice for those who don't necessarily have it in government because there's just not enough representation in government."

CONCLUSION

LGBTQ Americans also remain vastly underrepresented as political candidates and officeholders, though their numbers are getting slightly better. In 2022, the LGBTQ Victory Fund, a political action committee that supports LGBTQ candidates, reported that at least 1,065 LGBTQ candidates ran for political office nationwide, with 466 winning—up from 336 in 2020.[13] The Victory Fund also noted that the number of LGBTQ elected officials increased by 5.8 percent after the 2022 elections, with 1,043 openly LGBTQ officials serving in elected office.[14] The Victory Fund noted, however, that the United States would have to elect more than 35,000 additional LGBTQ people to reach truly equitable representation in the United States.[15]

While LGBTQ candidates set records in 2022, they face an increasingly hostile environment that saw an unprecedented number of anti-LGBTQ bills introduced in state legislatures, many of which target transgender individuals. Zooey Zephyr, the first trans woman to be elected to the Montana House of Representatives in 2022, told National Public Radio (NPR) after her election that such bills serve "as a reminder that LGBTQ people need to be in the room where the laws are being written."[16]

My 2019 survey found that LGBTQ Zoomers were just as likely as their straight counterparts to indicate that they would definitely run for office in the future, 9 percent versus 8 percent, respectively. By May 2022, however, LGBTQ Zoomers were only half as likely as their straight counterparts to say that they would definitely run for political office—3 percent compared with 6 percent, although 18 percent of LGBTQ Zoomers said that they might run for office if the opportunity presented itself compared with 14 percent of straight Zoomers.

The percentage of Gen Zers—women or men, LGBTQ or straight—who expressed any desire to run for office dropped between 2019 and 2022. This finding may speak to Gen Z's lack of faith in using established channels, through our two-party system, to effect political change. Gen Z is the least partisan generation, so it is worth considering their attitudes about the political parties in more detail and thinking about the challenges that both parties face in recruiting younger Americans to run for office and securing their votes in the years ahead.

CONCLUSION

DEMOCRATS, REPUBLICANS, AND GENERATION Z

Younger voters have always turned out at lower rates than older Americans.[17] Some scholars attribute this generation gap to changes in media consumption—older Americans are more likely to read about politics in newspapers or watch television news than younger Americans, resulting in older Americans being more knowledgeable about politics.[18] Voter turnout also increases as it becomes habitual; younger Americans simply have less experience with voting, and as those habits become inculcated, Americans begin to turn out at higher rates as they age—a function of the life-cycle effect.[19] Because younger Americans are more transient and are busy starting their adult lives, the opportunity costs of voter registration are higher for young people. In states where it is easier to register to vote—for example, where there is same-day voter registration—voter turnout is higher among younger Americans (and older voters, for that matter).[20] States that preregister teens to vote, combined with strong civics education that instructs students about how to vote, also have higher youth voter turnout.[21]

With younger voters, particularly college students, trending heavily Democratic in recent years, some Republican-led state legislatures have moved to make voter registration and voting more difficult. They have used tactics such as disallowing college student IDs as proof of identity, forbidding polling locations on college campuses, eliminating voting by mail, and forcing first-time voters to have enhanced identification such as a Social Security card.[22] Some bills have sought to penalize groups that mobilize voters with bureaucratic requirements that make voter registration drives, often a mainstay of college organizing, harder to conduct.[23]

Despite such barriers, in 2018, 2020, and 2022, the first elections in which Generation Z was eligible to cast ballots, turnout among younger voters hit historic highs. Data from the Center for Information & Research on Civic Learning and Engagement (CIRCLE), the Tufts University organization that tracks young voters aged eighteen to twenty-nine, shows that voter turnout among younger eligible voters surged from 13 percent in the 2014 midterm elections to 28 percent in 2018. Voters aged eighteen to twenty-nine also posted record high voter turnout rates in the 2020 presidential election, increasing from 39 percent in 2016 to 50 percent.[24] Although the youth vote did not quite reach the same turnout numbers in the 2022 midterms as the 2018 midterms, it was still the second-highest turnout of younger voters in the past three decades. Both Gen Zers and millennials, defined as those Americans born between 1981 and 1996, will make up approximately half of all eligible voters by 2024, then surpass older voters by 2028, according to the States of Change Project.[25] By 2036, Gen Z, which has far more members than millennials, are expected to comprise 35 percent of the electorate.[26]

In all three federal elections since Donald Trump was elected president, the youth vote—led by Gen Z women—voted mostly for Democrats. In the 2022 midterms, CIRCLE estimated, 71 percent of women aged eighteen to twenty-nine voted for Democratic House candidates compared with 53 percent of young men. Among LGBTQ youth, 93 percent indicated that they voted for Democratic House candidates.[27] Catalist, a Democratic research firm that compiles one of the most comprehensive databases of American voters, found that young voters were key to the Democratic Party maintaining its control of the Senate in the 2022 midterms, winning key governor's races, and keeping Democratic losses in the House to a minimum in what was expected to be a large Republican wave two years into Joseph Biden's presidency.[28]

Catalist found that 65 percent of voters between the ages of eighteen and twenty-nine supported Democrats. Key to this trend was the *Dobbs* decision. Exit polls from the 2022 elections showed that 44 percent of voters aged eighteen to twenty-nine said that abortion was their top issue, far more than any other age group; older voters tended to prioritize inflation.[29] Other experts noted record levels of voter registration among women after the *Dobbs* decision—one analysis of ten states in the aftermath of the Supreme Court's reversal of *Roe* found that 55 percent of newly registered voters were women.[30] While forecasting the political future can be risky, I expect that the current incarnation of the Republican Party will struggle to attract the votes of Generation Z, particularly Gen Z women and LGBTQ

CONCLUSION

Zoomers—a problem referred to by political writer Ron Brownstein as the Republican Party's "Demographic Doom."[31]

In August 2023, Public Religion Research Institute (PRRI) collected new data among Gen Z respondents nationally and found that the Democratic Party continues to hold greater appeal among the nation's youngest voters than the Republican Party—and future voters, too, as we also surveyed thirteen- to seventeen-year-old Zoomers. Gen Z women continued to be twice as likely to identify as or lean Democrat (56 percent) than identify as or lean Republican (23 percent); this was true for both Gen Z white women and Gen Z women of color. Gen Z women of color, however, were less likely to identify as or lean Republican (16 percent) than Gen Z white women (27 percent). Similar patterns emerged among Zoomer girls aged thirteen to seventeen, although a higher percentage identified as "true" independents (30 percent). The 2023 PRRI survey showed that about three in four LGBTQ Zoomers adults identified as or leaned Democratic; just 5 percent identified as or leaned Republican.

Democrats continued to hold an advantage with male Zoomer voters, too, despite many media narratives suggesting that Zoomer men are finding the Republican Party more appealing in recent years, particularly as a backlash to the spread of so-called woke politics. The 2023 PRRI Gen Z survey found that 45 percent of Gen Z men identify as or lean Democrat compared with 33 percent who identify as or lean Republican. Isolating the analysis to Gen Z teen males under age eighteen found that the same number—32 percent—identified as or leaned Republican. The racial breaks were slightly more pronounced among Gen Z men than they were for Gen Z women: 47 percent of Gen Z men of color identified as Democratic compared with 42 percent of white Gen Z men. Non-white Gen Z men are less likely to identify as Republican than their white counterparts, 24 percent versus 41, respectively. Overall, however, there is little indication that Gen Z men are suddenly bolting toward the Republican Party.

This bleak outlook about the Republican Party's future was shared by many of the Republican Gen Z women I spoke with, who often noted difficulties with identifying as a Republican. One Republican woman from Ohio State said identifying with the Republican Party was a "stigma" that "might deter other women in future generations." Others said that they avoid posting about their conservative views on social media because they are sometimes met with hostile reactions from more progressive classmates and friends. "I try to keep it on the downlow that I am a Republican and that I did vote for Trump," said a University of Texas woman. "I do get backlash sometimes."

Many young Republican women I spoke with said that their party needed to engage better with young women and young people of color. Said this Republican woman from the University of Maryland: "Let's put ourselves in uncomfortable situations and go listen. Maybe if we went into these communities and listened to what they want, we would understand what policies would help them better. We could actually be able to talk to them and then we can start incorporating their needs into our platforms." Other Republican women expressed a desire to see more women in prominent positions within their party. A Republican woman at the University of Maryland believes that the Democratic Party has been successful with young people partly because "they have been able to point to the Republican Party and say, 'Look at them, they're only white men.' And so if the Republican Party started adding more women, or more people of color, they'd be more diverse and then they wouldn't be able to do that anymore." She also believes that many of the economic policies promoted by the Republican Party would appeal to her generation, but they are often drowned out by an emphasis on racial and gender identity for many Gen Zers, particularly those on the political left.

Many Gen Z Republicans also wanted their party to do a better job addressing the concerns shared by many their age. One group, Gen Z Grow Our Platform (Gen Z GOP), developed a platform that calls for their party to deal better with climate change, environmental sustainability, student loan debt, and equal opportunity for racial minorities—all issues that Gen Z, especially Gen Z women, strongly prioritizes. (The group was active from 2018 to 2022.) Cofounder Ryan Doucette told me that he and several friends formed the group because they believe that otherwise, "[R]epublicans will just see our vote tally go down further, if we don't respond to the concerns that Gen Z has. Gen Z is not a politically homogeneous group, but when we're not even proposing solutions to their concerns, they are going to vote homogeneously." Doucette also said that the Republican Party needs to appeal to women voters and support female candidates. "I think the party is acknowledging that it failed with women in 2020 and 2016," he said. "I'm hoping that leaders take that extra effort to get more women involved."

The Democratic Party cannot take the votes and activism of Generation Z women or LGBTQ Zoomers for granted, however. There remains much frustration for the progressive Gen Z women activists that I spoke with concerning the slow pace at which the Democratic Party is moving to adopt their preferred policies on climate, guns, the economy, and equality. Believing that progressive women and people of color make up the backbone of the Democratic Party, these activists think that attempts to appeal to the white working class are ultimately futile.

A better strategy, they said, is for Democrats to pass *more* progressive legislation and get their base more motivated to come to the polls. Yale student Lauren Williams, who created The Young Vote, a social media platform that helped college students register to vote and who worked with the Democratic Congressional Campaign Committee (DCCC) said this:

> I like that the Democrats seem to know and embrace that they are a diverse coalition, both racially and socioeconomically. Sometimes I think those ideals don't live up to the reality all the time and that they could do better in actually serving the communities that they purport to represent. Sometimes I think they cater more toward "Let's get those coal miners in Pennsylvania" and not necessarily "Let's get those black voters in Philly."

Others expressed concern that the current leadership of the Democratic Party is too focused on its opposition to Trump. Naina Agrawal-Harwin, the environmental activist I profiled in chapter 2, worries that Democrats her parents' age remain fixated on how bad Trump is and how far right the Republican Party has gone. But for young progressives, Agrawal-Harwin said, "[t]here's no shock value because this was our normal, this is what we grew up under. I think Democrats still are very much in this place of using Trump bashing and using this sort of, 'Oh my God, the Republicans are so evil, donate now to stop them,' to try to get people engaged . . . But I don't think it works well with young people. . . . We have grown up with multiple economic recessions, with the shadow of the climate crisis, the Me Too era, and constantly being scared of school shootings and doing active shooting drills." From Agrawal-Harwin's perspective, shared by many Gen Z women I spoke with, the Democrats aren't doing nearly enough on these fronts.

Progressive Generation Z activists also grapple with our federalist system of government. Most Democrats live in larger urban centers, and the disproportionate voting power of rural residents in states with less population presents a structural challenge to Democrats. Political pollster Nate Silver estimates that the U.S. Senate, for instance, has more than two times as much rural representation as urban core representation although there are relatively equal numbers of voters who reside in both these areas nationally.[32]

I spoke with many Gen Z progressive women activists who hail from the South, including Anna Dean, from Little Rock, Arkansas, the founder LOUDwomen. She said that it is difficult sometimes to be a young progressive woman in the South, and it leads many highly educated women to leave the state after college. Dean, who was alarmed about the state of reproductive rights and racial justice in her state, lamented that "no one wants to come back and fix it," while she and others suffer from "the trauma that is created by living here and the discrimination that happens on a daily basis to different marginalized groups." Dean ultimately hoped to return to her home state after college and run for political office to challenge what she sees as a pervasive status quo: "I think it's very important to have that representation, not only of women, but of [individuals from] different races, different members of the LGBTQ community. . . . [Ot]herwise I think the policies are always going to look like who is representing the groups of people. And so everyone that's representing us are white, straight males."

It is clear that Democrats have an overwhelming advantage with LGBTQ Zoomers. Exit polls showed that nine out of ten opted to vote

CONCLUSION

for Democratic House candidates in 2022. Again, there was frustration among LGBTQ Zoomers that I spoke with about *both* parties. I conducted a Zoom focus group of LGBTQ Zoomers in the summer of 2020, well before many Republican-led state legislatures began introducing legislation targeting the rights of LGBTQ Americans, particularly transgender youth. One of the participants said that he identified as a Democrat because "that's the position we are forced to be in as queer people. You know, not voting Democratic is going to put us in danger."

Others acknowledged that, in their minds, the Democratic Party was the lesser of two evils. On what the Republican Party would need to do to earn their votes, one participant said they should just "go away," adding: "It is hard to appeal to queer young people when they believe that basic human rights are wrong. How are you supposed to compromise with that?" Some would like to see our two-party system abolished, including one participant, who said the current system "divides and disenfranchises people and makes it hard to get any good policy accomplished." Others focus group participants wanted Democratic leaders to listen to the more progressive members of the party, such as Alexandria Ocasio-Cortez.

Leaders of both parties should be wary about a growing sense of pessimism among younger Americans. Political analyst Philip Bump analyzed a 2023 poll by the Pew Research Center that found, while Americans hold increasingly dismal views of both political parties, this tendency is far more evident among Americans under the age of thirty, who are twice as likely as Americans aged sixty-five and up to view both parties negatively.[33] While two-thirds of older Americans believe there is a great deal of difference between the two parties, just about 40 percent of younger Americans do. Of course, as Bump and other observers note, younger Americans are far more likely than older Americans to eschew a variety of institutions in society, ranging from marriage to religious organizations, to civic groups—so their lack of enthusiasm for political parties is not necessarily exceptional.

These trends should be considered, however, in the context of political engagement among Gen Z writ large. Gen Z Americans participate in other forms of politics situated outside the formal channels of government institutions, such as protests, boycotts, and social media campaigns, at higher rates than older Americans. Such sustained engagement has the power to affect policy, even at the highest levels. In September 2023, for instance, the Biden administration announced plans to create the American Climate Corps and a White House Office of Gun Violence Prevention, largely in response to youth organizing on both issues but also in a nod to the need for Democrats to secure younger voters. David Hogg is a survivor of the shooting in Parkland, Florida, and cofounder of March for Our Lives. He went on to found Leaders We Deserve, a political group designed to support younger candidates. Hogg told the *New York Times* that, while young activists are frustrated at the slow pace of action to prevent gun violence, he recognizes that "there's a complex network of things that are stopping us from making more progress. But President Biden is with us, and that's the message he's sending today."[34]

One thing we have learned about Gen Z in the past few years is that younger voters will turn out when they have good reason. They don't vote at the rates of older Americans and they're not monolithic, but Gen Z voters have bucked historical turnout trends for young voters in recent elections because they are spurred by issues that are important to them. Restrictions of reproductive rights, escalation of the climate change and gun violence crises, and concerns about racial justice and gender identity are giving this generation plenty of reasons to remain engaged in politics.

THE PERILS AND THE PROMISE OF GEN Z WOMEN, LGBTQ ZOOMERS, AND POLITICS

Many of the young Gen Z activists that I spoke with started their own nonprofit political organizations while they were quite young, and they often continued to run them as full-time students. The work is exhausting, several told me, and many are frustrated with the incremental nature of policymaking. Others recognize the emotional downside that comes with reliance on social media, the currency that has allowed so many Gen Z women to build their own successful political groups and amass followers.

CONCLUSION

While a high school student in Tuscaloosa, Alabama, climate activist Isabel Hope started the Meddling Kids Movement, an online, youth-led organization that profiled Gen Z grassroots activists to inspire other young people on progressive political issues. While recognizing the power of social media, Hope, who is autistic, became overwhelmed and beset by anxiety. She shifted from political advocacy to journalism, writing about environmental issues and helping to edit her college newspaper. While social media is the lifeblood of the Gen Z political class, its negative attributes, including trolls and cyberbullying, could deter political online engagement. This was especially true for Gen Z women, who are more likely to be victims of online rumors or nonconsensual explicit messages than Gen Z men, studies showed.[35]

Other Gen Z women activists I spoke with fretted that their groups sometimes elevated style over substance. This was the case for Sabirah Mahmoud, profiled in chapter 3, who became involved while in high school with the US Youth Strike for Climate, a national youth-led organization cofounded by Representative Ilhan Omar's daughter Isra Hirsi. After spending more than a year as a national logistics director, Mahmoud left in frustration over "cloutavists," which she described as members who wanted to appear influential but ultimately didn't do the hard work of organizing. Mahmoud turned her attention to working with local environmental groups as she pursued a college degree. She also had no patience or hope for elected officials making the progressive changes she thinks are important, telling me, "I don't think politicians can be the ones to bring us to where we need to go. . . . We need to build community places and work together to strengthen our communities rather than putting faith in our politicians who, if anything, like most of our government, are just white men."

Many of the Gen Z political entrepreneurs profiled in this book got their start locally because they saw an injustice or problem that they felt compelled to address. In some cases, their groups continue to do meaningful work in the places they were founded. In other cases, local groups became larger and have had an even greater impact. I think of groups such as Amy Quichiz's organization Veggie Mijas, which started as a vegan co-op out of Quichiz's dorm and grew to eight chapters around the country that share vegan recipes, plant community gardens, and advocate for environmental justice and food security for marginalized groups. Ina Bhoopalam founded Dream Equal when she was a teen in Nebraska; she based it on her experiences with gender discrimination on her debate team. While the first iteration of Dream Equal started by offering after-school programs aimed at combatting negative gender stereotypes, its curriculum has spread to more than thirty-five cities here and abroad. High schoolers Rosie Couture and Belan Yeshigeta cofounded Generation Ratify—rebranded in late 2023 as the Young Feminist Party—after reading how their state, Virginia, had failed to ratify the Equal Rights Amendment (ERA). The Young Feminist Party has grown into a leading youth-led movement seeking ERA ratification, but it has extended its mission to advancing gender equality and women's rights issues more broadly. The group now has more than twelve thousand members in all fifty states and provides online and in-person activist training, inspiring their members to lobby elected officials and campaign on behalf of political candidates who support gender equality issues.

In other cases, Gen Z women have worked closely with their male counterparts to create truly national political movements—Gen Z women such as Jackie Corin, who was one of the cofounders of March for Our Lives along with other survivors of the shooting in Parkland. March for Our Lives was a keystone political event for many Gen Z Americans. Millions of them marched in solidarity shortly after the shooting, but it also provided, for most of the progressive Gen Z political entrepreneurs I interviewed, their first practical experiences as political organizers and leaders themselves. Many of them would go on to take that organizational experience and apply it to other progressive causes such as climate change, women's equality, LGBTQ rights, and racial justice. Maxwell Frost's involvement with March for Our Lives propelled him to become the first Gen Zer, and Afro-Cuban, elected to Congress in 2022. These early organizing experiences with gun violence prevention paved the way for Generation Z to flood the streets during the massive Black Lives Matter (BLM) protests that took place in the summer of 2020 after the police killing of George Floyd.

CONCLUSION

Generation Z women are not only providing new energy for existing racial justice organizations. They are also prompting the women's rights movement to incorporate their own passions, such as their advocacy for menstrual equity. Many Gen Z women and their allies are also fighting to extend gay rights to include more emphasis on the rights of transgender and nonbinary Americans—a cause that has become a wedge issue in conservative states, which rushed to pass legislation curtailing medical treatment for transgender youth or discussion of these issues in classrooms. Similar battle lines are also being drawn regarding the discussion of critical race theory in public schools.

As part of the most racially and ethnically diverse generation, however, Gen Z women have been at the forefront of promoting racial justice that is also intersectional. Many Gen Z women leaders remind other activists how the needs of young women of color are distinct from women overall. Still other Gen Z women have moved from the streets to more traditional forms of political advocacy, such as working with the political parties and pushing them to address their concerns regarding climate, equality, and education. Several years into the COVID-19 pandemic, Gen Z women were driving conversations about mental health, income inequality, and health disparities—challenging their elected officials to do more to address these concerns. Early indicators were that Gen Z women had closed the political ambition gap with their male counterparts in terms of thinking about running for political office themselves in the future, which remains one of the last bastions of male dominance in U.S. politics today.

Not all Gen Z women are politically progressive nor are Gen Z men completely absent from politics today—nor do we want that to be the case. My conversations with politically active Gen Z men on both sides of the political aisle and with conservative Gen Z women showed that no generation is politically monolithic and that there are passionate and politically motivated young Americans all along the political spectrum.

Yet, as Generation Z is poised to become our future leaders, it is progressive Gen Z women and LGBTQ Zoomers who are the most likely to shape the political future. While Americans certainly change their political affiliations from time to time, the political views and habits that young people develop in their late teens and early twenties—what scholars call the impressionable years—are generally far more likely to carry into their adult lives. The political trends we see among the members of this generation, with Gen Z women and LGBTQ Zoomers possessing a clear moral clarity about creating a safer, more just, and healthier world, will likely have spillover effects in the decades ahead to help create a more inclusive political future that protects and realizes the promise of the United States as a multiracial democracy—one that incorporates the talents and perspectives of all young Americans, including Gen Z women and LGBTQ Zoomers, in ways that previous generations have not.

METHODOLOGICAL APPENDIX

The source material for *The Politics of Generation Z* comes from interviews with eighty-seven Gen Z political activists, fifteen focus groups held with college women and men across the country and participants of IGNITE, and two national surveys of Gen Z Americans that I conducted in July 2019 and in May 2022. I began and completed most of the original research—the interviews, the focus groups, and the Qualtrics surveys—while I was a professor at Washington College, and each of these research approaches and methodologies were approved by Washington College's Institutional Review Board (IRB).

INTERVIEWS

From July 2020 through the spring of 2023, I interviewed eighty-seven Gen Z political activists who either started their own youth-led political organizations, held leadership positions in them, or were very active in partisan politics; three of the activists I interviewed just missed the cutoff to be part of Generation Z (those Americans born after 1996) because they were born in 1995; however, 70 percent of my interviewees were born in 2000 or later. Per IRB protocol, interviewees gave their written consent to be interviewed; in the cases of minors, their parents provided written consent. Interviewees were also given the opportunity to remain anonymous; in cases where interviewees are named, they gave their express permission, or their parents gave their express permission in the cases of minors. Interviewees spoke on the record; I also told them at the beginning of the interviews that I would be happy to keep any information off the record if they desired.

The activists profiled in the book are not meant to be representative of members of Generation Z more generally but instead to provide insight into the extraordinary actors engaged in the political process who are shaping political debates. While researching my book and seeking to profile Gen Z women political entrepreneurs specifically, I identified numerous youth-led Gen Z organizations online and through social media that touch on gender themes or had Gen Z women at the helm, and I reached out through email or social media to request interviews. In some cases, interviewees connected me with other activists, so many of the interview subjects come by way of what social scientists call a snowball sample. Most of my interviewees are female and progressive; seven identify as nonbinary, genderqueer, and/or transgender. I contacted the Human Rights Campaign (HRC), who put me in touch with several of their youth ambassadors for interviews. I also interviewed a dozen Gen Z male activists, either identified through my snowball sample or because I identified them as leaders in a youth-led organization online. Undertaken on Zoom, these semistructured interviews lasted between thirty and ninety minutes. Most of the activists I interviewed hold progressive political views and/or advocate for progressive policies; I also interviewed seven Republican Gen Z women activists and three Republican Gen Z men.

FOCUS GROUPS

I held fifteen focus groups, each of which lasted approximately ninety minutes, for Gen Z Americans from June 2019 through December 2020, both in person (prior to the onset of the COVID-19 pandemic) and via Zoom. The costs of the focus groups were generously underwritten by IGNITE; all

METHODOLOGICAL APPENDIX

participants were given a $75 Amazon gift card for participating. I held three focus groups in June 2019 with participants of IGNITE's annual conference in Washington, DC. In addition to wanting to understand more about the political views of their members, IGNITE also wanted to understand what students in college were thinking about politics, so we identified four college campuses with regional and political diversity to hold focus groups: Ohio State University; Georgia State University; the University of Maryland, College Park; and the University of Texas at Austin. I relied on political science faculty members teaching introductory courses in American politics to solicit volunteers from their classes for the focus groups. I held two Gen Z women focus groups (one Democratic, one Republican) on campus at Ohio State University in October 2019; two Gen Z women focus groups (one Democratic, one Republican) at Georgia State University in January 2020; and four Gen Z focus groups (two Democratic focus groups; one female, one male; two Republican focus groups; one female, one male) at the University of Maryland, College Park, in February 2020. I used a similar methodology to solicit students from introductory courses in American government at the University of Texas at Austin in December 2020, where I held three additional Gen Z focus groups (one with Democratic women, another with Republican women, and a third with Democratic men) online through Zoom because of COVID-19. (Attempts to find enough Republican men were difficult so I ended up canceling an online Republican male focus group at the University of Texas at Austin.) I also held an LGBTQ Zoom focus group in August 2020 by building a snowball sample and having activists I spoke with recommend friends or acquaintances who might be willing to participate in a focus group of LGBTQ Gen Zers. The identities of the focus group participants have been kept confidential.

SURVEYS

I designed two original, nationally representative surveys of Gen Z Americans. The first survey took place in July 2019 on a sample of 2,210 panelists aged eighteen to twenty-two provided by the survey firm Qualtrics, which

METHODOLOGICAL APPENDIX

includes opt-in panels. Qualtrics is a market research organization that recruits individuals to respond to surveys online for the purpose of achieving representative samples, although the participants in those panels are not randomly selected. Those surveys are conducted anonymously, which help guard against social desirability bias. The credibility interval for the 2019 sample, at the 95 percent level, is ±2.6 percent. In May 2022, I surveyed 3,200 Americans, which had an oversample of 1,600 Gen Z Americans aged eighteen to twenty-four. The credibility interval for the full sample, at the 95 percent level, is ±2.1; for the Gen Z sample, it is ±3.0 percent. In both cases, the data sets are weighted using benchmarks based on Pew Research Center's analysis of the U.S. Census Bureau's Current Population Survey (CPS) for age, gender, race/ethnicity, and income. The sample demographics for both surveys are listed in table A.1.

Independent studies of Qualtrics panels show that their samples are close to the demographic breakdown of the United States[1] and are more representative demographically and politically than Amazon's Mechanical Turk or Facebook, two other organizations that also allow for such recruitment of survey respondents.[2] However, opt-in panels have been shown to have larger absolute levels of error than surveys that are probability-based, based on random selection, especially among younger Americans, although probability-based samples also have errors when compared with high-quality government data sources.[3] At the same time, opt-in panels allow for the ability to survey harder-to-reach populations and are more cost-effective. Where possible, I used a variety of random, probability-based samples, such as the American National Election Studies (ANES), General Social Survey (GSS), and a survey from Pew Research Center, that are publicly available to allow for additional comparative data on Gen Z. I used several random probability-based surveys designed and conducted by the Public Religion Research Institute (PRRI) in 2022 and 2023. Information about those surveys, which are publicly available, can be found at PRRI's website (www.prri.org).

To capture levels of political engagement among Generation Z, in both surveys, I asked respondents to indicate which of seventeen political activities they participated in during the past year. Eight of these political activities I characterize as more "passive," such as political discussion or

METHODOLOGICAL APPENDIX

using social media for politics, and the rest I characterize as more "active," such as attending government meetings, attending marches, volunteering for campaigns, and contacting government officials. Activities were chosen based on previous scholarship and in consultation with IGNITE, which wanted data collected on specific measures of political participation. I chose *not* to include voting because, in the 2019 survey, I realized many Gen Z respondents would have not have been eligible to vote in a previous election. I also opted to keep the political engagement battery the same in the 2022 survey, so voting was omitted as a form of political participation. Those measures were added as part of a cumulative scale; the reliability of the scale for both surveys is good, with the Cronbach's alpha scores being .694 (2019) and .698 (2022).

CHAPTER 1 SOURCE MATERIAL

For tables A.3 and A.4, I used the ANES Cumulative Data File (1948–2020) to calculate the percentages of men and women who reported participating in at least one campaign-related political activity in the past year. These activities included volunteering with a campaign, attending a campaign rally or event, making a campaign donation, and/or trying to influence someone's vote choice. Table A.3 shows the percentages of Americans, by gender, who reported such participation. As table A.3 shows, men are significantly more likely to participate in campaign-related events compared with women in all years except 2008.

When it comes to younger Americans and participation in campaign-related events, however, there are relatively few gender differences stretching back to 1972. In three years, however, young men are significantly more likely to participate in campaign politics than young women (see table A.4).

My analysis of Pew Research Center's 2012 Civic Engagement in the Digital Age Study shows that there are no systematic gender differences in terms of overall levels of civic engagement in either offline or online political activities, although young men report being significantly more likely to attend a rally or contact a government official than young women, and

TABLE A.1 Demographic breakdown of Americans: Gen Z and U.S. population

	2019 GEN Z SURVEY	2022 GEN Z SURVEY	OTHER NATIONAL SURVEYS OF GEN Z	U.S. POPULATION
Race/ethnicity				
White, non-Hispanic	52	52	52[†]	59[‡]
Hispanic/Latinx	25	25	25	19
Black, non-Hispanic	14	14	14	13
Asian American	4	4	6	6
Multiracial/other*	6	6	5	4
Sexual orientation				
Straight	75	70	79[§]	87[∥]
Gay or lesbian	6	6	5	3
Bisexual	14	17	15	4
No opinion/other	5	6	5	7
Gender identity				
Cis female	50	46	n/a	n/a
Cis male	45	48	n/a	n/a
Transgender	2	2	2	.7
Nonbinary, genderqueer, or other	3	3	14.2	.1[#]
LGBTQ overall	25	30	n/a	n/a

* "Other" refers to Middle Eastern, Native American, or Pacific Islander or if someone said "other."
† Kim Parker and Ruth Igielnik, "On the Cusp of Adulthood and Facing an Uncertain Future: What We Know About Gen Z So Far," May 14, 2020, https://www.pewresearch.org/social-trends/2020/05/14/on-the-cusp-of-adulthood-and-facing-an-uncertain-future-what-we-know-about-gen-z-so-far-2/.
‡ U.S. Census Bureau, "Quick Facts," 2022. The figures for whites omit those who are not Hispanic or Latinx. https://www.census.gov/quickfacts/fact/table/US/PST045222.
§ Jeffrey Jones, "LGBT Identification in U.S. Ticks Up to 7.1%," 2022, https://news.gallup.com/poll/389792/lgbt-identification-ticks-up.aspx.
∥ Jones, "LGBT Identification."
The transgender and other non-cisgender numbers here come from Jones, "LGBTQ Identification." It is difficult to find nationally representative data on the percentage of Americans who identity as nonbinary, genderqueer, or some other category. The Williams Institute released a 2021 study showing that 1.2 million Americans age eighteen and older identify beyond the binary gender spectrum. Given that there are approximately 209 million Americans aged eighteen and older in the population, that means around 0.1 percent of the overall U.S. population identifies as nonbinary. The Williams Institute, "Nonbinary LGBTQ Adults in the United States," June 2021, https://williamsinstitute.law.ucla.edu/wp-content/uploads/Nonbinary-LGBTQ-Adults-Jun-2021.pdf.

TABLE A.2A General Social Survey (GSS) data: Partisanship among young women in 1972, 1990, 2006, and 2022

	1972	1990	2006	2022
Democrat	63	37	38	55
Independent	16	14	33	23
Republican	18	50	28	26
Other party/don't know	4	0	2	1
Number of Respondents	86	76	193	153

Note: Cohorts are age 18–24 in all groups except 1972; 1970 represents the year in which the entire cohort of 18–24 of boomers would reach adulthood, but the GSS starts in 1972.

TABLE A.2B General Social Survey (GSS) data: partisanship among young men in 1970, 1990, 2006, and 2022

	1972	1990	2006	2022
Democrat	54	35	41	24
Independent	19	13	26	21
Republican	20	33	30	52
Other party/don't know	6	1	4	3
Number of Respondents	113	66	171	128

Note: Cohorts are age 18–24 in all groups except 1972; 1970 represents the year in which the entire cohort of 18–24 of baby boomers would reach adulthood, but the GSS starts in 1972.

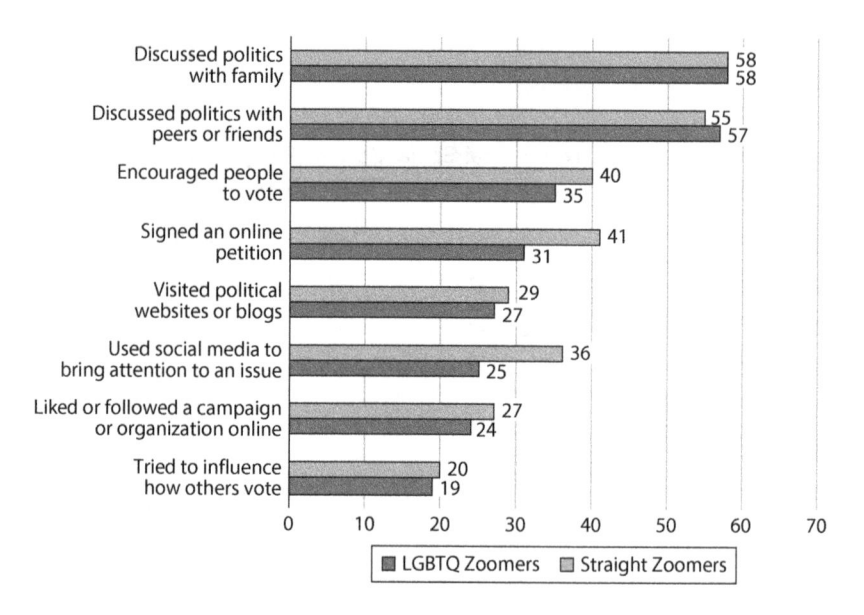

Activity	LGBTQ Zoomers	Straight Zoomers
Discussed politics with family	58	58
Discussed politics with peers or friends	55	57
Encouraged people to vote	40	35
Signed an online petition	41	31
Visited political websites or blogs	29	27
Used social media to bring attention to an issue	36	25
Liked or followed a campaign or organization online	27	24
Tried to influence how others vote	20	19

FIGURE A.1 Percentage of Gen Zers engaged in passive politics, by LGBTQ status, as of 2019. Qualtrics survey conducted by the author in July 2019, with a sample of 2,200 Americans aged eighteen to twenty-two.

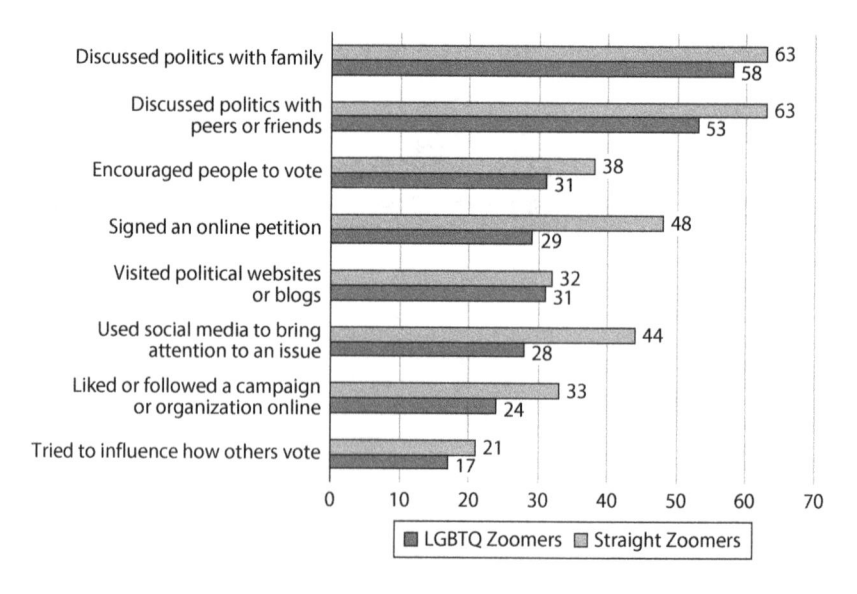

Activity	LGBTQ Zoomers	Straight Zoomers
Discussed politics with family	63	58
Discussed politics with peers or friends	63	53
Encouraged people to vote	38	31
Signed an online petition	48	29
Visited political websites or blogs	32	31
Used social media to bring attention to an issue	44	28
Liked or followed a campaign or organization online	33	24
Tried to influence how others vote	21	17

FIGURE A.2 Percentage of Gen Zers engaged in passive politics, by LGBTQ status, as of 2022. Qualtrics survey conducted by the author in May 2022, with a sample of 1,600 Americans aged eighteen to twenty-four.

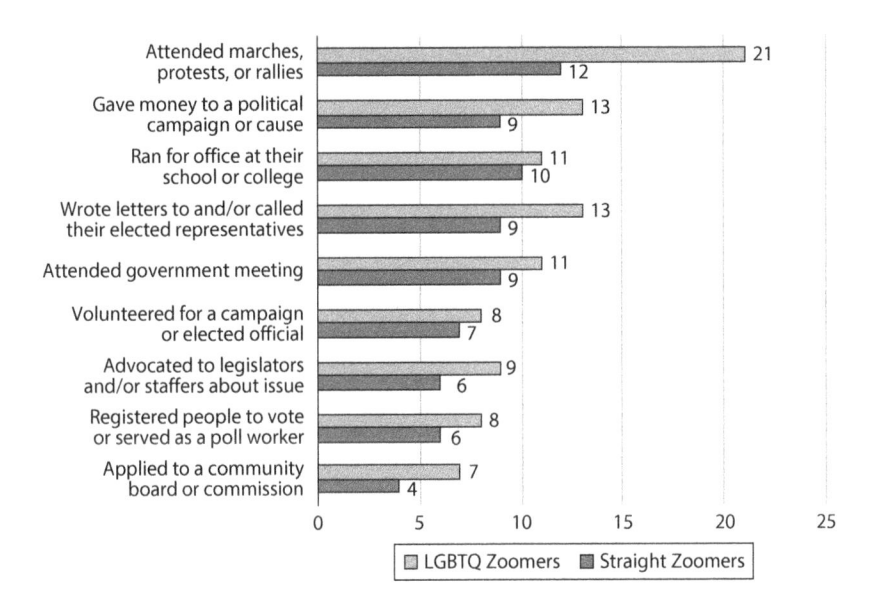

	LGBTQ Zoomers	Straight Zoomers
Attended marches, protests, or rallies	21	12
Gave money to a political campaign or cause	13	9
Ran for office at their school or college	11	10
Wrote letters to and/or called their elected representatives	13	9
Attended government meeting	11	9
Volunteered for a campaign or elected official	8	7
Advocated to legislators and/or staffers about issue	9	6
Registered people to vote or served as a poll worker	8	6
Applied to a community board or commission	7	4

FIGURE A.3 Percentage of Gen Zers engaged in active politics, by LGBTQ status, as of 2019. Qualtrics survey conducted by the author in July 2019, with a sample of 2,200 Americans aged eighteen to twenty-two.

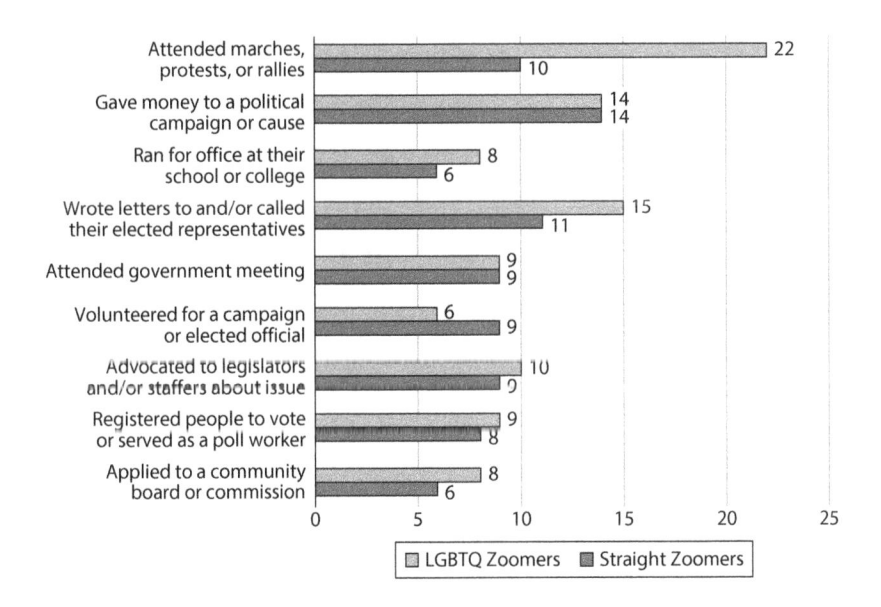

	LGBTQ Zoomers	Straight Zoomers
Attended marches, protests, or rallies	22	10
Gave money to a political campaign or cause	14	14
Ran for office at their school or college	8	6
Wrote letters to and/or called their elected representatives	15	11
Attended government meeting	9	9
Volunteered for a campaign or elected official	6	9
Advocated to legislators and/or staffers about issue	10	5
Registered people to vote or served as a poll worker	9	8
Applied to a community board or commission	8	6

FIGURE A.4 Percentage of Gen Zers engaged in active politics, by LGBTQ status, as of 2022. Qualtrics survey conducted by the author in May 2022, with a sample of 1,600 Americans aged eighteen to twenty-four.

TABLE A.3 Percentage of Americans of all ages participating in campaign-related activities by gender

	MEN	WOMEN	NUMBER OF RESPONDENTS
1952***	33	23	1,899
1956***	47	32	1,762
1960**	46	39	1,181
1964**	43	36	1,571
1968***	42	33	1,557
1972***	37	30	2,705
1976***	43	36	2,248
1980***	41	33	1,614
1984***	38	33	2,257
1988***	37	28	2,040
1992***	45	36	2,485
1996***	35	28	1,714
2000***	40	33	1,807
2004***	53	47	1,212
2008	49	49	2,322
2012***	47	43	5,914
2016***	49	46	4,270
2020***	53	51	8,210

Note: Data from American National Election Study (ANES). Differences in percentages are significant at the ***$p < .001$; **$p < .01$; *$p < .05$ level according to a chi-square test.

TABLE A.4 Percentage of Americans aged 18 to 24 participating in campaign-related activities by gender

	YOUNG MEN (18–24)	YOUNG WOMEN (18–24)	N
1972	40	39	403
1976	45	37	281
1980	42	39	232
1984	37	30	291
1988	27	19	202
1992	37	31	221
1996	15	20	117
2000	36	33	146
2004	54	43	127
2008#	47	36	221
2012***	44	31	511
2016**	54	42	328
2020	49	48	408

Note: Data from American National Election Study (ANES). Differences in percentages are significant at the ***$p < .001$; **$p < .01$; *$p < .05$ level, #$p < .10$ according to a chi-square test. In 2008, the gender difference is marginally significant ($p < .10$).

METHODOLOGICAL APPENDIX

young women report being significantly more likely to be an active member of a group influencing policy and contributing money to a candidate of cause; both young women and men report, on average, participating in 1.6 activities (see figure A.5).

While young women aged eighteen to twenty-four are significantly more likely to report using social media to encourage political activism, send text messages to others about politics, and like political stories online

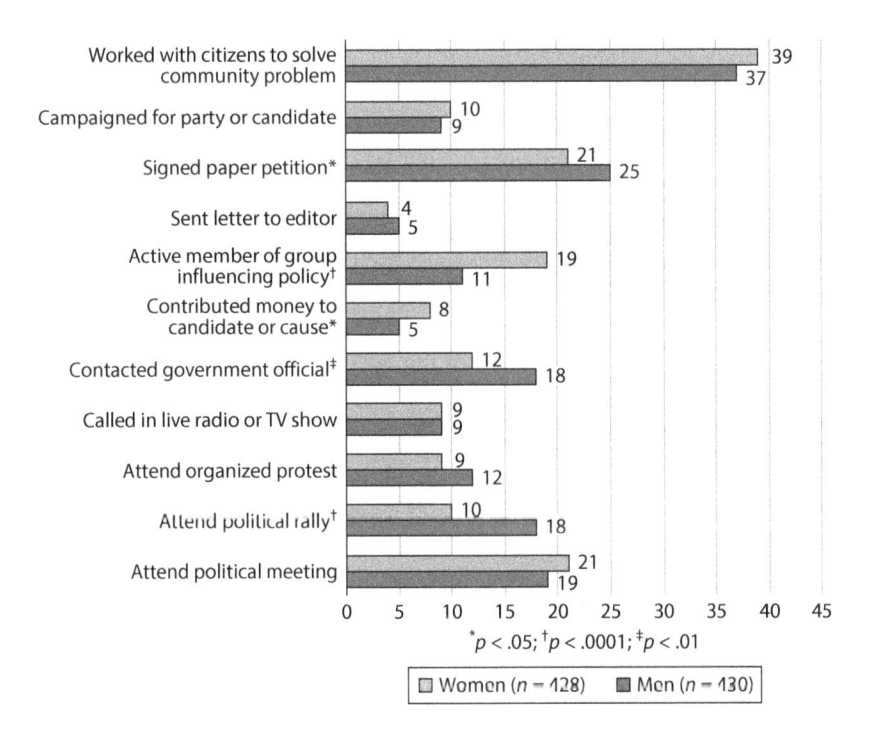

Activity	Women	Men
Worked with citizens to solve community problem	39	37
Campaigned for party or candidate	10	9
Signed paper petition*	21	25
Sent letter to editor	4	5
Active member of group influencing policy†	19	11
Contributed money to candidate or cause*	8	5
Contacted government official‡	12	18
Called in live radio or TV show	9	9
Attend organized protest	9	12
Attend political rally†	10	18
Attend political meeting	21	19

$^*p < .05;\ ^\dagger p < .0001;\ ^\ddagger p < .01$

☐ Women (n = 128)   ■ Men (n = 130)

FIGURE A.5 Percentage of Americans aged eighteen to twenty-four engaged in offline political activities, by gender. Pew Research Center, Civic Engagement Study, 2012.

METHODOLOGICAL APPENDIX

compared to young men, young men are significantly more likely to report contacting government officials via email or text. When I combined all these behaviors to form a political scale of online engagement, however, I found no statistically significant differences based on gender: young women engaged in 4.4 online political activities in 2012 compared with 4.0 online activities by young men, a difference that is not statistically significant (see figure A.6).

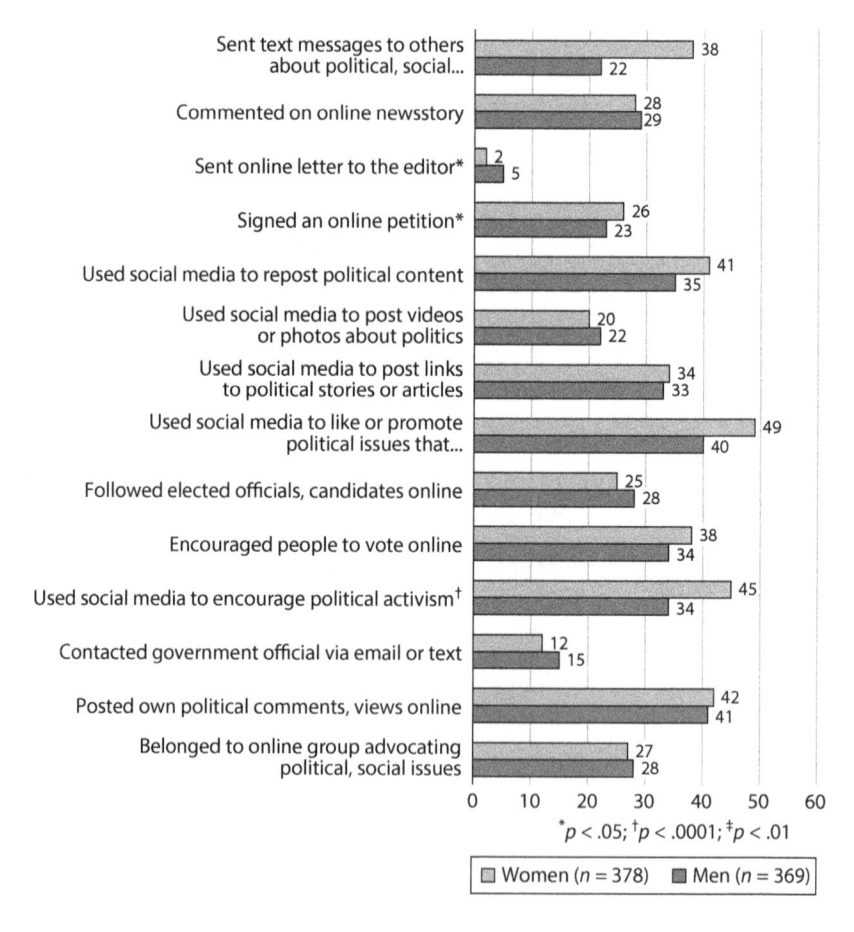

Activity	Women	Men
Sent text messages to others about political, social...	38	22
Commented on online newsstory	28	29
Sent online letter to the editor*	2	5
Signed an online petition*	26	23
Used social media to repost political content	41	35
Used social media to post videos or photos about politics	20	22
Used social media to post links to political stories or articles	34	33
Used social media to like or promote political issues that...	49	40
Followed elected officials, candidates online	25	28
Encouraged people to vote online	38	34
Used social media to encourage political activism†	45	34
Contacted government official via email or text	12	15
Posted own political comments, views online	42	41
Belonged to online group advocating political, social issues	27	28

*$p < .05$; †$p < .0001$; ‡$p < .01$

Women ($n = 378$)   Men ($n = 369$)

FIGURE A.6 Percentage of Americans aged eighteen to twenty-four engaged in online political activities, by gender. Pew Research Center, Civic Engagement Study, 2012.

METHODOLOGICAL APPENDIX

CHAPTER 2 SOURCE MATERIAL

TABLE A.5 Average number of political activities by numerous factors and gender for 2019 and 2022

	2019 GEN Z WOMEN	2019 GEN Z MEN	2022 GEN Z WOMEN	2022 GEN Z MEN
Education				
High school	3.20	3.07	3.55	3.92
Some college	4.17	3.62	3.94	3.85
College	4.64	3.42	3.92	3.91
Family income levels				
Less than $30,000	3.08	3.01	3.46	3.35
$30,000–49,999	3.95	3.14	4.08	3.80
$50,000–99,999	4.29	3.60	3.64	3.54
$100,000 or more	4.48	3.61	4.62	4.00
Race/ethnicity				
White, non-Hispanic	3.89	3.51	3.91	3.70
Black, non-Hispanic	3.57	2.89	3.41	3.00
Hispanic/Latinx	3.68	3.25	3.75	3.67
Asian American	4.45	3.22	3.65	3.45
Multiracial or other	3.96	3.74	4.18	3.87
High school activities				
1 activity or less	2.52	2.21	2.99	2.25
2 or 3 activities	3.76	3.47	3.96	3.52
4 or 5 activities	4.34	3.57	4.38	3.88
6 or more activities	5.04	5.34	5.50	5.07
Number of critical issues				
3 or fewer issues	2.68	2.73	2.53	2.78
4 to 6 issues	3.52	3.11	3.23	3.31
7 to 10 issues	4.19	3.58	4.74	3.66
More than 10 issues	4.30	3.97	4.68	3.96

(continued)

TABLE A.5 (*Continued*)

	2019 GEN Z WOMEN	2019 GEN Z MEN	2022 GEN Z WOMEN	2022 GEN Z MEN
Understands how government works				
Strongly disagree	2.04	1.89	1.97	1.91
Somewhat disagree	2.89	2.25	2.76	2.58
Unsure	2.65	2.83	3.13	2.62
Somewhat agree	4.26	3.38	4.54	3.65
Strongly agree	4.84	4.11	4.80	4.36
Party strength				
Independent	2.82	2.53	2.86	2.62
Weak partisan	3.79	3.54	4.27	3.48
Strong partisan	4.69	3.65	4.78	4.00
Contacted by party				
No	3.44	2.93	3.58	3.44
Yes	5.61	4.63	6.04	5.61
Contacted by campaign				
No	3.44	3.05	3.58	3.10
Yes	5.61	4.47	6.04	4.81
Contacted by political group				
No	3.44	3.17	3.87	3.31
Yes	5.61	4.55	5.31	4.67

TABLE A.6 Mean level of political activities by numerous factors and LGBTQ status for 2019 and 2022

	2019 LGBTQ ZOOMERS	2019 STRAIGHT ZOOMERS	2022 LGBTQ ZOOMERS	2022 STRAIGHT ZOOMERS
Education				
High school	3.45	3.07	4.07	3.15
Some college	4.76	3.71	4.84	3.67
College	3.97	3.95	4.61	3.72
Family income levels				
Less than $30,000	3.52	2.30	3.83	3.23
$30,000–49,999	4.51	3.29	4.72	3.67
$50,000–99,999	4.45	3.81	4.62	3.31
$100,000 or more	4.29	3.94	5.47	3.99
Race/ethnicity				
White, not-Hispanic	4.17	3.61	4.50	3.56
Black, not-Hispanic	3.63	3.09	3.73	3.12
Hispanic/Latinx	4.09	3.27	4.67	3.34
Asian American	3.49	3.76	3.17	3.74
Multiracial or other	3.89	3.81	4.67	3.76
High school activities				
1 or fewer activities	2.53	2.62	3.34	2.32
2 or 3 activities	3.82	3.51	4.41	3.40
4 or 5 activities	4.41	4.23	4.84	4.21
6 or more activities	4.94	5.89	7.19	4.80
Number of critical issues				
3 or fewer issues	2.41	3.09	2.78	2.90
4 to 6 issues	3.79	3.70	4.14	3.61
7 to 10 issues	3.68	3.74	4.46	3.49
More than 10 issues	4.33	3.93	5.01	3.73

(*continued*)

METHODOLOGICAL APPENDIX

TABLE A.6 *(Continued)*

	2019 LGBTQ ZOOMERS	2019 STRAIGHT ZOOMERS	2022 LGBTQ ZOOMERS	2022 STRAIGHT ZOOMERS
Understands how government works				
Strongly disagree	2.87	1.94	2.39	2.38
Somewhat disagree	3.17	2.77	4.17	2.52
Unsure	2.89	3.10	3.43	2.82
Somewhat agree	4.36	3.58	4.76	3.67
Strongly agree	4.34	4.47	4.99	4.26
Party strength				
Independent	3.12	3.07	3.80	2.82
Weak partisan	3.98	3.53	4.56	3.55
Strong partisan	4.12	4.11	4.98	3.82
Contacted by party				
No	3.48	3.29	4.15	3.14
Yes	4.90	4.59	5.54	4.52
Contacted by campaign				
No	3.46	3.19	4.10	3.11
Yes	4.59	4.60	5.25	4.33
Contacted by political group				
No	3.58	3.36	4.29	3.23
Yes	4.74	4.74	5.01	4.61

EMOTIONS SCALES

Rather than control for each *separate* positive or negative emotion that describes how Gen Z Americans feel about the way that things are going in the country today, I combined them into a negative emotions scale and a positive emotions scale. These additive scales have scores that range from 4 (meaning that respondents indicated that all four emotions in the scale "do not at all" describe their current emotional state about the country) to 16 (meaning that all four emotions in the scale describe their feelings about the state of the country "a lot." The Cronbach's alpha for the negative emotional scale for both 2019 and 2022 shows a reliability score of .82, and the

TABLE A.7 Description of key measures in Gen Z political engagement model and coding

VARIABLE NAME	DESCRIPTION
Political engagement scale	Additive scale (0 to 17 activities in the past year)
Respondent gender	1 = women; 0 = men (trans/nonbinary omitted from models due to small numbers)
Current education level	1 = high school or below; 2 = some college; 3 = college
Educational goals	1 = high school; 2 = associate degree; 3 = bachelor degree; 4 = graduate school
Family income	1=less than $5,000, 2=$5,000-$9,999; 3=$10,000-$19,999; 4=$20,000-$29,999; 5=$30,000-$39,999; 6=$40,000-$49,999; 7=$50,000-$74,999; 8=$75,000-$99,999; 9=$100,000-$149,999; 10=$150,000=$199,999; 11=$200,000 or more.
Racial identification	Racial and ethnic identification is captured by a series of dummy variables. "Black" is coded 1 if the respondent is Black/non-Hispanic and 0 otherwise. "Latinx" is coded 1 if the respondent is Hispanic and 0 otherwise. "Asian American" is coded 1 if the respondent is Asian American. "Multiracial American" is coded 1 for all other racial identification excluding whites. White is the baseline or comparison category.
LGBTQ	LGBTQ status coded 1 for those who are LGBTQ (gay, lesbian, bisexual; nonbinary; transgender); respondents are coded 0 if they are cisgender and straight.
Closely follows politics	1 = most of the time; 4 = hardly at all
Understands how politics works	1 = strongly disagree; 5 = strongly agree
Political system meets needs of the public	1 = strongly agree; 5 = strongly disagree
Party strength	1 = independent; 2 = independent leaner or weak partisan; 3 = strong partisan
Ideology	1 = extremely liberal; 7 = extremely conservative
High school activities scale	Additive scale, 0 to 9

(continued)

METHODOLOGICAL APPENDIX

TABLE A.7 *(Continued)*

VARIABLE NAME	DESCRIPTION
Issue publics/critical issues scale	Additive scale, 0 to 14
Party contact	1 = yes; 0 = no
Campaign contact	1 = yes; 0 = no
Political group contact	1 = yes; 0 = no
Positive emotions scale (see below)	4 = all four emotions do not at all describe their state; 16 = all four emotions describe their state a lot
Negative emotions scale (see below)	4 = all four emotions do not at all describe their state; 16 = all four emotions describe their state a lot
Church attendance	1 = never; 6 = more than weekly

Cronbach's alpha for the positive emotional scale for both years shows a reliability score of .85. In both cases, these scores denote a strongly reliable scale. A confirming factor analysis of the negative emotions in both years showed that they loaded on one factor, with loadings ranging from .79 to .82. Confirming factor analysis of the positive emotions also loaded on one factor for both years, with loadings ranging from .78 to .86.

In 2019, the average score for the negative emotions scale for Gen Z women is significantly higher (11.7) than it is for men (10.2) (t-test = −8.70; $p < .000$). The average score for the positive emotions scale for Gen Z women is significantly lower (8.8) than it is for men (10.9) (t-test = 7.83; $p < .000$.).

In 2022, the average score for the negative emotions scale for Gen Z women is significantly higher (11.5) than it is for men (10.5) (t-test = 5.26; $p < .000$). The average score for the positive emotions scale for Gen Z women is significantly lower (8.4) than it is for men (9.5) (t-test = 5.51; $p < .000$.).

The average score for the negative emotions scale for LGBTQ Zoomers is significantly higher (12.2) than it is for straight Zoomers (10.6) (t-test = 8.03; $p < .000$). The average score for the positive emotions scale for LGBTQ Zoomers is significantly lower (7.94) than it is for straight Zoomers (9.24) (t-test = 6.08; $p < .000$.).

TABLE A.8 Political engagement model for full model, Gen Z women and Gen Z men, in 2019

DEPENDENT VARIABLE: POLITICAL ENGAGEMENT SCALE	FULL MODEL	GEN Z WOMEN	GEN Z MEN
Female	0.343*	—	—
	(0.110)		
Current educational status	0.244	0.517	−0.086
	(0.312)	(0.432)	(0.442)
Family income	0.952**	0.969**	0.799**
	(0.188)	(0.255)	(0.272)
Black	−0.559**	−0.433*	−0.687**
	(0.138)	(0.194)	(0.200)
Latinx	−0.112	−0.102	−0.158
	(0.147)	(0.203)	(0.207)
Asian	−0.213	−0.148	−0.125
	(0.219)	(0.378)	(0.275)
Multiracial	0.307	0.142	0.549+
	(0.206)	(0.263)	(0.316)
LGBTQ	0.129	0.278	−0.115
	(0.138)	(0.176)	(0.213)
Follows politics closely	1.597**	1.979**	1.167**
	(0.203)	(0.288)	(0.286)
Understands how government works	1.206**	1.343**	1.109**
	(0.210)	(0.292)	(0.302)
Politics does not help people	0.584**	1.135**	−0.061
	(0.217)	(0.307)	(0.306)
Party strength	0.422↑*	0.674**	−0.007
	(0.164)	(0.208)	(0.217)
Ideology	0.782**	0.848**	0.552
	(0.258)	(0.328)	(0.371)
High school activities	2.687**	2.635**	2.707**
	(0.321)	(0.407)	(0.503)

(*continued*)

TABLE A.8 (Continued)

DEPENDENT VARIABLE: POLITICAL ENGAGEMENT SCALE	FULL MODEL	GEN Z WOMEN	GEN Z MEN
Number of critical issues	1.071**	0.726**	1.261**
	(0.220)	(0.259)	(0.361)
Contacted by political party	1.041**	1.153**	0.937**
	(0.156)	(0.237)	(0.209)
Contacted by campaign	0.834**	0.833**	0.829**
	(0.163)	(0.231)	(0.232)
Contacted by political group	0.600**	0.516+	0.766**
	(0.202)	(0.279)	(0.291)
Positive emotions scale	−0.199	−0.249	−0.039
	(0.225)	(0.301)	(0.332)
Negative emotions scale	0.371	1.022**	−0.116
	(0.229)	(0.298)	(0.337)
Church attendance	−0.602**	−0.603*	−0.533*
	(0.187)	(0.254)	(0.271)
Constant	−1.789**	−2.256**	−0.168
	(0.358)	(0.444)	(0.427)
Observations	2,014	1,071	943
R-squared	0.324	0.401	0.261

Note: Robust standard errors in parentheses.
**$p < 0.01$, *$p < 0.05$, +$p < 0.10$

TABLE A.9 Political engagement model, LGBTQ and straight Zoomers, in 2019

DEPENDENT VARIABLE: POLITICAL ENGAGEMENT SCALE	LGBTQ ZOOMERS ONLY	STRAIGHT ZOOMERS ONLY
Female	0.801**	0.241*
	(0.250)	(0.121)
Current educational status	0.210	0.260
	(0.622)	(0.362)
Family income	1.016*	0.942**
	(0.435)	(0.209)
Black	−0.415	−0.584**
	(0.320)	(0.153)
Latinx	−0.119	−0.122
	(0.345)	(0.164)
Asian	−0.456	−0.095
	(0.493)	(0.248)
Multiracial	0.306	0.352
	(0.425)	(0.237)
Follows politics closely	2.639**	1.350**
	(0.489)	(0.219)
Understands how government works	0.465	1.363**
	(0.435)	(0.236)
Politics does not help people	−0.015	0.659**
	(0.521)	(0.233)
Party strength	−0.014	0.462*
	(0.363)	(0.187)
Ideology	1.637**	0.534+
	(0.475)	(0.308)
High school activities	2.606**	2.795**
	(0.729)	(0.353)
Number of critical issues	1.652**	0.859**
	(0.481)	(0.245)

(*continued*)

TABLE A.9 (*Continued*)

DEPENDENT VARIABLE: POLITICAL ENGAGEMENT SCALE	LGBTQ ZOOMERS ONLY	STRAIGHT ZOOMERS ONLY
Contacted by political party	1.321**	0.964**
	(0.332)	(0.177)
Contacted by campaign	1.087**	0.774**
	(0.368)	(0.181)
Contacted by political group	0.699	0.564*
	(0.448)	(0.225)
Positive emotions scale	-0.203	-0.245
	(0.529)	(0.246)
Negative emotions scale	1.138*	0.203
	(0.470)	(0.260)
Church attendance	-0.607	-0.590**
	(.470)	(.208)
Constant	-3.317**	-1.352**
	(0.693)	(0.421)
Observations	451	1,563
R-squared	0.406	0.307

Note: Robust standard errors in parentheses.
**$p < 0.01$, *$p < 0.05$, + $p < 0.10$

TABLE A.10 Political engagement model, Gen Z Women and Men, in 2022

DEPENDENT VARIABLE: POLITICAL ENGAGEMENT SCALE	FULL MODEL	GEN Z WOMEN ONLY	GEN Z MEN ONLY
Female	−0.086	—	—
	(0.156)		
Current educational status	−0.282	−0.999*	0.523
	(0.412)	(0.482)	(0.635)
Family income	0.614*	0.675+	0.517
	(0.251)	(0.359)	(0.334)
Black	−0.358*	−0.278	−0.545*
	(0.156)	(0.221)	(0.228)
Latinx	0.050	−0.125	0.286
	(0.195)	(0.243)	(0.314)
Asian	0.160	0.117	0.281
	(0.282)	(0.395)	(0.386)
Multiracial	0.321	0.199	0.536
	(0.293)	(0.422)	(0.419)
LGBTQ	0.583**	0.798**	0.203
	(0.183)	(0.215)	(0.322)
Follows politics closely	1.144**	1.389**	0.792+
	(0.274)	(0.358)	(0.404)
Understands how government works	1.027**	1.028*	1.171*
	(0.310)	(0.406)	(0.460)
Politics does not help people	0.955**	1.152**	0.776*
	(0.275)	(0.405)	(0.381)
Party strength	0.097	−0.102	0.314
	(0.201)	(0.281)	(0.287)
Ideology	0.161	0.346	−0.052
	(0.292)	(0.385)	(0.413)
High school activities	3.185**	2.667**	3.593**
	(0.539)	(0.614)	(0.838)

(*continued*)

TABLE A.10 (*Continued*)

DEPENDENT VARIABLE: POLITICAL ENGAGEMENT SCALE	FULL MODEL	GEN Z WOMEN ONLY	GEN Z MEN ONLY
Number of critical issues	1.005**	1.204**	0.842+
	(0.307)	(0.370)	(0.491)
Contacted by political party	0.728**	0.643*	0.903**
	(0.206)	(0.318)	(0.273)
Contacted by campaign	1.043**	0.879**	1.256**
	(0.187)	(0.257)	(0.266)
Contacted by political group	0.764**	0.667*	0.854*
	(0.243)	(0.320)	(0.345)
Positive emotions scale	−0.317	−0.068	−0.578
	(0.286)	(0.453)	(0.365)
Negative emotions scale	0.305	0.785*	−0.178
	(0.285)	(0.381)	(0.408)
Church attendance	−0.303	0.357	−0.785*
	(0.270)	(0.374)	(0.377)
Constant	−0.478	−1.112*	−0.256
	(0.417)	(0.538)	(0.514)
Observations	1,409	713	696
R-squared	0.278	0.311	0.282

Note: Robust standard errors in parentheses.
**$p < 0.01$, *$p < 0.05$, +$p < 0.10$

TABLE A.11 Political engagement model, LGBTQ and straight Zoomers, in 2022

DEPENDENT VARIABLE: POLITICAL ENGAGEMENT SCALE	LGBTQ ZOOMERS	STRAIGHT ZOOMERS
Female	0.390	−0.229
	(0.365)	(0.170)
Current educational status	−0.742	0.050
	(0.736)	(0.481)
Family income	1.151+	0.291
	(0.595)	(0.269)
Black	−0.246	−0.371*
	(0.365)	(0.172)
Latinx	0.154	−0.037
	(0.444)	(0.209)
Asian	−0.293	0.556+
	(0.538)	(0.332)
Multiracial	0.252	0.326
	(0.613)	(0.316)
Follows politics closely	1.619**	0.878**
	(0.615)	(0.289)
Understands how government works	1.180+	1.005**
	(0.614)	(0.354)
Politics does not help people	1.648**	0.714*
	(0.621)	(0.300)
Party strength	−0.036	−0.017
	(0.491)	(0.217)
Ideology	1.383*	−0.282
	(0.629)	(0.324)
High school activities	4.281**	2.955**
	(1.132)	(0.601)
Number of critical issues	1.693*	0.853*
	(0.664)	(0.358)

(*continued*)

TABLE A.11 *(Continued)*

DEPENDENT VARIABLE: POLITICAL ENGAGEMENT SCALE	LGBTQ ZOOMERS	STRAIGHT ZOOMERS
Contacted by political party	0.369	0.875**
	(0.456)	(0.229)
Contacted by campaign	1.134**	1.017**
	(0.376)	(0.216)
Contacted by political group	0.624	0.895**
	(0.417)	(0.290)
Positive emotions scale	0.900	−0.543+
	(0.643)	(0.313)
Negative emotions scale	0.345	0.179
	(0.665)	(0.309)
Church attendance	−0.054	−0.315
	(0.635)	(0.293)
Constant	−3.368**	0.561
	(0.874)	(0.440)
Observations	356	1,053
R-squared	0.345	0.255

Note: Robust standard errors in parentheses.

**$p < 0.01$, *$p < 0.05$, +$p < 0.10$

TABLE A.12 Percentage who engaged in political activities from Public Religion Research Institute (PRRI) Gen Z survey (August 2023) by gender and LGBTQ status

	GEN Z WOMEN AND GIRLS	GEN Z MEN AND BOYS	LGBTQ ZOOMERS	STRAIGHT ZOOMERS
Signed an online petition	30**	23	44***	19
Liked or followed a campaign or organization online	23*	18	32***	15
Posted on social media about an issue that matters to you	30**	23	45***	19
Encouraged others to be politically active on social media	16	13	30***	8
Attended a public rally or demonstration	12	12	20**	7
Volunteered for a group or cause	33***	24	37**	25
Contacted an elected official	13	12	17**	9
Attended a community meeting such as a school board or city council meeting	15*	15	14	12
Avoided buying a particular brand or shopping at a certain store to register a protest	37**	30	41**	29

*$p < .05$; **$p < .01$; ***$p < .001$; Chi-square test

Source: Public Religion Research Institute (PRRI) Gen Z Survey (n = 1,500). "A Political and Cultural Glimpse into America's Future." https://www.prri.org/research/generation-zs-views-on-generational-change-and-the-challenges-and-opportunities-ahead-a-political-and-cultural-glimpse-into-americas-future/.

METHODOLOGICAL APPENDIX

CHAPTER 3 SOURCE MATERIAL

TABLE A.13 Political engagement model for all Zoomers, Gen Z women, Gen Z men, LGBTQ Zoomers, and straight Zoomers, with parents variable, in 2019

DEPENDENT VARIABLE: POLITICAL ENGAGEMENT SCALE	FULL MODEL	GEN Z WOMEN	GEN Z MEN	LGBTQ ZOOMERS	STRAIGHT ZOOMERS
Female	0.335**			0.867**	0.225+
	(0.109)			(0.244)	(0.120)
Discuss politics with parents	0.930**	1.041**	0.838**	1.428**	0.831**
	(0.166)	(0.218)	(0.248)	(0.374)	(0.186)
Current educational status	0.243	0.514	−0.077	0.208	0.272
	(0.309)	(0.423)	(0.440)	(0.603)	(0.359)
Family income	0.888**	0.883**	0.742**	1.010*	0.863**
	(0.187)	(0.254)	(0.269)	(0.425)	(0.208)
Black	−0.563**	−0.479*	−0.669**	−0.406	−0.589**
	(0.137)	(0.196)	(0.198)	(0.314)	(0.153)
Latinx	−0.130	−0.120	−0.184	−0.273	−0.120
	(0.147)	(0.200)	(0.208)	(0.342)	(0.164)
Asian	−0.211	−0.155	−0.116	−0.463	−0.083
	(0.216)	(0.375)	(0.272)	(0.514)	(0.243)
Multiracial	0.309	0.158	0.531+	0.350	0.342
	(0.202)	(0.258)	(0.308)	(0.393)	(0.235)
LGBTQ	0.126	0.302+	−0.147		
	(0.136)	(0.174)	(0.209)		
Follows politics closely	1.485**	1.747**	1.139**	2.468**	1.245**
	(0.203)	(0.287)	(0.287)	(0.483)	(0.219)
Understands how government works	0.992**	1.093**	0.925**	0.138	1.167**
	(0.211)	(0.294)	(0.305)	(0.426)	(0.242)
Politics does not help people	0.590**	1.149**	−0.061	0.031	0.649**
	(0.215)	(0.304)	(0.304)	(0.516)	(0.231)
Party strength	0.387*	0.665**	−0.052	−0.131	0.441*
	(0.164)	(0.207)	(0.248)	(0.356)	(0.188)

DEPENDENT VARIABLE: POLITICAL ENGAGEMENT SCALE	FULL MODEL	GEN Z WOMEN	GEN Z MEN	LGBTQ ZOOMERS	STRAIGHT ZOOMERS
Ideology	0.862**	0.959**	0.608+	1.886**	0.585+
	(0.254)	(0.322)	(0.367)	(0.473)	(0.304)
High school activities	2.521**	2.498**	2.529**	2.532**	2.623**
	(0.317)	(0.400)	(0.502)	(0.709)	(0.351)
Number of critical issues	0.966**	0.635*	1.156**	1.529**	0.761**
	(0.219)	(0.257)	(0.364)	(0.466)	(0.246)
Contacted by political party	1.010**	1.153**	0.886**	1.211**	0.949**
	(0.155)	(0.234)	(0.208)	(0.331)	(0.176)
Contacted by campaign	0.845**	0.858**	0.832**	0.994**	0.798**
	(0.161)	(0.227)	(0.230)	(0.354)	(0.179)
Contacted by political group	0.574**	0.521+	0.719*	0.677	0.539*
	(0.201)	(0.273)	(0.293)	(0.445)	(0.224)
Positive emotions scale	-0.282	-0.336	-0.130	-0.349	-0.320
	(0.223)	(0.296)	(0.330)	(0.514)	(0.244)
Negative emotions scale	0.282	0.952**	-0.222	1.013*	0.129
	(0.229)	(0.296)	(0.338)	(0.460)	(0.260)
Church attendance	-0.626**	-0.584*	-0.581*	-0.454	-0.637**
	(0.187)	(0.251)	(0.271)	(0.458)	(0.207)
Constant	-1.815**	-2.342**	-0.174	-3.683**	-1.330**
	(0.352)	(0.434)	(0.423)	(0.677)	(0.414)
Observations	2,013	1,070	943	451	1,562
R-squared	0.337	0.417	0.273	0.430	0.318

Note: Robust standard errors in parentheses.
**$p < 0.01$, *$p < 0.05$, +$p < 0.10$

METHODOLOGICAL APPENDIX

SURVEY INSTRUMENT: ROLE MODEL SURVEY EXPERIMENT

2019 QUALTRICS SURVEY DESIGN

Pretreatment Questions

How important is being a [man/woman] to you?

a. Extremely important
b. Very important
c. Not very important
d. Not important at all

When talking about [men/women] how often do you use "we" instead of "they"?

a. All the time
b. Most of the time
c. Some of the time
d. Rarely
e. Never

Posttreatment Questions

In the next year, how likely are you to engage in the following political or civic actions (Very likely, somewhat likely, a little likely, not at all likely)?

a. Volunteer for a political campaign
b. Participate in a protest or rally
c. Encourage people to vote
d. Discuss public affairs with friends and family
e. Follow political news
f. Run for political office
g. Attend a local public or community meeting
h. Use social media to bring attention to an issue in my community

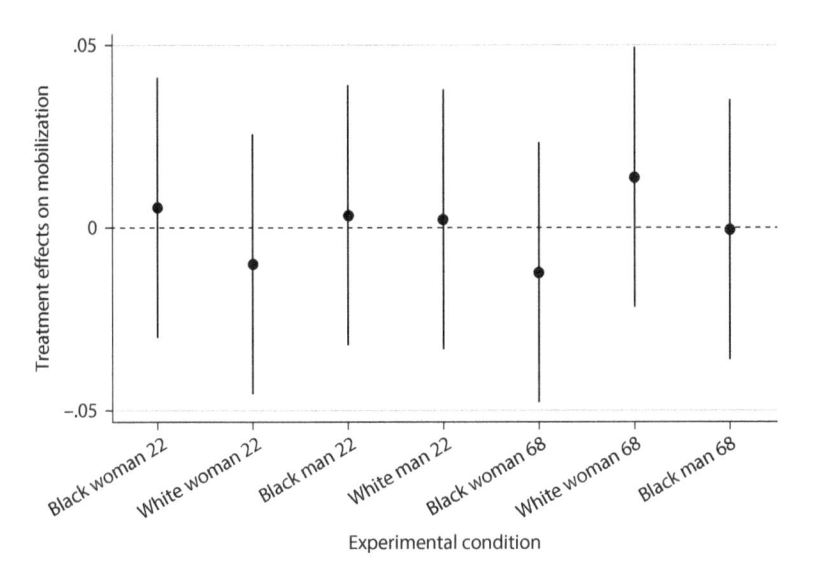

FIGURE A.7 Effect of treatment on mobilization: all Gen Zers (with white men aged sixty-eight as a baseline). Error bars represent 95 percent confidence intervals. Qualtrics survey conducted by the author in July 2019, with a sample of 2,200 Americans aged eighteen to twenty-two.

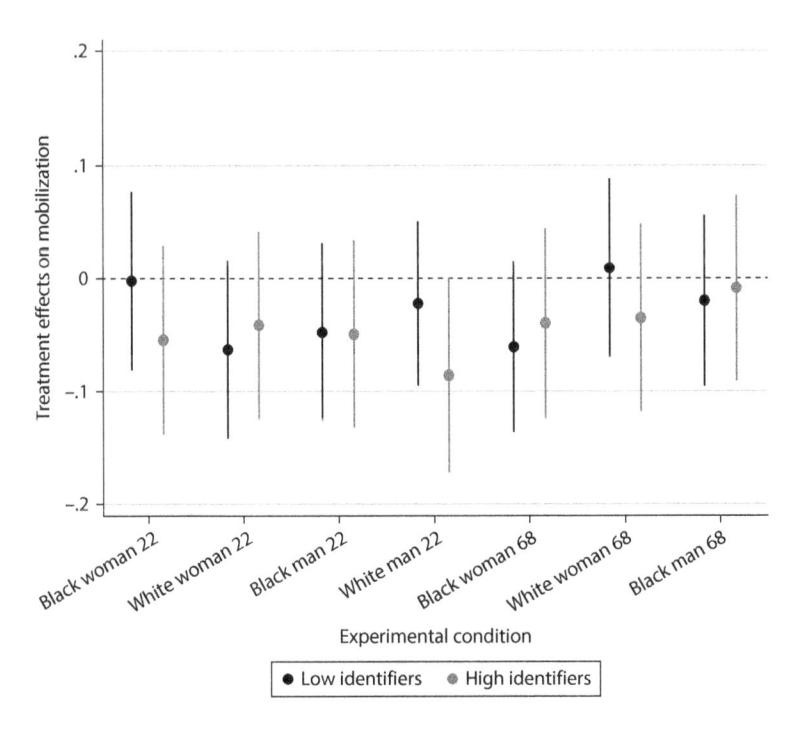

FIGURE A.8 Effect of treatment among Gen Z men by gender social identity (with white men aged sixty-eight as a baseline). Error bars represent 95 percent confidence intervals. Qualtrics survey conducted by the author in July 2019, with a sample of 2,200 Americans aged eighteen to twenty-two.

TABLE A.14 OLS regression coefficients-treatment and gender social identity on future political activity

VARIABLE	MODEL 1 MEN B/SE	MODEL 2 WOMEN B/SE
White-man-68 treatment	0.030	0.014
	(0.032)	(0.028)
Strong sense of gender social identity	0.053**	0.082**
	(0.015)	(0.014)
Treatment X gender social identity	0.013	−0.082*
	(0.044)	(0.038)
Constant	0.490	0.497**
	(0.011)	(0.010)
Prob>F	0.001	0.000
n	982	1,118

+Statistically significant at $p < 0.1$, two-tailed test.
*Statistically significant at $p < 0.05$, two-tailed test.
**Statistically significant at $p < 0.01$, two-tailed test.

TABLE A.15 Regression coefficients: treatment and gender social identity on future political activity, with control for partisanship

VARIABLE	MODEL 1 MEN B/SE	MODEL 2 WOMEN B/SE
Nonwhite-man-68 treatment	−0.028	−0.010
	(0.031)	(0.028)
Strong sense of gender social identity	0.073+	−0.003
	(0.041)	(0.035)
Partisanship (1 = Democratic, 7 = Republican)	−0.009*	−0.015**
	(0.003)	(0.003)
Treatment X gender social identity	−0.019	0.077**
	(0.044)	(0.037)
Constant	0.549**	0.566**
	(0.032)	(0.028)
Prob>F	0.000	0.000
n	982	1,116

+Statistically significant at $p < 0.1$, two-tailed test.
*Statistically significant at $p < 0.05$, two-tailed test.
**Statistically significant at $p < 0.01$, two-tailed test.

TABLE A.16 OLS regression—placebo interaction predicting future political activity as a function of ideology, treatment, and interaction of ideology and treatment

VARIABLE	MODEL 1 MEN B/SE	MODEL 2 WOMEN B/SE
Nonwhite-man-68 treatment	−0.023	0.082
	(0.064)	(0.056)
Ideology (1 = liberal, 7 = conservative)	0.009	0.008
	(0.014)	(0.012)
Treatment X ideology	−0.003	−0.012
	(0.015)	(0.013)
Constant	0.514**	0.482**
	(0.060)	(0.013)
Prob>F	0.233	0.221
n	958	1,090

+Statistically significant at $p < 0.1$, two-tailed test.
*Statistically significant at $p < 0.05$, two-tailed test.
**Statistically significant at $p < 0.01$, two-tailed test.

TABLE A.17 OLS regression—placebo interaction predicting future political activity as a function of partisanship, treatment, and interaction of partisanship and treatment

VARIABLE	MODEL 1 MEN B/SE	MODEL 2 WOMEN B/SE
Nonwhite-man-68 treatment	−0.033	−0.008
	(0.046)	(0.039)
Partisanship (1 = Democrat, 7 = Republican)	−0.007	−0.028**
	(0.010)	(0.009)
Treatment X partisanship	−0.001	0.012
	(0.011)	(0.010)
Constant	0.578**	0.608**
	(0.043)	(0.036)
Prob>F	0.047	0.000
n	982	1,116

+Statistically significant at $p < 0.1$, two-tailed test.
*Statistically significant at $p < 0.05$, two-tailed test.
**Statistically significant at $p < 0.01$, two-tailed test.

METHODOLOGICAL APPENDIX

CHAPTER 4 SOURCE MATERIAL

TABLE A.18 Political engagement model for all Zoomers, Gen Z women, Gen Z men, LGBTQ Zoomers, and straight Zoomers, with feminist variable, in 2019

DEPENDENT VARIABLE: POLITICAL ENGAGEMENT SCALE	FULL MODEL	GEN Z WOMEN	GEN Z MEN	LGBTQ ZOOMERS	STRAIGHT ZOOMERS
Female	0.269*			0.735**	0.169
	(0.113)			(0.258)	(0.124)
Feminist	0.430**	0.376*	0.054	0.343	0.422*
	(0.155)	(0.173)	(0.306)	(0.302)	(0.181)
Current educational status	0.206	0.459	−0.087	0.191	0.222
	(0.313)	(0.437)	(0.442)	(0.632)	(0.362)
Family income	0.947**	0.922**	0.805**	1.010*	0.941**
	(0.188)	(0.258)	(0.270)	(0.438)	(0.209)
Black	−0.562**	−0.437*	−0.688**	−0.402	−0.592**
	(0.138)	(0.193)	(0.200)	(0.318)	(0.154)
Latinx	−0.113	−0.105	−0.159	−0.119	−0.125
	(0.147)	(0.204)	(0.207)	(0.347)	(0.163)
Asian	−0.221	−0.159	−0.127	−0.463	−0.106
	(0.218)	(0.380)	(0.275)	(0.499)	(0.247)
Multiracial	0.329	0.165	0.550+	0.344	0.362
	(0.205)	(0.262)	(0.315)	(0.433)	(0.234)
LGBTQ	0.104	0.260	−0.119		
	(0.138)	(0.177)	(0.212)		
Follows politics closely	1.565**	1.942**	1.166**	2.604**	1.321**
	(0.202)	(0.287)	(0.285)	(0.488)	(0.217)
Understands how government works	1.164**	1.274**	1.107**	0.425	1.328**
	(0.210)	(0.291)	(0.303)	(0.435)	(0.236)
Politics does not help people	0.613**	1.111**	−0.050	−0.028	0.704**
	(0.214)	(0.305)	(0.299)	(0.519)	(0.231)
Party strength	0.376*	0.615**	−0.008	−0.047	0.418*
	(0.164)	(0.208)	(0.248)	(0.368)	(0.187)

DEPENDENT VARIABLE: POLITICAL ENGAGEMENT SCALE	FULL MODEL	GEN Z WOMEN	GEN Z MEN	LGBTQ ZOOMERS	STRAIGHT ZOOMERS
Ideology	0.686**	0.767*	0.543	1.567**	0.447
	(0.250)	(0.323)	(0.361)	(0.469)	(0.297)
High school activities	2.646**	2.633**	2.699**	2.626**	2.730**
	(0.322)	(0.407)	(0.502)	(0.729)	(0.356)
Number of critical issues	0.999**	0.657*	1.254**	1.584**	0.796**
	(0.217)	(0.259)	(0.356)	(0.482)	(0.242)
Contacted by political party	1.014**	1.137**	0.933**	1.308**	0.936**
	(0.156)	(0.235)	(0.213)	(0.330)	(0.178)
Contacted by campaign	0.825**	0.824**	0.828**	1.032**	0.779**
	(0.163)	(0.231)	(0.232)	(0.363)	(0.181)
Contacted by political group	0.587**	0.485+	0.765**	0.674	0.555*
	(0.203)	(0.280)	(0.291)	(0.444)	(0.226)
Positive emotions scale	−0.153	−0.188	−0.038	−0.134	−0.207
	(0.226)	(0.302)	(0.332)	(0.530)	(0.248)
Negative emotions scale	0.307	0.938**	−0.121	1.066*	0.146
	(0.229)	(0.296)	(0.337)	(0.468)	(0.259)
Church attendance	−0.608**	−0.593*	−0.536*	−0.623	−0.590**
	(0.187)	(0.255)	(0.269)	(0.472)	(0.207)
Constant	−1.571**	−2.109**	−0.164	−3.132**	−1.155**
	(0.358)	(0.442)	(0.426)	(0.726)	(0.411)
Observations	2,014	1,071	943	451	1,563
R-squared	0.327	0.405	0.261	0.408	0.310

Note: Robust standard errors in parentheses.
**$p < 0.01$, *$p < 0.05$, +$p < 0.10$

TABLE A.19 Political engagement model for all Zoomers, Gen Z women, Gen Z men, LGBTQ Zoomers, and straight Zoomers, with feminist variable, in 2022

DEPENDENT VARIABLE: POLITICAL ENGAGEMENT SCALE	FULL MODEL	GEN Z WOMEN	GEN Z MEN	LGBTQ ZOOMERS	STRAIGHT ZOOMERS
Female	−0.105			0.350	−0.222
	(0.171)			(0.380)	(0.192)
Feminist	0.067	0.194	−0.063	0.158	−0.026
	(0.181)	(0.190)	(0.353)	(0.327)	(0.215)
Current educational status	−0.289	−1.019*	0.529	−0.783	0.051
	(0.410)	(0.481)	(0.631)	(0.722)	(0.479)
Family income	0.616*	0.683+	0.517	1.148+	0.290
	(0.251)	(0.359)	(0.334)	(0.597)	(0.269)
Black	−0.359*	−0.284	−0.546*	−0.240	−0.370*
	(0.156)	(0.222)	(0.228)	(0.366)	(0.173)
Latinx	0.050	−0.134	0.283	0.160	−0.036
	(0.195)	(0.242)	(0.314)	(0.446)	(0.209)
Asian	0.158	0.116	0.283	−0.298	0.556+
	(0.282)	(0.394)	(0.386)	(0.542)	(0.332)
Multiracial	0.321	0.199	0.537	0.256	0.326
	(0.293)	(0.423)	(0.418)	(0.614)	(0.316)
LGBTQ	0.573**	0.775**	0.216		
	(0.188)	(0.217)	(0.340)		
Follows politics closely	1.131**	1.336**	0.799+	1.585*	0.882**
	(0.279)	(0.360)	(0.412)	(0.629)	(0.295)
Understands how government works	1.023**	1.019*	1.176*	1.168+	1.006**
	(0.312)	(0.406)	(0.469)	(0.618)	(0.355)
Politics does not help people	0.955**	1.154**	0.775*	1.648**	0.714*
	(0.275)	(0.402)	(0.381)	(0.623)	(0.300)
Party strength	0.088	−0.135	0.321	−0.052	−0.013
	(0.202)	(0.279)	(0.291)	(0.489)	(0.219)

DEPENDENT VARIABLE: POLITICAL ENGAGEMENT SCALE	FULL MODEL	GEN Z WOMEN	GEN Z MEN	LGBTQ ZOOMERS	STRAIGHT ZOOMERS
Ideology	0.146	0.304	−0.037	1.311*	−0.278
	(0.287)	(0.385)	(0.409)	(0.636)	(0.322)
High school activities	3.175**	2.635**	3.601**	4.236**	2.959**
	(0.541)	(0.615)	(0.842)	(1.149)	(0.601)
Number of critical issues	1.002**	1.206**	0.848+	1.713*	0.855*
	(0.306)	(0.370)	(0.478)	(0.664)	(0.353)
Contacted by political party	0.727**	0.646*	0.905**	0.372	0.875**
	(0.206)	(0.317)	(0.272)	(0.457)	(0.229)
Contacted by campaign	1.042**	0.883**	1.258**	1.137**	1.017**
	(0.187)	(0.257)	(0.265)	(0.377)	(0.215)
Contacted by political group	0.763**	0.662*	0.853*	0.637	0.896**
	(0.243)	(0.320)	(0.346)	(0.416)	(0.289)
Positive emotions scale	−0.322	−0.087	−0.576	0.870	−0.542+
	(0.287)	(0.454)	(0.367)	(0.650)	(0.314)
Negative emotions scale	0.305	0.794*	−0.176	0.327	0.178
	(0.285)	(0.382)	(0.408)	(0.660)	(0.309)
Church attendance	−0.300	0.376	−0.784*	−0.056	−0.317
	(0.271)	(0.374)	(0.377)	(0.634)	(0.295)
Constant	−0.437	−1.111*	−0.278	−3.265**	0.547
	(0.420)	(0.540)	(0.525)	(0.879)	(0.449)
Observations	1,409	713	696	356	1,053
R-squared	0.278	0.312	0.282	0.345	0.255

Note: Robust standard errors in parentheses.
**$p < 0.01$, *$p < 0.05$, +$p < 0.10$

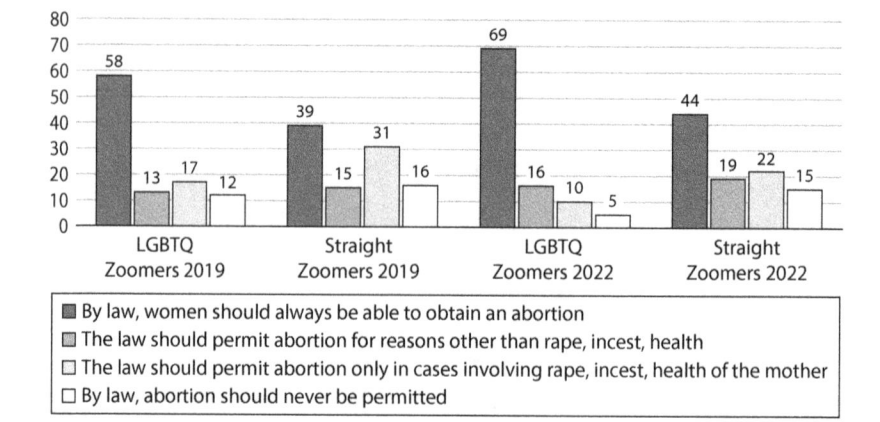

	LGBTQ Zoomers 2019	Straight Zoomers 2019	LGBTQ Zoomers 2022	Straight Zoomers 2022
By law, women should always be able to obtain an abortion	58	39	69	44
The law should permit abortion for reasons other than rape, incest, health	13	15	16	19
The law should permit abortion only in cases involving rape, incest, health of the mother	17	31	10	22
By law, abortion should never be permitted	12	16	5	15

FIGURE A.9 Abortion attitudes, by LGBTQ status, percentages as of July 2019 and May 2022. Qualtrics survey conducted by the author in July 2019, with a sample of 2,200 Americans aged eighteen to twenty-two; Qualtrics survey conducted by the author in May 2022, with a sample of 1,600 Americans aged eighteen to twenty-four.

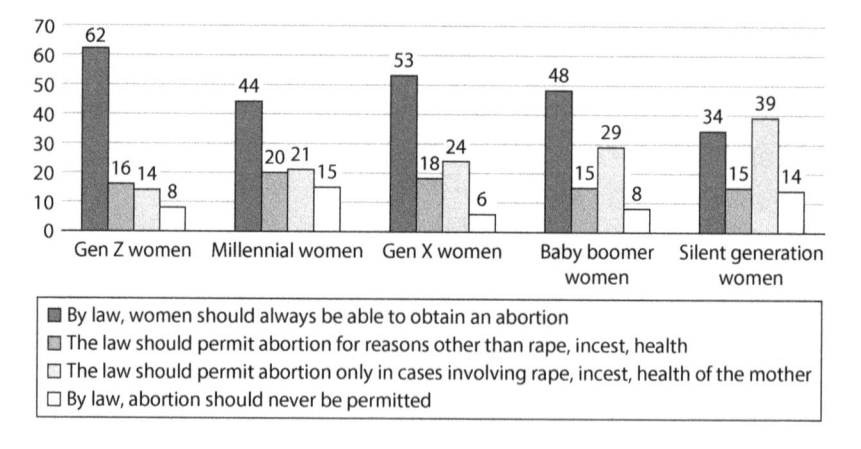

	Gen Z women	Millennial women	Gen X women	Baby boomer women	Silent generation women
By law, women should always be able to obtain an abortion	62	44	53	48	34
The law should permit abortion for reasons other than rape, incest, health	16	20	18	15	15
The law should permit abortion only in cases involving rape, incest, health of the mother	14	21	24	29	39
By law, abortion should never be permitted	8	15	6	8	14

FIGURE A.10 Abortion attitudes among women, by generation, expressed as percentages as of May 2022. Qualtrics survey conducted by the author in May 2022, with a sample of 1,600 Americans aged eighteen to twenty-four; 1,600 Americans aged twenty-five or older.

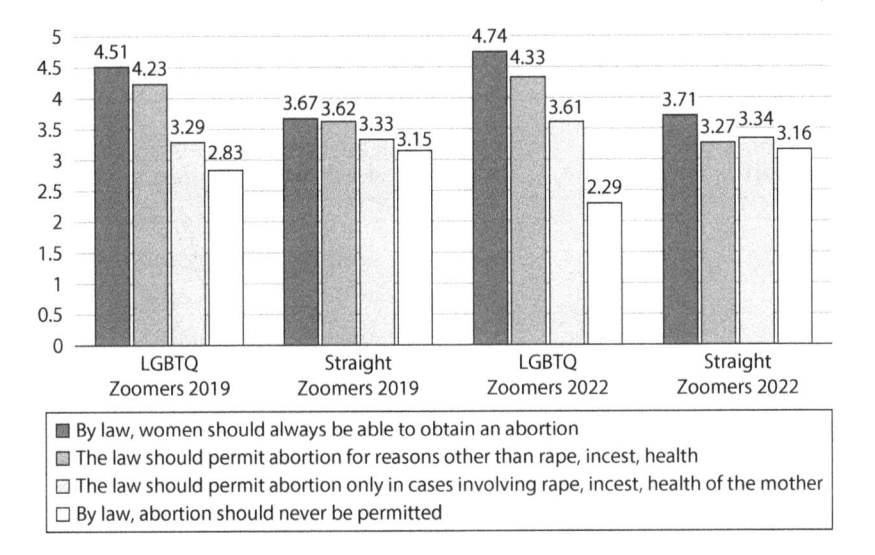

	LGBTQ Zoomers 2019	Straight Zoomers 2019	LGBTQ Zoomers 2022	Straight Zoomers 2022
By law, women should always be able to obtain an abortion	4.51	3.67	4.74	3.71
The law should permit abortion for reasons other than rape, incest, health	4.23	3.62	4.33	3.27
The law should permit abortion only in cases involving rape, incest, health of the mother	3.29	3.33	3.61	3.34
By law, abortion should never be permitted	2.83	3.15	2.29	3.16

FIGURE A.11 Average number of political activities, by abortion attitudes and by LGBTQ status. Qualtrics survey conducted by the author in July 2019, with a sample of 2,200 Americans aged eighteen to twenty-two; Qualtrics survey conducted by the author in May 2022, with a sample of 1,600 Americans aged eighteen to twenty-four.

TABLE A.20 Political engagement model for all Zoomers, Gen Z women, Gen Z men, LGBTQ Zoomers, and straight Zoomers, with abortion variable, in 2019

DEPENDENT VARIABLE: POLITICAL ENGAGEMENT SCALE	FULL MODEL	GEN Z WOMEN	GEN Z MEN	LGBTQ ZOOMERS	STRAIGHT ZOOMERS
Female	0.329**			0.819**	0.225+
	(0.111)			(0.242)	(0.121)
Abortion views	0.205**	0.299**	0.079	0.613**	0.114*
	(0.052)	(0.070)	(0.074)	(0.118)	(0.056)
Current educational status	0.249	0.490	−0.072	0.106	0.272
	(0.310)	(0.425)	(0.441)	(0.595)	(0.362)
Family income	0.907**	0.871**	0.779**	0.689	0.926**
	(0.190)	(0.259)	(0.272)	(0.428)	(0.211)
Black	−0.543**	−0.423*	−0.681**	−0.271	−0.580**
	(0.138)	(0.190)	(0.199)	(0.304)	(0.153)
Latinx	−0.133	−0.149	−0.171	−0.096	−0.141
	(0.148)	(0.207)	(0.207)	(0.334)	(0.165)
Asian	−0.283	−0.179	−0.172	−0.529	−0.142
	(0.220)	(0.377)	(0.276)	(0.485)	(0.250)
Multiracial	0.285	0.073	0.547+	0.182	0.344
	(0.204)	(0.263)	(0.314)	(0.421)	(0.235)
LGBTQ	0.122	0.293+	−0.135		
	(0.137)	(0.175)	(0.211)		
Follows politics closely	1.600**	1.957**	1.185**	2.825**	1.349**
	(0.202)	(0.283)	(0.285)	(0.468)	(0.219)
Understands how government works	1.233**	1.366**	1.114**	0.658	1.369**
	(0.210)	(0.293)	(0.303)	(0.441)	(0.237)
Politics does not help people	0.528*	1.087**	−0.081	−0.238	0.635**
	(0.218)	(0.307)	(0.311)	(0.490)	(0.235)
Party strength	0.415*	0.629**	0.001	−0.202	0.466*
	(0.164)	(0.205)	(0.247)	(0.356)	(0.187)

DEPENDENT VARIABLE: POLITICAL ENGAGEMENT SCALE	FULL MODEL	GEN Z WOMEN	GEN Z MEN	LGBTQ ZOOMERS	STRAIGHT ZOOMERS
Ideology	0.645*	0.635+	0.505	1.339**	0.457
	(0.259)	(0.331)	(0.375)	(0.476)	(0.308)
High school activities	2.596**	2.542**	2.676**	2.580**	2.736**
	(0.321)	(0.406)	(0.504)	(0.689)	(0.358)
Number of critical issues	1.014**	0.666*	1.227**	1.328**	0.835**
	(0.221)	(0.258)	(0.364)	(0.474)	(0.248)
Contacted by political party	1.063**	1.205**	0.943**	1.318**	0.978**
	(0.157)	(0.239)	(0.210)	(0.337)	(0.178)
Contacted by campaign	0.861**	0.901**	0.828**	1.145**	0.790**
	(0.163)	(0.228)	(0.232)	(0.357)	(0.181)
Contacted by political group	0.607**	0.504+	0.768**	0.799+	0.563*
	(0.202)	(0.278)	(0.292)	(0.425)	(0.226)
Positive emotions scale	−0.133	−0.086	−0.038	0.083	−0.216
	(0.225)	(0.303)	(0.332)	(0.512)	(0.246)
Negative emotions scale	0.294	0.876**	−0.125	1.038*	0.160
	(0.229)	(0.297)	(0.337)	(0.456)	(0.259)
Church attendance	−0.418*	−0.348	−0.451	−0.187	−0.483*
	(0.194)	(0.265)	(0.279)	(0.457)	(0.219)
Constant	−2.258**	−2.954**	−0.363	−4.953**	−1.602**
	(0.374)	(0.485)	(0.449)	(0.721)	(0.441)
Observations	2,007	1,066	941	449	1,558
R-squared	0.329	0.411	0.263	0.445	0.308

Note. Robust standard errors in parentheses.
*Abortion: 1 = most pro-life position; 4 = most pro-choice position.
**$p < 0.01$, *$p < 0.05$, + $p < 0.10$

TABLE A.21 Political engagement model for all Zoomers, Gen Z women, Gen Z men, LGBTQ Zoomers, and straight Zoomers, with abortion variable, in 2022

DEPENDENT VARIABLE: POLITICAL ENGAGEMENT SCALE	FULL MODEL	GEN Z WOMEN	GEN Z MEN	LGBTQ ZOOMERS	STRAIGHT ZOOMERS
Female	−0.143			0.369	−0.291+
	(0.157)			(0.369)	(0.170)
Abortion views	0.178**	0.184+	0.137	0.183	0.162*
	(0.067)	(0.102)	(0.086)	(0.185)	(0.070)
Current educational status	−0.333	−1.038*	0.472	−0.794	0.005
	(0.404)	(0.481)	(0.621)	(0.721)	(0.473)
Family income	0.592*	0.626+	0.516	1.122+	0.265
	(0.250)	(0.360)	(0.330)	(0.600)	(0.267)
Black	−0.370*	−0.308	−0.539*	−0.242	−0.389*
	(0.156)	(0.223)	(0.227)	(0.365)	(0.172)
Latinx	0.052	−0.126	0.289	0.127	−0.028
	(0.194)	(0.241)	(0.314)	(0.445)	(0.207)
Asian	0.148	0.133	0.252	−0.282	0.538
	(0.284)	(0.397)	(0.387)	(0.533)	(0.334)
Multiracial	0.345	0.206	0.558	0.234	0.358
	(0.292)	(0.421)	(0.419)	(0.612)	(0.316)
LGBTQ	0.539**	0.769**	0.153		
	(0.182)	(0.215)	(0.321)		
Follows politics closely	1.136**	1.347**	0.808*	1.626**	0.870**
	(0.274)	(0.362)	(0.404)	(0.620)	(0.288)
Understands how government works	1.036**	1.057*	1.166*	1.202+	1.018**
	(0.312)	(0.409)	(0.462)	(0.614)	(0.355)
Politics does not help people	0.949**	1.162**	0.763*	1.592*	0.717*
	(0.274)	(0.405)	(0.381)	(0.616)	(0.299)
Party strength	0.123	−0.066	0.328	−0.066	0.021
	(0.202)	(0.282)	(0.287)	(0.498)	(0.218)

DEPENDENT VARIABLE: POLITICAL ENGAGEMENT SCALE	FULL MODEL	GEN Z WOMEN	GEN Z MEN	LGBTQ ZOOMERS	STRAIGHT ZOOMERS
Ideology	0.050	0.201	-0.112	1.292*	-0.377
	(0.291)	(0.397)	(0.412)	(0.626)	(0.324)
High school activities	3.143**	2.662**	3.542**	4.268**	2.914**
	(0.532)	(0.608)	(0.833)	(1.113)	(0.595)
Number of critical issues	0.891**	1.080**	0.763	1.547*	0.759*
	(0.307)	(0.370)	(0.492)	(0.669)	(0.359)
Contacted by political party	0.729**	0.661*	0.888**	0.378	0.872**
	(0.204)	(0.316)	(0.270)	(0.461)	(0.226)
Contacted by campaign	1.023**	0.863**	1.235**	1.135**	0.989**
	(0.186)	(0.255)	(0.265)	(0.378)	(0.214)
Contacted by political group	0.753**	0.675*	0.829*	0.617	0.878**
	(0.241)	(0.316)	(0.345)	(0.416)	(0.288)
Positive emotions scale	-0.284	-0.017	-0.557	0.890	-0.499
	(0.283)	(0.446)	(0.361)	(0.644)	(0.309)
Negative emotions scale	0.315	0.761*	-0.140	0.268	0.213
	(0.282)	(0.380)	(0.402)	(0.683)	(0.303)
Church attendance	-0.186	0.446	-0.681+	-0.025	-0.188
	(0.270)	(0.384)	(0.375)	(0.632)	(0.292)
Constant	-0.835+	-1.576**	-0.599	-3.715**	0.203
	(0.432)	(0.592)	(0.553)	(0.925)	(0.462)
Observations	1,408	713	695	356	1,052
R-squared	0.282	0.314	0.284	0.347	0.259

Note: Robust standard errors in parentheses.
*Abortion: 1 = most pro-life position; 4 = most pro-choice position.
**$p < 0.01$, *$p < 0.05$, +$p < 0.10$

METHODOLOGICAL APPENDIX

TABLE A.22 Marginal values of political engagement scale for LGBTQ Zoomers and straight Zoomers, in 2019 and 2022

	2019 MARGINAL EFFECTS FOR LGBTQ ZOOMERS	2019 MARGINAL EFFECTS FOR STRAIGHT ZOOMERS	2022 MARGINAL EFFECTS FOR STRAIGHT ZOOMERS
By law, abortion should always be legal.	4.38 activities	3.63 activities	3.71 activities
Permittable for reasons other than rape, incest, health	4.30	3.54	3.23
Only permissible for reasons of rape, incest, or health	3.58	3.44	3.51
By law, abortion should never be permitted.	2.39	3.21	3.10

Note: Only in cases where abortion attitudes are significant.

CHAPTER 5 SOURCE MATERIAL

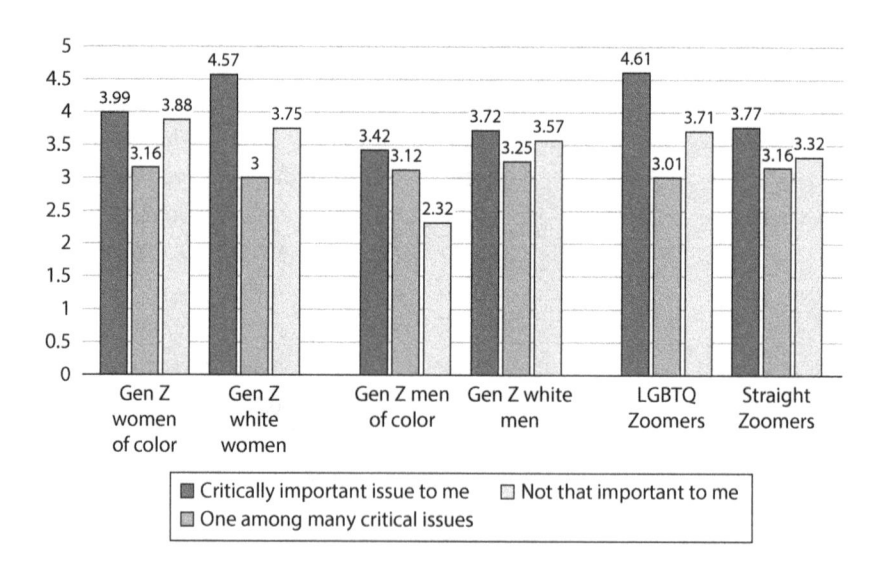

FIGURE A.12 Average number of political actions, by gender, race, LGBTQ status, and the importance of racial equality. Qualtrics survey conducted by the author in July 2019, with a sample of 2,200 Americans aged eighteen to twenty-two.

TABLE A.23 Political engagement model for all Zoomers, Gen Z women, Gen Z men, LGBTQ Zoomers, and straight Zoomers, with racial equality issue, in 2019

DEPENDENT VARIABLE: POLITICAL ENGAGEMENT SCALE	FULL MODEL	GEN Z WOMEN	GEN Z MEN	LGBTQ ZOOMERS	STRAIGHT ZOOMERS
Female	0.327**			0.806**	0.220+
	(0.110)			(0.248)	(0.121)
Racial equality is a critical issue	0.531**	0.473**	0.464**	1.022**	0.402**
	(0.117)	(0.145)	(0.179)	(0.251)	(0.130)
Current educational status	0.309	0.585	-0.007	0.453	0.294
	(0.310)	(0.427)	(0.441)	(0.601)	(0.363)
Family income	0.941**	0.946**	0.806**	0.967*	0.946**
	(0.188)	(0.253)	(0.273)	(0.431)	(0.209)
Black	-0.600**	-0.463*	-0.726**	-0.518	-0.618**
	(0.139)	(0.195)	(0.203)	(0.325)	(0.154)
Latinx	-0.136	-0.137	-0.161	-0.182	-0.142
	(0.147)	(0.202)	(0.207)	(0.349)	(0.163)
Asian	-0.283	-0.173	-0.212	-0.507	-0.155
	(0.223)	(0.382)	(0.281)	(0.492)	(0.253)
Multiracial	0.274	0.107	0.562+	0.252	0.321
	(0.208)	(0.264)	(0.320)	(0.415)	(0.239)
LGBTQ	0.127	0.293+	-0.141		
	(0.138)	(0.175)	(0.215)		
Follows politics closely	1.618**	1.994**	1.147**	2.760**	1.354**
	(0.204)	(0.289)	(0.292)	(0.497)	(0.220)
Understands how government works	1.217**	1.362**	1.140**	0.605	1.340**
	(0.209)	(0.290)	(0.304)	(0.437)	(0.236)
Politics does not help people	0.528*	1.098**	-0.131	-0.047	0.598*
	(0.216)	(0.303)	(0.307)	(0.511)	(0.233)
Party strength	0.414*	0.645**	0.003	-0.062	0.456*
	(0.164)	(0.208)	(0.248)	(0.367)	(0.187)
Ideology	0.792**	0.776*	0.639+	1.596**	0.564+
	(0.262)	(0.328)	(0.383)	(0.475)	(0.314)

(continued)

TABLE A.23 (*Continued*)

DEPENDENT VARIABLE: POLITICAL ENGAGEMENT SCALE	FULL MODEL	GEN Z WOMEN	GEN Z MEN	LGBTQ ZOOMERS	STRAIGHT ZOOMERS
High school activities	2.644**	2.589**	2.660**	2.574**	2.743**
	(0.318)	(0.402)	(0.504)	(0.709)	(0.352)
Contacted by political party	1.051**	1.176**	0.965**	1.387**	0.964**
	(0.156)	(0.236)	(0.208)	(0.325)	(0.178)
Contacted by campaign	0.826**	0.801**	0.825**	1.089**	0.771**
	(0.164)	(0.227)	(0.235)	(0.356)	(0.183)
Contacted by political group	0.630**	0.434	0.887**	0.720	0.606**
	(0.206)	(0.274)	(0.300)	(0.446)	(0.231)
Positive emotions scale	−0.112	−0.190	0.096	−0.079	−0.169
	(0.226)	(0.298)	(0.335)	(0.518)	(0.247)
Negative emotions scale	0.441*	1.026**	0.033	1.169**	0.266
	(0.224)	(0.289)	(0.333)	(0.442)	(0.255)
Church attendance	−0.620**	−0.581*	−0.576*	−0.582	−0.602**
	(0.187)	(0.253)	(0.271)	(0.459)	(0.207)
Constant	−1.604**	−2.144**	−0.006	−3.331**	−1.154**
	(0.357)	(0.441)	(0.426)	(0.682)	(0.419)
Observations	2,027	1,080	947	454	1,573
R-squared	0.320	0.401	0.255	0.412	0.302

Note: Robust standard errors in parentheses. I omitted the critical issues scale from this model because it is highly correlated with the racial equality measure.
*Racial equality is a critical issue: 1 = yes; 0 = no.
**$p < 0.01$, *$p < 0.05$, +$p < 0.10$

TABLE A.24 Political engagement model for Zoomers by gender and race, with racial equality issue, in 2022

DEPENDENT VARIABLE: POLITICAL ENGAGEMENT SCALE	GEN Z WOMEN OF COLOR	WHITE GEN Z WOMEN	GEN Z MEN OF COLOR	WHITE GEN Z MEN
Female	—	—	—	—
Racial equality is a critical issue	0.442*	0.409*	0.507*	0.416
	(0.220)	(0.189)	(0.218)	(0.276)
Current educational status	1.134+	−0.132	0.145	−0.230
	(0.609)	(0.594)	(0.539)	(0.705)
Family income	0.796*	1.053**	0.752*	1.004*
	(0.387)	(0.330)	(0.362)	(0.394)
LGBTQ	0.088	0.466*	0.190	−0.518
	(0.269)	(0.227)	(0.306)	(0.327)
Follows politics closely	1.622**	2.244**	1.206**	1.232**
	(0.461)	(0.363)	(0.393)	(0.429)
Understands how government works	1.429**	1.244**	0.766+	1.346**
	(0.379)	(0.421)	(0.410)	(0.464)
Politics does not help people	1.520**	0.729+	0.479	−0.657
	(0.470)	(0.389)	(0.365)	(0.476)
Party strength	0.274	0.962**	−0.046	0.137
	(0.314)	(0.272)	(0.313)	(0.365)
Ideology	0.516	1.007*	−0.277	1.690**
	(0.479)	(0.447)	(0.402)	(0.633)
High school activities	2.045**	2.935**	1.969**	3.044**
	(0.609)	(0.509)	(0.627)	(0.753)
Contacted by political party	1.432**	0.991**	1.369**	0.499
	(0.344)	(0.322)	(0.267)	(0.318)
Contacted by campaign	0.539+	1.026**	0.642*	0.990**
	(0.324)	(0.313)	(0.295)	(0.358)
Contacted by political group	0.533	0.362	0.769*	0.957+
	(0.372)	(0.399)	(0.332)	(0.491)
Positive emotions scale	−0.483	0.153	0.341	−0.098
	(0.405)	(0.436)	(0.424)	(0.484)

(continued)

TABLE A.24 *(Continued)*

DEPENDENT VARIABLE: POLITICAL ENGAGEMENT SCALE	GEN Z WOMEN OF COLOR	WHITE GEN Z WOMEN	GEN Z MEN OF COLOR	WHITE GEN Z MEN
Negative emotions scale	0.776+	1.362**	−0.045	0.057
	(0.421)	(0.408)	(0.414)	(0.513)
Church attendance	−0.250	−0.776*	−0.615*	−0.637
	(0.367)	(0.344)	(0.306)	(0.454)
Constant	−1.816**	−2.482**	0.181	−0.380
	(0.652)	(0.589)	(0.519)	(0.631)
Observations	540	540	536	411
R-squared	0.327	0.477	0.236	0.282

Note: Robust standard errors in parentheses. I omitted the critical issues scale from this model because it is highly correlated with the racial equality measure.
*Racial equality is a critical issue: 1 = yes; 0 = no.
**$p < 0.01$, *$p < 0.05$, + $p < 0.10$

TABLE A.25 Political engagement model for all Zoomers, Gen Z women, Gen Z men, LGBTQ Zoomers, and straight Zoomers, with racial equality issue, in 2022

DEPENDENT VARIABLE: POLITICAL ENGAGEMENT SCALE	FULL MODEL	GEN Z WOMEN	GEN Z MEN	LGBTQ ZOOMERS	STRAIGHT ZOOMERS
Female	-0.064			0.432	-0.213
	(0.152)			(0.366)	(0.162)
Racial equality is a critical issue	0.449**	0.467*	0.440*	0.504++	0.416*
	(0.147)	(0.205)	(0.212)	(0.352)	(0.165)
Current educational status	-0.323	-0.994*	0.454	-0.794	0.017
	(0.410)	(0.488)	(0.625)	(0.759)	(0.475)
Family income	0.673**	0.707+	0.591+	1.113+	0.363
	(0.253)	(0.362)	(0.335)	(0.606)	(0.271)
Black	-0.388*	-0.328	-0.572*	-0.222	-0.410*
	(0.158)	(0.225)	(0.227)	(0.361)	(0.175)
Latinx	0.097	-0.098	0.353	0.260	0.001
	(0.195)	(0.246)	(0.309)	(0.435)	(0.210)
Asian	0.163	0.111	0.283	-0.280	0.550+
	(0.286)	(0.406)	(0.387)	(0.560)	(0.333)
Multiracial	0.323	0.200	0.521	0.331	0.315
	(0.298)	(0.432)	(0.419)	(0.637)	(0.321)
LGBTQ	0.567**	0.786**	0.188		
	(0.184)	(0.217)	(0.321)		
Follows politics closely	1.204**	1.447**	0.859*	1.748**	0.925**
	(0.273)	(0.360)	(0.399)	(0.619)	(0.286)
Understands how government works	1.059**	1.063*	1.179**	1.100+	1.056**
	(0.310)	(0.413)	(0.456)	(0.615)	(0.349)
Politics does not help people	0.940**	1.110**	0.767*	1.587*	0.714*
	(0.276)	(0.409)	(0.380)	(0.651)	(0.298)
Party strength	0.131	-0.079	0.357	0.039	0.019
	(0.202)	(0.279)	(0.291)	(0.489)	(0.219)
Ideology	0.095	0.287	-0.130	1.249*	-0.325
	(0.296)	(0.397)	(0.417)	(0.633)	(0.330)

(*continued*)

TABLE A.25 (Continued)

DEPENDENT VARIABLE: POLITICAL ENGAGEMENT SCALE	FULL MODEL	GEN Z WOMEN	GEN Z MEN	LGBTQ ZOOMERS	STRAIGHT ZOOMERS
High school activities	3.194**	2.694**	3.600**	4.317**	2.952**
	(0.543)	(0.616)	(0.844)	(1.129)	(0.607)
Contacted by political party	0.737**	0.658*	0.906**	0.411	0.874**
	(0.207)	(0.317)	(0.275)	(0.452)	(0.228)
Contacted by campaign	1.013**	0.854**	1.222**	1.097**	0.989**
	(0.184)	(0.255)	(0.259)	(0.375)	(0.210)
Contacted by political group	0.724**	0.581+	0.842*	0.555	0.864**
	(0.241)	(0.326)	(0.338)	(0.434)	(0.284)
Positive emotions scale	-0.307	-0.029	-0.606+	0.860	-0.537+
	(0.290)	(0.459)	(0.364)	(0.654)	(0.315)
Negative emotions scale	0.448+	0.986**	-0.056	0.744	0.293
	(0.267)	(0.356)	(0.394)	(0.597)	(0.294)
Church attendance	-0.364	0.264	-0.836*	-0.257	-0.355
	(0.274)	(0.374)	(0.383)	(0.627)	(0.300)
Constant	-0.337	-0.845	-0.128	-2.935**	0.636
	(0.419)	(0.527)	(0.520)	(0.883)	(0.441)
Observations	1,409	713	696	356	1,053
R-squared	0.275	0.303	0.282	0.329	0.253

Note: Robust standard errors in parentheses. I omitted the critical issues scale from this model because it is highly correlated with the racial equality measure.
*Racial equality is a critical issue: 1 = yes; 0 = no.
**$p < 0.01$, *$p < 0.05$, + $p < 0.10$, ++ $p = .153$

TABLE A.26 Political engagement model for Zoomers by gender and race, with racial equality issue, in 2022

DEPENDENT VARIABLE: POLITICAL ENGAGEMENT SCALE	GEN Z WOMEN OF COLOR	WHITE GEN Z WOMEN	GEN Z MEN OF COLOR	WHITE GEN Z MEN
Female	—	—	—	—
Racial equality is a critical issue	0.474+	0.598++	0.476+	0.287
	(0.243)	(0.377)	(0.284)	(0.298)
Current educational status	−0.485	−1.940*	0.435	0.411
	(0.549)	(0.942)	(0.818)	(0.874)
Family income	0.208	1.823**	0.199	1.053*
	(0.428)	(0.613)	(0.537)	(0.447)
LGBTQ	0.743**	0.801*	0.141	0.315
	(0.254)	(0.401)	(0.581)	(0.381)
Follows politics closely	1.550**	1.423*	1.073+	0.694
	(0.423)	(0.621)	(0.593)	(0.507)
Understands how government works	0.833*	1.487+	1.560*	1.037+
	(0.420)	(0.881)	(0.690)	(0.601)
Politics does not help people	0.736	1.663*	1.149+	0.689
	(0.495)	(0.705)	(0.687)	(0.427)
Party strength	−0.588+	0.826+	−0.655	0.750*
	(0.348)	(0.472)	(0.481)	(0.345)
Ideology	0.599	−0.266	−0.987	0.418
	(0.502)	(0.730)	(0.623)	(0.574)
High school activities	2.632**	2.977**	4.359**	2.980**
	(0.809)	(0.910)	(1.453)	(0.962)
Contacted by political party	0.917*	0.345	1.100*	0.928**
	(0.385)	(0.511)	(0.434)	(0.347)
Contacted by campaign	1.006**	0.679	1.172**	1.145**
	(0.288)	(0.427)	(0.397)	(0.317)
Contacted by political group	0.792*	0.229	−0.036	1.355**
	(0.379)	(0.549)	(0.471)	(0.452)
Positive emotions scale	−0.319	0.236	−0.412	−0.693
	(0.526)	(0.800)	(0.536)	(0.503)

(continued)

TABLE A.26 (*Continued*)

DEPENDENT VARIABLE: POLITICAL ENGAGEMENT SCALE	GEN Z WOMEN OF COLOR	WHITE GEN Z WOMEN	GEN Z MEN OF COLOR	WHITE GEN Z MEN
Negative emotions scale	1.348**	0.112	−0.074	−0.036
	(0.408)	(0.612)	(0.502)	(0.554)
Church attendance	−0.159	0.899	−0.861	−0.679
	(0.454)	(0.627)	(0.599)	(0.459)
Constant	−0.642	−1.408+	0.361	−0.454
	(0.634)	(0.766)	(0.714)	(0.665)
Observations	497	216	338	358
R-squared	0.301	0.363	0.271	0.317

Note: Robust standard errors in parentheses.
*Racial equality is a critical issue: 1 = yes; 0 = no.
**$p < 0.01$, *$p < 0.05$, + $p < 0.10$, ++ $p = .114$

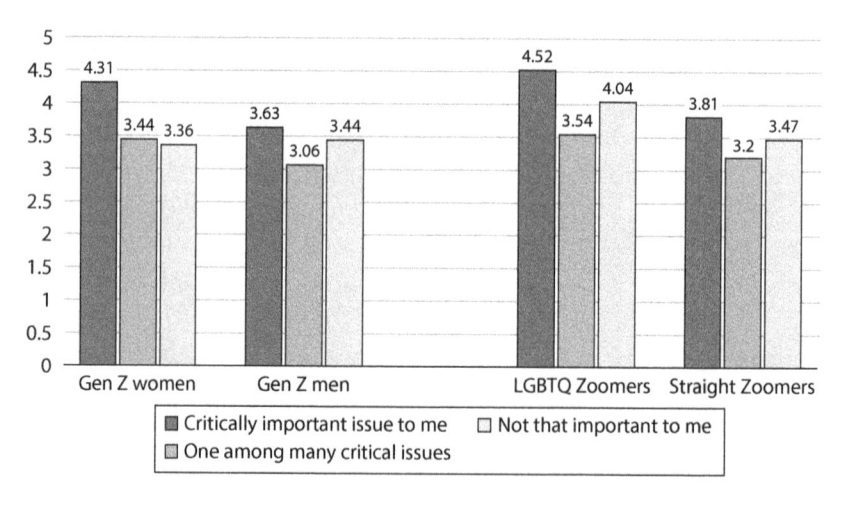

FIGURE A.13 Average numbers of political actions, by gender, LGBTQ status, and the importance of LGBTQ equality. Qualtrics survey conducted by the author in July 2019, with a sample of 2,200 Americans aged eighteen to twenty-two.

TABLE A.27 Political engagement model for all Zoomers, Gen Z women, Gen Z men, LGBTQ Zoomers, and straight Zoomers, with LGBTQ equality as a critical issue, in 2019

DEPENDENT VARIABLE: POLITICAL ENGAGEMENT SCALE	FULL MODEL	GEN Z WOMEN	GEN Z MEN	LGBTQ ZOOMERS	STRAIGHT ZOOMERS
Female	0.339**			0.818**	0.239*
	(0.111)			(0.254)	(0.121)
LGBTQ equality is a critical issue	0.222+	0.188++	0.139	0.642**	0.080
	(0.117)	(0.143)	(0.189)	(0.245)	(0.133)
Current educational status	0.221	0.487	-0.066	0.235	0.236
	(0.311)	(0.429)	(0.443)	(0.595)	(0.363)
Family income	0.942**	0.937**	0.806**	0.883*	0.958**
	(0.188)	(0.254)	(0.273)	(0.427)	(0.210)
Black	-0.577**	-0.438*	-0.709**	-0.365	-0.607**
	(0.139)	(0.194)	(0.203)	(0.321)	(0.154)
Latinx	-0.120	-0.106	-0.164	-0.091	-0.132
	(0.148)	(0.203)	(0.208)	(0.344)	(0.165)
Asian	-0.218	-0.081	-0.183	-0.496	-0.098
	(0.223)	(0.381)	(0.283)	(0.477)	(0.252)
Multiracial	0.340	0.153	0.640*	0.411	0.368
	(0.207)	(0.262)	(0.317)	(0.421)	(0.238)
LGBTQ	0.100	0.265	-0.152		
	(0.140)	(0.178)	(0.218)		
Follows politics closely	1.581**	2.013**	1.057**	2.599**	1.337**
	(0.205)	(0.289)	(0.289)	(0.497)	(0.220)
Understands how government works	1.257**	1.345**	1.224**	0.665	1.374**
	(0.211)	(0.291)	(0.307)	(0.434)	(0.237)
Politics does not help people	0.545*	1.116**	-0.119	-0.061	0.611**
	(0.217)	(0.304)	(0.308)	(0.515)	(0.234)
Party strength	0.424*	0.661**	-0.007	0.044	0.459*
	(0.165)	(0.208)	(0.249)	(0.364)	(0.188)
Ideology	0.852**	0.861**	0.664+	1.604**	0.637*
	(0.265)	(0.326)	(0.389)	(0.482)	(0.315)

(*continued*)

TABLE A.27 (Continued)

DEPENDENT VARIABLE: POLITICAL ENGAGEMENT SCALE	FULL MODEL	GEN Z WOMEN	GEN Z MEN	LGBTQ ZOOMERS	STRAIGHT ZOOMERS
High school activities	2.628**	2.606**	2.616**	2.525**	2.736**
	(0.320)	(0.402)	(0.508)	(0.709)	(0.355)
Contacted by political party	1.041**	1.160**	0.963**	1.351**	0.959**
	(0.157)	(0.238)	(0.211)	(0.327)	(0.178)
Contacted by campaign	0.808**	0.805**	0.795**	1.082**	0.753**
	(0.165)	(0.229)	(0.236)	(0.360)	(0.184)
Contacted by political group	0.610**	0.460	0.840**	0.668	0.597*
	(0.209)	(0.281)	(0.300)	(0.448)	(0.233)
Positive emotions scale	−0.137	−0.230	0.087	−0.134	−0.194
	(0.226)	(0.299)	(0.337)	(0.524)	(0.246)
Negative emotions scale	0.594**	1.171**	0.173	1.431**	0.399
	(0.218)	(0.283)	(0.324)	(0.444)	(0.247)
Church attendance	−0.616**	−0.605*	−0.545*	−0.706	−0.583**
	(0.188)	(0.254)	(0.273)	(0.472)	(0.208)
Constant	−1.530**	−2.064**	0.097	−3.135**	−1.127**
	(0.359)	(0.439)	(0.425)	(0.690)	(0.421)
Observations	2,029	1,081	948	455	1,574
R-squared	0.313	0.395	0.248	0.398	0.296

Note: Robust standard errors in parentheses.
*LGBTQ equality is a critical issue: 1 = yes; 0 = no.
**$p < 0.01$, *$p < 0.05$, + $p < 0.10$, ++ $p = .189$

TABLE A.28 Political engagement model for all Zoomers, Gen Z women, Gen Z men, LGBTQ Zoomers, and straight Zoomers, with racial equality as a critical issue, in 2022

DEPENDENT VARIABLE: POLITICAL ENGAGEMENT SCALE	FULL MODEL	GEN Z WOMEN	GEN Z MEN	LGBTQ ZOOMERS	STRAIGHT ZOOMERS
Female	−0.008			0.449	−0.151
	(0.156)			(0.374)	(0.168)
LGBTQ equality is a critical issue	0.171	0.343+	0.046	0.545++	0.117
	(0.161)	(0.199)	(0.261)	(0.348)	(0.178)
Current educational status	−0.301	−1.049*	0.503	−0.835	0.046
	(0.413)	(0.476)	(0.639)	(0.742)	(0.480)
Family income	0.670**	0.705+	0.581+	1.118+	0.362
	(0.255)	(0.364)	(0.339)	(0.615)	(0.273)
Black	−0.350*	−0.291	−0.513*	−0.215	−0.360*
	(0.159)	(0.223)	(0.238)	(0.358)	(0.176)
Latinx	0.130	−0.047	0.360	0.325	0.030
	(0.195)	(0.241)	(0.310)	(0.431)	(0.211)
Asian	0.179	0.144	0.309	−0.249	0.575+
	(0.289)	(0.414)	(0.392)	(0.555)	(0.337)
Multiracial	0.365	0.228	0.593	0.357	0.359
	(0.298)	(0.429)	(0.425)	(0.642)	(0.317)
LGBTQ	0.573**	0.747**	0.234		
	(0.191)	(0.218)	(0.346)		
Follows politics closely	1.175**	1.394**	0.824*	1.647**	0.899**
	(0.275)	(0.365)	(0.402)	(0.630)	(0.288)
Understands how government works	1.068**	1.049*	1.258**	1.109+	1.078**
	(0.310)	(0.413)	(0.452)	(0.616)	(0.348)
Politics does not help people	0.944**	1.085**	0.801*	1.584*	0.700*
	(0.277)	(0.410)	(0.380)	(0.645)	(0.300)
Party strength	0.121	−0.063	0.328	0.070	−0.006
	(0.202)	(0.280)	(0.287)	(0.488)	(0.217)
Ideology	0.190	0.314	0.032	1.321*	−0.242
	(0.289)	(0.389)	(0.405)	(0.627)	(0.317)

(continued)

TABLE A.28 *(Continued)*

DEPENDENT VARIABLE: POLITICAL ENGAGEMENT SCALE	FULL MODEL	GEN Z WOMEN	GEN Z MEN	LGBTQ ZOOMERS	STRAIGHT ZOOMERS
High school activities	3.217**	2.691**	3.644**	4.331**	2.972**
	(0.542)	(0.618)	(0.838)	(1.130)	(0.607)
Contacted by political party	0.756**	0.690*	0.925**	0.355	0.898**
	(0.209)	(0.321)	(0.277)	(0.449)	(0.234)
Contacted by campaign	0.991**	0.840**	1.208**	1.174**	0.957**
	(0.184)	(0.254)	(0.257)	(0.375)	(0.206)
Contacted by political group	0.705**	0.565+	0.808*	0.586	0.837**
	(0.242)	(0.323)	(0.345)	(0.427)	(0.286)
Positive emotions scale	-0.264	-0.080	-0.477	0.814	-0.467
	(0.287)	(0.461)	(0.362)	(0.670)	(0.310)
Negative emotions scale	0.530+	1.097**	-0.024	0.851	0.348
	(0.271)	(0.351)	(0.402)	(0.595)	(0.299)
Church attendance	-0.397	0.222	-0.834*	-0.221	-0.379
	(0.273)	(0.373)	(0.383)	(0.626)	(0.301)
Constant	-0.369	-0.713	-0.197	-3.077**	0.606
	(0.424)	(0.544)	(0.520)	(0.901)	(0.451)
Observations	1,409	713	696	356	1,053
R-squared	0.269	0.300	0.276	0.331	0.247

Note: Robust standard errors in parentheses.
*LGBTQ equality is a critical issue: 1 = yes; 0 = no.
**$p < 0.01$, *$p < 0.05$, + $p < 0.10$, ++ $p = .12$

METHODOLOGICAL APPENDIX

CHAPTER 6 SOURCE MATERIAL

TABLE A.29 Political engagement model for all Zoomers, Gen Z women, Gen Z men, LGBTQ Zoomers, and straight Zoomers, with mass shooting as a critical issue, in 2019

DEPENDENT VARIABLE: POLITICAL ENGAGEMENT SCALE	FULL MODEL	GEN Z WOMEN	GEN Z MEN	LGBTQ ZOOMERS	STRAIGHT ZOOMERS
Female	0.326**			0.807**	0.222+
	(0.109)			(0.246)	(0.120)
Mass shooting is a critical issue	0.505**	0.507**	0.451**	1.107**	0.324**
	(0.111)	(0.149)	(0.165)	(0.279)	(0.122)
Current educational status	0.301	0.629	−0.050	0.304	0.299
	(0.311)	(0.431)	(0.439)	(0.607)	(0.363)
Family income	0.923**	0.937**	0.776**	0.830*	0.945**
	(0.188)	(0.253)	(0.272)	(0.419)	(0.210)
Black	−0.566**	−0.420*	−0.709**	−0.400	−0.598**
	(0.139)	(0.192)	(0.201)	(0.315)	(0.154)
Latinx	−0.124	−0.097	−0.180	−0.105	−0.136
	(0.147)	(0.201)	(0.208)	(0.331)	(0.164)
Asian	−0.233	−0.093	−0.200	−0.451	−0.112
	(0.218)	(0.379)	(0.273)	(0.488)	(0.248)
Multiracial	0.317	0.153	0.586+	0.440	0.346
	(0.208)	(0.265)	(0.318)	(0.426)	(0.239)
LGBTQ	0.167	0.329+	−0.100		
	(0.137)	(0.175)	(0.213)		
Follows politics closely	1.639**	2.018**	1.153**	2.722**	1.373**
	(0.205)	(0.286)	(0.291)	(0.486)	(0.221)
Understands how government works	1.261**	1.356**	1.219**	0.613	1.381**
	(0.208)	(0.286)	(0.305)	(0.422)	(0.236)
Politics does not help people	0.585**	1.137**	−0.068	0.037	0.643**
	(0.215)	(0.303)	(0.306)	(0.500)	(0.233)
Party strength	0.389*	0.640**	−0.054	−0.113	0.441*
	(0.165)	(0.206)	(0.251)	(0.358)	(0.188)

(continued)

TABLE A.29 (Continued)

DEPENDENT VARIABLE: POLITICAL ENGAGEMENT SCALE	FULL MODEL	GEN Z WOMEN	GEN Z MEN	LGBTQ ZOOMERS	STRAIGHT ZOOMERS
Ideology	0.857**	0.859**	0.661+	1.755**	0.622*
	(0.262)	(0.325)	(0.383)	(0.465)	(0.313)
High school activities	2.627**	2.606**	2.606**	2.676**	2.721**
	(0.316)	(0.396)	(0.504)	(0.698)	(0.352)
Contacted by political party	1.053**	1.160**	0.976**	1.350**	0.967**
	(0.156)	(0.235)	(0.209)	(0.321)	(0.178)
Contacted by campaign	0.850**	0.852**	0.827**	1.118**	0.786**
	(0.165)	(0.229)	(0.236)	(0.365)	(0.184)
Contacted by political group	0.617**	0.481+	0.837**	0.721	0.594*
	(0.206)	(0.274)	(0.300)	(0.442)	(0.232)
Positive emotions scale	−0.136	−0.248	0.099	−0.168	−0.186
	(0.225)	(0.299)	(0.334)	(0.510)	(0.247)
Negative emotions scale	0.453*	1.021**	0.024	0.979*	0.309
	(0.220)	(0.290)	(0.322)	(0.477)	(0.248)
Church attendance	−0.615**	−0.595*	−0.548*	−0.598	−0.591**
	(0.187)	(0.251)	(0.272)	(0.455)	(0.207)
Constant	−1.723**	−2.298**	−0.069	−3.269**	−1.256**
	(0.359)	(0.444)	(0.427)	(0.684)	(0.425)
Observations	2,030	1,082	948	455	1,575
R-squared	0.320	0.402	0.255	0.416	0.300

Note: Robust standard errors in parentheses.
*Mass shooting is a critical issue: 1 = yes; 0 = no.
**$p < 0.01$, *$p < 0.05$, +$p < 0.10$

TABLE A.30 Political engagement model for all Zoomers, Gen Z women, Gen Z men, LGBTQ Zoomers, and straight Zoomers, with mass shooting as a critical issue, in 2022

DEPENDENT VARIABLE: POLITICAL ENGAGEMENT SCALE	FULL MODEL	GEN Z WOMEN	GEN Z MEN	LGBTQ ZOOMERS	STRAIGHT ZOOMERS
Female	−0.060			0.361	−0.190
	(0.155)			(0.375)	(0.166)
Mass shooting is a critical issue	0.536**	0.642**	0.387+	1.054**	0.376*
	(0.150)	(0.218)	(0.205)	(0.358)	(0.170)
Current educational status	−0.241	−0.832+	0.477	−0.463	0.058
	(0.407)	(0.480)	(0.634)	(0.743)	(0.477)
Family income	0.613*	0.658+	0.532	1.065+	0.314
	(0.251)	(0.361)	(0.336)	(0.591)	(0.271)
Black	−0.354*	−0.277	−0.531*	−0.220	−0.367*
	(0.156)	(0.221)	(0.226)	(0.365)	(0.173)
Latinx	0.069	−0.069	0.278	0.193	−0.016
	(0.192)	(0.242)	(0.304)	(0.428)	(0.207)
Asian	0.177	0.153	0.297	−0.287	0.568+
	(0.283)	(0.408)	(0.381)	(0.571)	(0.331)
Multiracial	0.344	0.219	0.574	0.339	0.343
	(0.294)	(0.421)	(0.422)	(0.617)	(0.316)
LGBTQ	0.627**	0.849**	0.244		
	(0.181)	(0.216)	(0.317)		
Follows politics closely	1.201**	1.419**	0.869*	1.776**	0.918**
	(0.270)	(0.357)	(0.395)	(0.588)	(0.286)
Understands how government works	1.122**	1.078**	1.271**	1.328*	1.090**
	(0.310)	(0.416)	(0.446)	(0.622)	(0.348)
Politics does not help people	1.007**	1.106**	0.879*	1.616**	0.762*
	(0.276)	(0.405)	(0.382)	(0.623)	(0.305)
Party strength	0.089	−0.084	0.291	0.032	−0.033
	(0.201)	(0.282)	(0.288)	(0.470)	(0.220)
Ideology	0.139	0.329	−0.053	1.201+	−0.282
	(0.294)	(0.390)	(0.420)	(0.613)	(0.334)

(continued)

TABLE A.30 (*Continued*)

DEPENDENT VARIABLE: POLITICAL ENGAGEMENT SCALE	FULL MODEL	GEN Z WOMEN	GEN Z MEN	LGBTQ ZOOMERS	STRAIGHT ZOOMERS
High school activities	3.280**	2.719**	3.718**	4.207**	3.059**
	(0.535)	(0.615)	(0.832)	(1.137)	(0.603)
Contacted by political party	0.768**	0.680*	0.943**	0.380	0.911**
	(0.208)	(0.316)	(0.277)	(0.437)	(0.234)
Contacted by campaign	1.009**	0.847**	1.219**	1.110**	0.979**
	(0.182)	(0.252)	(0.258)	(0.362)	(0.209)
Contacted by political group	0.755**	0.638*	0.849*	0.680+	0.869**
	(0.240)	(0.319)	(0.341)	(0.396)	(0.285)
Positive emotions scale	−0.281	−0.057	−0.509	0.756	−0.478
	(0.284)	(0.455)	(0.360)	(0.636)	(0.313)
Negative emotions scale	0.392	0.921*	−0.108	0.404	0.272
	(0.274)	(0.372)	(0.396)	(0.620)	(0.298)
Church attendance	−0.376	0.231	−0.827*	−0.377	−0.353
	(0.269)	(0.366)	(0.379)	(0.610)	(0.297)
Constant	−0.533	−1.047*	−0.317	−3.087**	0.490
	(0.417)	(0.531)	(0.523)	(0.872)	(0.441)
Observations	1,409	713	696	356	1,053
R-squared	0.278	0.308	0.281	0.348	0.252

Note: Robust standard errors in parentheses.
*Mass shooting is a critical issue: 1 = yes; 0 = no.
**$p < 0.01$, *$p < 0.05$, + $p < 0.10$

TABLE A.31 Political engagement model for all Zoomers, Gen Z women, Gen Z men, LGBTQ Zoomers, and straight Zoomers, with climate change as a critical issue, in 2019

DEPENDENT VARIABLE: POLITICAL ENGAGEMENT SCALE	FULL MODEL	GEN Z WOMEN	GEN Z MEN	LGBTQ ZOOMERS	STRAIGHT ZOOMERS
Female	0.356**			0.826**	0.247*
	(0.110)			(0.250)	(0.120)
Climate change is a critical issue	0.506**	0.381*	0.550**	0.932**	0.388**
	(0.116)	(0.156)	(0.165)	(0.271)	(0.128)
Current educational status	0.216	0.521	−0.131	0.190	0.236
	(0.309)	(0.426)	(0.439)	(0.609)	(0.360)
Family income	0.902**	0.902**	0.781**	0.666	0.937**
	(0.187)	(0.255)	(0.269)	(0.421)	(0.209)
Black	−0.520**	−0.408*	−0.637**	−0.312	−0.558**
	(0.139)	(0.194)	(0.202)	(0.316)	(0.154)
Latinx	−0.121	−0.092	−0.181	−0.049	−0.139
	(0.146)	(0.203)	(0.204)	(0.334)	(0.163)
Asian	−0.254	−0.116	−0.214	−0.392	−0.136
	(0.222)	(0.379)	(0.280)	(0.496)	(0.251)
Multiracial	0.317	0.135	0.609+	0.429	0.347
	(0.207)	(0.263)	(0.316)	(0.426)	(0.237)
LGBTQ	0.145	0.295+	−0.106		
	(0.137)	(0.175)	(0.214)		
Follows politics closely	1.532**	1.967**	1.033**	2.482**	1.301**
	(0.203)	(0.289)	(0.285)	(0.483)	(0.219)
Understands how government works	1.208**	1.330**	1.138**	0.556	1.338**
	(0.210)	(0.292)	(0.302)	(0.428)	(0.237)
Politics does not help people	0.526*	1.110**	−0.147	−0.092	0.601*
	(0.217)	(0.304)	(0.307)	(0.513)	(0.234)
Party strength	0.419*	0.647**	0.006	−0.041	0.457*
	(0.162)	(0.206)	(0.245)	(0.355)	(0.186)
Ideology	0.794**	0.841*	0.561	1.660**	0.557+
	(0.264)	(0.331)	(0.382)	(0.477)	(0.316)

(*continued*)

TABLE A.31 (Continued)

DEPENDENT VARIABLE: POLITICAL ENGAGEMENT SCALE	FULL MODEL	GEN Z WOMEN	GEN Z MEN	LGBTQ ZOOMERS	STRAIGHT ZOOMERS
High school activities	2.605**	2.581**	2.606**	2.566**	2.711**
	(0.319)	(0.401)	(0.503)	(0.708)	(0.353)
Contacted by political party	1.033**	1.150**	0.948**	1.347**	0.949**
	(0.157)	(0.237)	(0.208)	(0.329)	(0.179)
Contacted by campaign	0.831**	0.813**	0.829**	1.008**	0.783**
	(0.165)	(0.229)	(0.234)	(0.367)	(0.183)
Contacted by political group	0.647**	0.473+	0.890**	0.605	0.630**
	(0.208)	(0.279)	(0.301)	(0.464)	(0.232)
Positive emotions scale	−0.102	−0.179	0.088	−0.067	−0.169
	(0.226)	(0.298)	(0.336)	(0.529)	(0.247)
Negative emotions scale	0.503*	1.108**	0.043	1.499**	0.292
	(0.221)	(0.296)	(0.319)	(0.453)	(0.251)
Church attendance	−0.543**	−0.539*	−0.483+	−0.415	−0.540**
	(0.187)	(0.252)	(0.271)	(0.466)	(0.207)
Constant	−1.623**	−2.142**	0.057	−3.218**	−1.185**
	(0.358)	(0.439)	(0.422)	(0.681)	(0.421)
Observations	2,027	1,081	946	455	1,572
R-squared	0.319	0.398	0.259	0.408	0.302

Note: Robust standard errors in parentheses.
*Climate change is a critical issue: 1 = yes; 0 = no.
**$p < 0.01$, *$p < 0.05$, +$p < 0.10$

TABLE A.32 Political engagement model for all Zoomers, Gen Z women, Gen Z men, LGBTQ Zoomers, and straight Zoomers, with climate change as a critical issue, in 2022

DEPENDENT VARIABLE: POLITICAL ENGAGEMENT SCALE	FULL MODEL	GEN Z WOMEN	GEN Z MEN	LGBTQ ZOOMERS	STRAIGHT ZOOMERS
Female	-0.028			0.477	-0.175
	(0.153)			(0.366)	(0.165)
Climate change is a critical issue	0.430**	0.621**	0.234	0.737*	0.336*
	(0.145)	(0.192)	(0.208)	(0.364)	(0.156)
Current educational status	-0.312	-0.954+	0.467	-0.746	0.022
	(0.414)	(0.488)	(0.637)	(0.761)	(0.480)
Family income	0.657**	0.732*	0.558	1.098+	0.347
	(0.254)	(0.363)	(0.339)	(0.602)	(0.273)
Black	-0.342*	-0.268	-0.516*	-0.187	-0.360*
	(0.156)	(0.222)	(0.224)	(0.361)	(0.171)
Latinx	0.079	-0.105	0.330	0.247	-0.012
	(0.192)	(0.240)	(0.306)	(0.431)	(0.206)
Asian	0.110	0.020	0.288	-0.333	0.515
	(0.290)	(0.416)	(0.388)	(0.538)	(0.340)
Multiracial	0.372	0.257	0.586	0.431	0.350
	(0.294)	(0.417)	(0.424)	(0.609)	(0.318)
LGBTQ	0.603**	0.830**	0.221		
	(0.181)	(0.214)	(0.320)		
Follows politics closely	1.151**	1.327**	0.833*	1.625**	0.888**
	(0.275)	(0.363)	(0.399)	(0.622)	(0.288)
Understands how government works	1.045**	0.995*	1.235**	1.073+	1.058**
	(0.310)	(0.402)	(0.448)	(0.603)	(0.349)
Politics does not help people	0.889**	1.007*	0.776*	1.563*	0.651*
	(0.277)	(0.409)	(0.379)	(0.652)	(0.298)
Party strength	0.111	-0.101	0.329	-0.065	0.006
	(0.202)	(0.279)	(0.289)	(0.498)	(0.217)
Ideology	0.143	0.295	-0.013	1.296*	-0.273
	(0.298)	(0.388)	(0.432)	(0.634)	(0.334)

(continued)

TABLE A.32 *(Continued)*

DEPENDENT VARIABLE: POLITICAL ENGAGEMENT SCALE	FULL MODEL	GEN Z WOMEN	GEN Z MEN	LGBTQ ZOOMERS	STRAIGHT ZOOMERS
High school activities	3.213**	2.603**	3.671**	4.326**	2.966**
	(0.541)	(0.612)	(0.833)	(1.137)	(0.604)
Contacted by political party	0.723**	0.609+	0.914**	0.376	0.862**
	(0.207)	(0.320)	(0.277)	(0.449)	(0.229)
Contacted by campaign	1.015**	0.889**	1.211**	1.137**	0.981**
	(0.183)	(0.253)	(0.259)	(0.375)	(0.209)
Contacted by political group	0.708**	0.600+	0.806*	0.552	0.839**
	(0.238)	(0.327)	(0.335)	(0.433)	(0.280)
Positive emotions scale	−0.270	0.011	−0.516	0.824	−0.476
	(0.287)	(0.449)	(0.367)	(0.662)	(0.313)
Negative emotions scale	0.480+	0.986**	−0.038	0.675	0.329
	(0.266)	(0.353)	(0.395)	(0.589)	(0.293)
Church attendance	−0.323	0.269	−0.784*	−0.160	−0.320
	(0.279)	(0.371)	(0.394)	(0.634)	(0.305)
Constant	−0.387	−0.783	−0.210	−2.988**	0.586
	(0.423)	(0.540)	(0.515)	(0.864)	(0.448)
Observations	1,409	713	696	356	1,053
R-squared	0.274	0.308	0.278	0.336	0.251

Note: Robust standard errors in parentheses.
*Climate change is a critical issue: 1 = yes; 0 = no.
**$p < 0.01$, *$p < 0.05$, + $p < 0.10$

TABLE A.33 Political engagement model for all Zoomers, Gen Z women, Gen Z men, LGBTQ Zoomers, and straight Zoomers, with positive views of socialism, in 2019

DEPENDENT VARIABLE: POLITICAL ENGAGEMENT SCALE	FULL MODEL	GEN Z WOMEN	GEN Z MEN	LGBTQ ZOOMERS	STRAIGHT ZOOMERS
Female	0.359**			0.858**	0.247*
	(0.110)			(0.257)	(0.120)
Positive views of socialism	−0.016	0.255+	−0.355*	0.076	−0.043
	(0.108)	(0.143)	(0.159)	(0.252)	(0.119)
Current educational status	0.239	0.478	−0.002	0.265	0.249
	(0.310)	(0.424)	(0.441)	(0.593)	(0.363)
Family income	0.930**	0.962**	0.782**	0.782+	0.949**
	(0.189)	(0.255)	(0.273)	(0.431)	(0.211)
Black	−0.577**	−0.468*	−0.677**	−0.372	−0.610**
	(0.139)	(0.194)	(0.201)	(0.318)	(0.155)
Latinx	−0.115	−0.115	−0.169	−0.116	−0.126
	(0.147)	(0.204)	(0.208)	(0.345)	(0.164)
Asian	−0.219	−0.075	−0.175	−0.512	−0.099
	(0.223)	(0.377)	(0.285)	(0.483)	(0.253)
Multiracial	0.347+	0.136	0.658*	0.483	0.373
	(0.208)	(0.261)	(0.312)	(0.429)	(0.237)
LGBTQ	0.134	0.283	−0.121		
	(0.139)	(0.177)	(0.218)		
Follows politics closely	1.583**	2.023**	0.987**	2.635**	1.331**
	(0.205)	(0.289)	(0.285)	(0.505)	(0.220)
Understands how government works	1.271**	1.346**	1.233**	0.666	1.389**
	(0.212)	(0.289)	(0.306)	(0.436)	(0.238)
Politics does not help people	0.542*	1.144**	−0.149	0.003	0.608**
	(0.218)	(0.305)	(0.309)	(0.518)	(0.234)
Party strength	0.420*	0.639**	−0.001	−0.045	0.461*
	(0.164)	(0.208)	(0.248)	(0.370)	(0.187)
Ideology	0.904**	0.893**	0.769*	1.748**	0.667*
	(0.265)	(0.329)	(0.387)	(0.482)	(0.315)

(continued)

TABLE A.33 (*Continued*)

DEPENDENT VARIABLE: POLITICAL ENGAGEMENT SCALE	FULL MODEL	GEN Z WOMEN	GEN Z MEN	LGBTQ ZOOMERS	STRAIGHT ZOOMERS
High school activities	2.653**	2.601**	2.645**	2.590**	2.750**
	(0.321)	(0.402)	(0.503)	(0.716)	(0.354)
Contacted by political party	1.048**	1.144**	1.001**	1.341**	0.967**
	(0.157)	(0.239)	(0.208)	(0.337)	(0.179)
Contacted by campaign	0.814**	0.821**	0.797**	1.112**	0.755**
	(0.165)	(0.228)	(0.234)	(0.365)	(0.183)
Contacted by political group	0.605**	0.483+	0.822**	0.657	0.592*
	(0.208)	(0.280)	(0.299)	(0.464)	(0.231)
Positive emotions scale	−0.150	−0.232	0.062	−0.203	−0.196
	(0.227)	(0.300)	(0.336)	(0.537)	(0.247)
Negative emotions scale	0.670**	1.187**	0.244	1.765**	0.426+
	(0.216)	(0.283)	(0.315)	(0.441)	(0.245)
Church attendance	−0.623**	−0.584*	−0.538*	−0.708	−0.590**
	(0.188)	(0.255)	(0.270)	(0.472)	(0.208)
Constant	−1.562**	−2.161**	0.222	−3.159**	−1.136**
	(0.363)	(0.450)	(0.425)	(0.685)	(0.428)
Observations	2,028	1,079	949	454	1,574
R-squared	0.311	0.396	0.252	0.386	0.297

Note: Robust standard errors in parentheses.
*View socialism as positive: 1 = yes; 0 = no.
**$p < 0.01$, *$p < 0.05$, +$p < 0.10$

METHODOLOGICAL APPENDIX

CHAPTER 7 SOURCE MATERIAL

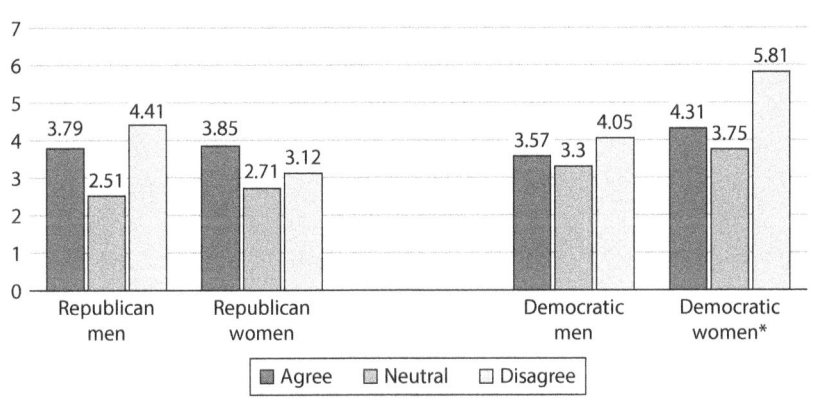

	Republican men	Republican women	Democratic men	Democratic women*
Agree	3.79	3.85	3.57	4.31
Neutral	2.51	2.71	3.3	3.75
Disagree	4.41	3.12	4.05	5.81

Differences are significant at $p < 0.5$

FIGURE A.14 Average number of political actions, by gender, party, and agreement that the political climate prevents them from saying things they believe. Qualtrics survey conducted by the author in July 2019, with a sample of 2,200 Americans aged eighteen to twenty-two.

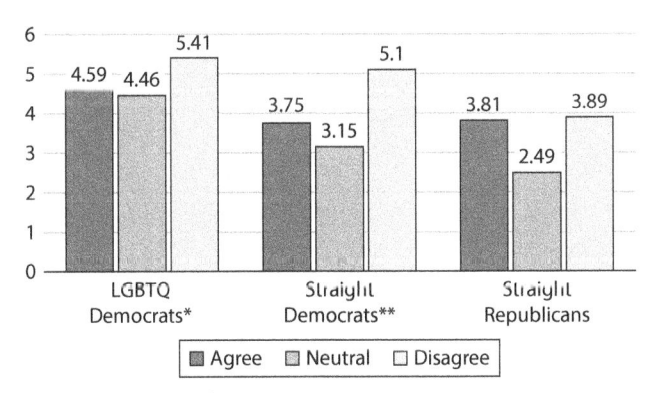

	LGBTQ Democrats*	Straight Democrats**	Straight Republicans
Agree	4.59	3.75	3.81
Neutral	4.46	3.15	2.49
Disagree	5.41	5.1	3.89

Differents are significant at $*p < .10$; $**p < .01$

FIGURE A.15 Average number of political actions, by LGBTQ status, party, and agreement that the political climate prevents them from saying things they believe. LGBTQ Republicans are omitted because there are fewer than one hundred cases. Qualtrics survey conducted by the author in July 2019, with a sample of 2,200 Americans aged eighteen to twenty-two.

TABLE A.34 Political engagement model for all Zoomers, Gen Z women, Gen Z men, LGBTQ Zoomers, and straight Zoomers, with America being soft and feminine measure, in 2019

DEPENDENT VARIABLE: POLITICAL ENGAGEMENT SCALE	FULL MODEL	GEN Z WOMEN	GEN Z MEN	LGBTQ ZOOMERS	STRAIGHT ZOOMERS
Female	0.265*			0.645**	0.182
	(0.112)			(0.248)	(0.123)
America is too soft and feminine (disagree)	0.184**	0.251**	0.102	0.391**	0.137**
	(0.046)	(0.060)	(0.070)	(0.114)	(0.051)
Current educational status	0.243	0.591	−0.116	0.349	0.254
	(0.311)	(0.427)	(0.445)	(0.600)	(0.363)
Family income	0.910**	0.887**	0.789**	0.839+	0.916**
	(0.187)	(0.253)	(0.272)	(0.437)	(0.209)
Black	−0.535**	−0.347+	−0.697**	−0.357	−0.565**
	(0.138)	(0.194)	(0.199)	(0.318)	(0.153)
Latinx	−0.102	−0.043	−0.173	−0.012	−0.123
	(0.147)	(0.201)	(0.206)	(0.345)	(0.164)
Asian	−0.253	−0.172	−0.165	−0.527	−0.127
	(0.222)	(0.380)	(0.278)	(0.515)	(0.251)
Multiracial	0.322	0.122	0.577+	0.242	0.371
	(0.208)	(0.269)	(0.316)	(0.426)	(0.239)
LGBTQ	0.099	0.239	−0.137		
	(0.137)	(0.174)	(0.213)		
Follows politics closely	1.582**	1.944**	1.167**	2.641**	1.333**
	(0.203)	(0.290)	(0.286)	(0.486)	(0.219)
Understands how government works	1.313**	1.451**	1.184**	0.649	1.445**
	(0.212)	(0.294)	(0.306)	(0.440)	(0.240)
Politics does not help people	0.411+	0.895**	−0.156	−0.341	0.528*
	(0.215)	(0.308)	(0.300)	(0.505)	(0.234)
Party strength	0.387*	0.616**	−0.023	−0.145	0.442*
	(0.163)	(0.206)	(0.247)	(0.361)	(0.187)
Ideology	0.593*	0.567+	0.463	1.423**	0.379

DEPENDENT VARIABLE: POLITICAL ENGAGEMENT SCALE	FULL MODEL	GEN Z WOMEN	GEN Z MEN	LGBTQ ZOOMERS	STRAIGHT ZOOMERS
	(0.265)	(0.330)	(0.385)	(0.463)	(0.320)
High school activities	2.643**	2.546**	2.702**	2.682**	2.755**
	(0.322)	(0.405)	(0.504)	(0.733)	(0.352)
Number of critical issues	1.024**	0.684**	1.227**	1.505**	0.829**
	(0.221)	(0.257)	(0.367)	(0.478)	(0.247)
Contacted by political party	1.056**	1.183**	0.938**	1.401**	0.972**
	(0.156)	(0.235)	(0.209)	(0.321)	(0.177)
Contacted by campaign	0.838**	0.868**	0.817**	1.137**	0.775**
	(0.163)	(0.229)	(0.232)	(0.364)	(0.181)
Contacted by political group	0.637**	0.576*	0.784**	0.809+	0.583**
	(0.201)	(0.276)	(0.291)	(0.431)	(0.225)
Positive emotions scale	−0.099	−0.090	−0.001	−0.018	−0.168
	(0.226)	(0.298)	(0.335)	(0.549)	(0.244)
Negative emotions scale	0.316	0.923**	−0.138	0.831+	0.179
	(0.231)	(0.297)	(0.339)	(0.475)	(0.261)
Church attendance	−0.519**	−0.510*	−0.479+	−0.303	−0.540**
	(0.185)	(0.250)	(0.271)	(0.495)	(0.204)
Constant	−2.094**	−2.861**	−0.390	−4.132**	−1.573**
	(0.360)	(0.454)	(0.449)	(0.754)	(0.418)
Observations	2,013	1,071	942	451	1,562
R-squared	0.330	0.412	0.263	0.426	0.310

Note: Robust standard errors in parentheses.
*America has become too soft and feminine: 1 = strongly agree; 5 = strongly disagree
**$p < 0.01$, *$p < 0.05$, +$p < 0.10$

NOTES

PREFACE

1. See Michael Dimock, "Defining Generations: Where Millennials End and Generation Z Begins," January 17, 2019, https://www.pewresearch.org/short-reads/2019/01/17/where-millennials-end-and-generation-z-begins/. Although sometimes referred to as iGen or the "Plurals," Generation Z or Gen Z is the moniker that has come to define this generation most often. Demographers typically delineate generations by roughly fifteen-year cycles; individuals born after 2012 are sometimes now described as Generation Alpha or Polars. For a thorough discussion of generational groupings, see Jean M. Twenge, *Generations: The Real Differences Between Gen Z, Millennials, Gen X, Boomers and Silences—and What They Mean for America's Future* (New York: Atria, 2023). In this book, I use the terms "Generation Z," "Gen Z," "Gen Zers," and "Zoomers" interchangeably.
2. See the appendix for more information about the interviews that I conducted and the other methods I use in the book.
3. See the appendix for more information about the original surveys I conducted.
4. See, among other studies, Richard Braungart and Margaret Braungart, "Life Court and Generational Politics," *Annual Review of Sociology* 12 (1986): 205–231; Stella M. Rouse and Ashley D. Ross, *The Politics of Millennials: Political Beliefs and Policy Preferences of America's Most Diverse Generation* (Ann Arbor: University of Michigan Press, 2018); Rouse et al., *Citizens of the World: Political Engagement and Policy Attitudes of Millennials Across the Globe* (New York: Oxford University Press, 2022).
5. Twenge, *Generations*.

PREFACE

6. Kim Parker and Ruth Igielnick, "On the Cusp of Adulthood and Facing an Uncertain Future: What We Know About Gen Z So Far," Pew Research Center, May 14, 2020, https://www.pewresearch.org/social-trends/2020/05/14/on-the-cusp-of-adulthood-and-facing-an-uncertain-future-what-we-know-about-gen-z-so-far-2/ See also Maddie Duley, "Gen Z or Boomers? Who Is Happier with How Their Tax Dollars Are Being Spent," *Yahoo News*, February 26, 2023, https://www.gobankingrates.com/taxes/gen-z-or-boomers-whos-happier-with-how-their-tax-dollars-are-being-spent/.

7. For a discussion of such challenges, see Pew Center, "How Pew Center will report on Generations Moving Forward," May 22, 2023, https://www.pewresearch.org/short-reads/2023/05/22/how-pew-research-center-will-report-on-generations-moving-forward/.

8. One of the most famous longitudinal studies that tracked the impact of formative political experiences of younger Americans involved a series of interviews with college women who attended Bennington College in the 1930s and 1940s. Although coming from more conservative families, these women became liberalized as college students and maintained those liberal political views well into their sixties and seventies. Duane F. Alwin, Ronald L. Cohen, and Theodore M. Newcomb, *Political Attitudes Over the Life Span: The Bennington Women After Fifty Years* (Madison: University of Wisconsin Press, 1991). See also M. Kent Jennings and Richard G. Niemi, *Generations and Politics: A Panel Study of Young Adults and Their Parents* (Princeton, NJ: Princeton University Press, 1981); Jon A. Krosnick and Duane F. Alwin, "Aging and Susceptibility to Attitude Change," *Journal of Personality and Social Psychology* 57, no. 3 (1989): 416–425; Duane F. Alwin and Jon A. Krosnick, "Aging, Cohorts, and the Stability of Sociopolitical Orientations Over the Life Span," *American Journal of Sociology* 97, no. 1 (1991): 169–195.

9. William Frey, "The Nation Is Diversifying Even Faster Than Predicted," *Brookings Institution*, July 1, 2020, https://www.brookings.edu/articles/new-census-data-shows-the-nation-is-diversifying-even-faster-than-predicted/.

10. Public Religion Research Institute (PRRI), "PRRI 2022 Census of American Religion: Religious Affiliation Updates and Trends," February 24, 2023, https://www.prri.org/spotlight/prri-2022-american-values-atlas-religious-affiliation-updates-and-trends/.

11. Kimberlé Crenshaw, "Demarginalizing the Intersection of Race and Sex: A Black Feminist Critique of Antidiscrimination Doctrine, Feminist Theory and Antiracist Politics," *University of Chicago Legal Forum* 1, no. 8 (1989): 139–167.

12. Kimberlé Crenshaw, "An Interview with Kimberlé Crenshaw on Intersectionality, More than Two Decades Later," News from Columbia Law School, June 8, 2017, https://www.law.columbia.edu/news/archive/kimberle-crenshaw-intersectionality-more-two-decades-later.

13. Center for Information and Research on Civic Engagement and Learning (CIRCLE), "The 2020 Election Is Over, but Young People Believe in Continued Engagement," January 12, 2021, https://circle.tufts.edu/latest-research/2020-election-over-young-people-believe-continued-engagement; CIRCLE, "Election Night 2018: Historically High Youth Voter Turnout, Support for Democrats," November 7, 2018, https://circle.tufts.edu/latest-research/election-night-2018-historically-high-youth-turnout-support-democrats.

1. GENDER, SEXUALITY, AND GEN Z'S POLITICS

14. CIRCLE, "State-by-State Youth Voter Turnout Data and the Impact of Election Laws in 2022 ." April 6, 2023, https://circle.tufts.edu/latest-research/state-state-youth-voter-turnout-data-and-impact-election-laws-2022.
15. William Frey, "Midterm Exit Polls Show That Young Voters Drove Democratic Resistance to the Red Wave," *Brookings Institution*, November 18, 2022, https://www.brookings.edu/articles/midterm-exit-polls-show-that-young-voters-drove-democratic-resistance-to-the-red-wave/.
16. Melissa Deckman, "The Numbers Show Gen Z Is Actually the Pro-Choice Generation," *The Hill*, July 21, 2022, https://thehill.com/opinion/civil-rights/3567581-the-numbers-show-gen-z-is-actually-the-pro-choice-generation/.
17. Frey, "Midterm Exit Polls Show."
18. Rob Griffin, William H. Frey, and Ruy Teixeria, "America's Electoral Future: The Coming Generational Transformation," *Center for American Progress*, October 19, 2020, https://www.americanprogress.org/article/americas-electoral-future-3/.
19. GLADD, "Election 2022: LGBTQs Deliver High Midterm Turnout Amid Fears of Political Safety in Current Climate," December 8, 2022, https://glaad.org/election-2022-post-midterm-poll.

1. GEN Z AND THE ROLE OF GENDER AND SEXUALITY IN THEIR POLITICS

1. William Frey, "Now, More Than Half of Americans Are Millennials or Younger," Brookings Institution, July 30, 2020, https://www.brookings.edu/articles/now-more-than-half-of-americans-are-millennials-or-younger/; Jean Twenge, *Generations: The Real Differences Between Gen Z, Millennials, Gen X, Boomers and Silences—and What They Mean for America's Future* (New York: Atria, 2023).
2. The term "Latinx" is a gender-neutral term that has been growing in popularity as a more inclusive term that includes Latinos (men of Latin American descent), Latinas (women of Latin American descent), and those Americans of Latin American descent who do not identify as male or female. This term is especially popular with younger Americans, although it is not without its critics, and most Latinos themselves prefer Latino or Hispanic to the term Latinx. See Mario X. Carrasco, "The Great Latinx Debate," *Think Now Blog*, December 18, 2019, https://thinknow.com/blog/the-great-latinx-debate/. By and large, demographers, including the U.S. Census Bureau, still use the term "Latino" or "Hispanic." In my book, I use the terms "Latinx" and "Latino/Latina" interchangeably.
3. Kim Parker and Ruth Igielnik, "On the Cusp of Adulthood and Facing an Uncertain Future: What We Know About Gen Z So Far," Pew Research Center, March 24, 2020, https://www.pewresearch.org/social-trends/2020/05/14/on-the-cusp-of-adulthood-and-facing-an-uncertain-future-what-we-know-about-gen-z-so-far-2/. Other categories include Middle Eastern, Native American, and Pacific Islander.

1. GENDER, SEXUALITY, AND GEN Z'S POLITICS

4. Identifying as cisgender means that one's gender identity matches the sex that they were assigned at birth. For example, if someone is assigned female at birth and continues to identify as a woman, then she is a cisgender woman. If someone is assigned male at birth and continues to identify as a man, then he is a cisgender man. By contrast, identifying as transgender means that one's gender identity does not match the sex they were assigned at birth. For example, if someone is assigned male at birth and later identifies as a woman, then she is a transgender woman. If someone is assigned female at birth and later identifies as a man, then he is a transgender man. The word "cisgender" is often shortened to "cis," and the word "transgender" is often shortened to "trans": cis woman, cis man, trans woman, trans man, trans person, trans youth, trans elder, and so on.

5. My Qualtrics surveys also found that the percentage of cisgender men who identify as LGBTQ ranges from 12 to 15 percent; for cisgender women, it ranges from 24 to 30 percent. In most subsequent analyses in the book, I omit showing data about Gen Z Americans who identify as transgender or as nonbinary because their numbers overall in my surveys are too small for the purposes of statistical inference. When discussing Gen Z women and men throughout most of the book, I am typically referring to those respondents who are cisgender. When reporting comparative data on LGBTQ versus straight Zoomers, however, I include *all* Gen Zers who self-identify as LGBTQ+, including trans and nonbinary individuals.

6. See, for instance, IPSOS, "Gender Identity and Sexual Orientation Differences by Generation," February 23, 2021, https://www.ipsos.com/en-us/gender-identity-and-sexual-orientation-differences-generation. See also Twenge, *Generations*, chapter 6.

7. Public Religion Research Institute (PRRI), "PRRI 2022 Census of American Religion: Religious Affiliation Updates and Trends," February 24, 2023, https://www.prri.org/spotlight/prri-2022-american-values-atlas-religious-affiliation-updates-and-trends/.

8. To understand the strong influence that political party has on shaping political choices, particularly as our nation has become more politically polarized and affected by negative partisanship, see Lilliana Mason, *Uncivil Agreement: How Politics Became Our Identity* (Chicago: University of Chicago Press, 2018); Alan Abramowitz, *The Great Realignment: Race, Party Transformation, and the Rise of Donald Trump* (New Haven, CT: Yale University Press, 2018). Another good source showing the strong link between party identification and vote choice is the validated voter file from the Pew Research Center. In the 2020 presidential election, for instance, Pew found that 92 percent of Republicans voted for Trump and 94 percent of Democrats voted for Biden. See Ruth Igielnick, Scott Keeter, and Hannah Hartig, "Behind Biden's 2020 Victory," Pew Research Center, June 30, 2021, https://www.pewresearch.org/politics/2021/06/30/behind-bidens-2020-victory/.

9. In measuring party identification among Gen Z Americans, I follow the American National Election Study measurement protocol, which asked survey respondents whether they consider themselves Democrats, Republicans, or independent of any party. Partisans are then asked whether they are strong or weak in their attachments to their parties. A significant number of Americans identify as independent of parties, but if prompted, they are generally likely to say that they "lean" toward one party or the other. Thus, the true

1. GENDER, SEXUALITY, AND GEN Z'S POLITICS

number of "pure" independents is relatively low among Americans. This figure aggregates independent partisan leaners with strong/weak partisans, resulting in a three-point scale, with independents who lean one way or the other being coded as partisans. This is a common practice in political science studies because research shows that "independent leaners" are more engaged in politics than weak partisans and exhibit political behavior more akin to strong partisans than weak partisans. See Bruce Keith et al., *The Myth of the Independent Voter* (Berkeley: University of California Press, 1992).

10. About 9 percent of respondents in my Qualtrics survey indicated that they think of themselves as something other than Democrat, independent, or Republican. Those respondents were also asked if they learned toward one party or another and are coded as leaners if they said yes. Those who did not were coded as part of the independent category.

11. The 2022 American Values Atlas (AVA) finds that, among women older than Gen Z, 50 percent identified as or leaned Democrat, 9 percent identified as independent, 37 percent identified as or leaned Republican and 4 percent refused to answer or didn't know. Among men older than Gen Z, 45 percent identified as or leaned Democrat, 11 percent identified as independent, 40 percent identified as or leaned Republican, and 3 percent didn't know or refused to answer.

12. See the appendix, Table 2.A and 2.B for this breakdown of data; the 1990 data should be interpreted with some caution because there are fewer than 100 cases of millennial women and men in the survey.

13. Pew Research Center, "The Generation Gap and the 2012 Election." November 3, 2011.

14. Lauren Young, "Gen Z Is the Most Progressive—and Least Partisan—Generation," *Teen Vogue*, October 2, 2019, https://www.teenvogue.com/story/how-will-gen-z-vote.

15. In all issues except for economic concerns, such as inflation and jobs and unemployment, the differences between Gen Z women and Gen Z men are statistically significant at the $p < .05$ level or higher.

16. Maddie Van Nes, "COVID-19 and Women's Mental Health: The Impact on Wellbeing, Disparities, and Future Implications," *Baylor University Community Connection Magazine*, April 1, 2021; Lindsey Dawson et al., "The Impact of the COVID-19 Pandemic on LGBT+ People's Mental Health," *Kaiser Family Foundation*, August 27, 2021.

17. Melissa Deckman, "The Numbers Show Gen Z Is Actually the Pro-Choice Generation," *The Hill*, July 21, 2022, https://thehill.com/opinion/civil-rights/3567581-the-numbers-show-gen-z-is-actually-the-pro-choice-generation/.

18. PRRI, "Diversity, Division, Discrimination. The State of Young America," January 10, 2018, https://www.prri.org/research/mtv-culture-and-religion/.

19. Melissa Deckman, "A New Poll Shows How Younger Women Could Help Drive a Democratic Wave in 2018," *Washington Post*, March 5, 2018, https://www.washingtonpost.com/news/monkey-cage/wp/2018/03/05/a-new-poll-shows-how-younger-women-could-help-drive-a-democratic-wave-in-2018/.

20. For a good overview with respect to patterns of political engagement among Americans, see Kay Lehman Schlozman, Sidney Verba, and Henry E. Brady, *The Unheavenly Chorus: Unequal Political Voice and Broken Promise of American Democracy* (Princeton, NJ: Princeton

1. GENDER, SEXUALITY, AND GEN Z'S POLITICS

University Press, 2013). Their work shows that Americans who possess higher socioeconomic status are disproportionately far more active in politics.
21. Julie Fenwick, "We're All Chronically Online Now," *VICE*, February 3, 2023.
22. My organization, PRRI, found in a March 2023 survey that 53 percent of Gen Z men and 58 percent of Gen Z women do not watch television news compared with just 19 percent of baby boomer men and 17 percent of baby boomer women. PRRI, "The Politics of Gender, Pronouns, and Public Education," June 8, 2023, https://www.prri.org/research/the-politics-of-gender-pronouns-and-public-education/.
23. Kevin Munger, *Generation Gap: Why the Baby Boomers Still Dominate American Politics and Culture* (New York: Columbia University Press, 2022), 86.
24. Nick Reynolds, "Women Lead Surge in New Voter Registrations Since Roe Overturned," *Newsweek*, August 22, 2022, https://www.newsweek.com/women-lead-surge-new-voter-registrations-since-roe-overturned-1735346; Amelia Thomson-DeWeaux and Meredith Conroy, "Women Have Swung Toward Democrats Since Dobbs Decision," *FiveThirtyEight*, September 28, 2022l, https://fivethirtyeight.com/features/women-have-swung-toward-democrats-since-the-dobbs-decision/.
25. Simone Carter, "Abortion Activist Mocked by Matt Gaetz Given Voice of the Year Award," *Newsweek*, December 14, 2022, https://www.newsweek.com/abortion-activist-olivia-julianna-mocked-matt-gaetz-given-voice-year-award-1767200.
26. "Social Media Fact Sheet," Pew Research Center, April 7, 2021, https://www.pewresearch.org/internet/2021/04/07/social-media-use-in-2021/.
27. These are data from Pew Research Center's May 2018 study "Teens, Social Media and Technology 2018"; Monica Anderson and JingJing Jiang, "Teens, Social Media and Technology 2018," https://www.pewresearch.org/internet/2018/05/31/teens-social-media-technology-2018/. The difference between Gen Z girls' and boys' use of Instagram is marginally statistically significant at the p = .076 level according to a chi-square. Pew's 2018 study also shows that Gen Z girls are more likely to use Snapchat than Gen Z boys, 72 percent to 67 percent, respectively, but this difference was not statistically significant (p = .137). Incidentally, 89 percent of Gen Z boys report using YouTube compared with 81 percent of Gen Z girls.
28. Linda Charmaraman, "Social Media Gives Support to LGBTQ Youth When In-Person Communities Are Lacking," *The Conversation*, September 28, 2021, https://theconversation.com/social-media-gives-support-to-lgbtq-youth-when-in-person-communities-are-lacking-166253.
29. Cristian Vaccari and Augusto Valeriani, "Digital Political Talk and Political Participation: Comparing Established and Third Wave Democracies," *SAGE Open* 8, no. 2 (2018), https://doi.org/10.1177/2158244018784986
30. For more on age and political engagement, see Amanda Barraiso and Rachel Minkin, "Recent Protest Attendees Are More Racially and Ethnically Diverse, Younger Than Americans Overall," Pew Research Center, June 24, 2020, https://www.pewresearch.org/short-reads/2020/06/24/recent-protest-attendees-are-more-racially-and-ethnically-diverse-younger-than-americans-overall/#:~:text=While%2064%25%20of%20U.S.%20

1. GENDER, SEXUALITY, AND GEN Z'S POLITICS

adults,are%20in%20this%20age%20group; Alec Tyson, Brian Kennedy, and Cary Funk, "Climate Engagement and Activism," Pew Research Center, May 26, 2021, https://www.pewresearch.org/science/2021/05/26/climate-engagement-and-activism/.

31. Combining these seventeen political participation items in the 2019 Gen Z survey produced a scale that ranged from zero activities undertaken in the past year to seventeen. That same scale was replicated in the 2022 survey; $t = 3.69; p < .000$. The Cronbach alpha score for both scales, which measures internal reliability and whether a collection of items is measuring similar things, is .68 for 2019 and .69 for 2022. Scores above .60 generally indicate that a scale is acceptable.
32. $t = 3.83; p < .000$.
33. $t = 5.62; p < .000$.
34. Geoffrey Skelley, "Few Americans Who Identify as Independent Are Actually Independent: That's Really Bad for American Politics," *FiveThirtyEight*, April 15, 2021. In 2019, independent Gen Z women reported participating in 2.68 political activities compared with 3.12 activities in 2022; independent Gen Z men reported participating in 2.53 political activities in 2019 compared with 3.07 political activities in 2022.
35. A *t*-test shows that the difference in mean scores between Democratic Gen Z women and Democratic Gen Z men is statistically significant for both years, as is the difference among Democratic Gen Z women and Republican Gen Z women for both years.
36. David Campbell and Christina Wolbrecht, "The Resistance as Role Model: Disillusionment and Protest Among American Adolescents After 2016," *Political Behavior* 42, no. 4 (2019): 1143–1168, https://doi.org/10.1007/s11109-019-09537-w.
37. In 2019, there were ninety-five Republican LGBTQ Zoomers compared with 319 LGBTQ Democrats in the sample; the difference in political engagement levels was significant ($t = 3.62; p < .001$); In 2022, there were ninety-two Republican LGBTQ Zoomers compared with 363 LGBTQ Democratic Zoomers in the sample; the difference in political engagement levels was significant ($t = 2.18; p < .05$)
38. Christina Wolbrecht and J. Kevin Corder, *A Century of Votes for Women: American Elections Since Suffrage* (New York: Cambridge University Press, 2020).
39. The appendix shows the breakdown of my analysis of these data starting in the 1950s; for ease of interpretation, I present just the last fifty years. (See Table A.3.)
40. For a great overview of the political participation habits of American women and men, read the classic book by political scientists Nancy Burns, Key Lehman Schlozman, and Henry Brady, *The Private Roots of Public Action: Gender, Equality and Political Participation* (Cambridge, MA: Harvard University Press, 2001).
41. Nancy Burns et al., "What's Happened to the Gender Gap in Political Participation?," in *100 Years of the Nineteenth Amendment: An Appraisal of Women's Political Activism*, ed. Holly J. McCammon and Lee Ann Banaszak (New York: Oxford University Press, 2019), 69–86. It should be noted that, for the past several decades, however, American women have turned out to vote more than American men. See Wolbrecht and Corder, *A Century of Votes for Women*.

1. GENDER, SEXUALITY, AND GEN Z'S POLITICS

42. Jo Freeman, *The Politics of Women's Liberation* (New York: Longman, 1975); Susan M. Hartmann, *From Margin to Mainstream: American Women and Politics Since 1960* (Philadelphia: Temple University Press, 1989).
43. Mary Ann Barasko, *Governing Now: Grassroots Activism in the National Organization for Women* (Ithaca, NY: Cornell University Press, 2004); Duchess Harris, *Black Feminist Politics from Kennedy to Clinton* (New York: Palgrave Macmillan, 2001).

2. POLITICAL CONTEXT, GENDER, AND SEXUALITY IN SHAPING THE POLITICAL ENGAGEMENT OF GEN Z

1. Kristen Soltis Anderson, *The Selfie Vote: Where Millennials Are Leading America (and How Republicans Can Keep Up)* (New York: Broadside, 2015), 8.
2. For more on how socioeconomic status is positively linked to higher rates of political participation, see Raymond E. Wolfinger and Steven J. Rosenstone, *Who Votes?* (New Haven, CT: Yale University Press, 1980); Sidney Verba, Kay Lehman Schlozman, and Henry E. Brady, *Voice and Equality: Civic Voluntarism in American Politics* (Cambridge, MA: Harvard University Press, 1995); Kay Lehman Schlozman, Sidney Verba, and Henry E. Brady, *The Unheavenly Chorus: Unequal Political Voice and the Broken Promise of American Democracy* (Princeton, NJ: Princeton University Press, 2013); Kay Lehman Schlozman, Henry E. Brady, and Sidney Verba, *Unequal and Unrepresented* (Princeton, NJ: Princeton University Press, 2018).
3. Nancy Burns, Kay Lehman Schlozman, and Sidney Verba, *The Private Roots of Public Action: Gender, Equality and Political Participation* (Cambridge, MA: Harvard University Press, 2001).
4. Nancy Burns et al., "What's Happened to the Gender Gap in Political Participation?," in *100 Years of the Nineteenth Amendment: An Appraisal of Women's Political Activism*, ed. Holly J. McCammon and Lee Ann Banaszak (New York: Oxford University Press, 2019), 69–86.
5. Derek Thompson, "Colleges Have a Guy Problem," *The Atlantic*, September 14, 2021, https://www.theatlantic.com/ideas/archive/2021/09/young-men-college-decline-gender-gap-higher-education/620066/.
6. Richard Reeves, *Of Boys and Men: Why the Modern Male Is Struggling, Why It Matters, and What to Do About It* (Washington, DC: Brookings Institution Press, 2022).
7. See the appendix for data on mean participation for gender, LGBTQ status levels by education.
8. Jan Leighley and Arnold Vedlitz, "Race, Ethnicity and Political Participation," *Journal of Politics* 61, no. 4 (1999): 1092–1114. More recent work suggests, however, that Black Americans are more likely to use social media to advocate for political offices than members of other racial groups. See Brooke Auxier, "Activism on Social Media Varies by Race and Ethnicity, Age, Political Party," Pew Research Center, July 13, 2020, https://www.pewresearch.org/short-reads/2020/07/13/activism-on-social-media-varies-by-race-and-ethnicity-age-political-party/.
9. See the appendix for data on mean participation for gender, LGBTQ status levels by race/ethnicity.

2. POLITICAL CONTEXT, GENDER, AND SEXUALITY

10. See, for example, Katty Kay, Claire Shipman, and JillEllyn Riley, *The Confidence Code for Girls: Taking Risks, Messing Up, & Becoming Your Amazingly Perfect, Totally Powerful Self* (New York: HarperCollins, 2018); Lisa Damour, *Under Pressure: Confronting the Epidemic of Stress and Anxiety in Girls* (New York: Ballantine, 2020); Reshma Saujani, *Brave, Not Perfect: Fear Less, Fail More, and Live Bolder* (New York: Currency, 2019); Reshma Saujani, *Girls Who Code: Learn to Code and Change the World* (New York: Penguin, 2018).
11. Girl Scout Research Institute, "The Girl Scout Alum Difference: A Lifetime of Courage, Confidence and Character," 2021, https://www.girlscouts.org/content/dam/girlscouts-gsusa/forms-and-documents/about-girl-scouts/research/GSUSA_GSRI_2021_The-Girl-Scout-Alum-Difference.pdf.
12. See Paul Allen Beck and M. Kent Jennings, "Pathways to Participation," *American Political Science Review* 76, no. 1 (1982): 94–108; Molly W. Andolina et al., "Habits from Home, Lessons from School: Influences on Youth Civic Engagement," *PS: Political Science and Politics* 36, no. 2 (2003): 275–280; M. Kent Jennings and Laura Stoker, "Social Trust and Civic Engagement Across Time and Generations," *Acta Politica* 39, no. 2 (2004): 342–379.
13. This 2019 mean difference with respect to levels of high school activities between Gen Z women and men is statistically significant ($t = 3.32$; $p < 0.001$).
14. This 2019 mean difference with respect to levels of high school activities between LGBTQ and straight Zoomers is marginally statistically significant ($t = 1.94$; $p < .10$).
15. See the appendix for data on mean participation for gender, LGBTQ status levels by high school activity level.
16. Linda Charmararam, "Social Media Gives LGBTQ Youth Support When In-Person Communities Are Lacking," *The Conversation*, September 21, 2021.
17. See, for example, Steven J. Rosenstone and John Mark Hansen, *Mobilization, Participation, and Democracy in America* (New York: Macmillan, 1993); Verba, Schlozman, and Brady, *Voice and Equality*; Lilliana Mason, *Uncivil Agreement: How Politics Became Our Identity* (Chicago: University of Chicago Press, 2018).
18. See Nancy Burns, Kay Lehman Schlozman, Ashley Jardina, Shauna Shames and Sidney Verba, "What Happened to the Gender Gap in Political Participation? How Might we Explain It?," in *100 Years of the Nineteenth Amendment: An Appraisal of Women's Activism*, ed. Holly J. McCammon and Lee Ann Banaszak, 69–104 (New York: Oxford University Press, 2018); Jennifer Wolak, "Self-Confidence and Gender Gaps in Political Interest, Attention, and Efficacy," *Journal of Politics* 82, no. 4 (2020): 1490–1501; Jennifer Wolak, "Conflict Avoidance and Gender Gaps in Political Engagement," *Political Behavior* 44 (2022): 133–156.
19. This difference is statistically significant: chi-square = 10.5; $p < .05$.
20. See Public Religion Research Institute (PRRI), "Political and Religious Activation and Polarization in the Wake of the Roe v. Wade Overturn," July 7, 2022, https://www.prri.org/research/political-and-religious-activation-and-polarization-in-the-wake-of-the-roe-overturn/.
21. This difference is statistically significant: chi-square = 22.9; $p < .000$.
22. Wolak, "Self-Confidence and Gender Gaps," 1490.

2. POLITICAL CONTEXT, GENDER, AND SEXUALITY

23. See Hahrie Han, *Moved to Action: Motivation, Participation, and Inequality in American Politics* (Stanford, CA: Stanford University Press, 2009). Han argues that individuals lacking in other resources that are often statistically linked to political participation yet who care deeply about a particular issue or set of issues can be compelled to engage in politics as members of what she calls issue publics.
24. See the appendix for data on mean participation for gender, LGBTQ status levels by number of issue publics.
25. These differences are statistically significant ($t = 4.99; p < .000$).
26. These differences are statistically significant ($t = 8.53; p < .000$).
27. These differences are statistically significant in 2019 ($t = 4.31; p < .000$) and 2022 ($t = 6.40; p < .000$).
28. See Verba, Brady, and Schlozman, *Voice and Equality*.
29. See, for example, M. Margaret Conway, Gertrude A Steuernagel, and David W. Ahern, *Women and Political Participation: Cultural Change in the Political Arena*, (Washington, DC: CQ Press, 1997); Lonna Rae Atkeson and Ronald B. Rapoport, "The More Things Change the More They Stay the Same: Examining Gender Differences in Political Attitude Expression, 1952–2000," *Public Opinion Quarterly* 67, no. 4 (2003): 495–521.
30. See the appendix for data on mean participation for gender by internal political efficacy scores.
31. This difference is statistically significant; chi-square = $6.5; p < .05$.
32. Research finds that this gender gap in political knowledge is also linked to risk aversion: men are more likely to guess answers on surveys that measure political knowledge; women are more likely to answer that they don't know the answer. This risk aversion by women likely results in the underestimation of women's knowledge of politics overall. See Mary-Kate Lizotte and Andrew H. Sidman, "Explaining the Gender Gap in Political Knowledge," *Politics & Gender* 5, no. 20 (2009): 127–151.
33. See the appendix for data on mean participation for LGBTQ status by internal political efficacy scores.
34. This question was developed by political scientists David E. Campbell and Christina Wolbrecht in their analysis of political engagement among young people. They asked respondents if they agree that the political system in this country helps the public with their genuine needs. Campbell and Wolbrecht find that higher rates of disillusionment with the political system enhanced the likelihood that Democratic teen girls will engage in protest politics in the future after the 2016 presidential election. David E. Campbell and Christina Wolbrecht, "The Resistance as Role Model: Disillusionment and Protest Among American Adolescents After 2016," *Political Behavior* 42, no. 4 (2020): 1143–1168.
35. This difference is statistically significant ($t = 2.05; p < .05$).
36. The *t*-test measuring whether differences in political engagement levels among LGBTQ Zoomers who disagree that government is meeting their needs (5.24 activities) compared with LGBTQ Zoomers who agree that the political system is meeting their needs (4.04) is statistically significant ($t = 3.50; p < .001$). The *t*-test measuring whether differences in political engagement levels among LGBTQ Zoomers who disagree that government

2. POLITICAL CONTEXT, GENDER, AND SEXUALITY

(5.24 activities) compared with straight Zoomers who disagree that the political system is meeting their needs (3.61) is statistically significant ($t = 5.38; p < .001$).
37. Mason, *Uncivil Agreement*.
38. $t = 4.77; p < .000$; likewise, Gen Z Democratic women leaners also report statistically significant higher rates of political engagement than Gen Z Democratic men leaners ($t = 2.32; p < .05$).
39. See the appendix for data on mean participation for gender and LGBTQ status by party strength.
40. See the appendix for more details.
41. See the appendix for more details.
42. This difference is statistically significant ($t = 2.67; p < .01$).
43. These differences are statistically significant ($t = 3.12; p < .05$).
44. These differences are statistically significant in both 2019 ($t = 4.04; p < .000$;) and 2022 ($t = 3.37; p < .000$).
45. See the appendix for data on mean participation for gender and LGBTQ status by contact with groups.
46. See Nicholas A. Valentino et al., "Election Night's Alright for Fighting: The Role of Emotions in Political Participation," *Journal of Politics* 73, no. 1 (2011): 156–170.
47. See Nicholas A. Valentino, Krysha Gregorowicz, and Eric W. Groenendyk, "Efficacy, Emotions, and the Habit of Participation," *Political Behavior* 31, no. 3 (2009): 307–330; Ted Brader, Nicholas A. Valentino, and Elizabeth Suhay, "What Triggers Public Opposition to Immigration? Anxiety, Group Cues, and Immigration Threat," *American Journal of Political Science* 52, no. 4 (2008): 959–978.
48. See the appendix for specific levels of emotions; all these differences with respect to expressing emotions between Gen Z women and Gen Z men are statistically significant in both 2019 and 2022. LGBTQ Zoomers also show statistically distinct emotional responses to the state of the country compared with straight Zoomers.
49. Normalizing or standardizing variables allows variables to share a common measuring scale, thus allowing for a more direct comparison of each of the variables' impact on the political engagement score.
50. Because social scientists estimate models based on representatives samples of data, there is always a chance that what we observe in the data is incorrect; conventionally speaking, however, statisticians rely on 95 percent confidence intervals, which indicates that the probability of us not finding the result that we do is 5 percent or less, known as the probability or p value.
51. I opted to keep all three measures of contact by political organizations (party, campaign, and political group) as separate controls in the model because those measures are not strongly correlated.
52. When I replace the strong partisan measure with dummy variables for Democrat and Republican among Zoomers in the full model in 2019, with independents being the reference category, Democratic Zoomers engage at higher levels than independent Zoomers, but Republican Zoomers do not.

2. POLITICAL CONTEXT, GENDER, AND SEXUALITY

53. While Gen Z Americans are following in the path of millennials in terms of leaving organized religion at much higher rates compared to older Americans, I include consideration of church attendance in my model because prior studies of women's political participation show historically that church activity fosters the development of the types of civic skills that are conductive to political participation. See Melissa Deckman, "Generation Z and Religion: What New Data Show," *Religion in Public*, February 10, 2020. https://religioninpublic.blog/2020/02/10/generation-z-and-religion-what-new-data-show/. See also Burns, Schlozman, and Verba, *The Private Roots of Public Action*.
54. Substituting party dummies for the overall party strength measure in the models, I find that Democratic Gen Z women engage in about one-half more political activities than Gen Z women who identify as independent; however, there are no statistical differences between Republican and independent women in the model. Neither party strength or partisanship matters to the political engagement levels of Gen Z men.
55. This difference is statistically significant; $t = 2.51$; $p < .05$.
56. This difference is statistically significant; $t = 2.95$; $p < .01$.
57. This difference is statistically significant; $t = 4.74$; $p < .001$.

3. NO MORE OLD WHITE MEN: HOW ROLE MODELS SHAPE THE POLITICAL ENGAGEMENT OF GEN Z WOMEN

1. Leila Ettachfini, "Isra Hirsi is 16, Unbothered, and Saving the Planet," *Vice*, September 19, 2019, https://www.vice.com/en/article/a357wp/isra-hirsi-ilhan-omar-daughter-climate-strike-profile.
2. K. K. Rebecca Lai et al., "The Faces of Change in the Midterm Elections," *New York Times*, October 31, 2018, https://www.nytimes.com/interactive/2018/10/31/us/politics/midterm-election-candidates-diversity.html.
3. Vanessa Williams, "Women of Color are Challenging Perceptions of Political Leadership," *Washington Post*, January 4, 2019, https://www.washingtonpost.com/nation/2019/01/04/women-color-congress-are-challenging-perceptions-political-leadership/.
4. See, for example, Lonna Rae Atkeson, "Not All Cues Are Created Equal: The Conditional Impact of Female Candidates on Political Engagement," *Journal of Politics* 65, no. 4 (2003): 1040–1061; David E. Campbell and Christina Wolbrecht, "See Jane Run: Women Politicians as Role Models for Adolescents," *Journal of Politic* 68, no. 2 (2006): 233–247; Richard L. Fox and Jennifer L. Lawless, "Uncovering the Origins of the Gender Gap in Political Ambition," *American Political Science Review* 108, no. 3 (2014): 499–519; Jeffrey Koch, "Candidate Gender and Women's Psychological Engagement in Politics," *American Politics Quarterly* 25, no. 1 (1997): 118–133.
5. See, for example, Amy C. Alexander and Farida Jalalzai, "Symbolic Empowerment and Female Heads of States and Government: A Global, Multilevel Analysis," *Politics, Groups, and Identities* 8, no. 1 (2020): 24–43; Tiffany D. Barnes and Stephanie M. Burchard, "'Engendering' Politics: The Impact of Descriptive Representation on Women's Political

3. NO MORE OLD WHITE MEN

Engagement in Sub-Saharan Africa," *Comparative Political Studies* 46, no. 7 (2013): 767–790; Fabrizio Gilardi, "The Temporary Importance of Role Models for Women's Political Representation," *American Journal of Political Science* 59, no. 4 (2015): 957–970; Shan-Jan Sarah Liu and Lee Ann Banaszak, "Do Government Positions Held by Women Matter? A Cross-National Examination of Female Ministers' Impacts on Women's Political Participation," *Politics & Gender* 13 (2017): 1–31; Christina Wolbrecht and David E. Campbell, "Leading by Example: Female Members of Parliament as Political Role Models," *American Journal of Political Science* 51, no. 3 (2007): 921–939.

6. Amy C. Alexander, "Change in Women's Descriptive Representation and the Belief in Women's Ability to Govern: A Virtuous Cycle," *Politics & Gender* 8, no. 4 (2012): 437–464.
7. Lonna Rae Atkeson and Nancy Carrillo, "More Is Better: The Influence of Collective Female Descriptive Representation on External Efficacy," *Politics & Gender* 3, no. 1 (2007): 79–101.
8. Hanna F. Pitkin, *The Concept of Representation* (Berkeley: University of California Press, 1972).
9. Research also finds that the role model effect applies for other underserved minorities, not just women. Minority representation can boost political empowerment, knowledge, and turnout among Latino and Black voters, for example. See, for example, Matt A. Barreto, Gary M. Segura, and Nathan D. Woods, "The Mobilizing Effect of Majority-Minority Districts on Latino Turnout," *American Political Science Review* 98, no. 1 (2004): 65–75; Adrian D. Pantoga and Gary M. Segura, "Fear and Loathing in California: Contextual Threat and Political Sophistication Among Latino Voters," *Political Behavior* 25 (2003): 265–286; Susan A. Banducci, Todd Donovan, and Jeffrey A. Karp, "Minority Representation, Empowerment, and Participation," *Journal of Politics* 66, no. 2 (2004): 534–556; Lawrence Bobo and Franklin D. Gilliam, "Race, Sociopolitical Participation, and Black Empowerment," *American Political Science Review* 84, no. 2 (1990): 377–393.
10. Jane Mansbridge, "Should Blacks Represent Blacks and Women Represent Women? A Contingent 'Yes,'" *Journal of Politics* 61, no. 3 (1999): 628–657.
11. Lonna Rae Atkeson, "Not All Cues Are Created Equal: The Conditional Impact of Female Candidates on Political Engagement," *Journal of Politics* 65, no. 4 (2003): 1040–1061; Nancy Burns, Key Lehman Schlozman, and Henry Brady, *The Private Roots of Public Action: Gender, Equality and Political Participation* (Cambridge, MA: Harvard University Press, 2001).
12. Amanda Clayton, Diana Z. O'Brien, and Jennifer Piscopo, "All Male Panels: Representation and Democratic Legitimacy," *American Journal of Political Science* 63, no. 1 (2019): 113–129.
13. See, for example, Kevin Denny and Orla Doyle, "Does Voting History Matter? Analysing Persistence in Turnout," *American Journal of Political Science* 53, no. 1 (2009): 17–35; Melissa R. Michelson, Lisa García Bedolla, and Margaret A. McConnell, "Heeding the Call: The Effect of Targeted Two-Round Phone Banks on Voter Turnout," *Journal of*

3. NO MORE OLD WHITE MEN

Politics 71, no. 4 (2009): 1549–1563; Richard G. Niemi and Kent M. Jennings, "Issues and Inheritance in the Formation of Party Identification," *American Journal of Political Science* 35, no. 4 (1991): 970–988.

14. Campbell and Wolbrecht, "See Jane Run"; Mack Mariani, Bryan W. Marshall, and A. Lanethea Mathews-Schultz, "See Hillary Clinton, Nancy Pelosi, and Sarah Palin Run? Party, Ideology, and the Influence of Female Role Models on Young Women," *Political Research Quarterly* 68, no. 4 (2015): 716–731.

15. Christina Wolbrecht and David Campbell, "Restoring Faith in American Democracy: The Effect of Women Candidates on Adolescents' Evaluations of Politics in 2018," paper presented at the Annual Meeting of the American Political Science Association, August 29, 2019.

16. David Campbell and Christina Wolbrecht, "The Resistance as Role Model: Disillusionment and Protest Among American Adolescents After 2016," *Political Behavior* 42, no. 4 (2019): 1143–1168, https://doi.org/10.1007/s11109-019-09537-w;" Jennifer Wolak and Michael McDermott, "The Roots of the Gender Gap in Political Knowledge in Adolescence," *Political Behavior* 33, no. 3 (2011): 505–533.

17. Annette Laureau, *Unequal Childhoods: Class, Race, and Family Life*, 2nd ed. (Berkeley: University of California Press, 2011).

18. See, for example, Richard E. Dawson and Kenneth Prewitt, *Political Socialization* (Boston: Little, Brown, 1969); Ron Warren and Robert H. Wicks, "Political Socialization: Modeling Teen Political and Civic Engagement," *Journalism and Mass Communication Quarterly* 88, no. 1 (2011): 156–175; M. Kent Jennings and Richard G. Niemi, "The Transmission of Political Values from Parent to Child," *American Political Science Review* 62, no. 1 (1968): 169–184. M. Kent Jennings, Laura Stoker, and Jake Bowers, "Politics Across Generations: Family Transmission Reexamined," *Journal of Politics* 71, no. 3 (2009): 782–799; Zoe Oxley, "Gender and the Socialization of Party Identification," in *The Political Psychology of Women in the United States*, ed. Angela L. Bos and Monica C. Schneider (New York: Routledge, 2017), 15–33.

19. A t-test = 2.63 ($p < .01$) shows that, among Gen Z women and men whose parents talk about politics very often, that difference is statistically significant. None of the other categories of political discussion among Gen Z Americans yielded statistically distinct gender differences in terms of the political engagement scale.

20. Melissa Deckman and Jared McDonald, "Uninspired by Old White Guys: The Mobilizing Factor of Younger, More Diverse Candidates for Gen Z Women," *Politics & Gender* 19, no. 1 (2023): 195–219, https://doi.org/10.1017/S1743923X21000477.

21. We chose to make all of the fictional candidates who were people of color Black, as opposed to Latinx or Asian American, because, in the real world, there are more Black candidates and elected officials than there are Latinx or Asian American ones. We were unable to include more conditions in our experiment because of sample size constraints.

22. This survey experiment design is known as a $2 \times 2 \times 2$ experimental design, with each treatment in terms of the characteristics of the candidate being discussed and pictured.

3. NO MORE OLD WHITE MEN

23. This battery of questions specifically includes eight items in which respondents rated how likely they would be in the next year to do the following: volunteer for a political campaign, participate in a protest or rally, encourage people to vote, discuss public affairs with friends and family, follow political news, run for political office, attend a local public or community meeting, and use social media to bring attention to an issue in their community. To assess the possibility of measurement error, I also generate a composite measure using a factor analysis (Cronbach's alpha = 0.823). This alternate method did not yield appreciably different results.
24. Because of the successful random assignment to the conditions, the differences we find can be attributed to the manipulations and not to other potential confounding factors. See Donald R. Kinder and Thomas R. Palfrey, eds., *Experimental Foundations of Political Science* (Ann Arbor: University of Michigan, 1993).
25. These questions are commonly used in studies measuring affective attachment to salient social identities. See, for example, Leonie Huddy, Lilliana Mason, and Lene Aarøe, "Expressive Partisanship: Campaign Involvement, Political Emotions, and Partisan Identity," *American Political Science Review* 109, no. 1 (2015): 1–17. I do not perform similar analyses for the race of the respondent because there were an insufficient number of racial minorities in our sample to estimate the heterogeneous effects confidently.
26. We normalize this measure from 0 to 1, although for ease of interpretation we categorized those who scored at 0.75 or higher as "high identifiers" and those who scored below as "low identifiers." We used the distribution of the variable as a guide to our categorization because roughly half our sample scored at a 0.75 or higher on gender social identity. Results do not change substantively if we treat this variable as continuous.
27. Although the 116th Congress, which was in session at the time of the survey experiment, was the most diverse in U.S. history, it remained 78 percent white and 76 percent male, and with a median age of fifty-eight.
28. When all seven treatment conditions are collapsed in a separate regression analysis (see the appendix), the interaction of the white–male–sixty-eight treatment with gender social identity is a significant predictor of whether women with a strong sense of gender social identity would be willing to engage in future political activity. Some may be concerned that gender identity is simply a proxy for partisanship among women. That is, women who have a strong sense of group identity based on womanhood are more likely to be Democrats and therefore are more motivated to get involved in politics when they see a politician who fits more closely with the Democratic coalition. In our data, however, we find that the gap between Democratic women and Republican women on gender social identity is relatively modest (a 64 percent to 55 percent difference in terms of high identifiers). The interactive effect among the treatments and gender social identity on future political activity is somewhat stronger among women who strongly identify as Republican than Democratic women, most likely because the politicians that the Democratic women are evaluating are all Democrats, and they are therefore more politically engaged across all conditions. The effect of gender social identity is most pronounced among Republican women who lack a similar partisan connection with the politician; among women who weakly identify as Republican, there is no effect of the treatment on future willingness to engage in politics. Yet women who

strongly identify as Republican are significantly more likely to get involved politically when the politicians they see are younger, women, or people of color—even if those politicians are Democrats. Taken together, then, we believe it is unlikely that gender social identity is simply a proxy for partisanship. Full results of analyses controlling for and modeling the effect of partisanship can be found in the appendix.

29. Cigdem V. Sirin, Nicholas A. Valentino, and José D. Villalobos, "Group Empathy Theory: The Effect of Group Empathy on US Intergroup Attitudes and Behavior in the Context of Immigration Threats," *The Journal of Politics* 78, no. 3 (2016): 893–908.

30. Our findings may not apply in situations in which young people are more motivated to become politically active writ large. Jared McDonald and I attempted a partial replication study of our experiment in late May 2020 using the same online methodology (although we excluded the four conditions involving a Gen Z candidate). We suspect base rates of political engagement may have already been high because of the nature of election-year politics and widespread frustration over the poor government response to COVID-19, yet this was further compounded by civil unrest throughout the country. During the survey administration, protests began over the murder of George Floyd, driven largely by Gen Z involvement. Because we found abnormally high levels of political engagement during the survey administration, the role model effect was considerably smaller, with some findings consistent with the hypothesis that the race, not the gender, of the candidate motivated young men in our sample. These findings suggest that gendered role model effects may be present more likely when current political engagement is not near its ceiling and when issues of women's rights are more salient in political discourse. See Deckman and McDonald, "Uninspired by Old White Guys."

4. "GROWING THEIR FEMINIST THING": HOW WOMEN'S RIGHTS AND REPRODUCTIVE RIGHTS ARE PROPELLING ACTIVISM AMONG GEN Z

1. Rachel Janfaza, "100 Years Later, We Still Don't Have an Equal Rights Amendment. This Generation's Leaders Want to Change That," *Elle*, March 23, 2023, https://www.elle.com/culture/career-politics/a43377381/equal-rights-amendment-2023-cori-bush-generation-ratify/; Olafimihan Oshin, "Bush, Pressly to launch Equal Rights Amendment Caucus," *The Hill*, March 26, 2023, https://thehill.com/homenews/3919468-bush-pressley-to-launch-equal-rights-amendment-caucus/.

2. NWA Media, "LOUDwomen organizer Anna Dean Speaks," July 4, 2022. https://nwamedia.photoshelter.com/image/I0000kOj71bVMc70.

3. Guttmacher Institute, "US Abortion Policies and Access After Roe," January 24, 2024, https://states.guttmacher.org/policies/georgia/abortion-policies.

4. See Christina Wolbrecht and J. Kevin Wolbrecht's excellent book *A Century of Votes for Women: American Elections Since Suffrage* (New York: Cambridge University Press, 2020) for an overview of women's voting patterns since 1920.

4. "GROWING THEIR FEMINIST THING"

5. Karen O'Connor, *Women's Groups Use of the Courts* (Lexington, MA: Lexington Books, 1980).
6. Phyllis Schlafly, *The Power of the Positive Woman* (New Rochelle, NY: Arlington House, 1977).
7. For a short history of Rush Limbaugh and his fight against feminism, see Monica Hesse, "Rush Limbaugh Had a Lot to Say About Feminism. Women Learned How Not to Care," *Washington Post*, February 19, 2021. See also Rush Limbaugh, *The Way Things Ought to Be* (New York: Pocket Books, 1992).
8. Dave Sheinin et al., "New Wave Feminism, Betty Friedan to Beyoncé: Today's Generation Embraces Feminism on Its Own Terms," *Washington Post*, January 27, 2016.
9. Catherine Morris, "Less Than a Third of American Women Identify as Feminists," Ipsos, November 25, 2019, https://www.ipsos.com/en-us/american-women-and-feminism.
10. Kristen Sollee, "6 Things to Know about 4th Wave Feminism," *Bustle*, October 30, 2015. https://www.bustle.com/articles/119524-6-things-to-know-about-4th-wave-feminism.
11. See, for example Katty Kay, Claire Shipman, and JillEllyn Riley, *The Confidence Code for Girls: Taking Risks, Messing Up, & Becoming Your Amazingly Perfect, Totally Powerful Self* (New York: HarperCollins, 2018); Lisa Damour, *Under Pressure: Confronting the Epidemic of Stress and Anxiety in Girls* (New York: Ballantine, 2020); Reshma Saujani, *Brave, Not Perfect: Fear Less, Fail More, and Live Bolder* (New York: Currency, 2019); Reshma Saujani, *Girls Who Code: Learn to Code and Change the World* (New York: Puffin, 2019).
12. See, for example, Sue Tolleson Rinehart, *Gender Consciousness and Politics* (New York: Routledge, Chapman and Hall, 1992); M. Margaret Conway, David W. Ahern, and Gertrude A Steuernagel, *Women and Political Participation: Cultural Change in the Political Arena*, 2nd ed. (Washington, DC: CQ Press, 1985); Arla G. Bernstein, "Gendered Characteristics of Political Engagement Among College Students," *Sex Roles* 52, no. 5/6 (2005): 299–310.
13. Quoted in Elizabeth R. Cole, Alyssa N. Zucker, and Joan M. Ostrove, "Political Participation and Feminist Consciousness Among Women Activists of the 1960s," *Political Psychology* 19, no. 2 (1998): 365.
14. In my 2019 survey, 47 percent of Democratic women identified as feminist compared with 17 percent of Republican. By May 2022, that gap had closed somewhat, with 59 percent of Democratic women identifying as feminist compared with 39 percent of Republicans.
15. Differences in political engagement levels among Gen Z women feminists and Gen Z women who supported women's equality but who are not feminists were significant in both 2019 ($t = 7.11$; $p < .000$) and 2022 ($t = 5.22$; $p < .000$). The same is true for Gen Z men feminists and men who support women's equality but who don't identify as feminists in 2019 ($t = 2.14$; $p < .05$) and 2022 ($t = 1.83$; $p < .10$).
16. In 2019, LGBTQ Zoomer feminists engaged in 4.5 political activities compared with 3.32 activities undertaken by LGBTQ Zoomers who support women's equality but who are not feminists ($t = 5.34$; $p < .000$); in 2022, those numbers were 5.04 activities versus 3.86 activities, respectively ($t = 4.07$; $p < .000$). In 2019, straight Zoomer feminists engaged in 4.5 political activities compared with straight Zoomers who support women's equality (3.32),

4. "GROWING THEIR FEMINIST THING"

a difference that is statistically significant ($t = 5.41$; $p < .000$). However, feminist identity did not differentiate levels of engagement among straight Zoomers in 2022.

17. I calculated this score using the margins command in Stata, holding all other variables at their mean score.
18. See the appendix, Table A.18, for full results.
19. See Public Religion Research Institute (PRRI), "The Politics of Gender, Pronouns and Public Education," June 8, 2023. Among millennial women, 22 percent are strongly committed feminists; 30 percent say that the term describes them but is not important to them (less committed feminists). Among Gen Z women, 21 percent are strongly committed feminists, and 23 percent are less committed feminists. Among baby boomers, 20 percent are strongly committed feminists and 33 percent are less committed feminists.
20. See figure A.9 in the appendix for full results.
21. See figure A.10 in the appendix for full results.
22. Melissa Deckman, "The Numbers Show Gen Z Is Actually the Pro-Choice Generation," *The Hill*, July 21, 2022, https://thehill.com/opinion/civil-rights/3567581-the-numbers-show-gen-z-is-actually-the-pro-choice-generation/.
23. While the 2023 Politics of Gender Survey does not have enough cases to isolate the views of LGBTQ Zoomers, PRRI's 2022 American Values Atlas, which has 744 respondents who answered about their abortion views, finds that 89 percent of LGBTQ Zoomers support abortion's legality in all or most cases, compared with 62 percent of straight Zoomers.
24. In 2019, differences in political engagement among Gen Z women who are the most supportive of abortion rights (4.33) compared with Gen Z women who are the most opposed to abortion rights (3.12) are statistically significant ($t = 6.36$; $p < .000$). By contrast, differences among Gen Z men in 2019 with respect to abortion attitudes and political engagement are not statistically significant. In 2022, differences in political engagement among Gen Z women who are the most supportive of abortion rights (4.07) are also significant compared with Gen Z women who are the most opposed (2.86 activities ($t = 3.65$; $p < .000$). These differences extend to Gen Z men in 2022 ($t = 2.76$; $p < .01$).
25. See figure A.11 in the appendix for full details.
26. In 2019, Gen Z women who believe that abortion should be legal in cases of rape and incest and to protect the life of the mother scored 3.52 on the political engagement scale, while the remaining Gen Z women who believe that abortion should be permitted when a need is established scored 4.15 on the scale. See the appendix for full regression model results.
27. See the appendix, Table A.22, for these model results and the marginal effects for the impact of abortion attitudes on participation levels of LGBTQ and straight Zoomers.
28. In 2022, Gen Z women who believe that abortion should be legal in cases of rape and incest and to protect the life of the mother scored 3.52 on the political engagement scale, while the remaining Gen Z women who believe that abortion should be permitted when a need is established scored 4.15 on the scale. See the appendix for full regression model results.

5. FIGHTING FOR RACIAL AND LGBTQ EQUALITY

29. See the appendix for these model results and the marginal effects for the impact of abortion attitudes on participation levels of straight Zoomers.
30. Tom Bonier, "How Abortion Changed the Kansas Electorate," August 3, 2022, https://insights.targetsmart.com/how-abortion-changed-the-kansas-electorate.html.
31. Rachel Janfaza, "Young Voters Tune into Wisconsin Supreme Court Election, Where Abortion Access Is Top of Mind," *The Up and Up*, April 4, 2023, https://www.theupandup.us/p/young-voters-tune-into-wisconsin; Lina Tran, "Voters Swipe Right for Wisconsin's State Supreme Court election," NPR. April 3, 2023, https://www.npr.org/2023/04/03/1167626232/wisconsin-supreme-court-election-abortion-dating-apps.

5. HOW GEN Z WOMEN AND LGBTQ ZOOMERS FIGHT FOR RACIAL AND LGBTQ EQUALITY

1. The term "intersectionality" was first developed by legal scholar Kimberlé Crenshaw. For an overview of her work, see Kimberlé Crenshaw, *On Intersectionality: Essential Writings* (New York: The New Press, 2017).
2. See Everytown for Gun Safety for statistics on the disproportionate impact of gun violence on marginalized communities. Everytown for Gun Safety, "Black History Month: Key Research Stats," everytown.org, January 25, 2024, https://everytownsupportfund.org/report/black-history-month-key-research-stats.
3. This difference is statistically significant (chi-square = 8.8; $p < .05$).
4. This difference is statistically significant (chi-square = 6.6; $p < .05$).
5. These differences are statistically significant for both years.
6. For white Gen Z women, differences in mean political engagement among those who say racial inequality is a critical issue to them personally and those who do not (combining the latter two categories) are significant ($t = 3.08$; $p < .01$); the same is true for Gen Z women of color ($t = 2.65$; $p < .01$).
7. For LGBTQ Zoomers who are not white, differences in mean political engagement among those who say racial inequality is a critical issue to them personally and those who do not (combining the latter two categories) are significant ($t = 2.62$; $p < .01$); the same is true for LGBTQ Zoomers who are white ($t = 3.03$; $p < .01$).
8. LGBTQ Zoomers of color who say racial inequality is critically important to them report engaging in 4.74 political activities in the last year compared with 4.87 activities undertaken by white LGBTQ Zoomers in 2022.
9. Public Religion Research Institute (PRRI), "More Acceptance but Growing Polarization on LGBTQ Rights: Findings from the 2022 American Values Atlas," March 23, 2023, https://www.prri.org/research/findings-from-the-2022-american-values-atlas/.
10. Justin McCarthy, "Same-Sex Marriage Support Inches Up to New High of 71 Percent," *Gallup*, June 1, 2022, https://news.gallup.com/poll/393197/same-sex-marriage-support-inches-new-high.aspx.

5. FIGHTING FOR RACIAL AND LGBTQ EQUALITY

11. PRRI, "More Acceptance but Growing Polarization on LGBTQ Rights," https://www.prri.org/research/findings-from-the-2022-american-values-atlas/.
12. PRRI, "Challenges in Moving Toward a More Inclusive Democracy: Findings from the 2022 American Values Survey," October 27, 2022, https://www.prri.org/research/challenges-in-moving-toward-a-more-inclusive-democracy-findings-from-the-2022-american-values-survey/.
13. Nico Lang, "2022 Was the Worst Year Ever for Trans Bills. How Did We Get Here?," December 29, 2022; https://www.them.us/story/2022-anti-trans-bills-history-explained; Solcyre Burga, "Tennessee Passed the Nation's First Drag Law," April 3, 2023, https://time.com/6260421/tennessee-limiting-drag-shows-status-of-anti-drag-bills-u-s/.
14. Hannah Natanson et al., "An Explosion of Culture War Laws in Changing Schools. Here's How," *Washington Post*, October 18, 2022, https://www.washingtonpost.com/education/2022/10/18/education-laws-culture-war/.
15. Nicole Narea and Fabiola Cineas, "The GOP's Coordinated National Campaign Against Trans Rights, Explained," *Vox*, April 6, 2023, https://www.vox.com/politics/23631262/trans-bills-republican-state-legislatures
16. Amanda D'Ambrosio, "AAP Stands by Policy on Gender-Affirming Care for Youth," August 23, 2022, https://www.medpagetoday.com/special-reports/features/100352.
17. Hannah Natanson, "Florida Bans Teaching About Gender Identity in All Public Schools," April 19, 2023, https://www.washingtonpost.com/education/2023/04/19/florida-bans-teaching-gender-identity-sexuality/.
18. Quoted in Christopher Wilson, "Scott Walker Blames Young Voters for GOP's Losses in Wisconsin, but Offers Few Solutions for Winning Them Back," *Yahoo News*, April 7, 2023, https://news.yahoo.com/republicans-young-voter-struggles-scott-walker-wisconsin-supreme-court-protasiewicz-203505242.html.
19. Adam Nagourney and Jeremy W. Peters, "How a Campaign Against Transgender Rights Mobilized Conservatives," *New York Times*, April 16, 2023, https://www.nytimes.com/2023/04/16/us/politics/transgender-conservative-campaign.html.
20. In my 2022 survey, ninety-three Gen Z Americans identify as nonbinary or trans. Although we should be cautious about generalizing from ninety-three cases, among these Zoomers who are not cisgender, 84 percent say LGBTQ rights are critically important. Similar trends emerged in the 2019 Gen Z survey, although the salience of this has gone up slightly. In 2019, 46 percent of Gen Z women, 28 percent of Gen Z men, 60 percent of queer Zoomers, and 31 percent of straight Zoomers say that LGBT rights in the survey indicated that this is a critical issue to them personally. The 2019 survey has 109 Zoomers who are nonbinary or trans; among those individuals, 74 percent say LGBTQ rights are critical to them personally.
21. Given that 85 percent of nonbinary or trans Zoomers indicate that such issues are critically important personally, and with so few cases of those Zoomers in my survey, I am opting not to report mean levels of engagement here by importance of LGBTQ equality. In May 2022, however, nonbinary or trans Zoomers reported engaging in 4.69 political activities. In July 2019, nonbinary or trans Zoomers engaged in 4.29 activities.

6. GUNS, CLIMATE CHANGE, AND INCOME INEQUALITY

22. For Gen Z women, differences in mean political engagement among those who say LGBTQ rights are a critical issue to them personally and those who do not (combining the latter two categories) are significant ($t = 4.18$; $p < .001$. For Gen Z men, those differences just miss conventional significance ($t = 1.53$; $p = .128$).
23. For LGBTQ Zoomers, differences in mean political engagement among those who say LGBTQ rights are a critical issue to them personally and those who do not (combining the latter two categories) are significant ($t = 3.10$; $p < .01$). For straight Zoomers, those differences just miss conventional significance ($t = 1.59$; $p = .113$).

6. HOW THE FIGHTS AGAINST GUN VIOLENCE, CLIMATE CHANGE, AND INCOME INEQUALITY HAVE BECOME GENDERED SPACES

1. Asher Stockler, "Gen Z, Millennials Twice as Concerned About Active Shooters as Baby Boomers," *Newsweek*, October 2, 2019, https://www.newsweek.com/young-people-mass-shootings-survey-1462787; Julia Mullins, "Poll: Gen Z Spurs Shift in Voter Support for Gun Control," RealClearPolitics, August 15, 2019, https://www.realclearpolitics.com/articles/2019/08/15/poll_gen_z_spurs_shift_in_voter_support_for_gun_control__141014.html; Cary Funk, "Key Findings: How Americans' Attitudes About Climate Change Differs by Generation, Party, and other Factors," Pew Research Center. May 26, 2021, https://www.pewresearch.org/short-reads/2021/05/26/key-findings-how-americans-attitudes-about-climate-change-differ-by-generation-party-and-other-factors/.
2. The differences on prioritization of mass shootings (chi-square = 16.8; $p < .001$) and climate change between Gen Z and older Americans (chi-square = 24.9; $p < .000$) are statistically significant.
3. Laura Wronski, "Axios|Momentive Poll: Capitalism and Socialism," Survey Monkey, June 15, 2021, https://www.surveymonkey.com/curiosity/axios-capitalism-update/.
4. Lisa Baumann and Manuel Valdes, "New Washington Law Bans Sale of Some Semi-Automatic Rifles. It's Already Facing Legal Challenge," *PBS NewsHour*, April 26, 2023, https://www.pbs.org/newshour/politics/new-washington-law-bans-sale-of-some-semi-automatic-rifles-its-already-facing-a-legal-challenge/.
5. The gender differences in support for such bans are statistically significant (chi-square = 111.5; $p < .001$). Similar gender gaps were found when I also asked that question in the 2019 survey.
6. These differences are statistically significant (chi-square = 26.0; $p < .000$). Similar gender gaps were found between queer and straight Zoomers when I also asked that question in the 2019 survey.
7. Steven Greene et al., "Do Moms Demand Action on Guns? Parenthood and Gun Policy Attitudes," *Journal of Elections, Public Opinion and Parties* 32, no. 2 (2021): 655–673, doi:10.1080/17457289.2020.1862130.
8. Mary-Kate Lizotte, "Authoritarian Personality and Gender Differences in Gun Control Attitudes," *Journal of Women, Politics & Policy* 40, no. 3 (2019): 385–408.

9. Philip Edwards Jones, "Political Distinctiveness and Diversity Among LGBT Americans," *Public Opinion Quarterly* 85, no. 2 (2021): 594–622; Kerith J. Conron et al., "Gun Violence and LGBT Adults," *The Williams Institute*, November 2018, https://williamsinstitute.law.ucla.edu/publications/gun-violence-and-lgbt-adults/.
10. Sandy Hook Promise, "Facts and Statistics About the Impact of Gun Violence on LGBTQ People," n.d., https://www.sandyhookpromise.org/blog/news/facts-and-statistics-about-the-impact-of-gun-violence-on-lgbtq-people/.
11. Human Rights Campaign, "Pulse 4 Years Later: LGBTQ, Gun Safety Groups Release Report," June 12, 2020, https://www.hrc.org/news/pulse-4-years-later-lgbtq-gun-safety-groups-release-report.
12. This difference is statistically significant according to a chi-square test (chi-square = 75.5; $p < .001$).
13. This difference is statistically significant according to a chi-square test (chi-square = 65.4; $p < .001$).
14. Sandy Hook Promise, "The Bipartisan Safer Communities Act: What's Next?," 2022, https://www.sandyhookpromise.org/blog/news/the-bipartisan-gun-safety-reform-bill-whats-next/.
15. Alex Tyson, Brian Kennedy, and Cary Funk, "Gen Z, Millennials Stand Out for Climate Change Activism, Social Media Engagement with Issue," Pew Research Center, May 26, 2021, https://www.pewresearch.org/science/2021/05/26/gen-z-millennials-stand-out-for-climate-change-activism-social-media-engagement-with-issue/.
16. Jamie Margolin, *Youth to Power: Your Voice and How to Use It* (New York: Hachette, 2020).
17. Jennifer Sperber, "Youth Climate Activists Press Companies to Become More Sustainable," April 22, 2021, https://www.forbes.com/sites/unicefusa/2021/04/22/youth-climate-activists-press-companies-to-become-more-sustainable/?sh=32baadfcaf85.
18. The gender gap in 2022 is statistically significant (chi-square = 48.2; $p < .000$). Gen Z women were also more likely to prioritize climate change than Gen Z men in my July 2019 survey (chi-square = 13.758; $p < .001$).
19. Balgis Osman-Elasha, "Women . . . In the Shadow of Climate Change," *UN Chronicle*, n.d., https://www.un.org/en/chronicle/article/womenin-shadow-climate-change#.
20. Mary-Kate Lizotte, *Gender Differences in Public Opinion: Values and Political Consequences* (Philadelphia: Temple University Press, 2020).
21. Lydia Saad, "Socialism as Popular as Capitalism Among Young Adults in the U.S," *Gallup*, November 25, 2019. https://news.gallup.com/poll/268766/socialism-popular-capitalism-among-young-adults.aspx.
22. Pew Research Center, "Modest Declines in Positive Views of 'Socialism' and 'Capitalism' in U.S," September 2022, https://www.pewresearch.org/politics/2022/09/19/modest-declines-in-positive-views-of-socialism-and-capitalism-in-u-s/.
23. This difference is statistically significant (chi-square = 38.885; $p < .001$)
24. This gender difference is statistically significant (chi-square = 8.984; $p < .01$).
25. This difference is statistically significant according to a t-test ($t = 2.43$; $p < .05$).
26. This difference is statistically significant according to a t-test ($t = 2.30$; $p < .05$).

7. GEN Z MEN AND POLITICS

1. Charlie Kirk, *Campus Battlefield: How Conservatives Can WIN the Battle on Campus and Why It Matters* (New York: Post Hill Press, 2018).
2. Charlie Kirk, *The College Scam: How America's Universities Are Bankrupting and Brainwashing Away the Future of America's Youth* (Lewes, DE: Winning Team Publishing, 2022).
3. Matt Stieb, "CPAC Cancels Speaker at 'America Uncanceled' Conference," *New York*, February 22, 2021, https://nymag.com/intelligencer/2021/02/cpac-cancels-speaker-at-america-uncanceled-conference.html.
4. Pew Research Center, "Americans and 'Cancel Culture': Where Some See Calls for Accountability, Others See Censorship, Punishment," May 19, 2021, https://www.pewresearch.org/internet/2021/05/19/americans-and-cancel-culture-where-some-see-calls-for-accountability-others-see-censorship-punishment/.
5. Meredith Conroy, "How 'Cancel Culture' Became an Issue for Young Republicans," *FiveThirtyEight*, March 22, 2021, https://fivethirtyeight.com/features/how-cancel-culture-became-an-issue-for-young-republicans/.
6. This difference is statistically significant (chi-square = 12.3; $p < .05$.)
7. This difference is statistically significant (chi-square = 43.0; $p < .001$.)
8. The difference between Republican Gen Z men and Republican Gen Z women is marginally statistically significant (chi-square = 9.4; $p < .06$.)
9. The difference between Democratic Gen Z women who strongly agree that the political climate prevents them from speaking out (19 percent) compared with Democratic Gen Z men (27 percent) is statistically significant according to a chi-square test (chi-square = 14.4; $p < .01$).
10. $t = 2.37$; $p < .05$.
11. $t = 2.25$; $p < .05$.
12. Models were run on the full sample of Gen Z Americans, and then Gen Z women and men separately, and on LGBTQ and straight Zoomers separately. In no cases were attitudes about political climate significantly related to overall levels of political activity while controlling for other factors.
13. Josh Hawley, "Senator Josh Hawley Delivers National Conservatism Keynote on the Left's Attack on Men in America," November 1, 2021, https://www.hawley.senate.gov/senator-hawley-delivers-national-conservatism-keynote-lefts-attack-men-america.
14. Josh Hawley, *Manhood: The Masculine Virtues America Needs* (Washington, DC: Regnery, 2023).
15. Hawley, *Manhood*, 8–9.
16. Kristin Kobes du Mez, *Jesus and John Wayne: How White Evangelicals Corrupted a Faith and Fractured a Nation* (New York: Norton, 2020).
17. Public Religion Research Institute (PRRI), "More Acceptance but Growing Polarization on LGBTQ Rights: Findings from the 2022 American Values Atlas," February 23, 2023, https://www.prri.org/research/findings-from-the-2022-american-values-atlas/.

7. GEN Z MEN AND POLITICS

18. Jordan Peterson, *Twelve Rules for Life: An Antidote to Chaos* (London: Penguin, 2018). *Twelve Rules for Life* has sold more than 5 million copies, according to Penguin Random House, its publisher.
19. PRRI, "A Christian Nation? Understanding the Threat of Christian Nationalism and American Democracy and Culture: Findings from the 2023 PRRI/Brookings Christian Nationalism Survey," 2023, https://www.prri.org/research/a-christian-nation-understanding-the-threat-of-christian-nationalism-to-american-democracy-and-culture/.
20. Melissa Deckman and Erin Cassese, "Gendered Nationalism and the 2016 US Presidential Election: How Party, Class, and Beliefs About Masculinity Shaped Voting Behavior," *Politics & Gender* 17 (2021): 277–300.
21. PRRI, "Fractured Nation: Widening Partisan Polarization and Key Issues in 2020 Presidential Elections," 2019, https://www.prri.org/research/fractured-nation-widening-partisan-polarization-and-key-issues-in-2020-presidential-elections/.
22. This difference is statistically significant (chi-square = 108; $p < .001$). There are not enough cases to isolate the 2019 PRRI American Values Survey (AVS) for Gen Z, who would have been aged eighteen to twenty-two in the survey ($n = 85$).
23. PRRI, "Fractured Nation."
24. Differences in mean political engagement between Gen Z Republican men who agree that America is too soft and feminine and those who disagree are not statistically significant. The same finding applies to Gen Z Democratic men. Gen Z Republican women who agree that America is too soft and feminine are not statistically distinct from those who disagree.
25. PRRI, "The Health of Democracy Ahead of an Unprecedented Presidential Election: Findings from the 2023 American Values Survey," October 25, 2023, https://www.prri.org/research/threats-to-american-democracy-ahead-of-an-unprecedented-presidential-election/.
26. Lucina Di Meco, "Monetizing Misogyny: Gendered Disinformation and the Undermining of Women's Rights and Democracy Globally," February 2023, https://she-persisted.org/wp-content/uploads/2023/02/ShePersisted_MonetizingMisogyny.pdf.
27. Cécile Guerin and Eisha Maharasingam-Shah, "Public Figures, Public Rage: Candidate Abuse on Social Media," October 5, 2020, https://www.isdglobal.org/isd-publications/public-figures-public-rage-candidate-abuse-on-social-media/.
28. Di Meco, "Monetizing Misogyny," 9.
29. Lindsay Dodgson and Bethany Dawson, "As His Beliefs Have Seeped into Homes and Classrooms, Children as Young as 11 Think Andrew Tate Is Their 'God,'" *Business Insider*, January 29, 2023, https://www.businessinsider.com/teachers-and-parents-talk-about-andrew-tates-influence-on-kids-2023-1.
30. Center for Countering Digital Hate, "YouTube Rakes in Millions in Ad Revenue from Videos of Misogynist Andrew Tate," August 19, 2022, https://counterhate.com/blog/youtube-rakes-in-millions-in-ad-revenue-from-videos-of-misogynist-andrew-tate/.
31. Kaiser Family Foundation, "Suicide Rate by Gender," 2021, https://www.kff.org/other/state-indicator/suicide-rate-by-gender/?.
32. The Violence Project, "Key Findings," 2023.

33. Glenn Thrush and Matt Richtel, "A Disturbing New Pattern in Mass Shootings: Young Assailants," *New York Times*, June 2, 2022, https://www.nytimes.com/2022/06/02/us/politics/mass-shootings-young-men-guns.html.
34. Vice, "Killer Incels: How Misogynistic Men Sparked a New Terror Threat," May 31, 2022, https://www.vice.com/en/article/bvnw3d/incels-elliot-rodger-misogyny-far-right.
35. Center for Countering Digital Hate, "The Incelosphere: Exposing Pathways into Communities and the Harms They Pose to Women and Children," September 23, 2022, https://counterhate.com/research/incelosphere/.
36. Taylor Lorenz, "The Online Incel Movement Is Getting More Violent and Extreme, Report Says," *Washington Post*, September 22, 2022, https://www.washingtonpost.com/technology/2022/09/22/incels-rape-murder-study/.
37. Center for Countering Digital Hate, "Digital Hate: Social Media's Role in Amplifying Dangerous Lies About LGBTQ+ People," August 10, 2022, https://counterhate.com/research/digital-hate-lgbtq/.
38. Anser Hassan, "Proud Boys Members Under Hate Crime Investigation After Disrupting East Bay Drag Queen Story Event," *ABC7News*, June 13, 2022, https://abc7news.com/drag-queen-story-hour-panda-dulce-san-lorenzo-library-proud-boys/11956109/.
39. Odette Yousef, "31 Members of the White Nationalist Patriot Front Arrested Near an Idaho Pride Event," *NPR*, June 12, 2022, https://www.npr.org/2022/06/11/1104405804/patriot-front-white-supremacist-arrested-near-idaho-pride.
40. Michael Kilmer, *Healing from Hate: How Young Men Get into—and out of—Violent Extremism* (Oakland: University of California Press, 2018).
41. Alan Feur and Zach Montague, "Four Convicted of Obstruction on January 6 in Final Oath Keepers Trial," *New York Times*, March 20, 2023; Dan Mangan, "DOJ Says at Least 1,000 Trump Supporters Arrested for January 6 Riot," *CNBC*, March 6, 2023.

CONCLUSION: THE POSSIBILITIES OF A MORE INCLUSIVE POLITICAL FUTURE

1. Center for American Women and Politics, (CAWP), "Women in State Legislatures 2023," 2023, https://cawp.rutgers.edu/facts/levels-office/state-legislature/women-state-legislatures-2024.
2. CAWP, "Women in State Legislatures 2023."
3. For a good summary of this scholarship, see chapter 8 of Julie Dolan, Melissa Deckman, and Michele L. Swers, eds., *Women and Politics: Paths to Power and Political Influence*, 4th ed. (Lanham, MD: Rowman & Littlefield, 2021).
4. Michele Swers, "Gender and Party Politics in a Polarized Era," in *Party and Procedure in the United States Congress*, 2nd ed., ed. Jacob R. Straus and Matthew E. Glassman (Lanham, MD: Rowman & Littlefield, 2017), 279–300.
5. See the Center for American Women and Politics for data on the partisan breakdown of elected women officeholders, "Find Elected Women Officials," n.d, https://cawpdata.rutgers.edu/.

6. Heiler Cheung, "Did First Female-Majority Legislature in the US Make a Difference?," *BBC*, March 4, 2020, https://www.bbc.com/news/world-us-canada-51623420.
7. Kelly Dittmar, *Measuring Success: Women in 2020 Legislative Elections*, Center for American Women and Politics, Eagleton Institute of Politics, Rutgers University, New Brunswick. NJ, 2021, https://womenrun.rutgers.edu/2020-report/.
8. Susan Carroll and Kira Sanbonmatsu, *More Women Can Run: Gender and Pathways to the State Legislatures* (New York: Oxford University Press, 2013).
9. Dolan, Deckman, and Swers, *Women and Politics*.
10. Jennifer L. Lawless and Richard L. Fox, "Running for Office Is Still for Men—Some Data on the 'Ambition Gap,'" *Brookings*, February 8, 2022, https://www.brookings.edu/articles/running-for-office-is-still-for-men-some-data-on-the-ambition-gap/.
11. Jennifer L. Lawless and Richard L. Fox, "Girls Just Wanna Not Run: The Gender Gap in Young Americans' Political Ambition," Washington, DC: Women & Politics Institute, March, 2013, https://www.american.edu/spa/wpi/upload/girls-just-wanna-not-run_policy-report.pdf.
12. IGNITE, "Igniting Young Women's Political Power," 2024, https://ignitenational.org/who-we-are.
13. Benjamin Ryan, "'Rainbow Wave' in U.S. Midterms Lifts LGBTQ+ Hopes but Battles Ahead," *Reuters*, November 18, 2022, https://www.reuters.com/article/usa-election-lgbt/analysis-rainbow-wave-in-u-s-midterms-lifts-lgbtq-hopes-but-battles-ahead-idUSL8N32B4ER/.
14. Victory Institute, "Out for America 2022: A Census of LGBTQ Elected Officials Nationwide," 2022, https://victoryinstitute.org/resource/out-for-america-2022-a-census-of-out-lgbtq-elected-officials-nationwide/.
15. Victory Institute, "Out for America 2022."
16. Halisia Hubbard, "What It Means That a Historic Number of LGBTQ Candidates Won Midterm Elections," *NPR*, November 14, 2022, https://www.npr.org/2022/11/14/1136165932/lgbtq-candidates-elections-winners.
17. U.S. Census, "Historical Reported Voting Rates," 2022, https://www.census.gov/data/tables/time-series/demo/voting-and-registration/voting-historical-time-series.html.
18. Martin P. Wattenberg, *Is Voting for Young People?* 5th ed. (New York: Routledge, 2020).
19. Erik Plutzer, "Becoming a Habitual Voter: Inertia, Resources, and Growth in Young Adulthood," *American Political Science Review* 96, no. 1 (2004): 41–56.
20. Meredith Rolfe, *Voter Turnout: A Social Theory of Political Participation* (New York: Cambridge University Press, 2012).
21. John Holbein and D. Sunshine Hillygus, *Making Young Voters: Converting Civic Attitudes into Civic Action* (Cambridge: Cambridge University Press, 2020).
22. Chris Walker, "Florida GOP Election Bill Aims to Make It Harder for Gen Z to Vote," *Salon*, April 7, 2023, https://www.salon.com/2023/04/07/florida-bill-aims-to-make-it-harder-for-gen-z-to-vote_partner/.
23. Walker, "Florida GOP Election Bill."

METHODOLOGICAL APPENDIX

24. Center for Information & Research on Civic Learning and Engagement (CIRCLE), "2020 Election Center: National Youth Voter Turnout," Tufts University, n.d., https://circle.tufts.edu/2020-election-center.
25. Rob Griffin, William Frey, and Ruy Teixera, "America's Electoral Future," Center for American Progress, October 19, 2020, https://www.americanprogress.org/article/americas-electoral-future-3/; Morley Winograd, Michael Hais, and Doug Ross, "How Younger Voters Will Impact Elections: Younger Voters Are Poised to Upend American Politics," February 27, 2023, https://www.brookings.edu/articles/younger-voters-are-poised-to-upend-american-politics/.
26. Griffin, Frey and Teixera, "America's Electoral Future."
27. Center for Information & Research on Civic Learning and Engagement (CIRCLE), "The Youth Vote in 2022," November 2022, https://circle.tufts.edu/2022-election-center#women,-youth-of-color,-lgbt-youth-give-democrats-strongest-support.
28. Catalist, "What Happened in 2022: An Analysis of the 2022 Midterms," 2023, https://catalist.us/whathappened2022/.
29. Center for Information & Research on Civic Learning and Engagement (CIRCLE), "The Abortion Election: How Youth Prioritized and Voted Based on Issues," November 14, 2022.
30. Francesca Paris and Nate Cohn, "After Roe's End, Women Surged in Signing Up to Vote in Some States," *New York Times*, August 25, 2022, https://www.nytimes.com/interactive/2022/08/25/upshot/female-voters-dobbs.html.
31. Ronald Brownstein, "The GOP's Demographic Doom," *The Atlantic*, October 23, 2020, https://www.theatlantic.com/politics/archive/2020/10/millennials-and-gen-z-will-soon-dominate-us-elections/616818/.
32. Nate Silver, "The Senate's Rural Skew Makes It Very Hard for Democrats to Win the Supreme Court," *FiveThirtyEight*, September 20, 2020, https://fivethirtyeight.com/features/the-senates-rural-skew-makes-it-very-hard-for-democrats-to-win-the-supreme-court/.
33. Philip Bump, "The Age Gap in Politics Contributes to the Cynicism Gap," September 19, 2023, https://www.washingtonpost.com/politics/2023/09/19/pew-polling-age-politics/.
34. Erica L. Green, "Biden Creates Federal Office of Gun Violence Prevention," *New York Times*, September 22, 2023, https://www.nytimes.com/2023/09/22/us/politics/biden-office-gun-violence-prevention.html
35. Monica Anderson, "A Majority of Teens Have Experienced Some Form of Cyberbullying," *Pew Research Center*, September 27, 2018, https://www.pewresearch.org/internet/2018/09/27/a-majority-of-teens-have-experienced-some-form-of-cyberbullying/.

METHODOLOGICAL APPENDIX

1. Miliaikeala S. J. Heen, Joel D. Lieberman, and Terance D. Miethe, "A Comparison of Different Online Sampling Approaches for Generating National Samples," UNLV Center for Crime and Justice Policy, September 2014.

METHODOLOGICAL APPENDIX

2. Taylor C. Boas, Dino P. Christenson, and David M. Glick, "Recruiting Large Online Samples in the United States and India: Facebook, Mechanical Turk, and Qualtrics," *Political Science Research and Methods* 8, no. 2 (2018): 232–250, doi:10.1017/psrm.2018.28.
3. Andrew Mercer and Arnold Lau, "Comparing Two Types of Online Survey Sampling," Pew Research Center, September 7, 2023, https://www.pewresearch.org/methods/2023/09/07/comparing-two-types-of-online-survey-samples/.

INDEX

50 Miles More (Milwaukee), 2, 102, 130–131

abortion/abortion rights: attitudes, 222; *Dobbs* decision on, 20–21, 29, 40, 100–101, 103, 174; Gen Z men on, 14; Gen Z women on, 14, 96–101, 272n26; and social media, 20–21
Abrams, Stacey, 61–62
Acevedo, Sylvia, 36
activism: climate, 61, 137; community, 109–110; conservative, 69; digital, 22, 28; and feminism, 84–96; Gen Z, 82–84, 112–116, 177; high school, 53, 93; LGBTQ, 59; LGBTQIA, 48; motivator for, 84–96; political, 3, 18, 22, 31–32, 35, 64, 71, 86, 89–94, 104–105, 109–110, 112–116, 195; social, 88; transgender, 155
activists: Gen Z, 3, 5, 9, 19–20, 23–24, 35, 53, 82–83, 87, 96, 104–105, 109, 111, 139–140, 144, 146–149, 177–183; LGBTQ, 57, 117, 127, 160; political, 3, 64, 73, 114; Republican women, 132; right-wing,

150; and role models, 64–67; social justice, 19
Agrawal-Hardin, Naina, 30–31, 177–178
Akanegbu, Zikora, 104–105
Amaral, Ana De Almeida, 36
American Academy of Pediatrics, 117
American National Election Studies (ANES), 27–28, 97, 98–99
American politics: feminism and future of, 101–103; reproductive rights and future of, 101–103
American Values Atlas (AVA), 8, 116, 259n11
Anderson, Kristen Soltis, 32
Anti-Defamation League (ADL), 163
AOC effect, 64–67, 74
Artis, Zanagee, 136
Asians Lead, 35, 88
Axios and Survey Monkey, 127

Backlash (Faludi), 161
"Bans Off Our Bodies" protest, 83
Bastida, Xiye, 61

INDEX

Bhoopalam, Ina, 5, 82, 135, 182
Biden, Joseph, 165, 174, 180
Big Brother, 162
Bipartisan Safer Communities Act, 135
Black Gen Z men, 34
Black LGBTQ Americans, 48, 107
Black Lives Matter (BLM) movement, 4, 9, 48, 70, 106, 108, 110, 182
Black Zoomers, 53
Blake, Jacob, 161
Blexit, 69
Bonier, Tom, 20, 101
Boy Scouts, 35, 37
Brady, Henry, 261n40
Brady: United Against Gun Violence, 107
Brown, Michael, 48
Brown Girl Magazine, 19
Bump, Philip, 179
Burns, Nancy, 261n40
Bush, Cori, 81
Bush, George W., 68
Byars, Patton, 151

California Menstrual Justice Network, 9
campaign-related activities, 27, 194
Campbell, David E., 63, 264n34
Campus Battlefield: How Conservatives Can WIN the Battle on Campus and Why It Matters (Kirk), 150
Campus Reform, 68
capitalism, 139–142
Cassese, Erin, 156
Census of American Religion, 6
Center for American Women and Politics (CAWP), Rutgers University, 168
Center for Countering Digital Hate (CCDH), 162–163
Center for Information and Research on Civic Learning and Engagement (CIRCLE), 102, 173, 174, 256n13
Century of Votes, A (Wolbrecht and Corder), 26
Chacko, Luke, 114–115

Chang, Claire, 128
Chun, Alexandria, 122
cisgender, 6, 92, 115–116, 131, 146, 258n4
cisgender Gen Z men, 6
cisgender men: as LGBTQ, 6, 258n5; white, 131
Civic Innovators Fellowship, 146
civic skills, and politics for Gen Z, 35–39
Civics Unplugged, 146, 152
Civil Rights Act of 1964, 115
climate activism, 61, 137
climate change, 127–128; gendered dimensions of, 135–138; Gen Z women on, 136–137, 138; intersectional approach to, 108–109; LGBTQ people on, 138
Clinton, Bill, 116
Clinton, Hillary, 39, 112
Clinton, Sophie, 67
cloutavists, defined, 181
community activism, 109–110
Concerned Citizens DC, 108
"concerted cultivation," 71
conservative activism, 69
Conservative Political Action Conference (CPAC), 150
Cooley, Mariah, 4
Corder, Kevin, 26
Corin, Jaclyn, 128, 131, 133, 135, 182; about gender dynamics of organization, 126; about Generation Z, 126; class research project on gun control, 125; cofounder of March for Our Lives, 125–126, 131; Jacobs, Kristin, 125; Kasky, Cameron, 125; at Marjory Stoneman Douglas High School, Parkland, 124; plea on Facebook and Instagram, 124
Couture, Rosie, 80–82, 115–116, 182
COVID-19 pandemic, 11, 38, 104, 128, 139, 183
Crawley, Joe, 64

D'Alacio, Isabella, 88, 128
Dean, Anna, 83, 102, 178

INDEX

Democratic Congressional Campaign Committee (DCCC), 177
Democratic Gen Z men, 158, 261n35
Democratic Gen Z women, 25, 45, 84, 91, 261n35
Democratic Party, 6, 177, 179; and Black Americans, 69; and Gen Z women, 8–9, 45; and youngest voters, 175–176
DeSantis, Ron, 117
Desaraju, Neha, 13
descriptive representation, 63
digital activism, 22, 28
Dilos, Thanasi, 145–146, 152, 164
di Meco, Lucina, 161
discrimination, 85, 105, 178; gender, 94, 182; job, 115–116; LGBTQ, 116–117; protections, 116–117; sexual, 29, 115
Dobbs decision on abortion rights, 20–21, 29, 40, 100, 101, 103, 174
Dobson, Sam, 140
domestic gun violence, 131
Do, Mai 9
Doucette, Ryan, 149, 159, 176–177
DREAM EQUAL, 5, 82, 135
Du Mez, Kristin, 155

Easly, Perri, 66
Eastmond, Aalayah, 107–108
Eder, Katie, 57–58, 70; LGBTQ community, 3; National School Walkout, 2; political organizing, 1–2
emotions: and political engagement, 49–50, 265n48; and Zoomers, 49
Equality Act, 115
Equal Rights Amendment (ERA), 21, 80–81, 85, 182
ethnicity: and Gen Z participation, 33–34; shape priorities/politics among Gen Z women, 105–108
external political efficacy, 42–45
extremism, 160–164

Fair Fight, 66
Faludi, Susan, 161
Fehsenfeld, Emily, 68, 90
female candidates and survey experiment, 73–78
"feminazi," 86
Feminine Mystique, The (Friedan), 85
feminism: and future of American politics, 101–103; as motivator for activism, 84–96; and political activism, 89–94; social media, role of, 87–88
feminists, 84, 272n19; Gen Z, 84–87, 89–90, 101, 271n15; LGBTQ Zoomers, 92, 271n16; motivations for Gen Z activism, 82–84; second-wave, 161; self-proclaimed, 92
Fleischer, Kathryn, 131–132
Florida: Department of Education, 118; Don't Say Gay bill, 117; General Assembly, 125
Floyd, George, 4, 106–107, 110, 182, 270n30
Fluke, Sandra, 86
focus groups, 186–187; IGNITE, 10, 31, 84, 185–187; Republican, 121–122; and role models, 64–67
formative politics, 256n8
Fox, Richard, 169–170
Foy, Jennifer Carroll, 80
French, Judi, 69
Fridays for Future (FFF), 61, 70, 127, 144
Friedan, Betty, 85
Frost, Maxwell, 182
Future Accelerator program, 2
Future Coalition, 2–3, 70, 114

Gaetz, Matt, 20
Gay and Lesbian Alliance Against Defamation (GLAAD), 82, 112
gender, 143–144; dynamics of organization, 126; and Future Coalition, 3; gaps, 15–16, 20, 26–29, 32–33, 40–43, 264n32; and partisanship, 24–25; political actions by, 251; stereotypes, 5

INDEX

gender discrimination, 94, 182
gender divide: in climate activism, 137; on gun violence, 129–135
gendered dimensions of climate change, 135–138
gender equality, 21; and Gen Z women, 5; and LGBTQ rights, 5, 14
gender identities, 57, 113–115, 117, 155, 176
gender social identity, 75–79, 215–216, 269n28
General Social Survey (GSS), 8, 95–96, 191
Generation Gap (Munger), 19
Generation Ratify, 81, 115. *See also* Young Feminist Party
Generation Z (Gen Z), 113, 255n1; and abortion rights, 96–101; activism, 82–84, 112–116, 177; activists, 3, 5, 9, 19–20, 23–24, 35, 53, 82–83, 87, 96, 104–105, 109, 111, 139–140, 144, 146–149, 177–183; civic skills shaping politics for, 35–39; Corin, Jaclyn, about, 126; data on, 127; and Democrats, 173–180; economic issues, 127–128; economy, 139–143; focus groups, 186–187; and gender, 143–144; General Social Survey (GSS) data, 191; income inequality, 139–143; interviews, 185–186; lack of engagement in workforce, 142; LGBTQ rights drive political activism for, 112–116; lockdown generation, 128; political engagement, 32–33, 47–48, 51–59, 96–101; political mobilization, 47–48; political priorities, 3; political views and social media, 18–26; psychological resources, 39–47; and racial equality, 109–112; Republicans, 173–180; on social media, 145; surveys, 187–189; in United States, 109–112; and U.S. population, 190; women of color, 88, 92, 105–106, 108, 110, 175
Gen X women, 8, 98–99
Gen Z American men, 166

Gen Z Americans, 35, 52–53, 71, 118, 120, 127, 152, 157, 185, 186, 266n53, 274n20; diverse generation, 3–7; least religious generation, 3–7; mass shootings, 127; and partisanship, 7–11; party identification, 258n9; policy priorities of, 11–15; political engagement of, 116–120; positive views of socialism, 141; prioritizing LGBTQ rights, 116–120
Gen Z Book, The (Goel), 141
Gen Z Democratic men, 133, 139, 153, 158
Gen Z Democratic women, 62, 132, 133, 139, 158
Gen Z feminists, 84–87, 89–90, 101, 271n15
Gen Z for Change, 102
Gen Z Grow Our Platform (Gen Z GOP), 122, 149, 151, 176
GenZHER, 104–105
Gen Z men, 8, 11, 13, 129–130, 136–137, 138, 144; on abortion, 14; activists, 148; crisis of masculinity, 154–160; culture and peer pressure, 150–152; Democratic, 25; effect of treatment, 215; extreme misogyny, 162–163; extremism, 160–164; *vs.* Gen Z women political engagement, 34, 54–57; high school participation, 38; ideology, 46; on mass shootings, 133; negative views of socialism, 143; political engagement, 15–17, 203–204, 207–208, 212–213, 218–221, 224–227, 229–230, 233–234, 237–253; political polarization, 165–166; and politics, 145–166; positive views of socialism, 141; semiautomatic weapons bans, 129, 130; violence, 160–164
Gen Z Republican men, 133, 151, 158
Gen Z Republican women, 133, 143, 150
Gen Z women, 5, 7, 11, 129–130, 138, 142, 143–144, 147, 170; on abortion, 14; climate change, 108–109; on climate change, 136–137, 138; and Democratic Party, 8–9, 25; dissatisfaction with

286

INDEX

political system, 43; feminist future, 94–96; gender equality, 14; Gen Z Democratic women, 132; *vs.* Gen Z men political engagement, 34, 54–57; on gun control, 132; gun violence, 13; high active engagement levels of, 24–26; high school participation, 37–38; ideology, 46; and LGBTQ candidates, 169–172; LGBTQ rights, 14; in March for Our Lives, 131; on mass shootings, 133; from May 2022 Qualtrics survey, 129; offline activities participation in, 21–24; participation in politics, 3, 15–17, 272n24; perils and promise of, 180–184; political ascendence of, in Trump era, 147–149; political engagement model, 203–204, 207–208, 212–213, 218–221, 224–227, 229–230, 233–234, 237–253; political entrepreneurs, 4; political surge, 26–29; political views/social media, 18–26; in politics, 146; positive views of socialism, 141; race and ethnicity, 105–108; Republican, 133; as Republicans, 10–11; role models shaping political engagement of, 60–79; semiautomatic weapons bans, 129, 130; on social media, 21–24

Ginsburg, Ruth Bader, 64
Girl Scouts, 35–36, 87
Girls Who Code, 87
Girl Up, 35, 87, 105
Global Girlhood, 19
Glover, Samantha, 168
Goel, Riya, 35, 37, 88, 141, 142
Gore, Al, 1
government responsiveness, 63
Greater Good Initiative, 67
Guillermo, Sara, 171
gun control, 127–128; Gen Z women on, 132; LGBTQ Zoomers on, 130
gun violence, 126–127; awareness march, 2; domestic, 131; gender divide on, 129–135;

Gen Z women, 13; LGBTQ Zoomers, 13; prevention, 136; prevention legislation, 134
Guttmacher Institute, 83

Haake, Sabrina, 67
Haley, Nikki, 68
Harper, A. Breeze, 109
Hawley, Josh, 154–155, 159
Healing from Hate: How Young Men Get into—and out of—Violent Extremism (Kimmel), 163
Heflin, Stella, 65, 137
Herod, Leslie, 67
high school activism, 53, 93
Hirsi, Isra, 181
Hogan, Larry, 142
Hogg, David, 126, 180
Homegirl Project, 65, 88, 106
Hope, Isabel, 181
Human Rights Campaign (HRC), 48, 106, 115, 186

identity politics: and Gen Z, 105; and zoomers, 121–123
ideology: Gen Z men, 46; Gen Z women, 46; LGBTQ Zoomers, 46; as psychological resources, 45–47
iGen, 255n1
IGNITE, 10, 31, 36, 47, 171, 185–187, 189
income inequality, 139–143
An Inconvenient Truth (Gore), 1
Institutional Review Board (IRB), 185
internal political efficacy, 42–43
intersectional approach to climate change, 108–109
intersectionality, 121, 273n1
Ivey, Kay, 69, 96

Jacobs, Kristin, 125
Jacobson, Ophelie, 10, 68
Jain, Pranjal, 19

287

INDEX

Jesus and John Wayne (Du Mez), 155
Jha, Devishi, 135–137
job discrimination, 115–116
Julianna, Olivia, 20

Kannan, Malavika, 65, 88, 105–106
Kasky, Cameron, 125
Kavanaugh, Brett, 112
Kelley, Ben, 149
Kemp, Brian, 66
Kerpen, Charlotte, 39
Khalil, Teya, 66, 139
Kids Tales, 1, 70
Kilby, Melissa, 18–19, 35
Kimmel, Michael, 163
King, Martin Luther, Jr., 136
Kirk, Charlie, 150

Laureau, Annette, 71
Lawless, Jennifer, 169–170
LeafPress, 136
Lee, Alvin, 148
LGBTQ+: activism, 59, 112; activists, 57, 117, 127, 160; advocacy, 113; candidates and Gen Z women, 169–172; cisgender men as, 6, 258n5; on climate change, 138; community, 114, 116; politics, 121; rights, 105
LGBTQ Americans, 115, 116, 117, 147–148, 166, 172
LGBTQ+ Americans of color, 115
LGBTQ discrimination, 116–117; in housing, 116; in jobs, 116; protections, 116–117; in public accommodations, 116
LGBTQ Gen Z Americans, 74
LGBTQ Gen Z people, 3, 8; Democrats, 26; online resources, 38–39; policy priorities, 11–13; political activities, 24; Republicans, 26
LGBTQIA activism, 48
LGBTQ people of color, 114

LGBTQ rights, 5–6, 29, 106, 113, 116, 118–120; Gen Z Americans, 116–120; Gen Z women, 14; and political activism for Gen Z, 112–116; Republican Party on, 10
LGBTQ Victory Fund, 112, 172
LGBTQ Zoomers, 6–7, 11, 13, 24, 49–50, 52, 72–73, 82, 90, 92–93, 97–98, 99–101, 103, 110–111, 117, 119–120, 129–130, 138, 141, 143–144, 146, 153, 157–159, 170, 180–184, 273n7; dissatisfaction with political system, 43, 45; feminists, 92, 271n16; on gun control, 130; high school activities, 38; ideology, 46; offline activities participation in, 21–24; political engagement, 15–17, 32, 57–58, 154, 205–206, 209–210, 212–213, 218–221, 224–227, 229–230, 233–234, 237–253, 264n36, 275n23; political interest, 40–41; and social media, 21–24; *vs.* straight Zoomers in political engagement, 32–33
LGBTQ Zoomers of color, 110, 273n8
Limbaugh, Rush, 86
Linktree of Generation Ratify, 21
Lizotte, Mary-Kate, 137
lockdown generation, 128
LoDuca, Isabel, 136
LOUDwomen, 83, 102
Lowther, Jeremiah, 152
Lu Lu, 140

Mahmud, Sabirah, 60–61, 78
Manhood: The Masculine Virtues America Needs (Hawley), 154
March for Our Lives, 4, 13, 80, 102, 104, 107, 112, 125–126, 129, 131, 134, 182
March On, 2
Margolin, Jamie, 136
Marjorie Stoneman Douglas High School (Parkland, Florida), 2

INDEX

Martin, Trayvon, 4
mass shootings: Democratic men, 133; Democratic women, 133; Gen Z Americans, 127; Gen Z men, 133; Gen Z women, 133; political activities, 134; at religious school in Nashville, 133
Maxie, Alise, 48, 106–107
McBride, Sarah, 67
McDonald, Jared, 73
McEnany, Kayleigh, 68
Meatless Mondays program, 37
Meddling Kids Movement, 181
Memon, Abdullah, 147
menstrual justice, 83
Me Too Movement, 31, 89, 101
Metullus, Yasmeen, 70
mobilization: effect of treatment on, 215; political among Gen Z, 47–48
Moses, Anne, 36, 82
Mott, Lucretia, 26
Muhammed, Ibtihaj, 35
Munger, Kevin, 19
Muslim American women, 62

Nagourney, Adam, 118
NARAL Pro-Choice America, 102. *See also* Reproductive Freedom for All
National Organization for Women (NOW), 85
National Public Radio (NPR), 172
National Rifle Association (NRA), 125
National School Walkout, 2
Native American women, 62
negative partisanship, 258n8
Network of Enlightened Women (NeW), 10, 37, 68, 132
Neville, Adam, 114
New York Times, 118, 180
NextGen America, 102
Nineteenth Amendment, 85
Nixon, Richard, 8–9

Not My Generation, 131
Nyugen, Antoilyn, 9

Ocasio-Cortez, Alexandria, 31, 62, 66, 179
Of Boys and Men (Reeves), 162
Okamoto, Nadya, 83
OLS regression, 217; coefficients-treatment, 216
Omar, Ilhan, 66, 181
Omeish, Abrar, 67
OneUpAction, 135
Owens, Candace, 69

Pant, Aarushi, 65, 113–114
parents as political motivators, 78–79
Parkland community, 124
partisanship: and gender, 24–25; and Gen Z Americans, 7–11; negative, 258n8; as psychological resources, 45–47
passive politics by Gen Zers, 192
Paul, Alice, 85
Pence, Mike, 165
Pennsylvania Youth Climate Strike, 60
Perino, Dana, 68
PERIOD., 83
Peters, Jeremy W., 118
Peterson, Jordan, 155–156
Peterson Report, The, 85
Pew Research Center, 139
Philly Earth Alliance, 60
political actions: by abortion attitudes, 223; by gender, 228, 236, 251; by LGBTQ, 199–200, 223, 228, 236, 251; from Public Religion Research Institute (PRRI), 211; by race, 228; by sex, 195–198, 211
political activism, 3, 18, 22, 31–32, 35, 64, 71, 86, 104–105, 109–110, 195; feminism and, 89–94; for Gen Z, 112–116; and LGBTQ rights, 112–116
political activists, 3, 64, 73, 114
political ambition, 169–171, 183

INDEX

political choices: role models and women's, 62–63
political context, 51–59
political engagement, 261n31; among Gen Z, 47–48, 59; and emotions, 49–50; of Gen Z Americans, 116–120; Gen Z men, 15–17, 54–57; and Gen Z psychological resources, 39–47; Gen Z women, 34, 54–57, 60–79; LGBTQ Zoomers, 15–17, 32, 57; model, Gen Z, 32–33, 51–59; straight Zoomers in, 32–33
political engagement model, 133, 137, 143, 154; and coding, 201–202; by gender, 231–232, 235–236; Gen Z men, 203–204, 207–208, 212–213, 218–221, 224–227, 229–230, 233–234, 237–253; Gen Z women, 203–204, 207–208, 212–213, 218–221, 224–227, 229–230, 233–234, 237–253; LGBTQ Zoomers, 205–206, 209–210, 212–213, 218–221, 224–227, 229–230, 233–234, 237–253; by race, 231–232, 235–236; straight Zoomers, 205–206, 209–210, 212–213, 218–221, 224–227, 229–230, 233–234, 237–253
political engagement scale, marginal values of, 228
political habits, 59, 63
political mobilization, 47–48
political motivators: parents as, 78–79; role models as, 78–79
political polarization, 165–166
politicians: not idols, 70; partisanship of, 74–75; white male, 63
politics: and Gen Z men, 145–166; identity, 121–123; LGBTQ, 121; reproductive rights and future of, 101–103
President John F. Kennedy's Commission on the Status of Women, 85
Pressly, Ayanna, 66
Pride in Running, 112–113

Private Roots of Public Action, The: Gender, Equality and Political Participation (Burns, Schlozman and Brady), 261n40
Pro-choice America (Reproductive Freedom for All), 131
Proctor, Maddie, 66–67
pro-social values, 137
Protasiewicz, Janet, 102
psychological resources: internal and external political efficacy as, 42–45; partisanship and ideology as, 45–47; and political engagement, 39–47
Public Religion Research Institute (PRRI), 6, 27, 40, 58–59, 98–99, 116–117, 118, 146, 155–157, 159, 165–166, 175, 188, 256n10; American Values Atlas, 8; American Values Survey (AVS), 156, 159; Census of American Religion, 6; conservative theology, 155; Politics of Gender Survey, 94

Quichiz, Amy, 108–109, 181

race: priorities/politics among Gen Z women, 105–108; socioeconomic status, 33–34
racial equality among members of Gen Z, 109–112
racial minorities, 63
Rahman, Afiya, 70
Rami, Norah, 70, 140
Reagan, Ronald, 161
Red Cross, 125
Reed, Riley, 43, 112–113
Reeves, Richard, 162
regression coefficients, 216
Reichardt, Gabby, 69
Reproductive Freedom for All, 102
reproductive rights and future of American politics, 101–103
Republican Party, 6–7, 9–10; Gen Z men, 45; on LGBTQ rights, 10

INDEX

Republican women: inspiration at home, 70–73; role models for, 68–73
reverse gender gap, 15, 26–29, 38; among Gen Z Americans, 48; Gen Z's, 43; historic, 52, 59, 62, 79, 92, 94, 101, 147; in political participation, 42, 159
right-wing activists, 150
Rittenhouse, Kyle, 161
Rodger, Elliot, 163
Roe v. Wade, 20, 81, 83, 102
role model effect, 63
role models: AOC effect, 64–67; as political motivators, 78–79; for Republican women, 68–73; shaping political engagement of Gen Z women, 60–79; shaping women's political choices, 62–63; view from activists/focus groups, 64–67
Romney, Mitt, 39
Rowling, J. K., 150
Running Start, 67

same-sex marriage, 116–117
Sanders, Bernie, 64–65
Schlafly, Phyllis, 85–86
Schlozman, Key Lehman, 261n40
Scott, Rick, 125
Second Amendment rights, 129
second-wave feminism, 85
second-wave feminists, 161
semiautomatic weapons bans, 129, 130
sexual discrimination, 29, 115
sexuality: and Gen Z, 1–29; and political engagement of Gen Z, 30–59
#ShePersisted, 161
Siegel, Jack, 148, 152, 159
Silver, Nate, 178
Sinema, Kyrsten, 66
Sistah Vegan (Harper), 109
social activism, 88
social justice activists, 19

social media, 161; *Dobbs* decision on abortion rights, 20–21; and feminism, 87–88; and Gen Z political views, 18–26; Gen Z women on, 21–24; and LGBTQ Zoomers, 21–24; political views and Gen Z women, 18–26
socioeconomic status: and Gen Z participation in politics, 33–34
Sofia, Maria, 142
Sparwath, Chloe, 11, 37, 132
Stanton, Elizabeth Cady, 26
STOP ERA movement, 86
straight Zoomers: *vs.* LGBTQ Zoomers in political engagement, 32–33; political interest, 40
Sunrise Movement, 13
survey experiment, and female candidates, 73–78
Swift, Taylor, 87

TargetSmart, 20, 101
Tate, Andrew, 162
Taylor, Breonna, 4, 106–108
Team ENOUGH, 107–108, 128–129
teenage girls, 63
Teen Vogue, 82
Tew, Madelaine, 136
Thelapurith, Priya, 83
Thunberg, Greta, 60, 61, 127
Tlaib, Rashida, 66
Torres, Selena, 167–168
transgender activism, 155
transgenderism, 91
Trump, Donald, 2, 4, 30, 62, 68, 121, 147, 148, 151, 156, 159, 174, 177–178
Turning Point USA, 69
Twelve Rules for Life (Peterson), 156
Twenty-eighth Amendment, 81

Uber Eats, 125
United Kingdom, 162

291

INDEX

United Nations (UN), 68; Commission on the Status of Women, 35; and Girl Up, 18; Nikki Haley as ambassador to, 68; women and climate change, 136–137

United States (US): House of Representatives, 66; racial equality among members of Gen Z in, 109–112

U.S. Census Bureau's Current Population Survey (CPS), 188

U.S. Constitution: Equal Rights Amendment (ERA), 80–81

U.S. Youth Strike for Climate, 60, 61

Veggie Mijas, 109
Vietnam War, 29

Walker, Scott, 118
Wallen, Morgan, 150
Washington, Tatiana, 102, 130
Washington Post, 117
Wellford, Susannah, 67
Williams, Lauren, 13–14
Wolak, Jennifer, 40–41
Wolbrecht, Christina, 26, 63, 264n34
women: LOUDwomen, 83, 102; Muslim American, 62; political choices, 62–63; role models for Republican, 68–73

Women Inspiring Social Harmony (WISH), 65
women of color, 4–5, 19, 66–67, 74, 79; Gen Z, 88, 92, 105–106, 108, 110, 175; in GOP, 122; Sabirah Mahmud, 61; second wave women's movement, 29
Women Republic, 66
Women's March, 71, 90, 106
Women's Republic, 139

Yanez, Rebecca, 171
Yeshigeta, Belan, 81, 182
Young America's Foundation, 118
Young Feminist Party, 81–82, 115. *See also* Generation Ratify
The Young Vote (theyoungvote.org), 13
youth-led organizations, 128–129, 141
youth-led progressive organizations, 115
Yuan, Aurora, 70

Zephyr, Zooey, 172
Zero Hour, 135–136
Zoomers, 45–46; and emotions, 49; and identity politics, 121–123; LGBTQ (*see* LGBTQ Zoomers); political engagement levels by, 49–50; in PRRI survey, 59; straight (*see* straight Zoomers)